The Magic Language
of the Fourth Way

The
Magic Language
of the
Fourth Way

Awakening the Power
of the Word

Pierre Bonnasse

Translated by Ariel Godwin

Inner Traditions
Rochester, Vermont

Inner Traditions
One Park Street
Rochester, Vermont 05767
www.InnerTraditions.com

Originally published in French under the title *Mode d'emploi de la parole magique* by Éditions Dervy
First U.S. edition published in 2008 by Inner Traditions

Library of Congress Cataloging-in-Publication Data
Bonnasse, Pierre.
  [Mode d'emploi de la parole magique. English]
  The magic language of the Fourth Way : awakening the power of the Word / Pierre Bonnasse ; translated by Ariel Godwin.—1st U.S. ed.
     p. cm.
  Summary: "An application of Gurdjieffian principles to fully and properly activate the power of language"—Provided by publisher.
  Includes bibliographical references and index.
  ISBN 978-1-59477-232-0
  1. Fourth Way (Occultism) I. Title.
  BP605.G92B6613 2008
  299'.93—dc22
                                                                    2008012168

Printed and bound in the United States by Lake Book Manufacturing

10 9 8 7 6 5 4 3 2 1

Text design by Jon Desautels and text layout by Virginia Scott Bowman
This book was typeset in Garamond Premiere Pro with Gil Sans and Garamond as display typefaces

Images on pages 298 and 299 used with the kind permission of the G. I. Gurdjieff Institute (Paris)
Excerpts from *A Night of Serious Drinking* by René Dumal, translated by David Coward and E. A. Lovatt, copyright 2003 by Overlook Press, reproduced with permission.

Inner Traditions wishes to express its appreciation for assistance given by the government of France through the National Book Office of the Ministère de la Culture in the preparation of this translation.

Nous tenons à exprimer nos plus vifs remerciements au government de la France et le ministère de la Culture, Centre National du Livre, pour leur concours dans le préparation de la traduction de cet ouvrage.

For more information about Pierre Bonnasse and his work visit:
www.pierrebonnasse.com and www.sophrobon.com

To all seekers of the truth

❧

Lord, I am not worthy that thou shouldest come under my roof: but speak the word only, and my servant shall be healed.

Matthew 8:8

Contents

Part 1

The Terror of the Situation: Devastation and Oblivion

Part 2

The Awakening of Hope: Rediscovery and Application

Part 3

The Esoteric Work: Transmission and Magic

Appendices

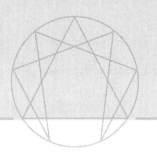

Acknowledgments

My sincere thanks for their assistance, support, and influence, whether it was material, intellectual, moral, or of another kind:

Jean-Yves Pouilloux, for whom I wish to express my eternal gratitude and deepest respect.

Bernard-Renaud de la Faverie and Alain-Jacques Lacot for publishing this book in France for Éditions Dervy; Jon Graham, Anne Dillon, and Inner Traditions for the U.S. edition; and Ariel Godwin for his translation into English.

The late Count de Maleville and Countess Graciela Pioton-Cimetti, Solange Claustres, Alexandre de Salzmann, Pierre Zuber, Jean Biès, Jean-Philippe de Tonnac, Basarab Nicolescu, Jean-Pierre Brach, Michel Cazenave, Xavier Dandoy de Casabianca, Jean-Luc Maxence, Karma Tsering, Judith Crispin, Jacky Bornet, Paul Baas and Helena Szenieer, Virginie Arramon, Claudine and Laurent Bonnasse-Gahot, René and Jacqueline Aris-Brosous, Sébastien Bonnemason-Richard, Isabelle Clerc, Frances Delbecq, Justes Emmanuel and Agnès Duits, Michel Vautelin, Véronique Messa, Tamar Karabetyan . . . and all those whose paths have crossed mine in this life and who have nourished me in one way or another.

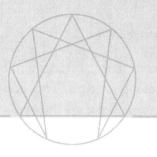

Who Is Speaking?

. . . You must begin by curing the soul; that is the first
thing. And the cure, my dear youth, has to be effected
by the use of certain charms, and these charms are fair
words; and by them temperance is implanted in the
soul, and where temperance is, there health is speedily
imparted, not only to the head, but to the whole body.

SOCRATES

Without knowing the power of words, it is impossible to
know men.

CONFUCIUS

At the beginning of time, words and magic were one and
the same.

SIGMUND FREUD

Why write a new preface? With the French version of this book having been published recently, I continue to ask myself the questions:
Who wrote this book—who in me? Who is speaking? Today, the true

question remains, extending to all things and becoming more pressing with each step I take along my path. This questioning, allowing those who practice the same in order to discover new, unexplored places within themselves, appears to me as something necessary to share with those who make the effort to read my writings and with all those in whom there persists an unappeased desire to understand and evolve.

This preface to the American edition of my book *Mode d'emploi de la parole magique* is intended less to offer "proof," affirmation, or other attempts at answering and more to open up new paths (unexplored at the time of the French publication of the work) that I leave for readers to follow. It is intended to pose some questions for readers to carry forth and explore further according to their own inner need.

Above all, this new preface is intended as an exercise impelling readers to preserve a critical view of *what they are reading* while also maintaining a good idea of *who is reading it* (regularly compelling them to ask the question "Who is reading this?" just as I always ask myself "Who is speaking?") so that they can approach the words with double attention: with the goal of being conscious simultaneously of the environment and of ourselves in this environment—in short, conscious of all the impressions that reach us simultaneously, both inwardly and outwardly, from our body and surroundings.

In this asceticism which is ideally permanent, in this remarkable effort—an act or "state" called, for example, *mushin* by Zen Buddhists, "stopping the world" by Carlos Castaneda, or "remembering ourselves" by Gurdjieff, generally referring to a state of self-awareness that the Hindus call *turya*—some see the key to consciousness of ourselves and thus, if we go by Socrates's famous phrase, to the "universe of the gods." As René Daumal wrote, this act is "the pivot of work on ourselves." "In truth," Meister Eckhart wrote, "if a man abandons a kingdom and the entire world but keeps himself, he has abandoned nothing"—perhaps because, as one yogi said, he has kept his self or, as Christ related, gained access to the kingdom of heaven which is in us, found his original face (Zen), his Buddha nature (Tibetan Buddhism), his transcendental "I" (Husserl), his essence, the innate part of himself which, just like his physical body, desires only to grow. We must therefore observe while preserving ourselves, and taking care not to fall into the traps of identification. "Carried by the eddy of affairs and occupations," as Seneca said, "each one consumes his life, always anxious of what will happen and bored of what he has. But he who dedicates every moment of his time to *growing,* who arranges each day as if it were his entire life, will not hopefully wait for tomorrow, nor will he fear it."

If we are to believe all the traditions, it is upon this *growing* that all development of "man" depends—if, as some say, he is truly worthy of this designation. As suggested in the parable of the sower told in the Gospels, perhaps the quality of speech grows in correlation with the growth of the seed—which must die in order to be born and begin to grow. Further, if Seneca insists on "every moment of his time," it is so that the "awakening," as René Daumal wrote, may be "not a state but an act." With practice and conscious effort, this consistent act of dividing our attention will grow in its depth (of what am I conscious?), its duration (for how long?), and its frequency (how many times?). Here, for certain, is the basic criteria allowing us to evaluate our degree of consciousness, which is defined as the faculty to know our own reality, the ability to use our attention in order to have the idea, the sentiment, and the sensation of this reality. Above all else, this action always requires returning to the sensation of our body (every time we remember to do so) without turning away from our exterior activities, a condition without which the rest is not possible. Sri Aurobindo says, "Corporeal consciousness becomes not only a means but a final objective." Yet, as René Daumal told one of his students, "also, do not forget that the Work is not a simple modification of ordinary life, something that takes its place; it is something added to it, it is something *more.* The more is what counts. Thus, the sign that your exercise is going in the right direction will be that you are not distracted from your ordinary tasks . . ."

Although this work explores the powers of speech in light of the Fourth Way, we must above all not lose sight of the fact that this Fourth Way is part of an ancient and nondual path, like the Advaita Vedanta. Consequently, it would be ridiculous and, more important, erroneous to reduce all to a single system that holds the truth. "All is One," as we are told by the famous anonymous text *Ellam Onru,* praised and recommended so many times by Ramana Maharshi. Night and day, we contain at the same time the wolf and the lamb, each thing and its opposite, the yin and the yang. Everything thus resides in conciliation, detachment, and transcendence, in this "third force" emerging from double attention. As the Bhagavad Gita tells us in that essential and practical passage relating simultaneously to the why and how of all inner work: "Our being in all things and all things in ourselves, this is what we perceive when we are detached, because at all times we keep an equal eye on all things." We cannot insist too much on the fact that the differences we perceive among the traditions (Christian, Buddhist, Hindu, Zen, Sufi, and any other faith or spiritual aspiration) are of a purely exoteric and popular nature; that they are due to education, sociocultural influences, and the equally theoretical and experimental misunderstanding of the processes of "realization." In their esoteric approach, all the traditions teach the importance of work on ourselves; they all arise from a *sophia perennis,* a "perennial religion," an eternal philosophy[1] coming from what we might call the womb or the primordial source. "The sleepers each live in their own worlds," writes Heraclitus. "Only the awakened have a world in common."

Indeed, to speak of awakening is to refer to a fundamental observation attested to by all traditions: the assumption that we are asleep and that our waking state is in reality a waking sleep. It matters little which metaphor or designation we use—mechanicalness, sleep, state of hypnosis, dream, Maya, illusion, exterior influences, confinement in a cave—the reality is always the same. Also of little importance is the name used for the awakening: *moksha, satori,* enlightenment, lasting joy, peace of the heart. The goal is always to liberate ourselves, to know ourselves, to evolve, to raise our level of consciousness, to see things *as they truly are* and not as we imagine or believe them to be or as we wish they would be. Dogma and belief aside, in their essence, the traditional teachings are addressed to all people. "There are no Russians, Englishmen, Jews, or Christians here," Gurdjieff said in one of his aphorisms. "There are only men pursuing the same goal: to become capable of being."

Being invited by the man who introduced the teaching of the

Fourth Way to the West, we seekers must experiment and verify for ourselves—beginning with the suggestions of the "master" and all he tells himself in his inner babbling—without taking into account anyone else's opinion, insisting on the necessity of questioning all things, even to the point of taking on a disconcerting perplexity. The only thing accepted as true is that which is lived and experienced with the whole of the being: It alone has the right to think and it alone—because it is sincere—has the right to speak. It is then another story whether one path is better adapted than another for its epoch and context, whether we are to make the choice of isolation or a social life—and each of us must choose to proceed according to his or her own aspirations. Remember only that what is important is consciousness of ourselves. An eternal philosophy, a practical thought traverses the ages, and all authentic teachings—if we are to refer to the etymology of the word *religion*—are, in a certain manner, linked. In an explanatory letter, René Daumal places emphasis on the unity of traditions: "If we compare the true religions in their inferior aspects of customs, speculative theologies, and popular beliefs, we see only differences, and in this sense all attempts at syncretism . . . are naive and erroneous. But if we consider the real thought, the practical thought (let us say the mystical, in the best sense of this word), we will find the same truths in all of them."[2] Gurdjieff insisted—as, in theory, is unanimously the case in every tradition—on the absolute necessity for cultivating benevolence toward other living beings and respect for "all the religions."[3] As he states many times in his works, "The highest goal and the very meaning of human life is to strive for the good of our fellow man."[4] In any case, no matter whether we are an atheist or a believer, this point of convergence is hard to dispute.

On the other hand, we should not forget that if books can be useful for our own evolution, they never replace the reality that is indicated. We must not confuse the moon and the finger that points to it. The book is to the reader as a geographical map is to a traveler, the cartographer in this case being the writer. Letters forming words and phrases are simply topographical signs showing roads, towns, mountains, or water. It is thus up to the reader-traveler to set forth, on condition, obviously, that the map must have real meaning. For this, on the one hand, the cartographer must have actually made the voyage whose itinerary he depicts and his words must be charged with true experience—in other words, the cartographer must be a traveler himself, just as a writer must first be a reader who has lived and verified what he has read. On the other hand, the traveler must also actually go on the trip, not contenting himself with the experiences of others and not imagining that he is traveling when really he is only looking at a map or reading a book. Only in action can he verify the validity of his basis and truly understand it with the whole of his being. In order for two people to understand each other truly, for their communication to have meaning, both must have taken the same path, both must have lived through a real and common experience.

René Daumal expressed these analogies perfectly. "The map is not the territory," as Alfred Korzybski said, and it is no coincidence that it is also the basis of neuro-linguistic programming (NLP). Yet a map is sometimes necessary—informing us of the destination, the various stages of the journey, the obstacles along the voyage, the possible resources, the exact point at which we currently are ("where am I?"), the path already covered and the path that remains to be taken. The way—especially the way to awakening, to the knowledge of our inner topography—can be found only with our own efforts. No one else can make the voyage for us. We are the only ones responsible for ourselves. "A great deal can be found by reading," Gurdjieff told Ouspensky.

> For instance, take yourself: You might already know a great deal if you knew how to read. I mean that if you *understood* everything you have read in your life, you would already know what you are looking for now. . . . But you do not understand either what you read or what you write. You do not even understand what the word *understand* means. Yet understanding is essential, and reading can be useful only if you understand what you read.[5]

If the reason for language to exist is, as some linguists say, "the accomplishment and perfection of communication between human beings," then is not the reason for communication to exist between human beings, according to initiatory tradition, the transmission of knowledge, the accomplishment and perfection of human beings themselves? Is it not starting at this moment—when it invites us to see into ourselves so that we might be capable of perfecting ourselves—that language gains its whole magical dimension? Driven by this fundamental question, we can now read Roman Jakobson's (1896–1982) theory of communication and the functions of language with a new, perhaps clearer point of view, especially his "general scheme"[6] (1963) inspired by the transmission of messages via telecommunication and consisting of six distinct poles, factors, and specific functions of language. This scheme can be completed in light of the reflections of René Daumal and Gurdjieff on the idea of evolution and a language that is, at the same time, new, clear, and exact.[7] We thus observe that what permits properly real understanding between two interlocutors is missing, namely what we might call the seventh factor: common experience. Heraclitus said, "the sleepers each live in their own worlds," meaning they do not understand each other, although they imagine they do. Each one of them lives in his own world with his subjectivity, and although all use common signifiers, that which is signified is specific to each one of them. This seventh factor, absent from Jakobson's scheme, can be associated with what we call the initiatory function—which insures the equilibrium between the "lines of knowledge and being," between theory and practice, between intellectual knowledge and lived experience. In light of the reflections put forward in this book, perhaps we may also associate a quality with each of Jakobson's factors and functions, with an eye to completing his brilliant scheme.[8]

Thus the power of the destinator-emitter (the speaker), which Jakobson associates with the expressive function—manifesting the attitude of the emitter in view of what he relates—depends inextricably on his quality of being, as does the destinatory (listener), with whom the conative function is associated—indicating the will of the destinator to act upon the destinatory, to interpellate him, to influence or excite him depending on his intentions, motivations, and personal goals. Gurdjieff said that "there is a law according to which the quality of what is perceived at the moment of transmission depends, as much for the knowledge as for the understanding, on the quality of the reference points constituted in the person who speaks."[9]

The quality of speech is thus linked inextricably to the quality of being of the *speaker* (with all that this implies), of *the person who speaks* (but who or what is speaking in *the person who speaks?*). All is not revealed in what the speaker knows he wants to say; the manner in which he says it is also important—the degree of sincerity (that which is said must be known, must have been lived and verified) and consciousness, and, above all, the level of attention and awareness. "If you put a human being in a good state of consciousness," Richard Bandler states, "there is nothing he will not be able to accomplish." Hypnosis, neuro-linguistic programming (PNL), sophrology, and all verbal therapies are a perfect illustration of this. The property of a speech of power, a "magic" speech, is that it is also an active and acting speech, a speech whose impact and meaning is measured by the effect produced upon the listener, the result obtained, or the reaction induced. "You must begin by curing the soul . . . by using certain charms, and these charms are fair words. By them, temperance (*sophrosune*) is implanted in the soul, and where temperance is, there health is imparted speedily—not only to the head, but to the whole body."

These words from Socrates in the *Dialogue of Charmides* speak to all the therapeutic power of speech, and in this domain, the efficacy is always dependent as much, if not more, on the "how" as on the "why." That said, let us not be mistaken: "[T]o want to induce faith by means of words," Gurdjieff tells us, "is like wanting to fill someone up with bread without ever looking at him."[10] Hence the primordial role of what we have called the initiatory function, implying, through perfect understanding, the personal initiation of the listener—his own work and his own experiences. But even if, once again, we cannot make an effort in someone else's place, it is possible sometimes for us—in whatever form we may express ourselves—to establish a relationship with someone else by inciting that person to respond, by inviting him or her to action, by making that individual hear a speech with all the force of an appeal.

As for what is said—that is, the message itself—Jakobson associates it with the poetic or stylistic function that resides in the setting forth of the message through itself with the aid of various processes. Independent from the informative aim, this function is related solely to the form of the message in that it has its own expressive and also artistic value. Further, the poetic quality of the message depends, as we have already seen, on the qualities of the person who constructs it. From this point of view, art—architecture, literature, poetry, the plastic arts, sculpture, theater—is not an end in itself but a means in service of consciousness, the transmission and evolution of the human being. As Alfred Orage, the famous English editor of *New Age* magazine, said to Margaret Anderson, editor of the avant-garde *Little Review,* art is a "power tool" that style must render more seductive.[11] Relative to communication, the style must serve the meaning and reinforce its impact, and the form (the way in which it is said) must reinforce the basis (content or that which is said), in order to heighten the *reception.*

According to this perspective, the *poetic* in itself—that is, the construction of the message—must have not only a *value or objective quality* (conforming to reality, to that which truly is, in the sense in which "the beautiful," as Plato said, "is the splendor of the true"), but also, above all, must have an *active quality* (on the entire being, not only on the intellect), serving a goal with mathematical precision.[12] The message and its function can thus have a *subjective quality* (when art is experienced as simple recreation or a simple work of aesthetic or social value or when communication is considered solely as an exchange of ordinary information including knowledge) or an *objective quality*—for the reasons outlined above, with certain privileged forms being poetry, aphorism, myths, theater, symbols, music, dance, koans, or legominisms, with a generally sapiential register.

Common to the destinator and the destinatory, the code, not necessarily linguistic, is the totality of the conventions permitting us to produce messages or, in other words, the list and the proper use of the signals used. Regarding the code, the metalinguistic function consists of explaining the components and functioning of the code, which is the usual role of dictionaries, grammars, and linguistic works. Gurdjieff uses it abundantly in *Beelzebub's Tales to His Grandson.* Further, if we live in what Gurdjieff called the "circle of the confusion of tongues," and if, as René Daumal writes, humanity has forgotten the "proper use of the spoken word," it is perhaps above all because we have lost this code or can no longer use it with the relative function. It is certainly easy to communicate on a primary level for the ordinary needs of life (to ask someone to pass you a bottle of water, to set up a meeting place), but things become complicated very quickly when the word is involved in our listening to each other and understanding certain more complex realities; studying a phenomenon with precision; transmitting knowledge, sensation, taste, the flavor of an experience with exactitude (even speaking of something simple, such as the flavor of a lemon)—as Antonin Artaud writes, when it is a matter of making our words agree with the "minutiae of [our] states."[13] Hence, according to Gurdjieff, the necessity for building the structure of language upon the principle of relativity in order to introduce relativity into all concepts and thus make possible "a precise determination of the angle of thought," explaining "immediately that which is said, from what point of view it is said, and in what context."[14] Moreover, in order to perfect this language, all ideas must be envisaged from the point of view of evolution. The metalinguistic function in a certain way expresses the reflection of the consciousness that the speaker has of his own code. Because human communication requires two beings at a minimum, the quality of this communication depends on the level of consciousness of these beings, the evolution of the human being, according to Gurdjieff, "the evolution of consciousness."[15] Thus an instruction manual for the proper use of communication is designed with a precise language, allowing, among other things, for us to "relate our thoughts to a rigorously mathematical definition of things and events, and to give us the possibility of understanding ourselves and each other."[16]

The channel of linguistic communication, oral or written, is associated with the phatic function that puts to use, establishes, maintains, or interrupts communication before the transmission of useful information. The typical example is the "Hello?" in a telephone communication, and it is also the role of many spoken expressions such as "so," "well," "there," "right," "you understand," and so forth, but also the mechanical "how are you?" and all futile, babbling conversations about insignificant subjects such as the weather that serve to introduce a conversation when these are not its actual subject. A conversation's quality in the framework of initiation might be efficacy and brevity, the condition of keeping to conscious salutations without the addition of automatic and habitual babbling and in the interest of reducing conversation to the essential.

The *context* or *referent* is the object (information in itself) or the group of objects to which the message relates—in other words, "the thing spoken of" designated by the referential function. When the referent of a communication is, for example, the table in the same room (in the same context), this poses no problem for understanding. But when the referent concerns a precise idea or a more abstract or complex reality such as the world, humans, or God, the understanding—which forever remains the first and principal goal of communication—is less obvious. Regarding the *quality* of the referent, we can say simply, along with Daumal, that the language must have a "real and possible *content*," which implies a common experience of the thing spoken of between the interlocutors. With a common experience and, more generally, the experience of the thing which alone will allow the consciousness to integrate it into the being, we are once again touching upon what has been designated as the seventh factor, the conciliation that is absolutely necessary and determinative not only in terms of understanding between two interlocutors in the framework of communication, but also on a more individual plane, in terms of adequation between the word and the thing, between the signifier and the signified.

When Charles Duits writes that "it is not the words that are dead, but the people," meaning—as Daumal wrote—that "we must not accuse the tool," he clearly gives us the key for what is behind the fault of languages and literature: ourselves, the quality of our experience of the thing spoken of, the consciousness with which the thing is experienced. How can someone who has never eaten a lemon speak of it objectively—that is, knowing what he speaks of? Even if he uses the signifier, even if he knows it, what knowledge can he have of the signified if he has only seen it, an image devoid of flavor? And if he has in fact eaten a lemon, in what manner did he eat it, taste it, appreciate it, assuming that there are at least two or perhaps more ways of absorbing food? And what would be his motivation for speaking of it—to what end and with what requirement, beyond mere babbling, speaking to say nothing while seeing nothing: for example, "the lemon I ate last night was good"? And if he knows the lemon thanks to the experience he has of this fruit, if he wishes to talk about the taste to a listener, how can the listener truly understand what she is speaking of, how can she have the taste herself, how can she have the idea, the sentiment, and the exact sensation connected with this flavor if she has never eaten a lemon herself—in other words, if she has no experience of it, that "gold reserve that confers an exchange value on the currency which words are"?

Without this common experience, there can be no true understanding.

In his May 1, 1937, letter to Jean Paulhan, René Daumal wrote:

". . . [Y]ou who have never eaten a leg of lamb, you once heard me speak of the taste of lamb. Another time you saw me eat lamb. Tell me that I am blabbering or that I am eating in a disgusting manner—that is your right—but how can you judge the flavor of the lamb? The restaurant nearby offers you woodcock; woodcock seems more interesting to you than lamb, but still you would have to taste it."[17] The word is to the thing itself as the restaurant's menu is to the dish, and the simple reading of the menu cannot nourish us, because reading is fundamentally not eating. The map is still not the territory. This said, the menu can awaken hunger and thirst, an irresistible desire to taste. From the sound and reception of words to the flavor and sensation of the content (things), there is a great gap that we can cross only with experience, and it must be observed that the transmission takes place at this price. To be, to understand, is to have the taste of the things that we know, to have the sensation and sentiment of our knowledge, of things both exterior and interior. *Being* requires necessarily, above all, "a certain taste for experimenting for ourselves . . ."[18]

To borrow Daumal's expression, everything is there: in the taste, in the ability we have to test a reality consciously, trying it out with our being in the simultaneous action of our body, thoughts, and emotions—that is to say, having the precise sensation, sentiment, and idea of this reality, our aptitude to know it (etymologically, *conscientia* means "knowledge") and thus to appreciate it objectively with its true flavor, such as it truly is, with its own qualities and defects and not as established sociocultural morals and norms conventionally define it. Gurdjieff said to Ouspensky:

> The chief method of self-study is self-observation. . . . But learning the correct methods for self-observation and self-study requires a precise understanding of the functions and characteristics of the human machine. To observe the functions of the human machine one must understand them in their correct divisions, and be able to define them exactly; the definition does not have to be verbal, but interior: by taste, by sensation, the same way we define for ourselves everything that we experience inwardly.[19]

He also insisted on the "taste of consciousness"—in the qualitative, not quantitative sense, as it is defined from the neuro-biological point of view—for the understanding of the various levels and degrees within ourselves. On a menu, we can read a description of the various states of consciousness possible for us, but we can never know their taste by reading alone; we can only imagine it. We are the only book in which we can learn, feel, and understand everything. "Good cooking," writes the gastronomic author Curnonsky, "is when things taste like what they are."

Another problem, as Daumal pointed out: "People are much more rarely awake than their words attempt to make us believe." We are always more severe with others than with ourselves, we always see the straw in our neighbor's eye without seeing the beam in our own. Thus it is of no use to think, "I am awake" or I am "this" or "that." In this case, it is always the ego speaking. Therefore, the only truly objective and palpable criterion—if we wish to prove something to others—is to speak but to embody our words. Simply, we must be an example. A teaching is true only when it is embodied. There is an enormous difference between calling ourselves something and *being* that thing. As Christ said to his disciples, "love one another as I love you, and in this way, everyone will recognize you as my disciples." There is no more correct evaluation and no more objective criterion than this: Evolution and progress are measured truly only by the attitude and quality of being. This is also the entire meaning of the myth of Hiram and the lost word. Here, we are touching upon the central question and key to Freemasonry. The initiatory function mentioned earlier explains this fundamental myth, which allows us in turn to understand—via the symbolic approach—all that is interesting in work on ourselves, the idea of death, birth into knowledge, and evolution.

The brilliant artisan Hiram Abi, recognized by Freemasonry as its master founder, is mentioned in the Bible in the first Book of Kings: "King Solomon sent and fetched Hiram out of Tyre. . . . He was filled with wisdom, and understanding, and cunning to work all works in brass. And he came to King Solomon, and wrought all his work."[20] Though he disappears from the Bible's succinct history after the reporting of his major deeds, Masonic legend latched onto him and made his existence, especially the assassination of Hiram (Adoniram or Adoram) by three evil brothers, an initiatory myth serving as the principal element in certain rituals developed in the eighteenth century. In 1850, Gérard de Nerval related a version of the story considered one of the finest in his *Voyage en Orient,* thus bestowing one of his best texts upon Freemasonry.

Seeking to obtain from Hiram by force "the password of the masters" in order to enter the Temple, three of his brothers, who had not been initiated to the secrets, assassinated him in the following manner: The first hit him on the head with a hammer (or the forehead, according to some versions), the second stabbed him in the side with a chisel (or dealt him a blow on the neck with his ruler), and the third plunged the point of a compass (or a square) into his heart. Then Hiram—a cosmic man—collapsed, his body covering three flagstones on the floor, the number three symbolizing the totality and unity of the world. After realizing that none of them had obtained the master's word, they were distraught at their useless crime. They hid the body, then buried it at nighttime near a forest and planted an acacia branch over the grave. Masonic ritual has made this murder into a symbolic drama inspired by ancient mysteries, and it is reenacted at initiatory ceremonies. Like Hiram, the initiate (to the degree of Master) must first die of his own will in order to "know." He must kill the "old man" in himself, on the mental, physical, and emotional planes.

This "triple death" symbolized the three blows dealt to Hiram in the legend. Such is the spiritual law: awaken, die, be born, grow, learn, and do. Thus it is possible to be reborn as a new man, replete with the qualities attributed to Hiram in the Bible: intelligence, knowledge, and wisdom. "Initiation is a process of individuation," note Chevalier and Gheerbrant. "Hiram's secret, the desired word of the master, resides precisely in this law of inner becoming. In a spiritual transformation and in the search for personal integrity invested with the qualities of Hiram, the initiate becomes master in his turn. We return to the symbol in the allegory, recalling that the three assassins represent ignorance, hypocrisy or fanaticism, and ambition or envy, to which are opposed Hiram's antithetic qualities: knowledge, tolerance, and detachment or generosity."[21] Concretely, the triple death—in other words, the awakening to ourselves that precedes birth into knowledge—is not a state, but an action in each moment that passes through conscious effort, through the sacrifice of our imaginary suffering (identification with obsessive thoughts, negative emotions) and the voluntary acceptance of our real suffering, as Hiram or Christ on the cross accepted.

The triple death is not merely the death of one of our functions, but the death of all our mechanical reactions together. When Adoniram (the speaker) tells his assassin (his listener), "You have not had your seven years of apprenticeship," it is because he knows that due to lack of experience (initiatory function), the man cannot understand his words (message), cannot have the taste and consciousness of his referent, which is symbolized in the legend by the triple death. Communication can be established only once the brother actually has the experience acquired through his seven years. In fact, Hiram does not need to speak, because he embodies his words. The traditional teachings tell us that it is not talking but *being* that counts. Hiram's brothers were asleep, just like Christ's disciples in the garden of Gethsemane. The ordinary traits of their personalities prevented them from understanding. We must awaken in order to die, and we must die in order to be born into knowledge. We must first awaken from sleep—that is, see that we are asleep. Then we must die of our own accord, leaving the body that we believe to be the self, leaving our negative emotions and mechanical thoughts. This is the meaning of the blows to the throat, side, and forehead. Then we can be reborn to a responsible life. But first, we must become our own master. Speech is not lost in nature; it is lost in ourselves. The desired word must be found in ourselves, then embodied by our actions. We are the architects of our being. Inner becoming, spiritual transformation, the alchemy of being: such is the secret of Hiram.

Finally, Hiram tells initiates to die just as he has died, for this word, the password of the masters, this secret, is to be found in ourselves, in our inner Temple. Letting himself be killed in this way, Hiram revealed to them—paying with his life—the path of initiation leading to knowledge and awakening. And for this, it is necessary to learn the new language, to be initiated into what Gurdjieff called the "lines of knowledge and being," to become our own architect working on our own construction, on our integral and total education. Hiram's words came from the totality of his being but were received by only the intellects of his assassins.

Gérard de Nerval's version of the myth of Hiram conveys magnificently all the things that characterize sleeping and mechanical humanity, all the things that drag our qualities downward, all that Gurdjieff called "negative emotions" or, more broadly, as in *Beelzebub's Tales to His Grandson,* the "crystallization of the consequences of the properties of the organ Kundabuffer": passion, fanaticism, envy, jealousy, hypocrisy, self-love, egoism, pride, and cowardice, but also all that characterize a person who merits the name "master"—that is, the quality of being, including tolerance, detachment, generosity, compassion. This individual differs from his blind assassins by reason of their ignorance, fanaticism, ambition, hypocrisy, envy, and their inability to understand the secret word. The goal of the initiatory path in the myth of Hiram, as well as in the Beelzebub myth, is to gather together human beings, whatever their strengths and weaknesses, to help them to grow inwardly, to divest themselves of their negative sentiments and to help their quality of being grow. "One man alone [and without goal(s)] can do nothing," Gurdjieff said. Through work on the self and through the perpetual examination of all that we believe ourselves to know, the initiatory path invites us to observe ourselves, to know and rule our own nature in order to use it to its full potential, and to use communication as a means of perfecting it.

Magic language—in the transcendental, divine meaning of the term—goes far beyond simple language in that it is in the beginning of all things, it bears all possibilities within itself, forming part of the miraculous logic of life. "Today we truly need to let go of all that hampers us, of all that tires us," writes Rudolf Steiner. "It is hard to want to see clearly. We must wait no longer to use ancient methods to see clearly. It is truly necessary that we develop the enthusiasm for it. Enthusiasm will do it all. It is from this that the following phrase acquires its meaning: Enthusiasm carries the spirit in itself; it is something entirely natural. We need enthusiasm; enthusiasm has something divine in it. It is the divine element of speech."

Speech has the power to transport us toward something higher, greater, and more true, namely to that part of ourselves that, in our blindness, we do not know. Yet in order for the words to contain the thing, perhaps the words themselves must be contained by something superior to us, by a force that pervades us and goes beyond us but for which we alone can be the vector, the channel. "Whatever you say you are capable of doing; wherever your dreams say you are capable of going, undertake it. Audacity has genius, power, and magic in it." These words from Goethe say a great deal. Before setting out on a path finally, whatever path it may be, before making a choice without return, the masters that rule are hesitation, the tendency to turn back, doubt, ineffectiveness, immobility, fear, and failure. In all domains and in all actions requiring initiative, determination, creation, boldness, and pertinence, there seems to exist a fundamental law that, through ignorance of it, has aborted innumerable ideas and caused fabulous projects and extraordinary lives to fail. This miraculous logic of life can be summarized: The moment we commit ourselves to the good, a superior energy—call it Providence, the absolute, conscious force, help from above, or whatever you like—comes into play, producing and manifesting all sorts of favorable circumstances that are definitely beyond chance and accident. Conscious decision appears to generate a positive current of events resulting in a variety of happenings, meetings, synchronicities, and supports as unexpected as they are beneficial and which no one would have dared to dream of or imagine. "It is not because things are difficult that we do not dare," said Seneca, "it is because we do not dare to see that things are difficult." Did not Christ tell us, "Ask, and it shall be given you; seek, and ye shall find; knock, and it shall be opened unto you"? He adds, "For every one that asketh receiveth; and he that seeketh findeth; and to him that knocketh it shall be opened."[22]

Now all that remains is to dare to do anything, to resolutely believe in all miracles.

In a letter to a friend, René Daumal mentioned a Hasidic story relating to the powers of speech: ". . . [A] St. Zaddik remained silent for long years, and everyone knew that he was in the glory of God. Because he was old, they begged him to speak, to say only one word of the wisdom to which he adhered, and he always refused. Finally, all the members of the community having pressed him to say one word, he made a sign that he was about to speak. He said only 'Fire,' and the whole house burst into flames and all was destroyed in the conflagration."[23]

It remains for each of us to seek out the speech we wish, pervading many and varied realities that are always relative and most certainly overlapping. It remains for each of us to gather together the scattered pieces of life, to create and use good glue to make them hold together. Each one of us, like a bee, must harvest artfully and transform many different pollens to make them into a single honey. "A landscape that preserves memory,"[24] speech can be an ear that sees much farther than the eye.

For the theoretical exposition of a proper use of the spoken word, there is most certainly a practical aspect, a concrete path leading to being, a nondualistic way which I will call the "yoga of speech" (including a "yoga of writing")—a way that searches beyond dualism for the union of the speaker and the thing he says, with the speaker's body and with the real part of himself, with each thing as well as with the All, for without union, without work, there can be no inner growth.

This work, which all traditions demand, is not only reserved for those who wish to evolve spiritually, as some put it, but also is for all people who aspire to knowledge of themselves and the universe, who aspire simply to see themselves as they are and to see the world as it is, without a prioris and prejudices, outside Plato's cave, beyond the prefabricated filters that blind us. It is for all people who aspire to create or, more simply, for all those who aspire to understand and to be, setting forth on the quest for reality. Jean-Yves Pouilloux writes:

> Swept up in the uninterrupted flood of impressions, we never cease to name the objects in the world. Without thinking of it, we attribute to them an identity, a form, a color, and we perceive ourselves only when we compose a fictitious world for ourselves in this manner, organized according to networks that do not belong to us even when we adhere to them spontaneously. I require accidents in order to become conscious of the somnambulism in which I live; I need ruptures, grief, in order that I may lose confidence in what I believe I see. I need accidents or else patient, calm, and exacting work in order to free myself from ready-made images.[25]

Let us not forget, finally, that beyond all systematization (which may turn out to be harmful and mistaken in that it has the desire and pretense of solidifying and imposing that which it imagines to be an absolute truth), whoever its auditor may be, whatever its quality of attention and consciousness, speech, which links beings to one another, remains a sharing. Thus we must always be vigilant of what the words are, half to the speaker, half to the listener, without letting ourselves be carried away by our own movement, our own enthusiasm, and the power of the energy we may feel in ourselves on certain occasions when the word is given to us. Others have touched upon being, and we must also arrive at understanding with the humility, attentiveness, and listening that are necessary, if others are available to listen to what we have to say to them.

In order to understand the mechanisms of speech as all human mechanisms, we must observe ourselves—body, emotions, and thoughts simultaneously, which implies necessarily observing our words and ourselves speaking, interrogating ourselves unceasingly as to the natures of the speaker and questioner. The question "Who am I?" implies necessarily being present in ourselves. Who is speaking? Who is reading? The energy of the question, which cannot crystallize into an answer, returns to the questioner (the little *"I"* of the false personality who is questioning in this case), and dissolves us, perhaps leaving the necessary space for seeing, feeling, and sensing the emergence of that which Hindus call the self. Perhaps it is then possible, for a few magic moments, to hear a fourth speech coming from the depths of what Zen Buddhists call the original face. This is a fourth voice coming from our essence on condition of pacifying our head, heart, and body for a few moments, on condition of first creating this sacred space within ourselves in order to see to its depths as we might peer into a lake that has become perfectly transparent, and moreover, see like a child, without prejudice, as if for the first time every time. This, without doubt, is one of the most important things: the taste of ourselves and the taste of the self, fundamentally difficult to separate. Above all and in all circumstances, let us therefore take the time to turn our view inward toward ourselves, and perhaps to listen there—as a result of conscious effort—for the speech that is offered as a gift by silence.

PIERRE BONNASSE
SEPTEMBER 2007

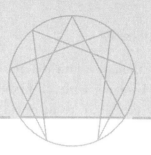

Preface to the First Edition

See, here is an open door; narrow and hard to access, but a door, and it is the only one for you.

ALEXANDRE DE SALZMANN,
ADDRESSING RENÉ DAUMAL (1930)

Why this book?

I shall answer this question straight away by defining this book's goal and necessity with a logic—as we will see—already developed by René Daumal in *A Night of Serious Drinking* and in some of his other marvelous texts, such as "Poetry Black, Poetry White." Bearing in mind the increasing "terror of the situation" at the dismal beginning of this new millennium, it is the writer's duty to offer a response to the prevailing mediocrity.

The fundamental task of this book is simple: to encourage the blossoming in the mentation and feelings of the reader of a veritable, non-fantastic representation of real language—the proper use of the spoken word in place of those illusory representations, the consequences of the crystallization of maleficent properties that we now perceive.

The goal of this book, then, is to open, for a few readers, a door leading to a more profound study of the teachings from which this text draws its essence, and possibly, by this approach, to restore hope. This syncretic book, intended as a study of art and language, condenses and crystallizes Gurdjieff's thoughts with the aid of objective reflections from certain initiates. I intend, with all my heart, to remain faithful to his "ideas" (as he wished them to be called), endeavoring to apply them as rigorously and as honestly as possible and as pertinently to this reflection on language. This is the aim and the objective of this work. This book has no other pretenses. It is solely an invitation to drink at the source. It is simply a taste of true hope, an initiation into esoteric wisdom, a reminder that the basis of all evolution is rooted in consciously guided self-observation.

At the beginning of this millennium, this work appears necessary in order to denounce the propagation of "word prostitution" while, at the same time, reframing what has been achieved by the greatness (and smallness) of literature and art in general since the dawn of time. The goal must not be fragmented or multiple: It is necessarily focused, concentrated on the essential—which is the essence of heaven and supreme meaning inherent to all "clear discourse." The tone of clear discourse which is that of blame, aims to give consistency and life to a theoretical language that is intended to be targeted, forming part of the great "objectively impartial criticism of the life of man." I hope that this book will answer truthfully to the logic of the goal for which it aims, itself inherent to all objective work. Perhaps it will add something more to the edifice of understanding. This is my dearest wish.

I also wish to pay homage to Charles Duits, who was the first to awaken my curiosity regarding the teachings, and to Michel Waldberg, who gave me the initial elements of my answer. These two were my guides, pointing to a path whose entrance I would never have found otherwise. Then, naturally, there were Ouspensky and Gurdjieff—but there was another guide: René Daumal, who, in light of the "system," lit up the regions that had remained dark for me previously. "There are many authors more famous than René Daumal," writes Jean Biès; "but few of them are so essential."[1] This statement is a striking truth.

In 1930, René Daumal, with the encouragement of his friend Luc Dietrich, was initiated into Gurdjieff's teachings by Alexandre de Salzmann, and later, after the latter's death on May 3, 1933, by Madame de Salzmann—who transmitted to him the essential elements of the

Work prior to his episodic meetings with Gurdjieff in 1938, which gave him less of a teaching than he had already acquired and more of a confirmation of certain truths.[2] Daumal's major works—initiatory tales, true myths impelling readers to think for themselves—bear witness to this teaching: *Mount Analogue* is an "entirely transparent transposition of the inner experience that Daumal and his friends pursued," an initiation to the Work, while *A Night of Serious Drinking* (1938) is an "objectively impartial criticism of the life of man."[3] Although plagued by a terrible illness—tuberculosis—Daumal continued to write many fundamental texts, including "Poetry Black, Poetry White," in which he defines his concept of true poetry, and the "The Holy War," in which he employs all his means to attain his goal. He met Lanza del Vasto in 1939 and worked on various translations, including D. T. Suzuki's *Zen Buddhism* and the *Teachings of Ramakrishna*. René Daumal, the awakener suffering from "an incurable need to understand,"[4] died in Paris on May 21, 1944, at the age of thirty-six—perhaps knowing, as he writes in *Mount Analogue,* why he had lived.

My intent here is not to write more biographies of the many characters who populate this book; this has already been done perfectly well by Jean-Philippe de Tonnac for Daumal and by James Moore for Gurdjieff.[5] Biographical references are inserted only as significant examples in order to support my reflections. For other seekers of the truth, all things will come in good time, for there is no such thing as chance, and recognition always comes to those who deserve it. Ask, and it shall be given you; seek, and ye shall find; knock, and it shall be opened unto you.[6] Have patience, then, in this regard.

My main task—de Tonnac having helped to make "the intentions of this father [Daumal]" more accessible and understandable by retracing his "terrestrial journey" carefully—is to throw a little more light on the question of the powers of language with the aid of this extraordinary work whose meaning and scope are simultaneously infinite and oriented toward the realization of *being* as Gurdjieff taught it to the West. This book, then, is not truly a commentary on his work or a critique in the generally accepted sense; this text is an exercise, an application of his work, or to be more precise, a continuation of the work. This is also what is accomplished by the incomparable grandeur of the texts that serve as references for this book: These works are living and active; they are invaluable tools for penetrating or at least grasping the secrets of knowledge. As for the main influences that fueled René Daumal's work, they are quite clear: Gurdjieff's teaching occupied the last fifteen years of his life and inspired his greatest texts. Thus, Gurdjieff must be given his proper place in the setting which concerns us here—and this has been well done by the magnificent biography cited earlier. Daumal was a writer and instructor, an archangel-poet, a warrior of silence, a bearer of speech who always knew how to set the record straight. This book is intended as a modest continuation of his work, an extension that, rendering unto Caesar that which is Caesar's, hopes to be significant.

"It is evident in my view," writes Charles Duits, "that if we need a 'guide,' we must necessarily turn to Gurdjieff." The master did not stop with a simple observation; he proposed a solution whereby we can exit this prison in which our consciousness is so horribly underdeveloped; he proposed that we should become independent, take our lives in hand, become our own masters. Therein lies his entire teaching. When Gurdjieff said that he had come to bring us knowledge, he was not joking—we need only note the attention his work has received in order to be persuaded of this. We need only start out upon the Fourth Way in order to transform our doubts conclusively into salvational certainties. Or almost . . .

The Fourth Way—that of the sly man—is the way of sincerity and true life (slyness does not preclude authenticity): the way by which we are no longer a passive machine subject to the "laws of accident and chance," but a conscious being liberated from the circle of the confusion of tongues, master of our life and all our actions, determined by a single goal and a single necessity at all times. Those of the Fourth Way aim for perfect control of life. It is the way of realization and bliss. From the moment we understand "with our being" that chance does not exist for those who are conscious, that it is only a pure invention of the ordinary person who attributes this word to exterior laws that are controllable, although laziness prevents such a person from controlling these exterior laws—we will have made a great step. Starting from this moment, it is truly possible to progress in our spirituality (in our "art of achieving union with God," according to Aldous Huxley's definition); life is a formidable challenge that we will then be ready to take on and, of course, to overcome.

When we truly understand why anything is possible, all dreams can become realities. It all depends on our degree of consciousness and on how far we have mastered esoteric wisdom. It is enough to create our life in the power of our words in order to take it in hand objectively—body, thoughts, and emotions together. This is the entire magic of the mystery. On the famous marble tablet, these words were inscribed: "Faith of consciousness is freedom."[7]

Happy is he who understands these words.

The Enneagram, Master Symbol of the Fourth Way

Everything can be included and read in the enneagram.
A man may be quite alone in the desert, and he can trace
the enneagram in the sand and in it read the eternal laws
of the universe.

G. I. GURDJIEFF, *IN SEARCH OF THE*
MIRACULOUS: FRAGMENTS OF
AN UNKNOWN TEACHING

The goal of this work is to present a new theory on language, which people have established "by means of intentionally producing from themselves corresponding consonants . . . or mutual intercourse."[1] I will explain this theory particularly with the aid of an ancient symbol that probably originated in Sufism and was introduced to the West by G. I. Gurdjieff: the enneagram, a sacred geometric figure and "master symbol" of the Fourth Way.

Let us first remember that it is a symbol used since the dawn of time by various occult and esoteric sciences, as well as by religions. The key to understanding it resides in the correct manipulation of those

1

tools that alone can open to us the doors of certain truths, certain fundamental laws. Because a symbol has the ability to transmit everything that ordinary language cannot transmit, it is therefore an effective aid in the quest for a universal language. Yet the understanding of symbols is correlative to the level of consciousness of those who seek to interpret them: "At first sight, a symbol is always a mystery, particularly for a man or woman whose inner senses are not yet sufficiently awakened, so that they perceive only that which is external, terrestrial, tangible, and material, and this only with the aid of the sensory organs of the human body."[2] A symbol permits us to test an individual or group's stage of evolution relative to something experienced. It has the power of unification and is therefore opposed to the ordinary and separative consciousness. "Finally, it is very important to know without any doubt and always to remember that a symbol's only life is borrowed from the person who works with it. Without human effort and will directed toward understanding and circumscribing it, any symbol—even the most ancient and most famous—has no reality by itself, means nothing, and has no power in and of itself. It is dead and remains so until it is animated and vivified by man."[3]

The enneagram, revealed by Gurdjieff, is a unique symbol that contains a multitude of meanings and uses. From the Greek *ennea* (nine) and *gramma* (letter, model), the enneagram is an extremely effective system for human development, allowing us to develop our consciousness. It is a master symbol in that it has the ability to show or demonstrate a single image and synthesize effectively a group of universal laws, embracing all other systems:

> Everything can be included and read in the enneagram. A man may be quite alone in the desert and he can trace the enneagram in the sand and in it read the eternal laws of the universe. And every time he can learn something new, something he did not know before. If two men who have been in different schools meet, they will draw the enneagram and with its help they will be able at once to establish which of them knows more and which, consequently,

stands upon which step, that is to say, which is the elder, which is the teacher and which the pupil. The enneagram is the fundamental hieroglyph of a universal language which has as many different meanings as there are levels of men.[4]

The "different levels of men" referred to should be understood as different levels of consciousness, bearing in mind that, as Gurdjieff said, "the evolution of man is the evolution of his consciousness." This great quotation says it all. Let us go a step further: this universal law of consciousness does not spare us from the use of language. Far from it. Because it has become banal and conventional to speculate on the powerlessness of language, we must learn how to set the record straight. After Boileau's example, René Daumal refuses "to accept that a clear thought can ever be inexpressible."[5] And as Théophile Gautier said to Baudelaire: "Any man who cannot express an idea, however elusive or unexpected it may be, is not a writer. The inexpressible does not exist."

The powerlessness of language is revealed as nothing but an apparition, a maleficent illusion which the writer likes to evoke when, by reason of an unconfessed deficiency, he finds himself incapable of saying something that in fact he does not understand: "If human discourse is capable of expressing perfectly no more than a mean level of thought, it is because the mean of humankind thinks with this degree of intensity; it is to this level that it assents, it is to this measure of exactness that it agrees."[6] In other words, let us not chastise language ("we should not blame the tool we use"), but rather chastise the mediocre level of consciousness and therefore the reality in which the ordinary among us live. "As with magic," writes René Daumal, "poetry is black or white, depending on whether it serves the subhuman or the superhuman."[7] We should not be shocked by his use of subhuman and superhuman, nor should we hasten to draw false interpretations from it. It is clear that in "subhuman," Daumal means what Duits calls the "pseudoanthrope" or, more simply and relevantly to the source (Gurdjieff), the "average ordinary man"—whether a writer or an artist. There is no elitism in this; here we must see—however difficult it may appear—a correct and objective observation of reality, specifically the terror of the situation.

In "superhuman," Daumal therefore means the man who has attained a level of consciousness elevated enough for him to claim that title that has no value but in that which it represents—namely, a reality.

Let us return, however, to the enneagram. Notes Tereshchenko, "The enneagram, although it is a symbol, is also a tool that permits us to test everyone's ideas, hypotheses, and reflections. Only that which is true and real can be placed upon the enneagram without distortion and without constraint. It is therefore a highly valuable and immensely valid test for our ideas." This is the new starting point for our studies, the basic postulate: If "everything can be included and read in the enneagram," why not read in it the laws ruling language? How can the powers of speech be translated with this ancient tool?

If we are lost and we draw the enneagram on a blank page—that great desert of creation—perhaps we will see there, in light of the texts of Gurdjieff, René Daumal, and a few other initiates, the eternal laws of language. This is a proposition, a hypothesis and a test that, at our own level of understanding, we modestly seek to explore. In my line of work, I have therefore developed specifically an "enneagram of language," crystallizing my theories on the powers of speech. This schematization attempts to show clearly the reasons why language is all too often powerless and, conversely, what makes its many-sided force and power. This illustration would not have been possible without the prior study of certain books of power, certain fundamental works that allow us to materialize the essence of this thought today.

"What do you look for in a book? A pocket tutor: all the advantages of a teacher with none of the disadvantages."[8] Thus we pay legitimate homage to G. I. Gurdjieff as well as to René Daumal and all the other authors cited in this book for the quality and strength of their writings, which bear witness to the crystallization of certain properties of their psyches—and this could not be any more positive.

Having now drafted a dismal report bearing witness to the increasing terror of the situation, I will now attempt to regain the "proper use of the spoken word" referred to by René Daumal, in order to leave its free usage to the good will of the reader.

"The first water always gives birth to the vessel that must contain it."[9]

PART ONE

The Terror
of the Situation

DEVASTATION AND OBLIVION

*. . . The rhetorical, technical, philosophical, algebraic,
logistic, journalic, romanic, artistic, and aesthetishoo
usages of language have led humankind to forget the
proper use of the spoken word.*

RENÉ DAUMAL

*But there should be some restraint of law against foolish
and impertinent scribblers, as well as against vagabonds
and idle persons. . . . [S]cribbling seems to be a symptom
of a disordered and licentious age.*

MONTAIGNE, *ESSAYS*, III, 9

Father, forgive them; for they know not what they do.

LUKE 23:34

1

The Man-Machine
and the Circle of
the Confusion of Tongues

Awake thou that sleepest . . .

Ephesians 5:14

In ancient times, near the beginning of Creation, words possessed strange magical powers that, when they were pronounced, could lead to astonishing consequences. Today, however, language is presented generally as powerless by the great majority of writers. Yet have they truly questioned the causes of this powerlessness? This question must be posed at the start, before any serious investigation begins. René Daumal notes that ". . . the rhetorical, technical, philosophical, algebraic, logistic, journalic, romanic, artistic, and aesthetishoo usages of language have led mankind to forget the proper use of the spoken word."[1] The mechanicalness of humans is the principal cause of this forgetting. We must acknowledge the evidence and draw an objective report, here at the beginning of this book: Indeed, man is a machine—sheeplike, asleep, blind, conformist—incorporating as many synonyms and pleonasms as are necessary to express the full terror of the situation.

Man as Machine (as described in the title of the work *Man a Machine* by the physician and philosopher La Mettrie) lives in a quasi-permanent lethargy, a paralyzing sleep, involutive for his being. Part 3 of *A Night of Serious Drinking* explains this topic pertinently, as the narrator awakens from his follies and finally sees, or almost sees, "the cold light of day." The night of drinking is like this sleep: We know not what we do and cannot take charge of our actions; we live from vanity to vanity, and anything can happen to us at any time—because we are inexorably subject to the laws of chance and accident. Everything is mere falsehood, machinery, and multiple "I"s, because "all people are machines governed by external influences."[2] Those who doubt this terrible statement need only look around in newspapers and television in order not only to find sufficient examples to legitimize these scandalous statements, but also to disgust themselves with this dramatic situation. The evidence rises before the eyes of the "drinker" the morning after his great binge: "the drinking party had not just been a dream."[3] Alas, far from it! It is no less than the wars, bloody revolutions, and all the atrocities committed by unconscious man.

Awakening is very rare and often difficult, because it throws us violently "in the face of the facts," leading us to the rude reality to be grasped and the dreadful hostility of things. Since the time of the Tower of Babel, we have well and truly been prisoners of the circle of the confusion of tongues, as Gurdjieff calls it. Such is the reality: We suffer from incomprehension due to our sleep, and we cannot truly communicate. "Fidgeting, fabricating, or clarificating"[4]—such is our daily lot: an immense babbling. "Be quiet," says the ancient sage in an authoritative tone. To close our mouth and open our consciousness: Therein lies salvation. We, like the narrator, are "held as fast as a bee in a strongbox."[5] Because it is not enough simply to awaken, we must also know what to do and where to go once our eyes are wide open. We are prisoners of our condition, as Gurdjieff said: "You do not realize your own situation. You are in prison. All you can wish for, if you are sensible, is to escape." We must first become aware of our "nullity" (in other words, our incapacity to do, to act), and finally attempt to be objective with ourselves: "And I, who had believed myself to be a poet, could not find words with which to call the Sun."[6] This is a terrible recognition, for what use is a poet who does not know how to use the magic powers of speech? In fact, he is not a poet. Such is the meaning Daumal intended to transmit regarding art and the objective approach:

> As I was burning my trousers, thread by thread, stirring them constantly with the poker to maintain the unburnt parts of the cloth in contact with the reluctant flames, I saw the fire turn curiously pale. I felt a light cool breeze caressing my naked shoulders. A milky glimmer melted the shadows around me. I raked together the still glowing embers and covered them with cinders so that the fire would last for some time yet. I went to the window and saw in the depths of the bluish air teeming masses of pink clouds and suddenly, flushing on the horizon, a beam of gold, a tiny burning dome slowly rising into a blinding scream.[7]

Daumal's poetic power is a testimony to this great incineration of ordinary consciousness, the prelude to all true learning in which glimmers hope on the horizon. While discussing the powers of language, Daumal gives an excellent illustration of what language should be: clear and purified of all useless dross. The narrator necessarily passes through the various states of dreaming, drowsy quiescence, and waking,[8] drawing in and inviting the reader's total participation with him in the levels of evolution. Literature is the art of serving the thing to be said, the art of circumscribing our target with words before striking it right in the heart. But art, poetry, and thought are phenomena of the same order as those who claim to pursue these: "These activities," Gurdjieff explains to Ouspensky, "are just as mechanical as everything else. Men are machines and nothing but mechanical actions can be expected of machines."[9] The same goes for actions, words, habits, opinions, and sentiments. This is why we should speak not of psychology, but rather of mechanics. Psychology can come only too late. What humanity needs, above all, are some mechanics that are able to repair broken machines, and God knows there is work to be done there. We all must become the master of ourselves, but for this, we must first learn to know ourselves. Then we must become responsible and take charge of our actions entirely—because they are performed consciously. Yet in order to act, we first must understand; understanding is essential. Understanding requires studying everything in depth, setting aside all desire for superficiality. Only then does it become possible to speak, to exchange, to communicate—truly to transmit an idea to the very heart of another. As Gurdjieff said to Ouspensky: "When you understand this it will be easier for us to talk."[10] What is urgent is therefore to exit the circle of confusion—as is so magnificently materialized by Daumal's narrative. Herein lies all our hope. Nihilistic and materialistic thought destroys every chance of freedom: Even if it begins with an objective recognition—namely, that of a cancerous humanity—it ignores the hope that is the entire subject of Gurdjieff's teachings. In this dismal circle, "nobody here is capable of staying awake for two seconds together."[11] The narrator asks, "How can I get out of this vicious circle? What would it be like if I woke up?"[12]

Sometimes, *Homo ignorantus* pretends to make art, giving evidence of the blind subjectivity of, at best, a "half sleep." This is the height of suggestibility of the masses.

2

Necessary Digressions on Art

Let them alone: they be blind leaders of the blind. And if the blind lead the blind, both shall fall into the ditch.

MATTHEW 15:14

The question of art is unavoidable for those who wish truly to understand the laws of speech, and consequently to attempt to understand what we call conventionally "literature" or "poetry." It is necessary to be aware that most of the time, art, which includes those activities known to be "creative," can lead us only further—often to a very great degree—into in confusion and blindness. True art, useful art, is entirely different.

Like everything connected with the man-machine, art can be only mechanical, an inevitable projection of what is perceived in the state of sleep. On the occasion of their first meetings, Gurdjieff and Ouspensky had "several interesting talks"[1] on the subject of art. As was his tendency, Gurdjieff shattered the conventional reflections that had crystallized in Ouspensky. Once again, the reality was difficult for Ouespensky to accept: "Just as there are very different levels of men, so there are different levels of art."[2] Yet ordinary men are not conscious of it, although they say generally that they are capable of seeing and understanding these differences in levels. How ironic! Reality is aligned with the vertical and not, as Ouspensky had believed, with the horizontal—a grave illusion. True art has nothing to do with the art we call "modern" or "contemporary," which is all too often detached from the source, from the sacred. True, objective art is distinct from subjective art, a Manichaeism whose precise legitimization comes from the mouth of Gurdjieff:

> In your art everything is subjective—the artist's perception of this or that sensation; the forms in which he tries to express his sensations and the perception of these forms by other people. In one and the same phenomenon one artist may feel one thing and another artist quite a different thing. One and the same sunset may evoke a feeling of joy in one artist and sadness in another. . . . And the spectators, listeners, or readers will perceive, not what the artist wished to convey or what he felt, but what the forms in which he expresses his sensations will make them feel by association. Everything is subjective and everything is accidental, that is to say, based on accidental associations—the impression of the artist and his *creation* [he emphasized the word *creation*], the perceptions of the spectators, listeners, or readers.[3]

The man to whom everything happens can create only a subjective work—a circumstance of exterior influences. And this work will be interpreted in multiple ways—we need think only of all the opposing theses that have been written about a given work, neglecting to seek true, instructive meaning, which does not exist in the multitude of subjectivities. The meanings attributed to it are simply the inner projections of the viewers or readers who arbitrarily and unconsciously transpose the frail viewpoint of the *"I"* seated in their machine at this particular moment. Subjective art crystallizes the dreams or imagination of the artist, his inventions, which are purely arbitrary but nevertheless claim authentic meaning.

In *A Night of Serious Drinking,* René Daumal calls these aspiring artists "the fabricators of useless articles," or, "for brevity and to avoid wounding their dangerous susceptibilities," simply "the Fabricators."[4] These fabricators are the target of objective, biting, and sarcastic irony: Those who "never call things by their name" often live in their ivory towers—a prison within a prison—gripped by a certain manifest irritability. If Daumal refers to their characteristic "susceptibilities,"[5] then Gurdjieff gives us the recipe for undermining this maleficent property of their presences, evoking the "means of tickling which infallibly act on the psyche of these unfortunate favorites."[6]

Yet as he points out himself, not all truths are good to speak: "Any kind of truth makes them extremely indignant, and their animosity toward others almost always begins from such indignation."[7] Who enjoys titillating their envy, pride, self-love, vanity, or lying? The explanation resides in the crystallization—mentioned at this point—of the "consequences of the properties of the organ Kundabuffer," which makes people perceive reality in reverse: "With such an already quite automatized 'consciousness,' and completely 'nonsensical' feelings, they feel themselves to be immeasurably superior to what they really are."[8] The habitual expressions of these "nonentities," their favorite exclamations such as the substantives "genius," "talent," or "gift," which they love to attribute to themselves, are "words empty also like themselves." These empty beings nevertheless proclaim the greatest achievement of art: making "the most useful things quite unusable."[9] Consequently, all their art consists ultimately of giving our "fellow man a desire without giving him the means to satisfy it"[10] and in depicting "imaginary and unproductive human lives."[11]

They are also known as fabricators of frustrations and false dreams—and to cap the situation, the public has "nothing but admiration for these Fabricators of useless objects,"[12] even when the fabricators paint fruits—literally—which the public will never eat. Subjective art has no decisive impact on the being who observes it, rarely even passing beyond the narrow frame of the intellect (never mind emotion). By contrast, objective art penetrates the entire mass of the being, merging with the totality of that which constitutes man:

. . . The true painter, as you know, possesses within himself—in his muscles, his sensibility, even in his thinking—the golden number or numbers and the laws of color; he possesses them, he has earned them, he makes them live through everything he experiences and sees, not just on the canvas: his work is therefore both useful and universal. What's more, the painter, like any artist, thinks before he paints, while this lot—and you'll see that the same thing applies in various ways to every one of our Fabricators—begins by painting in the hope of discovering subsequently, without ever needing to think, what they might have thought before setting brush to canvas if they'd had the slightest desire to think in the first place.[13]

The same goes for theater: Afflicted by "the illness of dramatizacring,"[14] "sick" artists never cease to "wiseacre," improving, as an objectively maleficent consequence, the quality of their sleep[15]—that is, the terror of the situation—because they lead the public into their sinister snoring. They know only how to "swagger," influenced by fashions, that "maleficent custom of theirs, which began there since the Tikliamishian civilization and which has now become one of those being-factors which automatically gives them neither the time nor the possibility to see or sense reality."[16] In fact, they do nothing but modify periodically "the covering of their nullity," changing masks mechanically depending on what exterior influences tell them to do. Writes Peter Brook:

A good actor never thinks completely in character, while a bad actor throws body and soul into his interpretation to the point of losing himself entirely. He often leaves the scene convinced that he has given the best of himself, while it is clear to those who have seen him that he has been excessive, artificial, and false. Yet he cannot realize this at all, for he is blind; he has not the least distance between himself and the image he projects, he has been swallowed by what Gurdjieff calls "identification."[17]

The other pitfall, even more ghastly, is that of consideration—that is, "identification with someone else's opinion as your own."[18]

Consideration pushes us into "permanently playing a role intended for someone else," which is "constantly interiorly dependent on the esteem or antipathy that it elicits."[19] Writes Georges de Maleville: "He no longer has his own being; he is the opinion people have of him, and will adapt his behavior accordingly. . . . Anyone can observe the ill effects of such behavior in men of politics . . . or in stars of the stage. These characters fabricated for public opinion truly live only in this opinion. Often enough, they have no other being of their own."[20] Although more marked among public people, this situation remains the lot of everyone, explaining many conflicts, especially those generated by our susceptibilities. Hence the vigilance, the necessity to undertake work on ourselves in order to remind ourselves to keep that distance which alone allows for mastery and control.

By contrast, objective art aims for a very specific impression or sensation that cannot be subject to exterior influences:

> In real art there is nothing accidental. It is mathematics. Everything in it can be calculated, everything can be known beforehand. The artist knows and understands what he wants to convey and his work cannot produce one impression on one man and another impression on another, presuming, of course, people on one level. It will always, and with mathematical certainty, produce one and the same impression.[21]

In other words, the artist has a target clearly in view, and the arrow must strike right to its heart or rather to its center,[22] the art being aimed specifically at the emotion. The differences in understanding that arise from an objective work of art depend simply on our level.[23] Charles Duits, author of the unparalleled *Pays de l'éclairement*—a truly objective text—observed the "mechanicalness" of people looking at paintings in museums, especially at the Louvre: "Alas, God was no more hidden in the dead beauties among which they wandered, limply perplexed, than he was behind the curtains of the tabernacles."[24] In this double critique, he showed that people seek God without ever finding him, because they form a false image of him. Their blindness is born of this erroneous perception:

> Their blindness was exasperating and tragic at the same time. When they passed before a window, they hastened their pace, gripping their guides as if they were prayer books. Sometimes the vertiginous desire came to me to make a violent gesture, to shatter these idols, to destroy these canvases—almost all of them, it is true, made by men who have seen—but offering, however beautiful they may be, only the pallid reflection of the Absolute Marvel.[25]

The objective work of art can be born only from a man who has seen and understood certain things, and who has then known how to crystallize their substance. The mescaline taker's brief revelation, for example, is similar to the everyday experience of some mediums. Aldous Huxley made a similar observation on the subject of Van Gogh's *Chair*, a testimony to the painter's visionary state: "The chair Van Gogh had seen was obviously the same in essence as the chair I had seen. But, though incomparably more real than the chairs of ordinary perception, the chair in his picture remained no more than an unusually expressive symbol of the fact. The fact had been manifested Suchness; this was only an emblem."[26] Like language, pictorial illustration, however expressive it may be, appears to reach its limits when endeavoring to represent what Huxley called "manifested Suchness." If Van Gogh came close to this, it was because he breathed the essence into the work of art, the respiration inherent to itself, imperceptible by ordinary perception, but palpable for the more evolved consciousness. Duits adds, "Van Gogh obviously lived in that world of energies that I could enter only under the influence of peyote."[27] Likewise for Huxley: "What the rest of us see only under the influence of mescaline, the artist is congenitally equipped to see all the time. His perception is not limited to what is biologically or socially useful. . . . For the artist as for the mescaline taker, draperies are living hieroglyphs that stand in some peculiarly expressive way for the unfathomable mystery of pure being."[28]

What is essential is to make the symbol projected onto a canvas or a page (or into the sounds of an instrument) as expressive as possible, bringing the emblem to life. Van Gogh, as Artaud notes, painted "not lines or forms, but things of inert nature as if in the throes of convulsions."[29] Through the dissolution (denuding) of the symbol—as occurs for the *"I"* under the influence of mescaline or certain exercises—it is possible to gain access, via representation, to that which constitutes the essence of Suchness in all its true meaning. This is difficult to believe, for the symbol is never the thing and nothing can be substitute for this thing. Huxley noted that few "great knowers of Suchness" have been interested in art—because they know, deep down, that above all, art is aimed at the "beginners" and at "those resolute dead-enders, who have made up their minds to be content with the ersatz of Suchness, with symbols rather than with what they signify, with the elegantly composed recipe in lieu of actual dinner."[30] Charles Duits said the same regarding Van Gogh and the perception of the "world of energies": "[H]e gave a correct image of it, but he could not do any more, even with all his genius. I still lament this cruel fact or, to be more exact, this banality: The reflection of a thing is not that thing. Art is—and only is, as the Orientals say—a finger pointing at the moon. The exorbitant importance we give to art today is due simply to our mistaking the finger for the moon, the indicator for the thing indicated."[31]

Objective art points to a reality that is attached to the meaning of human life. It cannot be otherwise. Duits notes—and perhaps this is what is ultimately essential (the "essence of heaven")—that "the works express with a sublime fidelity what those who made them have understood."[32] This reflection, far from being limited to plastic creation, extends to all forms. Faced with a work of art, a single question should be asked: What did the creator understand and what did he wish to show? To ask ourselves such a question is to dispense with babbling: "Van Gogh was one of those beings with a superior lucidity that permitted him, in all circumstances, to see farther, infinitely and dangerously farther than the immediate and apparent reality of things."[33] In order to earn the title of objectivity, the work of art, must be able to transmit knowledge via our emotional center, beyond the blinding circumvolution of the intellect:

I discovered the grandeur of the ancients little by little: They did not know merely how to see; they knew how to manipulate the substance. They possessed the science of signs which alone protected the magician against domination by the forces he unleashed. They knew how to take and give, they knew the words and gestures, the oblations and sacrifices that allowed man to change the circulation of effluvia without disturbing the laws of harmony.[34]

But objective works of art are rare, and many observers are conclusive regarding the artist's failure and unavoidable powerlessness in this domain: ". . . the glory and the wonder of pure existence belong to another order, beyond the Power of even the highest art to express."[35] Is objective art even possible, and do works capable of expressing such existential things exist? Yes, Gurdjieff tells us: These include the great Sphinx of Egypt, certain famous architectural works (the abbey of Mont-Saint-Michel),[36] and certain statues of gods. "There are figures of gods and of various mythological beings that can be read like books, only not with the mind but with the emotions, provided they are sufficiently developed."[37] This involves reading and sensing a cosmological system in the work—where possible, of course—that can be deciphered by the few who possess the right tools. The work is a system that leaves no room for chance, something that does not exist for the evolved human being. Everything must make sense, leaving the creator's intentions transparent. Those who observe must feel, with their entire "bulk," the ideas, sentiments, and sensations of the person who originated the work. This was the case for Charles Duits as he viewed the famous sculpture representing the Aztec god Quetzalcoatl: "The most striking image of the relationship we develop with the universe under the influence of peyote is, in my view, the one offered to us by a Mexican sculpture, a cast of which was exhibited . . . about four years ago, at the Petit Palais. From the massive pedestal formed by its overlapping rings sprouts the head of a feathered serpent, and inside its gaping mouth there appears, noble and serene, the head of a warrior."[38]

Given that this sculpture, for Duits, signified "the absolute fact, simultaneously speakable and unspeakable, to which he was suddenly initiated," the work can claim objectivity. The feathered serpent, god of vegetation and wind, is the son of the sun god and Coatlicue, one of the five goddesses of the moon. He is represented as a bearded man wearing a mask from which two pointed tubes stick out in front, two earrings with pendants, a pectoral "wind jewel," and a conical hat. Quetzalcoatl is the force of life which emerges, as Duits said, "just as the fruit emerges from the flower."[39] This god went with his twin, Xolotl, to the subterranean world, where he found the bones of the ancient dead. He brought them up, crushed them, and mixed them with his blood. The remains came to life and gave birth to humanity. Quetzalcoatl was a benevolent god who reigned over Tula, refusing human sacrifices. A lawmaker and civilizer, he gave the people his faithful maize farming, arts, crafts, sculpture, and writing. He taught them to measure time with calendars and to study the movements of the stars. He was the origin of civilization. As the king of Tula, he brought peace and prosperity. One day, Tezcatlipoca presented himself and showed the king the drunkenness that can be gained from consuming *pulque,* showed him his wrinkled face, and tried to seduce his daughter. Quetzalcoatl refused to leave his palace, then decided finally to take the path of exile. The intruder's malicious and evil spells destroyed the king's power and the land's prosperity. The king headed to the east, to the ocean, where he fasted for forty days, then dressed in fine clothes and readied a pyre for himself. Then he threw himself into the fire. Birds emerged from the flames, and in their midst, the heart of the king could be seen rising to the sky and becoming the planet Venus. According to Duits, "the universe makes humans as it makes the plants, the animals, the wind. Thus no conflict exists between what we call nature, or Quetzalcoatl, and us."[40]

Objective art crystallizes a divine essence, a testimony to the macrocosm and, of course, to the universal laws:

> . . . The principal object of art (and also of true religion?) is to preach, via the image, the doctrine of interpenetration (I borrow this word from the Avatamsaka). In this regard, the sculpture I speak of is exemplary, but every work worthy of the name com-

bines these two apparently contradictory elements—the human and the inhuman—in such a way that their marriage gives birth to the vision of the superhuman, the being that is simultaneously man and stone: God.[41]

The secret resides in the understanding of symbols. Let us take a few significant examples. Xochipilli was the Aztec prince of flowers, dreams, ecstasy, and visions. Recently, on the slopes of the Popocatepetl, at Tlamanalco, there was discovered a magnificent statue of Xochipilli dating to the sixteenth century. His face has an ecstatic expression, as if he is having visions, and his head is slightly inclined, as if he is trying to hear far-off voices. On his body are engraved stylized flowers, among which sacred plants have been identified. The pedestal on which he is seated is decorated with cross-sections of the caps of *Psilocybe aztecorum*. Surely, Xochipilli thus represents not only the prince of flowers, but, more specifically, the prince of the flowers that intoxicate—that is, the mushrooms which, in Nahuatl poetry, are indeed called "intoxicating flowers."

It is perfectly clear for those who know how to read it that this statue is a map of the ecstatic experience, offering some keys not only to the function of consciousness but also, above all, to the means for acting upon this consciousness. On the same order of ideas and examples, we are reminded of the rite of the mysteries of Eleusis practiced in ancient Greece. We must hear the hypotheses of some contemporary initiates in order for the secret of these mysteries to be finally revealed—at least, in part. Some engravings and images from the time lead us to believe that the *kykeon,* the famous sacred and initiatory beverage drunk during these rituals, may have obtained its visionary and alchemical essence (in the sense of a transmutation of being) from a concoction of mushrooms of the genus *Psilocybe* or else was derived from rye ergot or perhaps even from certain varieties of *Ipomoea*—in short, from a substance of vegetable origin with the salvational power of modifying the consciousness at its depths in order to make it receptive to cosmic phenomena.

Everything lies in the ability to read these symbols—especially ancient symbols, the fruit of ancient schools, "that Archetypal World, where men have always found the raw materials of myth and religion."[42] We must note that this capacity is accessible to all people who truly want it—but this work requires a great deal of attention and intensive concentration of our inner powers, as is the case for every authentic esoteric method. It requires both efforts and super-efforts. Nothing is easy and nothing is given freely: We must pay with all our being. Only in this way will the objective work deliver its initial truths: doctrines; techniques (as in the case of Xochipilli); cosmology (in the case of Quetzalcoatl); secrets; and all that certain prophets, visionaries, and priests have understood integrally. Van Gogh saw clearly that all is vibration and that all is connected in the universe. To be persuaded of this, we have only to look attentively (with the eyes of the heart!) at his *Fisherman* or his *Blossoming Apricot Trees*.

Certain architectural structures also relate to universal laws. The Sphinx is one example of an exceptional richness in this regard.[43] What a symbol contains, no book can replace. Who can read *The Adoration of the Magi* or *The Birth of Venus* by the Florentine Botticelli? Who can read the works of the visionary William Blake or the great Leonardo da Vinci?[44] A number of objective works—crystallizing some keys to inner evolution—can also be found in caves on all the continents. Let us take as a single example the caves of Lascaux: The horses drawn there mean much more for humans, for the laws of creation, and for the maintenance of the world than a great stack of books on psychology or science.

Slowly and patiently assembling the original correspondences offered to the human race, the disciple acquired the true means for examining any given ancient symbols in order to understand them and discover their spiritual significance. Studying the combinations and juxtapositions of the symbols, he was able to tell easily whether they formed a coherent whole and thus transmitted truths or were merely invented, fanciful combinations, transmitting merely imaginary human teachings.[45]

Finally, we turn to the particular case of icons, which, on many points, correspond to Gurdjieff's definition of objective art. According to Orthodox tradition, an icon (from the Greek word for "image") is a painting that is supposed to invoke Christ, the Virgin, or the saints and that is executed on a wooden panel. Beyond being a simple depiction, this "vision of the world transfigured" evokes a presence with remarkable efficacy. Simultaneously message and messenger, it conveys a living and transforming speech to those who look at it or, to be more exact, to those who see it. It produces a precise effect upon those who view it in that they appear to harmonize with the icon generally in (and for the purpose of) prayer.

To produce an icon is work in itself: Much more than a painting, it is a scripture that connects us to the sacred. A true spiritual exercise, this work (which begins long before the actual making of the icon) educates those who view it and elevates the consciousness. Icons belong to the world of the visionary, to those who maintain an inner view. In this way, they differ from subjective representations that have solely an aesthetic purpose. Writes Jean-Yves Leloup:

> Pious images, even those which, from an aesthetic point of view, are the most successful and remain in the sphere of taste and emotion without necessarily opening the human psyche to transcendence. The icon, however, through the remarkable process of colors, symbols, and inverted perspectives, has no function other than this opening to transcendence. It is a school of seeing which, beginning with the visible, introduces us patiently to the invisible.[46]

The emotion evoked by the icon is in no way haphazard and cannot function through associations. It always unleashes a precise feeling in those who are prepared for it, with the purpose of instructing about supreme reality. It is image and speech all at once and works not through imitation, but through vision. Entirely unlike idols, the "downfall of seeing," icons widen our view of the invisible and unnamable. "The idol makes us blind, while the icon makes us see," writes Leloup.[47] Obviously, there are as many degrees of reading for icons as there are degrees of consciousness. Through the difficulty imposed by their reading, icons teach humility and show us that to see things as they truly are (*yatabutam*), it is necessary to understand. As Gurdjieff taught, "only understanding leads to God." An icon is a door to the divine, a window through which the infinite of all things appears, because it teaches us to "read the invisible in the visible, the presence in the appearance."[48] In other words, it unveils: It impels the gaze not to stop with what it sees, just as reflection should not stop with what it knows; it pushes the consciousness toward higher levels of being, stimulating our senses. It takes the place of nothing and no one; on the contrary, it cedes its place to something much greater, making us receptive to forces from above. Finally, calling us back to the Other—herein, perhaps, lies its power—it calls us back to ourselves.

Objective art is esoteric. It is a *legominism,* an initiatory mode of transmission for a truth.[49] Everything depends on the deciphering. The same goes for all the arts: sculpture, theater, painting, and music.[50]

"The true value of art lies not in what it is," writes Peter Brook, "but in what it suggests. It makes us able to discover new degrees of lucidity within ourselves, which can rise to a culminating level of consciousness in which all images are nothing more than fleeting shadows."[51] In other words, as René Daumal wrote, "art is not an end in itself; it is a means in the service of understanding." Art clearly exercises a positive and luminous magnetization which, in certain cases, leads to elevation.

Next, let us study more closely the literature and poetry that take form in language, for these too—because they form part of art—can be either objective or subjective.

3

The Propagation
of "Word Prostitution"

*I am in a good position to say here, and too bad if I
betray the brotherhood, that the literary exercise known
today as poetry is, more than nine times out of ten,
a barefaced bluff, a masquerade that is ignorant of
everything having to do with words and images (the
language; the importance; the life; the ideas, if there are
any; the craft, the tools and above all, the goal). It is
irresponsible, vain, guilty of ten million forms of self-
love, and lazy. . . . Otherwise, yes, it would be a possible
path. But this would be the only path, and would no
longer be a literary exercise.*

RENÉ DAUMAL

If man is a machine and consequently art is mechanical, we may well
doubt that it could be different for literature. And this is exactly
what Gurdjieff tells us in his famous introduction to *Meetings with
Remarkable Men.* Conscious that "one of the chief means for developing the mind of man is literature," he nevertheless recognizes that the

literature of contemporary civilizations—here we will venture to add that there are some rare exceptions—is useful for "nothing whatever, except for the development of, so to say, . . . 'word prostitution.'"[1]

This terrible revelation is confirmed—all the more so at the beginning of this new millennium—if we look carefully at the shelves of any library. Unfortunately, we find nothing there other than the dismal testimony of a commodification that not even the greatest mediocrity can stop. Instead, it must be recognized: Often enough, the more mediocre a book is, the more buyers it will have. Perhaps ordinary people find in this some meager consolation for their own mediocrity, for these books mirror such people. There is no hope, of course—no hope at all—that these people will seek the hammer that will reduce the mirror to shards. The trap of prostitution has closed upon them, prostituting them in their turn. In making and buying these books, publishers and readers take part actively in the author's prostitution. They reveal themselves, exposing their mediocrity. A simple, focused etymological search shows to what point we live under the reign of images, ease and appearances, the laws of minimal suffering and minimal effort. Yet beyond certain conditions of current society (politics emerging from all books, television newscasters, participants in so-called reality shows—descending from the ordinary into complete nothingness), the writer's problem is that he has wiseacred: "The fundamental cause of this corruption of present-day literature is, in my opinion, that the whole attention in writing has gradually, of itself, come to be concentrated not on the quality of thought and the exactitude with which it is transmitted, but only on the striving for exterior polish or, as is otherwise said, beauty of style—thanks to which there has finally resulted what I called *word prostitution*."[2]

The cleavage of the breast of poetry, dividing poets of the signifier and poets of the signified, demonstrates and reinforces this idea. The former devote themselves to materiality; the latter devote themselves to meanings. The *ouroboros* poetry of the former, in cases of overly intense exacerbation, closes in upon itself and perishes in an emptiness without face or expression, as if in a closed vessel, tailless and headless by definition, or else dies in a rhetoric that devours its tail with its head.

. . . In short, it pours ever more from the empty into the void, without ever making it overflow. For these poets, the meaning, if there is one, is always accidental and haphazard. This is why no true literature can exist without the goal of truth. Such is the law. It is not the symbol that is arbitrary, but rather the consciousness of those who believe in it. There are many ways—a multitude of different languages and dialects—to use in naming the same object, but this does not prevent some people from understanding each other even though they do not have the same mother tongue. The principal incomprehension is not the consequence of all the tongues, but of the different levels of consciousness that animate them—above all, the sleeping state of the ordinary consciousness. Neither Cratylus nor Hermogenes (no more than Plato!) were right. Both were wrong, because the former believed blindly that the word possessed the qualities of the thing designated and the latter believed that absolutely no connection existed between the two. Such binary reasoning proves ignorance of the Law of Three upon which is based the existence of all isolated phenomena. Thus, the thought of the former is a matter of intuition and that of the latter is a matter of logical reasoning. In this sense, both are right and both are wrong. The adequation between words and things is in fact possible only with the presence of the third force, the "holy conciliation" without which nothing is possible. In other words, this adequation depends on the level of consciousness—but we will return to this later.[3] We must not sell Cratylus's skin without first having crucified him.

The propagation of word prostitution poses many problems of which readers are often unaware: At best, they realize, after having dedicated precious time to useless reading, that they have lost something more valuable—a moment of their lives: "And in fact you can spend a whole day reading a lengthy book and not know what the writer wished to say, and only when you have nearly finished, after having wasted so much of your time—already insufficient for the fulfillment of the necessary obligations of life—do you discover that all this music was built up on an infinitesimal, almost null idea."[4]

Gurdjieff arranges contemporary literature into three categories "according to its content": *scientific domain, narrative,* and *description.*

Within this classification we find what Daumal calls, paraphrasing "Fabricators of useless articles," the fabricators of useless utterances—by definition, prisoners of the circle of the confusion of tongues.[5] Their creations are completely mechanized and mechanizing.

The first, relative to the scientific domain, consists of a remodeling of old hypotheses that are formulated differently, expounded and commented upon, and subjected to a few slight variations of a purely formal nature. Needless to say, originality and pertinence are excluded from these rhetoricians' rhetoric. These are what Daumal calls the "clarificators" or "savants," made up of the "scienters," who attempt to explain things and the "Sophers," who explain anything the first are unable to explain.[6] We might as well eat our tail! The "Purificators of Accounts,"[7] prisoners of the circumvolutions of the intellect, represent people of theories, argumentation, vain dialectic, and inopportune babbling. They are the weavers of illusions, the mental onanists who fill libraries, burying the essence of things beneath futile commentaries that have been written a thousand times. Daumal calls them "logologists." They are "Clarificators of clarifications, who strain their ingenuity stripping down the observations of other people in order to extract from them some truth which is useless and insubstantial."[8] These men can only spawn pathological "ouroboros expressions," which will fall into the vicious circle of babbling and confusion of tongues in which all is inverted, confounded, or unknown.

Even in a cathedral, Daumal notes, signifier and signified are inverted and confounded: "In these same buildings, large crowds congregate from time to time to sing and to glorify the name of the Lord. It is the *name* of the Lord that they glorify and not the Lord himself . . ."[9] In such a context, the author of *A Night of Serious Drinking* adds, it is no longer a matter of *prière* [prayer] but rather of *plière* [bending over]! These people bend not only their knees and their bodies to beg the Almighty for "two plus two not to equal four"—an impossibility, we must agree— but also for the meaning of words, emptying them of their real content. Absolutely everything has fallen into confusion. The greatest irony is that by persisting in their wish to state the past and the future, these people skip over the present tragically. They know not what they do or where they go, and they suffer from a great imbalance of the being, the consequence of the multitude of *"I"*'s that animate them. Everything happens to them and nothing can be done, despite the repeated efforts of those "certified inspectors of dustbins"[10] commonly known as psychologists. Lentrohamsanin, "the great culprit of the terror of the situation," as Gurdjieff told us in *Beelzebub's Tales to His Grandson,* only perpetuates the suggestibility of the masses and, through this evil property, their blindness. He preaches liberty, but in reality he only adds more bars to a prison from which it is already extremely difficult to escape. As the parable says, one blind man cannot lead another . . . and as Gurdjieff said to Ouspensky: "It is possible to think for a thousand years; it is possible to write whole libraries of books, to create theories by the million, and all this in sleep, without any possibility of awakening. On the contrary, these books and these theories, written and created in sleep, will merely send other people to sleep, and so on."[11]

Narratives or novels are the most numerous of writings. They often tell stories of ordinary men and women revolving around the notion of love, "that sacred feeling which has gradually degenerated in people, owing to their weakness and will-lessness."[12] It is by reason of their loving one another—or in the name of love—that men destroy, do violence, and sometimes assassinate each other or make war. They do so for the love of their women or their gods, their children or their freedom. The main problem here, besides the trap of the imagination, is the powerful identification that paralyzes the reader's consciousness. Writes Georges de Maleville:

All modern, Romanesque, or theatrical literary production is . . . based on identification. Unlike ancient writings, which almost always had a didactic or even sacred character, all modern literature, for many centuries, has tended to fix readers' attention upon a hero with whom they must identify sympathetically and whose adventures they must experience through the pages, hoping that all will end well for him. For the reader, the novel is a dream followed along the page. Dramatic art proceeds with the same principle today: Except in certain pieces, from the beginning of the action, spectators are begged to identify with the sympathetic character whose experiences they will follow from act to act and whose final success they will enjoy as their own. The public's pleasure is therefore the most perfect identification possible.[13]

These remarks do not mean that we should reject all novels and plays at a stroke—far from it! But those who seek spiritual elevation must be aware of all the factors that force us to forget ourselves and lose concentration.

Finally, with regard to *description,* this writing achieves only vulgar imitation of nature, animals, voyages, adventures, and even situations that do not merit the least interest. The most distressing aspect for those who search in such writing, be it only for a mere hint of authenticity and sincerity, is that these texts "are generally written by people who have never been anywhere and have never in reality seen anything."[14] This is the whole terror of the situation. Those who aspire to the real achieve only ersatz reality that is completely contaminated by the simple projection of their dreams, imaginings, inventions, phantasms, fantasies, borrowings, and subjectivities. In other words, they are victims of exterior influences over which they have not the least control and, often enough, not the least awareness. For a text to be authentic, above all, it must its author must be sincere—and being sincere requires having experienced and understood whatever is said. Without this fundamental condition, all literature is mere babbling, hollow words devoid of meaning.

Contemporary writers, "with this puny understanding of the responsibility and significance of literary works," sacrifice meaning for the beauty of style and "the exquisite sonority of the rhyme." The true objective of sonority is to serve meaning, to accompany it to the heart of another person, to stimulate the action of the centers of being in order that these centers may receive the liberating message.[15] According to Gurdjieff, the principal poison in literature is generated by grammars that participate actively in the "'common malphonic concert' of contemporary civilization."[16] These, as Daumal puts it, are the "aesthetishoo" and aesthetic uses which have caused humanity to forget the proper use of the spoken word. The main cause of this forgetting seems due to the "category of people who, in respect of understanding real life and the language evolved from it for mutual relations, are quite 'illiterate.'"[17] The link between life and language is inextricable, and we cannot be understood or have our thoughts carried out skillfully without understanding both. Everything is connected. Like the beauty of style, grammar aids in the dismemberment and death of meaning. Obscuring the text, it veils the essential truths that might emerge from an idea and imposes them as a barrage upon understanding—which, however, is essential for our evolution. True grammar should crystallize a cosmic essence and draw its coherence from the laws of the universe; but this is not the case, because most linguists prefer confusion to illuminating clarity. Moreover, these absurdities uttered by the *"flower of contemporary civilization"* are what "prevent the literature of today from serving as the basic means for developing the minds of those people who are considered representatives of this civilization."[18] How could it be otherwise, when the reader, by the fault of an "incorrectly employed word," understands "something quite different from what the sentence was intended to express"? And who other than Gurdjieff and Daumal will denounce this masquerade orchestrated by machines?

Michel Waldberg's book *La Parole putanisée* is a remarkable response to the ideas put forward by Gurdjieff in the introduction to his second series, a perfect and concrete application of his thoughts to literature and to literary criticism. This tract not only sets the record straight, denouncing "false merchandise," but also—and this is essential when we deal with language—dots the *i*'s and crosses the *t*'s. It goes without saying that Michel Waldberg has done these things for us and done them well, even if I decline to cite, at this point, those who fill publishers' coffers without scruple. As Waldberg's editor writes, he debunks, with an incomparable verve, some of the great values of contemporary literature that have steered this magnificent art into the realm of "I-don't-know-what and almost-nothing." Rare are those who do not propagate word prostitution, and there is no lack of candidates for the position of universal Hasnamuss. As Antonin Artaud writes, we have had "enough individual poems benefiting those who write them more than those who read them."

Such things are not literature, but bulk mechanics, which is why Waldberg wastes no time performing critical pseudo-psychology or other exercises of the poetic poetician, instead performing true debunking on a grand scale. He shows simply why contemporary literature is a broken-down motor, and offers a few interesting paths to follow for its possible repair: "'Who am I?' remains, in fact, the only worthwhile question—not that it should lead to solipsism. On the contrary, everything both inside and outside is visible in a glass house, and there is no basis for otherness beyond self-knowledge—whether or not it is gained via the abyss."[19]

Let us stop for the moment with this terrible realization, the terror of which must not make us disgusted with literature. Sufficient unto the chapter is the evil thereof. The time will come for the necessary explanations when we seek to understand the proper use of the magic word, as Daumal himself put it. Some clarifications are necessary beforehand. Not admitting the divisions and gradations that define us, and therefore art, will always and forever amount to "a pouring from the empty into the void." As Ouspensky writes, "All discussions about art without the recognition of these divisions and gradations seemed to me empty and useless, simply arguments without words." Here, indirectly, he points to an entire criticism that continues to live in blindness and illusion for lack of initiation and understanding. To understand art and language requires first understanding the ideas of relativity and evolution. There can be no clear discourse without this understanding. As we shall see, according to Gurdjieff, there exist seven categories of men and knowledge, but also seven categories of art, and therefore seven categories of speakers who make up humanity, and some of these apply themselves to what we call literature and poetry.

PART TWO

The Awakening of Hope

REDISCOVERY AND APPLICATION

And I, who have no other weapon, no other coin in Caesar's world than words—am I to speak? I shall speak to call myself to the holy war. I shall speak to denounce the traitors whom I nourished. I shall speak so that my words may shame my actions until the day comes when a peace armored in thunder reigns in the chamber of the eternal conqueror.

RENÉ DAUMAL, "THE HOLY WAR"

I am certain the day will come when the physiologist, the poet, and the philosopher will all speak the same language and understand each other.

CLAUDE BERNARD

For a precise study, a precise language is necessary.

G. I. GURDJIEFF

4

Evolution and the Principle of Relativity

The Seven Types of Speakers

Men are mortal gods and gods are immortal men. Happy are those who understand these words, for they possess the key to all things.

ÉDOUARD SCHURÉ, *THE GREAT INITIATES*

If an entire section of contemporary literature is "soulless," according to Gurdjieff, this is because it is produced by blind machines who do not know why, how, or where they are going. But all is not lost; hope is glimmering on the horizon.

"Horribly awake," the narrator of *A Night of Serious Drinking* observes, not without surprise, "the daylight and the violent tremors which shook the building changed the entire look of the place,"[1] a place to which we must adapt ourselves in order for evolution to be possible. The third part of this allegory, "The Cold Light of Day," imposes a picturesque, pertinent reflection on the idea of evolution profoundly influenced by Gurdjieff's teachings, because it marks the starting point of a realization: Humanity is asleep and governed by mechanical and ouroboros thoughts. It is a terrible realization for which Daumal's metaphors are binge drinking and delusions of paradise. Real work is possible only when we finally understand our dismal condition in the cold light of day. This evolution takes place at first through an upheaval, an overturning, and then a reharmonization of the three centers of being: the *intellectual center,* the *physical center,* and the *emotional center:* "In moments of great danger, the emotions sometimes are anesthetized and the mechanisms of speech paralyzed. Thought, free of words and fear, then acts with its own certainty and clarity—coldly, logically."[2] The emotional center, through its momentary anesthesia, paralyzes the physical center that governs the emission of language (which, in terms of its development, depends on the intellectual center). Here, this appears to have a favorable action upon clarity. The man-machine is compared to a house composed of three stories that must be reorganized: Before embarking on the path of evolution, we need a perfect knowledge of the function of its machine on which language also depends. That is why it is necessary, before anything else, to focus on this idea of the center in order to understand its mechanism:

In a flash, I realized that I had plummeted down into the lowest levels of the house. I could see huge pressurized boilers, engines, and complicated assemblages of ropes and levers, all made of pliable materials and awash in warm lubricant. Fuel was piped in from the floor above, where a crusher first ground and mixed it. At the lower level, the resulting pulp passed through a series of stills, which purified it and extracted a red liquid. On the middle floor, a pump sucked up this liquid and sent it coursing towards the boilers where it was burnt. The flames were fanned by two large foundry bellows installed on each side of the pump. The air entered the bellows through two holes made in the top just below the fuel pipe.[3]

Here, Daumal gives us a complex picture of our physical center. In his *Beelzebub's Tales to His Grandson,* Gurdjieff refers to "three-brained beings"—beings composed of three great centers—which, as we shall see, are in turn divided into several fundamental elements.[4]

The lower—physical—story functions according to the Law of Triamazikamno (Law of Three)—the *sexual center* being the polarizing or neutralizing force.[5] The *motor center* is the seat of the human body's voluntary movements. The *instinctive center* governs and coordinates the body's reflex movements and organic functions such as respiration, digestion, and blood circulation. Metaphorically, the body is an assembly of "complicated assemblages of ropes and levers" in which all is interconnected—just as in the universe. In order to function, it requires three types of fundamental nourishment: air (which "enters the bellows"), animal and vegetable food, and received impressions. In ordinary life, however, we ignore the existence of our higher centers, although, paradoxically, they alone are always well developed, under all circumstances—but they suffer from a lack of nourishment, which distorts the awareness we have of them. Ignorant of the machine, we mistreat it. And along with the three types of fundamental nourishment of the being, our machine—"like every living being," Gurdjieff affirms—needs to be nourished with "hydrogens," combustible substances necessary for the use of the centers.[6]

In his visit to the house, Daumal finally arrives at the top story—a metaphor for the *psychic center*: "With difficulty, I succeeded in reaching the room above. It was a sort of operation-cum-observation post. The only means of seeing out was provided by two lenses embedded in the wall like a pair of binoculars. The room was cluttered with levers, handles, gauges, and dials by means of which it was presumably possible to direct the movements of the mobile house."[7] It could not be clearer: We coordinate our movements with the brain and its complex mechanism, controlling our perception and memory. This is the *intellectual* or *psychic center,* whose seat is in the head—or "room above." The intellect gathers impressions in order to classify them and direct the machine, working over the impressions with the memory and interpreting and transforming them.

Only through an attentive self-study does it become possible to evolve and reharmonize the machine. This process takes place through voluntary suffering and conscious effort—the famous being-partkdolg-duties referred to by Gurdjieff. Daumal's description can refer to nothing other than this human factory. One of his paragraphs confirms this idea and emphasizes the importance of the *emotional center:* "An unexpected jolt would sometimes throw me right out of my seat down to the floor below where my fall created great confusion: the pump and the bellows would begin to race—for once the moment of great danger is passed, the anesthetized emotions start getting their own back—and I had very great difficulty climbing back up again."[8]

Here, Daumal shows how the centers interact with one another. An emotional shock triggers a disturbance of the physical and intellectual centers automatically, unsettling the machine somewhat. It is not unusual to see a depressive person become affected by a violent emotional shock (such as bereavement) or a person whose cerebral activity is overly intense so that he or she suffers such physical problems as spasmophilia (which makes breathing labored) or difficulties of the heart (infarcts, heart attacks), not to mention serious illnesses such as cancer. The influence of emotion on an agitated mind tends to disrupt the body's functioning to the point of seriously damaging it. Sometimes the impact of these repercussions is benign; sometimes it is deadly: fatal somatization. Hence the importance of aligning and mastering the various parts that make up the human being.[9]

Let us take a simple example: Who of us, influenced by anger, has not said words that we regretted after the fact? In this particular case, emotion overrides the mind, and the results can be catastrophic. First of all, Gurdjieff tells us, we are like the ape—able only to imitate vulgarly what we see outside of ourselves. Only training enables us to train the ape or apes that live through us, and thereby reestablish equilibrium between the centers. We do this not without difficulty: "Training apes to maintain and work the machine is not easy. Training them to keep a steady balance between the machine's input and output is less easy still. But to train apes to drive the vehicle—I cannot imagine when I will even dare hope to manage such a thing. But only then will I be the master, free to go where I like without ties or fears or illusions. But I'm dreaming again."[10] And yet, only if we become our own master can we achieve effectively the famous "detachment"—the essence of the noble truths—praised by the holy Buddha. But how, indeed, can we claim detachment if we are ignorant of the functions of our machine, if we are the unceasing victims of identification?

Everything has its place and must fulfill its own role. There is no nihilism in Gurdjieff's and Daumal's criticism: They prepare a statement and go beyond it, they show the door to our relief and suggest that we accompany them in order to delight in our own freedom for ourselves:

> How beautiful the world was—except for mankind! Each moment each thing did what was required of it without demur. The unique uniqueness of things unchangeably repudiated its being indefinitely in an infinity of unities which joined once more into one-ness: the river was lost in the sea, the sea in the clouds, clouds in rain, rain in sap, sap in wheat, wheat in bread, bread in man—but at this point there was resistance as man looked on with that air of bewilderment and discontent, which sets him apart from all other animals on our planet. High and low, everything everywhere turned on the wheel of its own transformation—except mankind.[11]

Everything is interdependent; one nourishes the other and vice versa. We might compare this to the "food chain of the universe," in which everything is simultaneously predator and prey—in other words: food. But in this marvel of creation, it is the creature made in the creator's image that plays the role of obstruction, shoving a stick in the spokes of the cosmic wheel: We are ill, and humankind, "resisting transformation, attempted with great travail to live for itself in the tiny, cancerous tumor it made on the universe."[12] All is substance, all is food: Everything is nourished by something and must in turn nourish something else, but we perturb this good system—or, to be more precise, we are incapable of nourishing ourselves correctly. Moreover, we have no awareness of the fact that we serve as substance in our turn. We allow ourselves to be manipulated by the laws of the universe without knowing that they exist, let alone that we can use them for our own transformation. The moon takes care of the leftovers . . . let those who can, understand.

In any case, man's "mechanicalness" is sufficient for the mineral functioning of the planet and the universe. Not all people have to evolve in order to satisfy general functioning, and this is impossible anyway (such is the law). Beyond a certain degree, Gurdjieff tells us, man's evolution is "not necessary for nature at a given moment in its own development."[13] In other words, "humanity, like the rest of organic life, exists on earth for the needs and purposes of the earth. And it is exactly as it should be for the earth's requirements at the present time."[14]

But these statements, scandalous as they may seem, do not negate the possibility of our evolution. Quite the contrary. Happily, Daumal tells us, all is not lost: Certain people—belonging to a "superior humanity"—can help us escape from this prison, from this maleficent influence; people such as Totochabo, "an ordinary sort of man, only he knew a bit more than you or I."[15] We are "less than nothing," "nil," "dirt," even "absolute dirt," as Gurdjieff said. Only by returning to ourselves, by recognizing our nullity, will we be something: "Is it not a great comfort to the caterpillar to learn that she is a mere larva, that her time of being a semi-crawling digestive tube will not last, and that after a period of confinement in the mortuary of her chrysalis, she will be born again as a butterfly—not in a nonexistent paradise dreamed up by some caterpillary, consoling philosophy, but here in this very garden, where she is now laboriously munching on her cabbage leaf?"[16] All the hope is there. With this caterpillar's metamorphosis, Daumal describes the possible evolution of humankind. But this is a matter of banishing the dream—that maleficent illusion, that irresistible trap that we must learn to resist—and of concentrating on the real, the here, and the now in which we live, suffer, and die: "I understood then that these dreams were one of the principal obstacles on our possible way to the miraculous."[17] Man is a caterpillar, Daumal tells us, and he skillfully used the lexical field of the larva to develop his metaphor:

> We are all caterpillars, and it is our misfortune that, in defiance of nature, we cling with all our strength to our condition, to our

caterpillar appetites, caterpillar passions, caterpillar metaphysics, and caterpillar societies. Only in our outward physical appearance do we bear, to the observer who suffers from psychic shortsightedness, any resemblance whatsoever to adults; the rest of us remain stubbornly larval. Well, I have very good reasons for believing (indeed if I didn't there'd be nothing for it but to go off and dangle from the end of a rope) that man can reach the adult stage, that a few of us already have, and that those few have not kept the knack to themselves. What could be more comforting?"[18]

No need for suspense, then; the hope is there, with liberty at its end—and all we need is enough will and courage to seize it finally and to fly like a butterfly that knows where it is going and why it is going there. René Daumal—who did not "want to die without having understood why [he had] lived"[19]—was insistent on the subject of man's metamorphosis, his transmutation on which he placed all his hope. And indeed, thanks to his encounter with Gurdjieff's teachings, he attained this: "Even if, in spite of my certainty, I were the victim of a monstrous illusion, I should lose nothing in the attempt. For apart from this hope, all life lacked meaning for me."[20] Aware on the one hand of "a superior type of man, possessing the keys to everything which is a mystery to us,"[21] and on the other hand "that we cannot reach truth directly nor all by ourselves," he devoted body, mind, and thought to the teachings of the Fourth Way. It was there that he found, like many men, what other religious sects and mystic cults had been unable to give him: the hope of understanding the meaning of human life.

Yet this hope required an intermediary who was "still human in certain respects yet transcending humanity in others."[22] He first found this guide in Father Sogol, the most respectable Alexandre de Salzmann, with whom he began—not without difficulty—the climb up *Mount Analogue,* which was "inaccessible by ordinary human means." Then he worked at length with Madame de Salzmann, who instilled in him all the foundations of the teaching before his episodic meetings with Gurdjieff, "the Envoy from above," living evidence of a "superior humanity." Once there, suffering from an "incurable need to understand," he understood, before being led to death tragically by a terrible illness. Yet happily for him, he found what he sought, and severe though his tuberculosis may have been, he was able to die in peace, in an entire presence in the world.

But let us return to us sheep (machines). The question of evolution is subject to differing interpretations, as *A Night of Serious Drinking* confirms: that of the narrator, which is erroneous, and that of Totochabo (the ferryman), which is quite correct. Our metamorphosis, which suggests the alchemical work, aims for the transmutation of personality (lead) into essence (gold)—or at least to a preliminary rebalancing: "You would also need him—and this is vital—to give up his caterpillariness and to want to mature of his own volition."[23] In other words, we must recognize our ignorance, our incapacity; we must desire truly to learn. "And education?" says Totochabo: "[I]f schools are not able to stimulate and direct this transformation, there's always the teaching that goes on from one larva to another."[24] The same goes for literature and art in general, which should have no goals other than human evolution and awakening. This is precisely what Gurdjieff tells us in *Beelzebub's Tales to His Grandson* regarding education: "To teach and to suggest to their children how to be insincere with others and deceitful in everything, has become so ingrained in the beings of the planet Earth of the present time, that it has even become their conception of their duty towards their children; and this kind of conduct towards their children they call *by the famous word 'education.'*"[25] Daumal also emphasizes the fundamental fact that "we see or rather imagine everything back to front."[26] This observation is explained by the myth of the organ Kundabuffer central to Gurdjieff's *Beelzebub's Tales to His Grandson,* because it is responsible for the maleficent state of ordinary consciousness, which sees everything topsy-turvy.

Let us touch briefly upon the accidental genesis of the moon as per Gurdjieff's mythology. It was the consequence of a primordial mistake: The comet Kondoor collided with Earth due to erroneous calculations by a certain "sacred individual," and two great fragments split off from the planet. After this "general cosmic misfortune," a "most high commission" was sent to our solar system, where it members made sure that under the influence of the "law of catching up," the fragments from the planet would orbit around the planet of origin (rather than causing further catastrophes). Moreover, in order to prevent the fragments from escaping this influence at some future point, the most high commission took certain measures that in fact explain the emergence of life. Returning to our solar system to perfect their salvational task and fearing that humans might understand prematurely the real reason for their existence in the world (to keep the detached fragments in place), the commission decided, as a provisional measure, to implant in the three-brained beings a certain organ that would cause them to perceive reality in reverse. When this organ, known as the Kundabuffer, was suppressed—which the most high commission had not foreseen—its maleficent properties disappeared with it, but its consequences had already begun to be crystallized in their presences. Gurdjieff states that this is why we suffer "from the crystallization [in the psyche] of the consequences of the properties of the maleficent organ Kundabuffer," Gurdijeff's intent being to help us escape the terrible condition that explains why we are not human but are instead machines subject to exterior influences.

Faced with such statements, at first sight, this condition appears to be something to revolt against. In fact, this is exactly what one of the characters does in *A Night of Serious Drinking*: "You thay we all walk on our headth and thee everything back to front? What giv'th you the right to thay that? What ith your criterion for telling the back from the front? Anthwer uth and thith time uthe a concrete egthample. Don't give uth any of your vague comparithonth and analogieth!"[27]

By what right may we claim that we see everything backward? Indeed, what is backward and what is forward? The answer lies all around us, in everyday reality: It is enough to read newspapers and watch television to realize the terror of the situation. The principal cause of all misfortune, particularly "mutual destruction," resides in the confusion of tongues whereby people are not even understood by themselves, let alone by others. As already mentioned, people kill each other and commit atrocious massacres and irreparable holocausts for, they say, love. How, then, can we not think that people see reality backward?

Our consequences for the properties of the maleficent organ Kundabuffer are not limited to love. Far from it. War and everything connected with violence (ever increasing in this new millennium) is where progress leads—maleficent illusion. Einstein said (and he knew what he was saying), "I do not know if there will be a third world war, but this much is certain: If there is one, then in the fourth, men will fight with rocks and clubs." This is where the crystallization of the consequences of this terrible organ's maleficent properties can lead us. In addition, it leads to egoism, envy, hatred, hypocrisy, contempt, servility, ambition, duplicity, the remorse of conscience, narcissism, vanity, pride, presumption, credulity, susceptibility, notoriety, celebrity, snobber, the inability to think for ourselves, intellectual rigidity, pernicious identification with our own passions, the inability to imagine the process of our own death, the absence of a will leading freely to a goal, the misunderstanding of cosmic laws and the means to influence our destiny as ordinary humans, scientific speculation, falsehood, imitation, rejection of experience. . . . All these serious defects, catastrophic for humanity, are reinforced by a singular property: suggestibility. "This singular trait of their psyche—which consists in holding single-mindedly to what Mr. Jones said to Mr. Smith, without making the effort to know better—has been rooted in them for ages, and they no longer seek to learn those things that can only be understood through activities of personal reflection."[28]

As Gurdjieff said, "Such is the average ordinary man: an unconscious slave entirely in the service of designs of universal order, which have nothing to do with his individuality." In the ordinary man, who spends most of his time "wiseacring," there is not unity, but rather a multiplicity of contradictory "*I*"s. Nick makes a decision, but it is Pete who has to take responsibility. Yet he does not accept it. "*I* is another," Rimbaud said. "*Me* is a crowd," said Michaux. Considerably earlier, as Jean-Yves Pouilloux notes, "Montaigne had the same awareness of the abuse inherent in assuming one unity of being for one individual ('*I now* and *I anon* are two persons.')"[29] In ordinary life, it is the social *I*, tyrannical and false (the personality—not our own, but one that is acquired), that takes over. This is, in fact, composed of a multitude of little "*I*"s, which "are each kings in their turn." If they all speak at once, we cannot understand them. If they speak one after the other, we cannot rely on their authenticity, knowing that Dave is saying one thing now, but Jerry will say something else in five minutes. This is a lot for one man: Dave wants to be faithful to his wife (he really does want to), but Jerry sleeps with his neighbor . . . and it is Dave—or maybe even Simon—who must carry out this action without considering the remorse of Matt's conscience. . . .

We are the product of exterior influences (identification, consideration, negative emotions): Everything happens to us; we can only argue blindly with inept words that we are able to do and say. This, by definition, is impossible and is a lie. Who would want to trust in a lie? No one. Yet that's life. The man who is unaware and is not a complete being has three possible futures: evolution, stagnation, or degeneration. This is why the true *"I"* must be freed, keeping in mind that our true *"I"* can grow only starting from its essence (that which it is in itself, that which is innate). In this way, our speech can contain a true power: "Every serious literary enterprise is an endeavor to express the whole of the man. Every serious literary enterprise must therefore begin with a categorical refusal to express, as part of the real being, the successive *I*'s and this other *I*—just as illusory—of the writing writer."[30] The key to all secrets resides not only in self-awareness, but also in the use of a clear, exact, and objective language. This is the key to inner evolution, without which nothing is possible (conciliation).

But let us elaborate, at the risk of aggravating the terror of the revelation: A few handfuls of evolved beings are enough, although they are powerless in the face of the "process of mutual destruction" known as war. We must not evolve "apart from surrounding nature, or have regarded the evolution of man as a gradual conquest of nature. . . . humanity as a whole can never escape from nature, for, even in struggling against nature man acts in conformity with her purposes."[31] The most surprising aspect at first, what might seem the most unacceptable, is the idea that only a small percentage of us "may be in accord with nature's purposes" or, in other words, that this evolution, accessible only to some people, might be impossible for the masses. Holy moon! But Gurdjieff explains this impossibility:

The advantage of the separate individual is that he is very small and that, in the economy of nature, it makes no difference whether there is one mechanical man more or less. We can easily understand this correlation of magnitudes if we imagine the correlation between a microscopic cell and our own body. The presence or absence of one cell will change nothing in the life of the body. We cannot be conscious of it, and it can have no influence on the life and functions of the organism. In exactly the same way a separate individual is too small to influence the life of the cosmic organism to which he stands in the same relation (with regard to size) as a cell stands to our own organism. And this is precisely what makes his "evolution" possible; on this are based his "possibilities."[32]

Yet what interests us here is knowing that "possibilities of evolution exist" and that "they may be developed in separate individuals with the help of appropriate knowledge and methods."[33] This is the treasure of Gurdjieff's teachings, and this is precisely the object of what he called the Work. Evolution is strictly individual, and no one can do it in our stead—but we must go against planetary forces and evade their traps, their obstacles which, far from being useless, are necessary for this evolution: "If they did not exist they would have to be created intentionally, because it is by overcoming obstacles that man develops those qualities he needs."[34] Evolution cannot be mechanical (as we may imagine); in order to develop powers and faculties out of the ordinary, it must be conscious—for "the evolution of man is the evolution of his consciousness."[35] There are no other possibilities, Gurdjieff tells us. This implies, first and foremost, the evolution of our will and our "power of doing." But in order to do, we must stop being those "to whom everything happens"; we must liberate ourselves from the confusion of tongues, consciously diverting the laws of chance and accident to make them serve us and not enslaving ourselves to them. Do not let things happen, but do things. This is a fundamental nuance—and these powers, accessible to us, are not instinctive or innate. Indeed, they are no more instinctive than medicine, chemistry, or any other scientific discipline. Knowledge is not given, but requires a great deal of effort. Without apprenticeship, there is no real action and any attempt to do will result in an accident—fortunate or unfortunate, but still accidental.

Moreover, our evolution, our harmonic development, operates along the "line of knowledge and the line of being," and learning a superior language means being initiated along the two lines which "develop simultaneously, parallel to, and helping one another."[36] If one rules over the other, our development stops at a certain point. Like knowledge, *being* belongs in various categories on different levels, and "knowledge depends on being." What is unfortunate is that only knowledge is valued, especially in the West, and consequently this knowledge, merely "theoretical and abstract and inapplicable to life," only complicates things.

By definition, this inappropriate knowledge remains partial and superficial. As Gurdjieff told us, people "do not understand that a our knowledge depends on the level of our being." Now all true evolution, all authentic development, takes place by way of the harmony of the two. This is why we have within us not one unity, but a multitude of sleeping *"I"*s—which prevent us from changing our *being* and *doing* to the point that, "People whose being can still be changed are very lucky. But there are people who are definitely diseased, broken machines with whom nothing can be done, and such people are in the majority. If you think of this, you will understand why only few can receive real knowledge. Their being prevents it." This is a distressing observation. It is far better for the two lines to be balanced than for one of them to be too developed to the detriment of the other, even though "it is precisely this one-sided development that often seems particularly attractive to people." Some go through higher education without ever being interested in what they are studying, while others attend blindly to one action after another without knowing anything: "If knowledge outweighs being a man knows but has no power to do. It is useless knowledge. On the other hand if being outweighs knowledge a man has the power to do, but does not know—that is, he can do something but does not know what to do. The being he has acquired becomes aimless, and efforts made to attain a goal prove to be useless." It is all a question of equilibrium, stability, and realigning. Without this balance, it is impossible to understand anything whatsoever. To understand that fire burns means on the one hand knowing intellectually the properties that govern fire, and on the other hand having experience with it. Those who learn to swim from a book and then jump into the water will drown, because such people *know*—they can recite the book word for word, like parrots—but they cannot do. Thus, equilibrium exists between knowledge and *being,* and it then becomes possible to speak of it (equilibrium) with knowledge of the facts.

The problem comes from the fact that people confuse *knowledge* with *understanding*—which not only "depends on the relation of knowledge to being" but also "grows only with the growth of being." Accumulating knowledge does not mean we are accumulating understanding. This is explained by the notion of centers: Knowledge depends only on the intellectual (formative) center, while understanding requires the action of the three centers of which we are composed. "Thus," Gurdjieff tells us, "the thinking apparatus may *know* something. But *understanding* appears only when a man feels and senses what is connected with it." This is what distinguishes theory from practice, knowledge from doing. We may know the biggest dictionary by heart, but this does not mean we understand anything, though our lexical knowledge may be immense. Without that perfect adequation with the real, all our understanding will remain nil and our knowledge will be useless.

We have come to it: All people's problems come from the language with which they endeavor to communicate, which is "one of the reasons for the divergence between the line of knowledge and the line of being in life, and the lack of understanding which is partly the cause and partly the effect of this divergence."[37] In ordinary language, all is distorted due to the differences of "levels" between us:

And the chief thing is that, owing to the essential characteristics of ordinary thinking, that is to say, to its vagueness and inaccuracy, every word can have thousands of different meanings according to the material the speaker has at his disposal and the complex of associations at work in him at the moment. People do not clearly realize to what a degree their language is subjective, that is, what different things each of them says while using the same words. They are not aware that each one of them speaks in a language of his own, understanding other people's language either vaguely or not at all, and having no idea that each one of them speaks in a language unknown to him. People have a very firm conviction, or belief, that they speak the same language, that they understand one another. Actually this conviction has no foundation whatever. The language in which they speak is adapted to practical life only. People can communicate to one another information of a practical character, but as soon as they pass to a slightly more complex sphere they are immediately lost, and they cease to understand one another, although they are unconscious of it. . . . As a matter of fact, no one understands anyone else. Two men can say the same thing with profound conviction but call it by different names, or argue endlessly together without suspecting that they are thinking exactly the same. Or, vice versa, two men can say the same words and imagine that they agree with, and understand, one another, whereas they are actually saying absolutely different things and do not understand one another in the least.[38]

There are a number of examples of this shrewd analysis in everyone's life. We have all had the experience of incomprehension, especially in debates relating to metaphysics or religion.

I offer a personal example here to illustrate this point. Curiously, when the event occurred, I was just concluding the writing of this book's first chapter. My oldest friend (whom I could not possibly have held in higher esteem) was invited to my table to share some basic "being nourishment" and to drink some exceptionally good wine ("just like baby Jesus peeing in your mouth," as my dear grandmother would have said). He left in a huff, however, the victim of that famous incomprehension due to language itself: Barely had I uttered the name "Gurdjieff" than he attacked me with simplistic sectarianism, and he subsequently attacked all those who did not share his vision of things. To clarify: Without leaving me time to speak or to suggest the least idea, he declared to me—with a fanatical evangelism and an unprecedented intolerance—that "Gurdjieff was the enemy of God, Christ, and the Gospel." I retorted that he had understood absolutely nothing of what he had read (if he had indeed read and not simply repeated the statements of Mr. Jones or Mr. Smith—maleficent "suggestibility"!), and that the master of the Fourth Way had himself called his teachings "esoteric Christianity," which could not be in contradiction to the message of Christ.

At these objective words, he redoubled his intolerance, to which I responded simply in a reprimanding tone: "I forbid you to say that!" I also added that my interest had been merely in exchanging ideas for a deeper understanding of the Holy Scriptures and that in any case, I was not seeking to "convert" him or to perform any kind of proselytism—unlike him, with his mechanical and blind "pseudo-preachings" based on the imitation of other machines. His final rhetorical question—interrupting my attempt at reconciliation—was dismissive and obviously, by definition, did not call for any answer, even though he provided one: "Answer this question: Did Gurdjieff state that only faith in Jesus Christ—and in nothing else—could save us? No, certainly, because he is the enemy of the Gospel, just as you are its enemy." Because enough was enough, I stopped him outright, answering politely that the blind and sheeplike sectarianism that he called "faith" prevented any communication between us (despite my repeated efforts), even though I was only trying to make clear to him that, like Daumal, I suffered from an "incurable need to understand"—something he did not understand. At this point, he rose mechanically and left my flat like an enraged robot, preferring to sacrifice a ten-year friendship to words that he had emptied of their meaning.

I might add that it was an occasion of my happily receiving him after several months' absence, to share a meal at my table, which turned out to be the last. (The dinner was aborted after fifteen minutes.) Quite a Last Supper for an alleged Christian! Thus alone, abandoned by one who, in the absolute, had the same goal as I, I consciously—and without remorse—finished the wine, which had lost none of its holy taste in my estimation. *In vino veritas!*

To a great degree, the consequences of this confusion of tongues are catastrophic because they sometimes lead to what Gurdjieff calls the "process of mutual destruction" or war. Men kill each other for the same god, whom they imagine to be different. This example is typical of the so-called monotheistic religions. If we read *Beelzebub's Tales to His Grandson,* we will understand why all this is merely a grievous illusion. Says Gurdjieff, "The religions do not exist" in the same manner that "*men* are not men"! The word *world,* for example, is thus subject solely to the perspective or specialty of the person who uses it: The definition will be different for a historian, an astronomer, a physicist, a believer in some given religion . . . and in vain they will try to exchange ideas and to think the same thing.

As an example, let us take the word *man,* already analyzed by numerous initiates to the Fourth Way (including Ouspensky), and endeavor to transcend common considerations (which remain pertinent and necessary to the understanding of our hypothesis), applying this analysis to the laws that govern language. We each have our own definition for the word *man,* and these do not necessarily have anything in common. For some, it is defined according to the Manichaeism man–woman; for the believer, it may be defined as Christian–non-Christian; for the doctor, healthy–sick; for the spiritualist, astral body–physical body; for the moralist, it will be good or bad depending on his conception of good and bad.[39] These considerations can be continued ad infinitum. Even science, Gurdjieff tells us, becomes lost in confusion, with a multitude of different terminologies. So what to do? How do we make ourselves understood? How do we truly communicate?

> For exact understanding exact language is necessary. And the study of systems of ancient knowledge begins with the study of a language which will make it possible to establish at once exactly what is being said, from what point of view, and in what connection. This new language contains hardly any new terms or new nomenclature, but it bases the construction of speech upon a new principle, namely, the principle of relativity; that is to say, it introduces relativity into all concepts and thus makes possible an accurate determination of

the angle of thought—for what precisely ordinary language lacks are expressions of relativity.[40]

This new language will guarantee the transmission of knowledge, intransmissible in ordinary language. But there is another question: On what angle of thought should this new language hinge? The answer is contained in this teaching: "The fundamental property of the new language is that all ideas in it are concentrated round one idea, that is, they are taken in their mutual relationship from the point of view of one idea. This idea is the idea of *evolution*. Of course, not evolution in the sense of mechanical evolution, because such an evolution does not exist, but in the sense of a conscious and volitional evolution, which alone is possible."[41]

The pertinence of this idea is confirmed in reality: Everything evolves or degenerates, rises or falls, develops or declines, from the solar system down to the atom. Only evolution is conscious and "only degeneration and destruction proceed mechanically." "The language in which understanding is possible is constructed upon the indication of the relation of the object under examination to the evolution possible for it; upon the indication of its place in the evolutionary ladder."[42]

Thus, to return to and apply the example of the word *man* in terms of a division conforming to the stages of this evolution as defined by Gurdjieff: There are seven possible degrees of evolution of the *"I"* which, we must clarify, have nothing to do with the famous Law of Seven that we will study later in this book. To the seven levels of men, knowledge, and arts defined by Ouspensky there may correspond seven types of speakers (and also literature and poetry)—constituting all of humanity—so that in fact all activities relating to man can be divided into seven categories.[43] Only this division will allow us to understand each other when we speak of *man* and his activities.

Concretely, what is objective language? Let us take an example inspired by messages read in discussion forums on the Internet. A user started a debate with a historian intending to demonstrate the arbitrary nature of words:

"One day, a young disciple went to see his master and said to him: 'Master, I beg you, tell me the whole truth, for I have not been able to find it!'

"His master took an apple which was there, and said: 'Tell me, then, what this is.'

"The young monk, believing his master to be mocking him, answered: 'It's an apple!'

"'No!' answered the master. *Apple* is the word that has been invented to designate the thing that is in front of you, but what is it?'

"The young monk, taken aback, thought for a few moments and said: 'It's a fruit . . .'

"'*Fruit* is also a word, and what is in front of you is certainly not a word, so what is it?'

"The monk turned over the question in all directions, but the answers that came to his mind were still only words, and so, resigned, he asked his master to tell him the answer.

"The master said: 'When the mind no longer has an answer to give and is faced with its powerlessness, then comes the truth. Do you think the tree in front of you is really a tree? It is no more than the apple, because *tree* is a word. If you look at this apple again in a few days, it will be rotten. You will believe yourself still to be in the presence of the same apple, but you will have missed out on the process of life that animates what you call *apple*.'

"You who read these lines, are you certain you are in front of a computer screen?"

To this another user responded ironically: "Could we also claim that an eggplant is a purple calf that hasn't opened its eyes yet?"

This example is highly instructive, and it seems necessary to quote it (though the series of conversations fell subsequently into total confusion, becoming "dialogs between deaf people," or rather, between people not understanding each other). Regarding the apple story: The problem is not knowing whether we must name something *apple, bean, ape,* or *parrot,* but rather knowing the thing through experience. In other words, the thing (here, an apple) has as many degrees of reality as there are levels of people (on the plane of the evolution of consciousness and perception; according to Shakespeare, "That which we call a rose by any other name would smell as sweet"). We merely must place the apple on the target in order to obtain its exact definition. (See the cosmological chart of the target in appendix 1.) For a subjective person, the apple will be only what he or she projects into its signifier—and of course, what he or she knows about it. This may relate to the variety of apple, its color, its size, all kinds of associations or ideas (such as apple trees and orchards), its taste ("I like it" or "I don't like it").

Yet all this remains extremely subjective. Certainly, the example is very simple; the range of meanings attributed generally to an apple are very narrow compared to words such as *god, truth,* and *liberty.* In cases where two people have a common experience of the thing that is being talked about (let us stick with apple), the exchange becomes easier. If these two people share the apple, they can then say whether it is tart or sweet, understanding each other on this point—but whether they perceive the essence of the apple, what it truly is, depends on the state of consciousness. Even if the apple is called a *dog* or a *cat,* if the consciousness joins the word to the thing, then the speaker is situated in reality and not in illusion. Conversely, those who say that an apple might just as well be called an *eggplant* without truly understanding why they say this (or if they repeat this like a parrot) will be in illusion and confusion; they call the apple an eggplant while saying, right from their heart, that it is an apple because it has always been called *apple.* The objects are there, the words are there, but the lucid consciousness seems to have vanished. There are only arbitrary and powerless people: "The words contain the things."

The idea of relativity is the speaker's most valuable tool; it allows objective classification of ideas and, by measuring speech on the scale of evolution, allows the speaker to give the words exact meaning. Thus, each time, the speaker gives a precise indication of the way in which a given concept is envisaged, and because of common experience, the listener is in a position to receive the words and to understand them.[44]

According to Gurdjieff, there are three fundamental types of humans constituting the circle of the confusion of tongues, and we must observe which are the most numerous. Here we see three fundamental types of speakers (if we characterize each person from birth) constituting mechanical humanity, itself prisoner of this maleficent circle.[45]

Speaker 1 corresponds to man 1. This is the *physical* being. The knowledge of man 1 depends on the motor center and is based on imitation, instincts, and knowing by heart or repeating. The functions of instinct and movement always prevail over the functions of sentiment and thought. Speaker 1, who has no personal thought, is like the ape or the parrot. This human being knows only how to imitate, repeat, and mechanically reproduce what he sees and hears, understanding nothing. The organ of language serves only for repeating what Mr. Jones or Mr. Smith has told him. He thus requires a considerable amount of time in order to understand even the most elementary things. All creation is merely imitation. "Tame the apes," writes Daumal; that is the only thing to be done. Men 1—we "apes" or "parrots"—must train ourselves to use different parts of our machine in order to become our own masters (a master of the house!) and to go where we want, when we want, and how we want. This legitimizes the necessity for self-observation, calling to ourselves in order truly to evolve. We will call speaker 1—the ordinary speaker—the Pseudoanthrope,[46] the greatest victim of suggestibility.

Speaker 2 corresponds to man 2. This is the *emotional* being who is interested only in what he loves (or what he loathes, if he is sick), and thus speaks only of what he loves, with all his maleficent subjectivity. Emotion always prevails over the other centers. He is animated by a blind faith. This is the human of obsessions and whims, of whining and of vocal effusions of subjective sentiment. This is also the way of the monk. He is the writer of love stories and horror stories. Art, for him, is nothing but the projection of his desires and fears, his sentiments and phobias. He loves to titillate his emotional center, making himself cry (at a film, for example) or scaring himself. All his writing is merely sensual and primitive, without any foundation. We will call him the Romantic, because of his susceptibilities, exaltation, and reveries.

Speaker 3 corresponds to man 3. This is the *mental* being for whom everything starts from mental considerations. This is the man of theory, interminable argumentation, invention, construction, and the "propagation of word prostitution." As *A Night of Serious Drinking* demonstrates, there are several types of these speakers. Their knowledge is based on literal understanding, subjective logic, and vain dialectic. They are what Daumal calls, among other things, "clarificators of clarifications," or "Purificators of Accounts." This human being speaks only to flaunt his intellect, and his statements are built on marshes and sandbars whose lack of stability and foundation he is incapable of seeing. He is what is popularly called a good speaker: many nice phrases, well-polished rhetoric—but at the foundation, there is nothing. The signifier masks the gaping void of the signified—devoid of all true intentions. He knows but can do nothing, creating an imbalance among his centers simply by the fault of his intellect. He writes only to explain, theorize, argue—in short, to babble. He is convinced of the solidity of his hypotheses because they have first been passed through the sieve of his reason. We will call him the Savant.

Speakers 1, 2, and 3—"fabricators of useless objects and utterances"—are prisoners of the circle of the confusion of tongues. They know neither where they are going nor what they are saying and they have no "permanent center of gravity," which occupies a center only according to its category. They remain on the level where they were born and know only how to lie, babble, imagine, and identify themselves with their negative emotions. The literature of these speakers is part of the slumber of the masses, and all meaning of their words—if there is any—is always accidental and haphazard. Unfortunately for those who read, they write the most abundant literature. By nature they cannot possess the knowledge of superior men. "Whatever you may give him," Gurdjieff said, "he may interpret it in his own way, he will reduce every idea to the level on which he is himself."[47] This is one of the reasons why knowledge acquired through the Work cannot be divulged publicly, lest it be misinterpreted and distorted. Each level has its own knowledge, and it cannot be otherwise.

Speaker 4 corresponds to man 4. He is not born as man 4, but becomes it as a result of conscious and voluntary work. He is on the threshold between the circle of confusion and the esoteric circles. His centers are balanced; he is the "product of schoolwork": He has a permanent center of gravity and draws his knowledge from men 5, 6, and 7. On the path toward objective knowledge, he may use his higher centers. He knows where he is going and also knows what he is saying; he has taken the path of "voluntary suffering" and "conscious effort." He knows the shortest way. His words are motivated by a precise goal and his will leads him to the means of achieving it. He begins to understand and can thus claim to write literature or be a poet: He knows what to say, whom to say it to, and why and how to say it. Guided by understanding, his creation is freed from all nutritive or cultural values that might pervert the validity of what he says. All the things he puts forward have been verified by experimental study. His work—reinforced by a permanent center of gravity—crystallizes a life, not some kind of education or imagination. Writing becomes a spiritual exercise, a true asceticism that forms part of his transformation. We will call him the Apprentice Speaker.

Speaker 5 corresponds to man 5 and belongs in the exoteric circle. He is the product of a crystallization. His multiple "I"s are unified: He has achieved the unity that is so lacking in ordinary men. What he knows, he knows with all his being. His knowledge is total and indivisible and his consciousness belongs entirely to his finally unified "I." His words can thus lay claim to true authenticity, because this speaker is sincere toward himself and others. He can therefore divulge his knowledge in public, albeit very sparingly (exoterically). He is conscious of himself and his words, and he knows how to use his higher centers. We will call him the Authentic.

Speaker 6 corresponds to man 6, who has acquired "objective consciousness" and the "entirety of knowledge accessible to man." Yet his knowledge may still be lost, even if he knows how to use his second higher center. We will call him the Objective.

Speaker 7 corresponds to man 7. His "I" is permanent and his knowledge is eternal. His knowledge is objective and entirely practical in all ways. His speech is complete, permanent, and immortal.

He alone can preside over the esoteric circle. He alone can lay claim to real teaching. The literature of this fully evolved man, beyond literature (*transpoetic* and *transpersonal*—"beyond the personality," in contact with the essence, alchemical), has a single goal: the transmission of objective knowledge acquired in his existence. His forms have a legominism (in esoteric logic), materialized in writings through myths and symbols.[48] This is the passing on of the torch, the offering of the keys to the universal language. We will call him the Master. Was not Gurdjieff the most exemplary embodiment of speaker 7? After an unremitting search, did he not dedicate his life to the transmission of this knowledge, whether it was through his dance lessons, his reprimands, his books, his dinners, and even his famous toasts to the idiots—and did he not do so even on his deathbed at more than eighty years of age? Is it not surprising that the physical body of this unique speaker had barely expired when his books (beginning with Ouspensky's *In Search of the Miraculous: Fragments of an Unknown Teaching*), the continuation of his teachings, were published? Why? And how can we decipher his legominism, which is by definition hermetic?

We may well wonder how to evaluate a speaker. We can do so simply by listening to him—even if he does not utter words, "[f]or by thy words thou shalt be justified, and by thy words thou shalt be condemned."[49] But here let us take care not to fall into the trap of the ego. It is easy enough to judge others and lie to ourselves! We must remember the words of Christ: "And why beholdest thou the mote that is in thy brother's eye, but perceivest not the beam that is in thine own eye?"[50]

Each of the circles (confusion of tongues, exoteric, mesoteric, and esoteric) corresponds to a language, and in each one, all people speak the same language. To be initiated is therefore to learn the language of a higher circle along the lines of knowledge and *being*. To know the system intellectually is not enough; we must also know experientially the functioning of the human machine, practicing self-observation—because only a rigorous and impartial observation of ourselves can allow us to understand our mechanisms.

"It is very important to understand this division of man into seven categories," writes Ouspensky, "because it has applications in all the possible forms of study of human activity. It provides an instrument or a tool, powerful and precise in the hands of those who understand it, and it allows us to define manifestations which are impossible to define without it."[51]

This tool is conceived initially through self-study, and not through the judgment of others. This is not a matter of seeing a sectarian categorization. Those who think so have understood nothing. The gradation is seen within the logic of work on ourselves and is a matter of our own personal evolution. There is nothing pejorative or degrading in recognizing ouselves as man 1, 2, or 3—far from it! On the contrary, the sooner we locate our dominant and subversive center, the sooner we will be able to work on rebalancing our being in hope of a better life. The Work exists not to enslave us, but to serve us; it contributes to our general well-being and our evolution toward something spiritually superior. Those who imagine themselves to be free and saved or who believe they have understood everything have lost their way. The Work is not for them; it is for those who, conscious of their ignorance and weaknesses, wish to understand and become. The choice is up to each individual.

The act of speaking, which is movement, is a capacity of the motor center functioning under the impulse of the psychic center (in cases where speech is a materialized thought) or under the impulse of the emotional center (in the case of a cry arising from fear, arising from effusions of sentiment, or under an impulse from another center belonging to an inferior level—a cry of joy from the sexual center or a cry of pain from a physical shock passing through the mental center). In the case that interests us here, namely oral or written language, nothing is possible without the motor center (the mouth for speech, the hand or hands for writing), directed by thought—because every word has its origin in the intellectual center. But those of us who identify with negative emotions cannot stop expressing them. In doing this, however, not only do we create useless suffering, but we speak it and project it, wasting more and more energy in a babbling that is nothing but lies. Apprentice Speakers struggle against exterior influences not simply to stave them off in order to enjoy inner peace, but to transform them into a positive energy that will serve their speech, ultimately drawn from silence.

The seven types of speakers can be illustrated on an inverse enneagram. Keep in mind, however, that this classification has nothing to do with the Law of Seven. This schematic illustration simply allows us to represent this idea clearly:

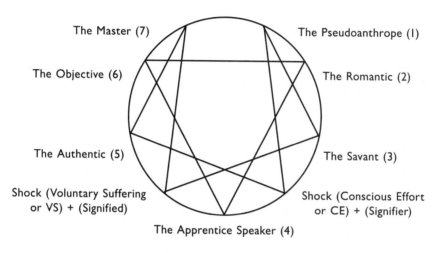

The seven types of speakers

The speaker evolves in the same direction as the hand of a watch (the symbol for a human being here). The first shock arises from conscious effort (CE), allowing the speaker to go beyond the simple approximation of the signifier. The second, requiring voluntary suffering (VS), including struggle against lies, touches upon what is truly signified and the adequation between the word and the thing designated. Between the two, on the threshold, speaker 4, the Apprentice Speaker, gains awareness of this evolution little by little and begins to stop speaking to say nothing. This work, however, is difficult, and the task that awaits the speaker is enormous: "To unlearn daydreaming, to learn to think, to unlearn philosophizing, to learn to say, this is not done in a single day."[52]

In order to do, speak, or say effectively, we must *be,* and *being* requires learning this "special language" inherent to all true evolution. In parallel, we work on the harmony of the lower centers in order to access the powers of the higher centers. Thus, for example, speakers who attain a sufficient degree of development know that they must use the intellectual part of their emotional center in order truly to stimulate their artistic creation. If they use only their intellectual center for such a task, they will fall into confusion. To each center, its essential task.[53] Certain writers or speakers know and master these faculties. They are able to write books of power that act upon all the centers of the being, that are capable of overturning the entire lives of their readers. These are, in a way, magic books, pocket masters that dispense a teaching and imprint a salvational message on the heart of every reader, aiding in self-realization.

Certain poets known as oral poets know how to make the poem leap from the page, striking the eardrums of their automaton specta-tors with hammer blows from their vocal cords. They make us waver between the dark and light sides of speech simply by enveloping the audience with their voices, hypnotizing them with their gestures, imprinting a real message on their presence. These poets signal the death of the idea word, the descriptive word, to reactivate the archaic powers of magic words, participating in the recovery of the "proper use of the spoken word" as a source of salvation.[54]

But how can language—and therefore literature and poetry—as iso-lated phenomena evolve in their turn? By what processes? How does it work? How can we find the proper use of the spoken word? The answer lies in a profound understanding of the fundamental laws of the universe, beginning with the Law of Three, or Triamazikamno. But in order truly to understand what is happening, the understanding must be not only intellectual, but also emotional and corporeal. Only a being-understanding (embracing all the centers of the being) in har-mony with the lines of knowledge and being can lead to the recovery of the lost powers of speech.

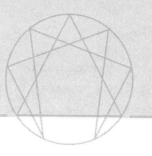

5

Reflections in Light of the Law of Triamazikamno

The Powers of Speech according to the Law of Three

Its name remains unknown. It is called Tao.

LAO-TZU

Language, like everything that exists, is ruled by universal laws. The same is true for the macrocosm and the microcosm. The idea of evolution can be understood and then assimilated only via a perfect understanding of the laws relating to language.

As a preliminary introduction, let us recall that the enneagram is made from the workings of the double universal, fundamental, and sacred Law of Triamazikamno (the Law of Three) and Law of Heptaparaparshinokh (the Law of Seven or the the Law of the Octave). This tool's originality lies in the fact that it provides an explanatory global vision of all the processes at work in the cosmos. Gurdjieff was the first to reveal its existence to the West around 1915; it had never before been the object of a written tradition or even of an oral tradition. Besides being a graphical projection of the laws of the universe, the enneagram also serves as a "musical protractor" for the teachings to which it relates. In fact, every conscious endeavor corresponds, in its sequential order, to the points located on the rotating circle, while at the same time the inscribed triangle manifests the three "holy forces" present everywhere—the Law of Three:

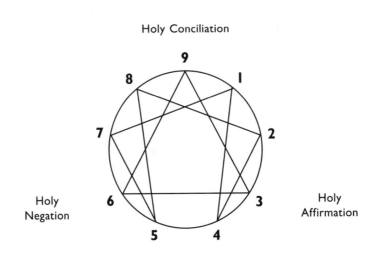

The Law of Three, or Triamazikamno (a term combining Slavic, English, and Sanskrit roots and meaning "I am the triple work between the yes and the no"), postulates that every phenomenon, wherever it is produced, results from the meeting of three forces, which Gurdjieff called holy affirmation (assertion; the Father), holy negation (the Mother; the Son), and holy conciliation (reconciliation; the Holy Ghost). It is because of these forces that everything becomes possible. Ouspensky more simply calls them the active force, the passive force, and the neutralizing force. In the ordinary circumstances of existence, however, we are blind to the existence of these forces; we can recognize them only if we undertake work on ourselves. According to Gurdjieff, we are subject to the same laws as the universe—and as such, we are an image of the world, a microcosm subject to the same laws as the macrocosm. By observing ourselves, we can then understand and use these fundamental laws.[1] Let us clarify right away (this is an ongoing source of confusion): Conciliation is not the result, but the force by which the result is possible. Metaphorical images allow us to illustrate the third force. In a windmill, for example, it is the blade—the wind being the active force and the structure the passive force. And in language?

Before showing how the Law of Triamazikamno applies to language as well as to all other isolated phenomena, let us first investigate the causes of what certain intellectuals call "the limits of description"—wherein, by definition, the Triad is not realized, which consequently dooms every exchange to failure. Here is a highly revealing example: How can we describe a powerful ecstatic experience? How can we describe a voyage through the states of consciousness when it is provoked chemically? Let us examine the experience of taking peyote. Between his initiation and the publication of *Pays de l'éclairement,* Charles Duits read a great deal about "unlimiters of consciousness," but he was still disappointed by the descriptions—both his own and those of others: "I had never been able truly to say what made peyote a sacred plant comparable to the fabled soma of India, which, as the Vedas say, the gods themselves consumed 'to maintain their divinity.'"[2]

Yet this avowal of inability conceals a mark of intense humility that speaks eloquently to the powers of language—demonstrated by the force of Duits's writing, which is incomparably revealing and highly significant. Writes Thierry Guichard, "Charles Duits is one of those rare writers the reading of whom can upturn entire lives. This is perhaps the reason for the rejection he has faced for so long." Let us clarify further that the reader is not upturned by hollow and void language, but by a speech of life directed toward awakening: "Charles Duits's work," writes Michel Camus, "is that positively dangerous writing which (Jean Paulhan refers to in his preface to *The Story of O*) does not leave us as we are, that awakens and transforms us." Such is the true purpose of writing. All the power of its phrasing is at the service of the goal or goals for which the writer aims. (We will return to this later.) According to Duits, description must first throw light upon the subject in order for it to be visible from all its angles: "My description necessarily has a goal which . . . illuminates the things of which I speak like a lamp, bringing out their contours and edges."[3] But it must be noted that there are some experiences that are hard to relate:

> [I]t is evident that the more one excites the reader's curiosity, the more difficult it is to appease it. The longer the wait, the more prodigious must be the event required to satisfy it. Now when describing the world revealed by peyote, it is impossible to satisfy the expectations aroused by this description. The reader remains necessarily unsatiated. He understands that for the investigator, the things seen there had an extreme, exorbitant importance, but the reason why they had this importance escapes him.[4]

The only means for satisfying readers' hunger, ultimately, will be sharing the same experience and eating the sacred cactus! If they wish to satisfy this metaphysical hunger, readers must become participants and no longer simple spectators in a world that eludes them.[5] What may have appeared optional at the beginning of the reading becomes, in fact, an absolute necessity, so important are the things seen by the investigator. They have a significance apparently unequaled by language: "Every shrub contains an angel," writes Duits, "but an angel with closed lips, not confiding any message, not dictating any law, not charging with any apostolate the person to whom he reveals himself." The goal of the writer, like that of the master, is to be the finger pointing to the moon. It is up to each person to make his or her own way, to discover what is hidden in the bush. Only lived experience allows us to find ultimate meaning—and peyote appears to be one of the effective means, among many, for balancing the "lines of knowledge and being" mentioned by Gurdjieff, an indispensable operation for all true evolution: "The essential effect of peyote is to make us feel what we ordinarily only know."[6]

In fact, peyote is an effective tool for the being-understanding of what causes the powerlessness of the idea word and the formidable force of the magic word. Is speech hallucinogenic, illusory, or psychedelic, revealing the spirit and the divine in ourselves? In fact, it can be both liar and deceiver and revealer of consciousness. It is like magic, as

Daumal said—white or black, objective or subjective. It can heal or kill, give sight or make us blind. If the effects of peyote are so disturbing at first, it is because, according to Duits, they "manifest through an involution of the signifying power of speech," revealing the apparent emptiness of language while causing the investigator to experience a "crucifixion of speech."[7] This stage is difficult and alarming, giving the illusion that language is powerless to say. But this is not at all so, as we will see.

Since the time of Baudelaire, Duits notes, "the very possibility of verbal exchange has been often and seriously called into question."[8] Here the poet poses the question—already posed in Ouspensky's *In Search of the Miraculous: Fragments of an Unknown Teaching*—of communication between individuals: When two people (speaker and listener) converse, are they talking ultimately about the same thing? Do they give the same value to the words, the same profundity, the same meaning?[9]

> Nothing, in fact, proves that I give to words—at least, to essential words: love, justice, God, liberty, salvation—the same meaning as my interlocutor. The agreement that discussion reaches in principle is perhaps illusory. Ultimately, every word rests upon an act of faith, which the too-often-justified skepticism of our times renders more difficult every day. We can no longer content ourselves with believing that we understand; and we prefer honest obscurity to deceptive illumination.[10]

It is all a question of understanding. It is clear that based on these "essential words," all communication remains very fragile. Is it not enough to listen to certain reflections on liberty, for example, to perceive very quickly that this signifier embraces various realities, various things signified, often very different from each other depending on the different people who use this word? The question of language, of speech, is an eternal debate, an eternal question that has forever haunted the writer. Duits writes, "On the blank page, a membranous shadow." Yet he also notes, "sometimes it happens that the uncertainty inexplicably fades away," a "joy comes," and a "music reaches the depths of the language, animates them, illuminates them." He takes care to clarify, however, that these moments are brief. This is why the idea of evolution discussed in chapter 4 must be understood with the entire measure of being. Analysis of the foreword to *A Night of Serious Drinking* in light of the Law of Three will help us considerably in this respect.

Emphasizing the fragility of the relationship that exists between the "events [dimensions] and the sentiments [intensity]," Duits shows how, for those who consume an unlimiter, the "description of the event" is no longer sufficient, because the investigator "feels and sees differently."

> Infinitesimal, in fact, this event (a bird flew by, a leaf fell) resounds in the soul of the adept with a violence that appears exorbitant to the profane. There is no connection between dimension and intensity. A distance asserts itself, making the reader profane, a humiliating word which rightly awakens indignation. By what right, he asks himself, does the other decorate himself with the fine name "initiate"? Calling him sick would be more fitting. The writer does what is thus possible for him; he describes the "cloak of Magnificence" (Rûzbehân's expression). But this cloak is entirely immobile; no breath will move a single fold of it.[11]

Those who consume an awakener will find themselves alone, apart from others, and they must bear the indelible mark of this singular experience—like Jacob after his fight with the angel—because between others and them "the magic blood that gives exchanges to their value does not circulate."[12] And yet, it is all a matter of circles. Duits's metaphor, very significant paradoxically, speaks to the whole obscurity of ordinary language: "Here, then, is the obstacle, impassable and simple. During a long journey, almost nothing happens to us, in the end, on the objective plane. There is absolute silence. Manifesting itself is a disproportion for which language cannot compensate and which apparently indicates a new weakness in language. I am even more alone than I thought. In vain I shake the dark lamp of speech."[13] Charles Duits is not alone, but he lives—we must admit—in a circle from which ordinary people are absent, which explains his dismay and his apparent solitude.

Is there a state in which words no longer speak? Many authors who endeavor to describe ecstatic, psychedelic, or paranormal experiences show that it is a state in which language seems useless and ineffective, in which speech seems no longer to speak . . . which does not mean that speech has no power. Far from it! True, the word-idea appears powerless in retranscribing ecstasy. Sure enough, we have been able to observe this throughout these many questionings. But what if, rather than always doubting language, we question the person who uses it? It seems, if we stand by Gurdjieff's observation, that all problems of communication are connected to us ourselves—precisely because, as he tells us, "men are not men" but machines, enslaved and imprisoned robots. This powerlessness of language comes from the fact that the normal, ordinary person lives in what Gurdjieff calls the circle of the confusion of tongues. To reactivate the powers of speech, to restore to words their vibratory and magical forces, the poet or writer must evolve his or her level of consciousness, must "find the nectar at the heart of the poison" if his or her questioning requires it, in order finally to find the true, Adamic, crystalline word. By purifying his or her perception, the poet purifies speech. Everything arises from the same movement in which the consciousness occupies a central place.

How can language signify something to an ordinary consciousness, blind and hallucinating? The problem comes not from the words in the end, but from the man-machine, unconscious as we are of our mechanicalness:

> At first, we would think Gurdjieff to be joking. But no, he is not joking at all. I can no longer go for a walk, so atrocious is the spectacle. On the street we meet only with madmen, dying people, phantoms, automatons, and walking stomachs. With the best will in the world, I cannot call them men. And I can no longer speak to them . . . or address myself to them. We write for others—for ourselves as well, for sure, but mainly for others—most often because we wish to awaken ourselves or sometimes because we

wish to transmit a teaching. But we cannot write for . . . for things, you understand. Spirits are lucky: They have interlocutors. Not I. All writers—writers worthy of the name—run into this dilemma sooner or later. It is not the words that are dead, but the people.[14]

And if the people are dead, we must—if still possible—awaken them.[15] Once again, this is the goal of art. In purifying his perception, the poet purifies his speech, giving words a "being semblance" in order that they may recover their profound meanings. Because I invoke it, the pigeon appears; because I apply the forces to it, the word *dog* dies. Those who "pass through the door in the wall" will leave the circle of the confusion of tongues and reach the clear discourse referred to by Daumal in his foreword to *A Night of Serious Drinking*. As Michel Waldberg notes, the "new language" whose absolute necessity Gurdjieff emphasizes "has undoubtedly never been better defined than by René Daumal in his foreword."[16]

This remark deserves elaboration. The key may reside in this fundamental observation: In order to understand one another, people must truly be in the same world, or rather, in the same circle (which is more accurate, considering we all live in the same world, although it is all a question of definition!). This will give language its entire force of meaning: "The sleepers each live in their own worlds," writes Heraclitus; "only the awakened have a world in common"—and for a common world (or circle), a common language! Only those who have a high enough level of consciousness can gain access to the magical powers of speech and delight in the energy inherent in language. Hence the necessity for this common language. "The truth is entirely simple, but it is unspeakable. To formulate it, we must invent a new grammar, and therefore also a new logic. Currently, because it is impossible to formulate, we must content ourselves with expressing it. This is what poets do."[17]

For saying it, a new system is needed that can make up for this absence. This is what Gurdjieff made. "You can describe a unicorn," writes Duits, "but how to describe the world from the unicorn's point of view?" Begin by studying yourself! According to Rimbaud, "The first stage for the man who wishes to be a poet is his own entire consciousness: he searches his soul, he inspects it, he tempts it, he learns about it."[18] Gurdjieff states, "The chief method of self-study is self-observation. Without properly applied self-observation, a man will never understand the connection and the correlation between the various functions of his machine." Experiential knowledge of the functioning of the human machine requires rigorous self-observation ("analysis + method of observations"). Rimbaud, and some others, understood it, because they had seen. Writes Daumal, "The white poet seeks to understand his poetic nature, to free himself from it and make it serve. The black poet uses it and becomes its slave."[19] Only properly guided self-observation can allow us to recover the proper use of the spoken word. Gurdjieff, Ouspensky, and Daumal indicated a few of its fundamental features and provided its foundations—scattered fragments that we intend to reassemble here and to forge at the fire of a new teaching, to weld with the strength of a new formula.

Rightly denying "that a clear thought can ever be inexpressible," René Daumal—who, although he does not refer to it, knew of the Law of Triamazikamno—formulated the basic conditions for claiming clear discourse. Let us remember that although he was one of the greatest and most inspired writers of the twentieth century, he was also, above all, the disciple of Father Sogol, who helped him crystallize those fundamental properties in himself, the luminous traces of which we find in his texts.

Language, like everything else, is subject to the fundamental cosmic Law of Triamazikamno. This is precisely what René Daumal reveals implicitly in his foreword to *A Night of Serious Drinking* and in "Poetry Black, Poetry White" for the few who know how to decipher these texts, aided by the proper tools. These two fundamental texts have the same meaning and express the same "proper use": that of speech. Ouspensky relates that for Gurdjieff, "each completed whole, each cosmos, each organism, each plant, is an enneagram. . . ." We might add to this list each clear discourse. "[B]ut," Gurdjieff adds, "not each of these enneagrams has an inner triangle. The inner triangle stands for the presence of higher elements according to the scale of hydrogens in a given organism." In other words, depending upon which axis we are concerned with, all language does not necessarily have an inner triangle. Only what Daumal calls clear discourse is composed of the three holy forces (holy affirmation, holy negation, and holy conciliation), which are also, symbolically, the "three presupposed conditions" that Daumal refers to in his foreword. "Clear discourse presupposes three conditions: a speaker who knows what he wishes to say, a listener in a state of wakefulness, and a language common to both."[20] Furthermore, more subtly, there are the "three phases of the poetic operation" for white poetry, which correspond in a certain manner to the aforementioned three conditions and which activate the powers of speech. "I will distinguish three phases of the poetic operation: the luminous seed, the clothing in images, and verbal expression."[21] This idea can be illustrated on the triad.

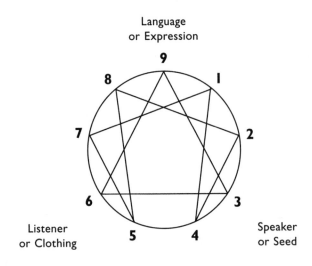

It is only "by studying himself, the manifestations of his thought, consciousness, activity—his habits, his desires, and so on" that "man may learn to observe and to see in himself the action of the three forces."[22] "If we could see the manifestation of three forces in every action," Gurdjieff adds, "we should then see the world as it is (things in themselves)."[23] The same is true for objective language: The triad embodies the three conditions (the three forces) for a true rehabilitation of the powers of speech; the exchange (result) becomes possible when the speaker (active force) and listener (passive force) share the same language (conciliatory force).

The three represents the "speaker who knows what he wishes to say" or the "luminous seed"—the holy affirmation, the active and acting force, which in this particular case affirms: If the wind does not blow powerfully, it cannot make the windmill's blades turn quickly. In the same way, if the speaker does not know what he truly wishes to say or how to say it, he can have no true action upon language and the psyche of the listener: "Every poem is born of a seed, dark at first, which we must make luminous for it to produce fruits of light. With the black poet, the seed remains dark and produces blind, subterranean vegetation. To make it shine, one must create silence, for this seed is the Thing-to-be-said itself, the central emotion that seeks to express itself through my whole machine."[24] It is the speaker who carries the "seed" inside himself: Only the speaker can make it brilliant and inundate the being—to its very depths—with light. Conversely, the black poet cannot make the seed luminous any more than the ordinary man; it remains dark and produces blind, subterranean vegetation—in other words, it propagates word prostitution, encouraging the suggestibility and blindness of the masses. The black poet is Lentrohamsanin in *Beelzebub's Tales to His Grandson,* the great culprit of the terror of the situation. He is the intellectual (the educator) in the Western sense of the term ("learned being of new formation"), symbolized in *Beelzebub's Tales to His Grandson* by the "subsequent universal Hasnamuss." He is the "destroyer of the very saintly labors" of Ashiata Shiemash, he is at the origin of the subjectification of values performed in the name of liberty, which produced Babel and the circle of the confusion of tongues in which we live. These culprits corrupt the spirit of the *obyvatels.* Lentrohamsanin embodies the beings we are, in contrast with Ashiata Shiemash. He is the man of confusion par excellence, stating without understanding, the fruit of his parents' vanity. He is the opposite of the conscious person. He favors ambition over love of truth.

With Lentrohamsanin, Gurdjieff harshly criticized writing that speaks to say nothing or, worse yet, aggravates the situation in which humanity is stuck. Writes Daumal, "Writing, for me, is a very serious exercise full of risks, saying what I know, never more or less."

The seed, the thing to be said, passes through silence—that crucible of revelations—in order to shine. This central emotion is expressed through the "machine":

> So far, you've only talked about inanimate objects. What about animate objects, then?—Oh them! You know as well as I do how sensitive they are to *articulated language*. For instance, a man walks down the street; he is preoccupied with his *inner ticklings* (thoughts, he calls them). You yell out: "Hey!" Immediately, the whole complex *machine,* with its *mechanisms* of muscles and bone, blood channels, thermo-regulation, gyroscopic gadgets . . . all this complicated *equipment* does a half-twist, the jaw drops, the eyes bulge, the legs wobble and the whole *thing* stares at you like a calf or a viper or a visor or a bucket or a rat, it all depends. And the inner ticklings (well, what do *you* call them?) are suspended for a moment and perhaps the direction they take will be permanently changed as a result. You are also aware that the word: *"Hey!"* if it is to produce this effect, must be pronounced with a particular intonation. Generally speaking, people talk as they might fire a gun, at random, every ear for itself.[25]

Daumal does not neglect to point out, after the fashion of his own master, that men are not men ultimately, that we are machines that must free ourselves from this dismal condition in order to enjoy true freedom, which is "faith in consciousness," according to the first line of the marble tablet. "So be quiet, machine! Work and shut up!"[26] It is a machine that fully legitimizes the use of the word *that.* Because we are not people, this is not dehumanization. We should speak not of psychology, but of mechanics. To bring about a possible gain of consciousness, hammering is necessary, and if language is imprecise, it is because thought is imprecise and inexact. It is the thought of the speaker that determines the precision of his speech, the force of his luminous seed.[27]

No. 6, the listener in a drowsy quiescence, but also "clothing in images," is the passive force: Just as the structure supports the blades of the windmill, so speech is anchored and imprinted on the listener-spectator. "But once the order is established, we must let the seed itself choose the plant or animal in which it will clothe itself by giving it life."[28]

Without a precise target, it becomes useless to speak, lest we fall into babbling and the confusion of tongues. "It takes two to make a poem." The poem must be heard in order to exist; it requires the presence of a listener who is the target.

> There is another manner of speaking. It consists first of having a clearly defined *target*. Next of taking careful aim. And then, fire! Every ear for itself. But if I've aimed carefully, I'll score a bull's ear. It's even better when your words begin to suggest images, that is to sculpt the psychophysical waste produced by *walking stomachs,* carving it by means of various stirrings of the animal spirits, but I can't explain everything to you at once. Besides, you don't need to do much; you've only to think a bit.[29]

Let us then reflect: Part 1, chapter 10, of *A Night of Serious Drinking* is unreadable for those unfamiliar with Gurdjieff's teachings, but it is incredibly succulent, rich in illustrations and teachings for those who do know this secret. The same can be said for Charles Duits's *Le Pays de l'éclairement.* These are not unreadable works in the sense that readers will understand nothing of what is read. Far from it, for these are works of genius in themselves and are rich in meaning—but in the sense that the something that readers understand will not be the essential thing that will be understood by those who know this secret. Again, every ear for itself.

Point 9 on the enneagram symbolizes the common language, otherwise known in "Poetry Black, Poetry White" as verbal expression—the holy conciliation or neutralizing force. It is to language as the blade is to the windmill (someone or something—an active force—is needed to make it turn) or as the beam is to the balance. This common language matches what Ouspensky calls the new language, implying understanding of the ideas of evolution and relativity. We have already approached this idea many times, and this new knowledge requires observing ourselves. To activate this polarizing force, it is important to take care of not only "internal work, but also external science and know-how"—in other words, the power of action of speaking, the seed's own respiration: "Its breath takes possession of the expressive mechanisms by communicating its rhythm to them. . . . This power is exercised thanks to the particular relation that exists between the various elements of the poet's machinery, and that unites matters as different as emotions, images, concepts and sounds in a single living substance. The life of this new organism is the poet's rhythm."[30]

Though black poetry opens a number of worlds, these worlds may appear to some to be "without Sun" and "decorated with mirages." The black poet remains a prisoner of the circle of the confusion of tongues. This is why only "[w]hite poetry opens the door to only one world, that of the unique Sun, without false wonders, real."[31]

Daumal confesses seeking to achieve this whiteness that forms all the force of true poetry. Grayness takes hold of writing, sullied by the "mixture of light and darkness." Now the poet rereads his sentences to purify them: "In my sentences, I see words, expressions, interferences that do not serve the thing-to-be-said."[32] Now begins the great poetic cleansing that alone allows this liberating whiteness to be accessed: "Language itself seems set up in such a way as to detect the intruders for me. Few mistakes are purely technical. Almost all of them are my mistakes. And I cross out, and I correct, with the joy one can have at cutting a gangrenous limb from one's body."[33] This is precisely what Charles Duits did when he sought to restore the "academic value" to words: "I no longer had any reason to doubt that the universe was exactly what language says it is—an order with its origin in divinity at whose heart man occupies the central place. Having no other motive for doubting, I doubted no longer. I believed in speech as we believe in an oracle whose predictions are always proved correct."[34] According to Duits, it is the true hope in the action of communicating—or obsession—that makes poets of those who write. Style is necessary and determines an author's quality,[35] but, we must clarify, not style for the sake of style, but the form that serves what Daumal calls the thing to be said, the seed, or the central emotion signifying by its very structure. In other words, the style must serve the meaning, "the beautiful being the splendor of the true."

But all this would not be enough, Daumal adds, without the fourth double condition (requirement)—already implicitly mentioned—relating to the idea of evolution taught by Gurdjieff: "[I]t is not enough for a language to be clear in the way that an algebraic proposition is clear. It must also have a real, not simply a possible, content. Before this happens, the participants must have, as a fourth element, *a common experience of the thing which is spoken of.*"[36] This common experience, symbolized by the circle itself (again, literally and in all senses), defines the contour of the enneagram as well as the triangle itself, which implies clear discourse. It should be explained: The circle can be that very same circle of the confusion of tongues (which has no triangle) in which the ordinary common experience is subject to the same confusion—always linked to an incapacity of consciousness. Two people can use the same words without speaking of the same reality, continuing to live, without realizing it, on distorted misunderstandings. Everything depends on the signifier, but the signified is not shared. Those who have never burned themselves, for example, may very well use the word *fire* in a conversation with someone who knows the sensation produced by burning, but because they have never experimented with it themselves, they can never understand its mechanism—because they do not know the sensation that results from it. Without this common experience, language is fundamentally doomed to failure—for there is incomprehension and a difference in levels of reality. Again, "only the awakened have a world in common," as Heraclitus said. This is why clear discourse requires first an evolution of consciousness, and this evolution implies a being-understanding of its mechanisms, bearing in mind that "understanding is acquired . . . from the totality of information intentionally learned and from personal experiencings."[37]

Hence the crucial importance of experience, according to Daumal, in keeping with Hindu poetry, which alone allows for an authentic and fruitful exchange:

This common experience is the gold reserve that confers an exchange value on the currency of words. Without this reserve of shared experiences, all our pronouncements are checks drawn on insufficient funds. Algebra, in fact, is no more than a vast intellectual credit exercise, a counterfeiting operation which is legitimate because it is acknowledged: Each individual knows that it has its object and meaning in something other than itself, namely arithmetic. But it is still not enough for language to have clarity and content, as when I say, "that day, it was raining" or "three plus two make five"; it must also have a goal and an imperative.[38]

The goal, given as clearly by Daumal as it was avowed and claimed by Gurdjieff, is to allow us to free ourselves from our mechanicalness and thus from our slavery, passivity, illusion, sleep. "My father had a very simple, clear and quite definite view on the aim of human life. He told me many times in my youth that the fundamental striving of every man should be to create for himself an inner freedom towards life and to prepare for himself a happy old age. He considered that the indispensability and imperative necessity of this aim in life was so obvious that it ought to be understandable by everyone without any wiseacring."[39]

"To create for himself an inner freedom," the ultimate goal of human life, involves plenty of effort, plenty of suffering. Those who wish to evolve must follow the path of the warrior without tarrying, like Arjuna on his battlefield who, seized by a profound dismay, falling victim to his abulia and vertigo, to his fear and his principles, rose up from his ashes, thanks to the words of Krishna, to confront his own brothers and let his own blood flow. The "Song of the Blessed" has only a single goal: to liberate us from our illusory torments and machine-like reactions, forcing us to confront our own phantoms.[40] Such is the prize of this inner liberty: the mastery of emotions, body, and thought, as is suggested—once again—by the metaphor of the chariot, horses, and reins, the coachman and his passenger. Krishna, the incarnation of consciousness and healing speech, is the double holy conciliation of the holy affirmation, thanks to which action becomes possible and, through action, moksha—true liberation. Krishna symbolizes the Tao regulating the alternation of yin and yang, the fusion and harmony of the being which reveals its essence and becomes its master.

Likewise, the goal of all true speech, of all literature in the noble sense, is to work actively on this journey of realization, to free the speaker from his babbling, to wake him up—in short, to remove the speaker one way or another from his "abnormal being conditions of ordinary existence," a great many of which arise from the "crystallization of the consequences of the properties of the organ Kundabuffer." The single goal of the awakening poet is simply to awaken people to absolute sentiment and to the sacred, as Michel Camus writes:

> In the eyes of seekers of the truth, initiatory poetry—magicians' and diviners' poetry, awakening poetry—oriented toward unitive knowledge, aims to reconnect the essence of man with the essence of the universe. Only the awakened poet knows that the living are of the same essence as the dead. Yet most awakening poetry today is not living in the catacombs of an era that falls prey to the disintegration of all values, the degeneration of all religions, the breakdown of the last myths such as Marxism and the utopian eschatology of science. In a world that has lost all its reference points, there are still, here and there, heretical carriers of the sacred fire, alchemists of silence, and visionaries. The media are afraid of silence. Insensitive to higher poetry, the men who live on the surface of life are incapable of sensing the secret of the living silence hidden in all the silence of death. . . . The diviner poets know on which side they fight. The paradigm of transcultural poetry is above all the necessity of awakening man to what constitutes him, to what passes through him and transcends him.[41]

All true poetic experience is by definition transpersonal, carrying the goal within itself, intending to go "beyond personality" in order to attain the essence that lies at the heart of the being, beyond the multiplicity of the "*I*"s:

> Every serious literary enterprise is an endeavor to express the whole of the man. Every serious literary enterprise must therefore begin

with a categorical refusal to express, as part of the real being, the successive *"I"*s and that other *"I,"* just as illusory, of the writing writer. [. . .] I have become conscious of this mechanicalness, of my fear of existence. I write only to affirm that I am not its dupe, and to invite others to become conscious of it for themselves. I do nothing but describe this illusory existence, woven from hollow threads, in its extreme complexity. I write *Ulysses*, I write *À la recherche du temps perdu*, or I write *Waiting for Godot*. I write to make myself nauseous and to make my readers equally nauseous.[42]

Indeed, who wants to wait in vain for someone who will never come, not knowing who they are waiting for or when or where or why that person will arrive? Who wants to start each day just like the day before it and the day after, like a sick robot—tedious, sterile, and oppressive? No one, no one would want to lead such an unfortunate existence, answers the first person to whom we pose this question. In this way, the responder imagines him- or herself to be conscious or intelligent enough not to be subject to such absurdity. And yet, this is exactly what the majority of us do. We wait, not knowing why, for things to happen instead of triggering them and then seizing them. We wait for the "luck" that by definition will never come (or will come only by accident), blindly submitting to the law of chance. Everything happens to us; we control nothing in our lives, preferring—unconsciously, for the most part—for someone else to do things in our place, even at the price of our own freedom. Otherwise, we would no longer be waiting but doing—endeavoring to control the universal laws rather than being subject to them. We would no longer be killing time, like Vladimir and Estragon, with vain actions and pointless chatting.

Finally, in all seriousness, what can we think television is for—especially those programs that are insulting to true human potential—if not to kill time, which serves these puppets of flesh and bone only for their profound subjugation to the days that pass, while they passively wait in their anguished fate for the hour of death? "I can't go on like this," "That's what you think," declare the indecisive bums in *Waiting for Godot*. They would like to put an end to this terrible situation, but they cannot. As they themselves admit, they are only machines, going on "like this." They move, urinate, make noises with their mouths. They believe that sometimes they think or that they exist, they believe, they believe—but it means nothing. Pauwels might have added to his list *The Bald Soprano,* a piece in which the dramaturge exorcises his babbling in the production of an empty and hollow speech given in the terrible theater of the confusion of tongues, in an illusory language full of holes.

Writes René Daumal, "The poet makes us help him fight his battle against illusion. He speaks of himself, of his torment; he talks of his passions, his mania, his feelings in order better to fight them, conquer them, and shut them in the tomb of a measured word." Like Arjuna in the Bhagavad Gita, the poet must confront his phantoms, battle his passions, destroy his desires, conquer his abulia—without these conditions there can be no pretense to writing. For this, he must combat exterior influences, turn away from negative nourishment, force himself to hunt down and annihilate his nutritive values in order to open himself to true life, and finally, dare to take up his pen once again before a page that is free of vanity. Writes Pauwels, "I do not know if I will manage to create this great *"I,"* but what I have accomplished, in the revolt against the nonexistence of myself and all things around me, will end by giving my language a creative value which ordinary human language, the language of submission, the language of accepted absence, cannot have."[43]

The same is true for reading as for writing, for readers as for the writer. Every work that aims for evolution must be experienced as a spiritual asceticism that seeks to raise consciousness to a higher level. Those who seek *diversion*—according to the etymology of the word—will turn themselves away from the essential, from the essence of heaven, the source of salvation, condemning themselves forever to confusion and incapability:

A great deal can be found by reading. For instance, take yourself: you might already know a great deal if you knew how to read. I mean that, if you understood everything you have read in your life, you would already know what you are looking for now. . . . But you do not understand either what you read or what you write. You do not even understand what the word *understand* means. Yet understanding is essential, and reading can be useful only if you understand what you read.[44]

Here, we would be tempted to add: We must read again or do something correctly with our entire consciousness—but we are too lazy and insincere. With the tough and demanding qualities of a master, Gurdjieff said to one of his writing students: "It would be a thousand times better for you to wash the floor just once the way it ought to be done than to write twenty books." This was not a gratuitous declaration; its primary goal was to cause the birth in his student's psyche of some aggravating truths about himself. Its secondary goal was to awaken his consciousness, "[f]or to love the disciple," writes Michel Waldberg, "means not to console but to heal him. And the more serious the disease, the more violent the cure."[45]

The necessity Daumal mentions corresponds ultimately to this goal: Only an identical language will allow for an understanding of the idea of evolution,[46] which must be conscious and voluntary, according to the principal laws of Gurdjieff's cosmology. We must always remember, "the evolution of man is the evolution of his consciousness," implying necessarily will, conscious effort, and voluntary suffering:

> Otherwise, from language we descend into chatter, from chatter to babble, and from babble to confusion. In this confused state of languages, men, even though they have a common experience, have no language with which to exchange its fruits. Then, when this confusion grows intolerable, universal languages are invented, clear and hollow, where words are but counterfeit coins no longer backed by the gold of authentic experience, languages which allow us from childhood to swell our heads with false knowledge.[47]

The circle of the confusion of tongues contains almost all of humanity, subject to the laws of chance and accident, wandering without a target, without a goal, and without necessity, in contrast with the esoteric circles in which people know not only where they are going but also why and how, because they are conscious and masters of themselves and consequently masters of their destiny and their words.[48]

The proper use of the magic word corresponds to the Law of Three applied according to the following algebraic proposition: language = (clarity + content) + (goal + necessity). The triad allows us to test any idea that, without this concrete application, would fall into confusion and into false ideas.

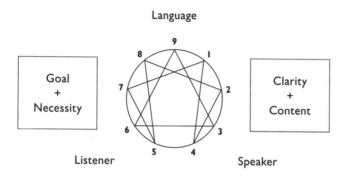

In the case of a comparative analysis, which must precede every statement, the comparer "playing the game" will also note the importance of this triangular relationship. Let us use the example of someone approaching texts with the goal of drawing some given meaning from them. This is a matter of intertextuality in the sense given to it by L. Jenny in *Poétique:* "[n]ot a confusing and mysterious summation of influences, but a project of transformation and assimilation of many texts, operated through a central text that preserves leadership over the meaning."[49] In other words, two texts, incomparable a priori, can reveal themselves to be full of interesting connections with the mediation of a third text which polarizes them and plays the role of a conciliating force. If sulfur and mercury seem to have nothing in common, then, according to alchemical logic, adding salt can allow us to achieve the Great Work. The seeker's entire task is to find the holy conciliation that makes all things possible.

In chapter 3, there was also the question of adequation between words and things, and of course the famous—though sterile—debate between Cratylus (a disciple of Heraclitus), the intuitive partisan of this concordance, and Hermogenes, the materialistic opposing thinker who is devoted to chance, overzealously proclaiming the triumph of the arbitrary because he has not put the "sign" upon the cross:

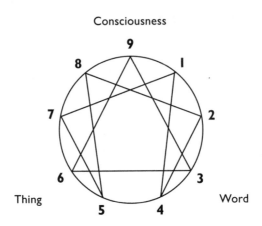

Due to the polarizing or neutralizing force—which is conscious-ness in this case—holy conciliation, symbol of the Holy Ghost, is resur-rected to meaning by Cratylus, language is resacralized, and the word regains its primordial, creative power. Finally, the word can embody the thing in its essence; consciousness insures correct mediation between the two.[50] Without this superior consciousness, all true communica-tion is condemned, and we must observe all literature and all poetry as unable to claim to be anything but fuel for the lethargy of the masses and futile descriptions of disembodied things. For this adequation to be possible at all, we must no longer look at the thing and attempt hap-hazardly to give it a name, but rather see it in order finally to say it and name it:

> . . . Yes, when I now write *tree,* the word I use is no longer a word;
> it is the action by which the tree receives the name *tree* for the first
> time and truly becomes a tree. I no longer refer to things, I no lon-
> ger appeal to them as witnesses to the discharge of the perpetual

process of my false life, I no longer tell stories about them, I no longer make literature. I name them. . . . Thus, for us, this is no longer a matter of describing, but of creating, and in order to create, we must first create ourselves. Afterward, we can allow ourselves to write. I write *tree*. It is a tree. I write *friendship*. It is friendship. I write *love*. It is love. It is a matter of renaming things, animals, beings, and the relationships between the beings.[51]

In order to succeed in creating things, however, the poet must bear in mind, always in keeping with the logic of the system, that "poetry (in fact, all writing restored to its sacred character) is an instrument of knowledge," that true knowledge is experiential, "the identity of the subject and object," and that it must be "that of the absolute" without forgetting that "the production of a poem (the writing of the least phrase) is analogous to the genesis of the world."[52] In this way, objective speech can be born.

The efficacy of language, its power of creation, is therefore the consequence of the law of "Fundamental-First-degree-Sacred-Triamazikamno,"[53] which regulates the manifestation of all isolated phenomena—that is, the current and complete existence of an object or event as well as all other things. But this result is not conciliation—which is the common language (without which nothing is possible), the new language. Instead, the capacity for communication, which must be perfect and faultless in order for a true exchange to occur, must reach the point of doing and, if possible, awakening. Just as water and flour do not make bread unless they are joined by fire, so Mr. Smith and Mr. Jones do not really understand each other—and are thus not capable of acting—unless they are joined by the fire of the same language and thus the same level of consciousness.

This new language is to true communication much as the Holy Ghost is to Christians or history is to Marxists. Through the polarizing force, everything becomes possible, particularly the revival of what Daumal called the proper use of the spoken word. Further, if the Law of Three governs the causality of every isolated phenomenon, it is the highly complex Law of Seven that rules the trajectory of every process or series of phenomena. In other words, if it is Triamazikamno that makes true exchange possible, then sure enough, it is Heptaparaparshinokh that determines the real consequences that the progression of this series of exchanges can have at the very heart of the humanity in which we live. Everything is inextricably linked, and consequently every isolated phenomenon is included without delay in the weaving of a process that is itself subject to this Law of Seven. As the Emerald Tablet tells us: ". . . [t]he higher blends with the lower in order to actualize the middle and thus becomes either higher for the preceding lower or lower for the succeeding higher."[54]

6

Reflections in Light of the Law of Heptaparaparshinokh

or How to Reach Your Target (Goal)

The words of the sage are like the seven notes on the lyre,
which contain all music, along with the numbers and
laws of the universe.

ÉDOUARD SCHURÉ, *THE GREAT INITIATES*

If all realities come from the primordial triad, then the order of their progression is determined not by chance (which does not exist in the Work), but rather by the Law of Heptaparaparshinokh[1] (a mixture of Greek and Slavonic roots, meaning "family of the seven units of measure that follow one after the other"), otherwise known as the Law of Seven or the Law of Octaves, which, along with Triamazikamno, constitutes the most original element that Gurdjieff brought to the West around 1915. It synthesizes the complexity of his teachings in a single figure: the enneagram—a formidable symbol that expresses the two fundamental laws in the universe and consequently offers infinite possible interpretations. Some trace its origin back to Pythagoras, around 600 BCE. It is said to be the ninth of the ten seals, but nothing is proved, for this symbol was kept highly secret and was not made the object of any tradition, written or oral, before Gurdjieff's arrival.

The mystery is still unsolved, but the master tool is at our disposal, alive and revealing certain truths to those who truly wish to see them. This is what is essential. It is not enough to have a goal; we must also know how and by what means to realize it. This observation is true not only for the speaker. Everything depends on "quality," as Peter Brook defines the "maker who gives way to human experience": "There is no better field of study than this curious phenomenon we call art, which transforms the very nature of our perceptions and opens a feeling of wonder in us that sometimes makes us breathless. Certain *frequencies of vibration*—in colors, shapes, geometric figures, and above all, proportions—evoke frequencies in us corresponding to their quality and particular flavor."[2] According to Gurdjieff, we must see "the universe as consisting of vibrations,"[3] and language—which forms part of art—does not escape this rule. Speech, both oral and written, is composed of sonorous vibrations which bear a meaning, because "these vibrations proceed in all kinds, aspects, and densities of the matter."[4] The phenomenon is more perceptible in the voices of the spoken word, more subtle in the written word. In this latter case, the vibrations act, under certain conditions, like a groundswell, reaching readers unconsciously, penetrating their entire being. Once again, "all is material," including speech, and therefore all is controllable.

Yet—and this is what makes things more difficult than they seem—there is discontinuity in every phenomenon in that these vibrations can be ascending or descending, with accelerations and retardations. All is explained by the Law of Seven. The octave represents this line of development of the vibrations. The seven-tone musical scale, developed by ancient schools, is applicable to language as well as to music, because the "laws are everywhere the same."[5] This Law of Octaves "gives us an entirely new explanation of the whole life, of the progress and development of phenomena on all planes of the universe observed by us."[6] Says Gurdjieff, "That is, we do not have to prove the existence of this law or of the Law of Three." In any case, it is clear enough that the proof will emerge for those who make the effort to decipher it and to understand its simultaneously symbolic and practical meaning. This law shows the progress and development of language, of exchanges, of the transmission of a teaching. Without it, we can "neither think nor do," and consequently can neither speak nor say. Everything happens to us, and the impact of our words will have a radically different effect from the goal we desire and seek to attain. Our "art" can be only subjective and its emotional or psychic repercussions can be only accidental. We may point out long paths that lead nowhere, to be followed "at your own risk," without ever having gone along them or seen them ourselves. Not knowing where we are going, how can we tell others where to go?

These consequences are the result of the phenomena mentioned earlier: "retardations in the development of vibrations."[7] This can be depicted graphically, with the musical scale being a symbolic representation of the Law of Seven:

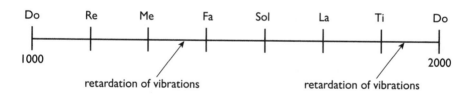

"The true quality," Peter Brook writes, "is an objective reality ruled by three exact laws. Each phenomenon rises and falls, degree by degree, according to a scale of natural values."[8] Thus, when these retardations occur, there is a deviation from the original direction. In the octave, we can observe deviations between *mi* and *fa* and between *ti* and *do,* corresponding to the semitone in the musical scale. "This law," Gurdjieff explained to Ouspensky, "shows why straight lines never occur in our activities, why, having begun to do one thing, we in fact constantly do something entirely different, often the opposite of the first, although we do not notice this and continue to think that we are doing the same thing that we began to do."[9] The line—which might symbolize speech—starts out straight, but deviates around the first interval:

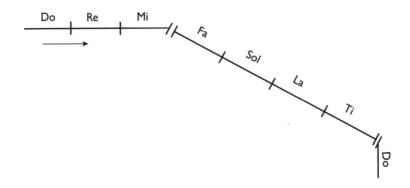

Everything can be explained by the Law of Octaves, as long as we understand the role and significance of the intervals, which "cause the line of the development of force constantly to change, to go in a broken line, to turn round, to become its 'own opposite' and so on."[10] Gurdjieff adds, "Such a course of things, that is, change of direction, we can observe in everything. After a certain period of energetic activity or strong emotion or a right understanding a reaction comes, work becomes tedious and tiring; moments of fatigue and indifference enter into feeling; *instead of right thinking a search for compromises begins*."[11] The consequences of these compromises can be found in the speech, which weakens, balks, slackens, halts, wavers, strays, and finally misses its target. Curved thought results in circular speech. And because the deviation is intensified at each octave, "the line of octaves may at last turn around completely and proceed in a direction opposite that of the original direction," and "in developing further, the line of octaves or the line of development of vibrations may return to the original direction, in other words, make a complete circle."[12] In *Beelzebub's Tales to His Grandson*, Gurdjieff gives a definition for this, a formula resulting from "objective cosmic science": "The-line-of-the-flow-of-forces-constantly-deflecting-according-to-law-and-uniting-again-at-its-ends."[13]

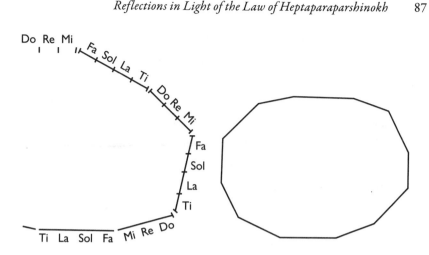

This is precisely the definition of *ouroboros speech:* "eating its tail," a bent, holed, effaced speech abased to the level of ordinary events. Thought becomes dogmatic and literal, dragging down language with it: all is subjectified, "thought goes round in a circle, repeating what was known before, and the way out which had been found becomes more and more lost."[14] The speaker, subject to the influences of his thought, repeats himself, turns around, and becomes ever more bogged down in the circle of the confusion of tongues, marching into perdition: "The serpent eating its tail, revolving unceasingly, is confined to its own cycle, evoking the wheel of existence, the samsara, condemned never to escape from its cycle and rise to a higher level. It symbolizes the perpetual return, the indefinite circle of reincarnation and continual repetition, revealing the predominance of a fundamental death wish."[15]

This curved speech embodies what Daumal calls black poetry—produced by "pride, imagination, and laziness."[16] For the most part, we are already dead, condemned to remain in the original circle of confusion. Consequently, we will never be able to reach the esoteric circles in which speech forms a straight line—the speech of life and of beneficial rebirths into being and spiritual elevation. White poetry is superior in that it awakens and fights deviations in order to achieve its goal: "The white poet prefers reality, even paltry reality, to these rich lies. His work is an incessant struggle against pride, imagination and laziness.

Accepting his gift, even if he suffers from it and suffers from suffering, he seeks to make it serve ends greater than his selfish desires: the as-yet-unknown cause of this gift."[17]

This is entirely the inverse of the black poet, who is blind and unconscious of his blindness. He is the poet-machine who refuses to look reality in the face and who, by the force of circumstances, sees it "in reverse"—condemned, dare we say it, by the maleficent influence of the organ Kundabuffer. Incapable of making his own choices, never knowing what to do or how to do it, his poetic aspirations are caterpillary and he crawls, an automatized larva, on the "natural, sub-human slope."[18] His laziness prevents him from acting in the upward direction, which in all ways represents too great an effort for him—but this is necessary for anyone who claims to speak or to do. What he writes, he writes like a robot that does not even have the intelligence of a sophisticated device. Even when he repeats like a parrot, imitates like an ape, or records appearances like a tape recorder, there is nothing but distortion, amplification, projection, and illusion. "One need not make an effort to brag, to dream, to lie and be lazy; nor to calculate and scheme, when calculating and scheming are for the benefit of vanity, imagination or inertia."[19]

White poetry, on the other hand, which is literature and objective speech, requires the poet to undertake preliminary work on himself. He must be capable of calling to himself consciously; he must not let himself be carried by the current, by human mechanisms, by his routine habits. He must go against nature, making the necessary efforts that are the price to pay for elevating himself and claiming to elevate others. He must force himself to undergo voluntary suffering, to sacrifice his vanity, his noxious reveries, and his caterpillary laziness in order to confront the real in its reality and not in its illusory representation: "White poetry goes uphill. It swims upstream like the trout to go spawn in its birthplace. It holds fast, by force and by cunning, against the whims of the rapids and the eddies. It does not let itself be distracted by the shimmering of passing bubbles, nor be swept away by the current toward soft, muddy valleys."[20]

—◦—

"The same thing happens in all spheres of human activity,"[21] Gurdjieff tells us: in literature, science, art, philosophy, religion, and individual, social, political, and religious life. Nothing escapes this law. All movement, in its development, deviates after a certain amount of time from its original direction, going then in the opposite direction. Further, when words contain a teaching, even an authentic one, it cannot be otherwise. Gurdjieff alludes to the change in the history of religion from the teachings of love in the Gospels to the hate of the Inquisition: The path gradually deviated from the starting goal to become its exact opposite. Little by little, the white words of Christ became tainted with black until the light could no longer pass through them, leaving humanity in chaos and conflict. Democracy turns into tyranny, love into hate, faith into intolerance, flexibility into rigidity . . . and good wine into vinegar!

The Law of Octaves explains how teachings become distorted over time and how civilizations fall and disappear. If Buddha were to return today, Gurdjieff tells us, he would not even recognize his own teachings! Nothing has escaped this law, not even the teaching that constitutes the material of this very book. As Michel Waldberg remarks correctly, the word *turn* is used as a synonym for *degenerate*. The subjective word turns around, confines itself to the impassable frontiers of the circle of the confusion of tongues, and degenerates into repetition and babbling, eventually falling into nothingness. Through lack of energy, it rolls up, winds around itself, becomes muddled, tangled, and knotted, spirals and twists itself, and becomes woven inextricably into the curtain of Maya: "We are gyrovagues, and I wonder at what point the ellipse appearing above will open, changing eventually into a spiral, that spiral with which Pere Ubu's 'august and tubiform *gidouille*' will be decorated for all eternity, and whose triumph over the era has been sufficiently demonstrated."[22] "Under these conditions," Peter Brook writes, "the level of our consciousness is low, the power of our thought is limited, and the available energies fuel one vision, one direct motivation."[23] All these weaknesses arise from the natural fact that nothing in the universe can remain stable.

To summarize, the Law of Octaves is composed of four great

principles: the *deviation of forces,* the fact that *nothing in the world stays in the same place* (everything goes up or goes down; there is a discontinuity of vibrations), the *inevitability of either ascent or descent,* and "the *periodic fluctuations,* that is, rises and falls"[24]—the inevitable cosmic conditions of all action. These principles or phenomena are the causes of our illusions about ourselves, because we are blind to them or because we have no consciousness of the Law of Octaves. "No development is possible by mechanical means," Gurdjieff repeated unceasingly to his students. Our moods "become better or worse" and "all from time to time pass through periods of ascent or descent, become stronger or weaker."[25] The fluctuations of thoughts, feelings, moods, and words "are periods of the development of forces between intervals in the octaves as well as the intervals themselves." "Upon the law of octaves depends upon the imperfection and the incompleteness of our knowledge in all spheres without exception, chiefly because we always begin in one direction and afterwards without noticing it proceed in another."[26] All things thus obey Heptaparaparshinokh: the days of the week, the biblical myth of Creation in six days (an expression or "incomplete indication" of the Law of Octaves), our imperfections, our incompleteness, our limits, our incomprehension, our babbling, our vanity, and our confusion of tongues.

But how, under such dismal conditions, can we achieve our goal, become master of our actions, speak in order truly to say, and escape this vicious circle? What reason is there to do or say if we will only ever miss our target and inexorably be the victim of failure?

Gurdjieff's teachings in this regard might amount to the following: Although victims of our exterior influences, we can act upon these laws, given a certain amount of effort, and evade them or, better, use them to realize our own goals. The system is fueled entirely by hope: "[O]bservations show that a right and consistent development of octaves, although rare, can be observed in all the occasions of life and in the activity of nature and even in human activity."[27] Thus we are saved . . . almost. We must still make the effort necessary for understanding and then mastering the laws that allow us to enjoy this salvation. Reaching the target thus becomes a possibility and a realistic objective. Acting along the development of the line allows the poet to rectify the effects of speech, giving those effects a regular and stable direction that follows the original direction without deviation in order to achieve the intended goal. This technique, acting upon the frequencies of vibrations, allows us to activate the powers of speech that are otherwise lost—a speech evoking "frequencies in us corresponding to their quality and particular flavor." Peter Brook, who applied this teaching to his calling as a director and actor, gives a highly significant definition of this Law of Octaves:

> This is a radical and very surprising notion: it means that all *energy,* and consequently all human *action,* can rise only to a certain point via its own initiative, just as an arrow shot into the sky, after exhausting the force of momentum that carries it, reaches its highest point and is forced to bend its trajectory and fall back to earth. Nevertheless, if the crucial point where the initial energy begins to weaken is observed with precision, there can be applied at this same point what Gurdjieff called a *shock*—that is to say, the conscious introduction of an *appropriate impulse* whereby the movement will break through the barrier and can continue its ascending development. This image allows us to understand why human enterprises collapse, why empires fall into decadence, why the best predictions reveal themselves to be false, and why immense revolutions reverse their movement and betray their great ideas. The same laws show that a certain force, applied with precision, could have prevented this return to zero. But the fundamental principle is only rarely recognized, and all that remains for us is to blame others and ourselves in bitterness and frustration.[28]

All the subtlety of this technique depends clearly on the dosage and precision of this "appropriate impulse." Gurdjieff said that "[o]bservation of such rightly developing octaves establishes the fact that if at the necessary moment, that is, at the moment when the given octave passes through an 'interval,' there enters into it an 'additional shock' which corresponds in force and character, it will develop further without hindrance along the original direction, neither losing anything nor changing its nature."[29] An additional shock thus permits a correct development, providing what Brook calls "the necessary quality and thrust," but on condition that the introduction of this new vibration must be applied at the opportune moment, and with exactitude—that is, "at the moment when the given octave passes through an interval." Herein resides all the difficulty, because it is also necessary to differentiate between ascending octaves (in which the first interval is between *mi* and *fa*) and descending ones (in which the greatest interval is right at the octave's beginning, after the first *do*) and to know that the shock must be strongest between *ti* and *do*. The great cosmic octave is inscribed in regularity and is the image of the ray of creation—the foundation of the Gurdjieffian system: The absolute is *do,* and shock 1 corresponds to the "will of the absolute," while shock 2 is "organic life on earth."[30] The objective speech that is also installed in this regularity respects this law. Additional shocks are also necessary for its creative power, but they will have to be artificial—created artificially.

These shocks thus allow the lines of forces to reach a projected goal, but because they are very uncertain, they can take place "accidentally."[31] Those who wait for accident or "luck" have little chance of achieving their goal. On the contrary, they will only be perpetuating their mechanicalness. The unconscious have the illusion that *doing* is possible and that the lines are always straight by definition. Yet this is all wrong. "He thinks that straight lines are the rule and broken and interrupted lines the exception."[32] Quite the opposite, Gurdjieff tells us! Here, we cannot help but think of the organ Kundabuffer, which makes us see reality backward. By our own fault, we are not even aware that our actions go against our own goal. What irony! "A man *can* win at roulette. But this would be accident."[33] The majority of people play at roulette their whole lives, and gather only the fruits of chance. By contrast, those of the Fourth Way choose their square and their number; they are master of what befalls them and they assume the consequences of their own actions. If they "win," it is neither accidental nor due to a third person; it is due to themselves alone. If they "lose," it is their own failure.

People ordinarily blame others for their misfortunes, problems, faults, powerlessness, misery, and their state in general. Yet with the exception of phenomena of a cosmic order (and sometimes even then), it is always their own fault, it is always their weakness that is at the origin of their failure. It cannot be otherwise. Everything is connected, we all pay for the consequences of our own actions, and sometimes the bill is hard to accept. It then remains for us to take charge of ourselves, to realize our extreme nullity in order to free ourselves from all accidents. Life is not a roulette game in which the result always appears immediately before our eyes. At the height of our blindness, we can also "very easily deceive ourselves and take the result obtained as the result desired," and thus "believe that we have won when on the whole we have lost." We may think we have been understood when in fact no one understands anything; we may think we have created when, on the contrary, we have destroyed. This is the Kundabuffer again. How, under such conditions, can this be explained to us for our good when we will inevitably take it as something bad, as an aggression toward our person and our own faculties? How many machines have badmouthed Gurdjieff after having been broken to pieces, after having been subjected to the technique of "corn removal" after having suffered from a bitter truth?

> The greatest insult for a man-machine is to tell him that he can do nothing, can attain nothing, that he can never move towards any aim whatever and that in striving towards one he will inevitably create another. Actually of course it cannot be otherwise. The man-machine is in the power of accident. His activities may fall into some sort of channel which has been created by cosmic or mechanical forces and they may by accident move along this channel for a certain time, giving the illusion that aims of some kind are being attained. Such accidental correspondence of results with the aim we have set before us or the attainment of aims in small things which can have no consequences creates in mechanical man the conviction that he is able to attain any aim, "is able to conquer nature" as it is called, is able to "arrange the whole of his life," and so on.[34]

The last straw for the man-machine is that he is unconscious of his nullity, he is blind in his own condition and is surrounded by a veil. His belief that he can do something is set in stone, though in fact he can do nothing at all. He even believes that the thing has been attained, already accomplished, that the goal is already achieved when this is not so at all. In the same manner, he thinks that he speaks the right words and that they have a certain influence on his listeners. Again, this is not so at all. On the contrary, he falls again and again into confusion, entangled in his curved speech. For the cause, we need look no further than the phenomenon of deviations.

In *Psychologie de la motivation*, Paul Diel shows how people stray from the path, losing themselves due to false targets and false motivation, in "affective deformation."

> The conscious being, man, can validate his desires, and validated desires become the inner determinants of reactions: the motives. Validation can be right or wrong. We often do not want to become aware of our false validation. We justify it falsely and, thus robbing it of conscious control, we make it subconscious, and it becomes false motivation. False validation is thus a powerlessness of spiritual function, a pathological deformation of the spirit. It is not essential to human nature; *it is accidental.*[35]

Only self-observation, objective introspection, can allow us to become aware of our nullity and blindness: "Introspection becomes more objective the more we dare to delve into the cause of affective and subconscious obscuring, the more we become conscious of our false motivation. To become conscious of false motivation means to disperse affective obscuring, to see ourselves as we truly are, to take hold of truth in the human psyche, to understand the objective of scientific research."[36]

The theory of false motivation can be explained in Gurdjieffian terms: We are overburdened with little "I"s—as we have seen—which all respond to different motivations to which is added the Law of Octaves, which makes every endeavor to deviate unceasingly from attaining its goal. It is difficult truly to do anything under these conditions. All our unconscious choices are ruled by false motivation, because we exalt only these "multiple desires to the detriment of the essential desire."[37] Hence our dismal indecision. True freedom is accessible only at the price of demanding inner work. This requires combating useless considerations, identifications, and projections and mastering our excitations, passions, false desires, vain envy—in short, mastering the various functions of our machine in order finally to control them and use them judiciously for the harmonious and harmonic development of all. All the great masters—as well as the great psychologists—are unanimous on this observation: Solutions must be found to remedy divergence. Yet those who seek shall find.

Ordinary humans are incapable of doing or saying; but this observation, which we will interpret as an "insult" through the broken prism of our subjectivity, is the basis of all true apprenticeship. Only by realizing that we are less than nothing can it become possible for us to become something or, rather, someone whose consciousness enjoys its full potential. In other words, we can become beings capable of controlling both exterior things and things within. Gurdjieff tells us, "A man who cannot control himself or the course of things within himself can control nothing."[38] He does not control the powers of speech and does not know the proper use which permits us to do; he never ceases speaking and saying nothing. He is a dreaming robot that never awakens (never realizes that it is a robot and a broken one to boot) and takes itself for a human.

But if a shock intervenes at the moment of the retardation of vibrations, the impact will assure continuity in the action undertaken, thus attaining its goal. Anything is possible. There is no misfortune for him who knows the necessity of additional shocks. "[H]e can learn to recognize the moments of the 'intervals' in all lines of his activity and learn to create the 'additional shocks,' in other words, learn to apply to his own activities the method which cosmic forces make use of in creating 'additional shocks' at the moments necessary."[39]

We must learn to control the laws in order to attain our goals. It is the only hope a machine can have. We must not submit to them passively, serving them blindly. We must make use of them consciously within ourselves, with all the tools available to us, in the presence of some of our contemporaries who can be gathered together in a school or in the pages written by a teacher. It is also possible for all these conditions to be united. "The possibility of artificial, that is, specially created, 'additional shocks' gives *a practical meaning* to the study of the law of octaves and makes this study obligatory and necessary if a man desires to step out of the role of passive spectator of that which is happening to him and around him."[40] This practical meaning constitutes the very substance of the proper use of the magic word, because it signifies concrete and performing action. Is it not also the proper use of white poetry? Knowing the Law of Octaves, knowing the moments of the intervals and creating the corresponding additional shocks, allows the speaker, the creator, and any other individual who has a precise goal, to speak, create, and reach the target at the center, in a regular continuity—in other words, to do effectively. The arrows shot by the conscious archer do not fly haphazardly, get lost, or end up striking something for which they were not aimed. They move in the direction willed by the necessary force, and if the archer is experienced, nothing can stop their course. The arrow pierces the target just as the speech penetrates the listener who glimmers on the horizon of speaker 4, 5, 6, or 7.

But like all things, the success of this endeavor against nature often requires a preliminary formation that can be found only in a school or through a competent master—it is created or formed upon these principles of the universal laws inherent in all phenomena.[41] As Gurdjieff said to Ouspensky, man 4 may lead man 2 or 3 out of the circle of the confusion of tongues, and man 4 may very well have man 5 as his teacher—in other words, as a guide toward another level of evolution. This is the metaphor of the staircase: Those of us on a higher step can help another, a person on the step just below, to ascend. Likewise a simple Apprentice Speaker can act as the salvation for a Romantic or a Savant, but the last two cannot have any objective action upon others.

It is necessary to feel and understand this law with all the centers of our being.[42] This law is so important, so revolutionary for those who discover its properties, that it becomes impossible to ignore it, because it is the magic key—combined with Triamazikamno—that opens all the doors. Ouspensky tells us that at the beginning, when he studied the system, he was obsessed constantly with this law and that all Gurdjieff's students considered everything from this point of view. Herein, we should note, lies an excellent exercise that allows us to move toward better understanding, and thus toward a greater evolution of consciousness on the basis of all human powers.

Let us describe the ray of creation or the cosmic octave, synthesizing *In Search of the Miraculous: Fragments of an Unknown Teaching* and *Beelzebub's Tales to His Grandson*.[43] *Shock 1* in the cosmic octave comes between *ti* and *do* and therefore corresponds to the will of the absolute—in other words, the conscious apparition of the force plus the conciliation filling the interval between the positive and negative forces of Triamazikamno. It is interesting to note that a relevant parallel or significant connection can be established between the conciliation that fills the interval of the cosmic octave and the conciliation that prevails over all clear discourse in the octave of speech. Due only to the will of the speaker—an absolute necessity—can a common language be imposed. In other words, due only to the will of the speaker can the word be imposed that is a direct emanation from the absolute and that alone permits this interval to be filled.[44] In order to make the word live, however, this will must serve the consciousness here and now: The speaker must call to himself to be consistent with a total, fundamentally eternal being-presence that alone permits him to say.

Shock 2 must be between *mi* and *fa*. In the cosmic octave, it is "organic life on earth" that fills this interval, planetary influences acting upon the events of the human masses while these masses take in these influences.[45] Regarding the octave of speech, the shock may correspond to techniques, to certain powers of speech, and to mastery of names, sound, rhythm, or phrasing in writing.[46] We might say that in this case, the shock is the power that must seek to unite into a single living substance "matters as different as emotions, images, concepts." And this living substance, the "life of this new organism," is what Daumal calls the poet's rhythm.[47] If it is a new organism that has been intentionally created, is it not also organic life on earth? This organic life—whose "role . . . in the structure of the earth's surface was indisputable"[48]—is nothing other than the rhythm of nature: "There was the growth of coral islands and limestone mountains, the formation of coal seams and accumulations of petroleum; the alteration of the soil under the influence of vegetation, the growth of vegetation in the lakes, the 'formation of rich arable lands by worms,' change of climate due to the draining of swamps and the destruction of forests, and many other things that we know of and do not know of."[49] *Rhythm* is therefore also a conciliatory force in that it takes part in realizing a double operation that is impossible to conciliate via the intellectual path or via the instinctive path. It permits the thing to be said not only to bend "the sounds of language to its breath," all the while compelling them "also to contain its images."[50] Hence the crucial importance, according to Daumal, of that which permits this otherwise

ABSOLUTE SUN	I	Origin of all things	DO	Protocosmos	Shock I: Will of the absolute (the strongest shock)
ALL WORLDS	3	All galaxies	TI	Hagiocosmos	
ALL SUNS	6	Our galaxy (the Milky Way)	LA	Macrocosmos	
SUN	12	Our sun	SOL	Deuterocosmos	
ALL PLANETS	24	Our solar system	FA	Mesocosmos	Shock 2: Organic life on earth
EARTH	48	Our planet	MI	Tritocosmos	
MOON	96	Our satellite	RE	Tessarocosmos (Microcosmos)	

———————————————————————— Do

impossible union: the "particular relation that exists between the various elements of the poet's machinery." Note that the struggle against negative emotions—which is also transformation or transmutation of gross matter into subtle matter—works to fill this interval, uniting the living substance. Those who fall into the trap of uncontrollable emotions generate suffering uselessly, using their inferior centers mechanically and fallaciously. They can therefore do nothing objective, falling ever more into confusion, speaking to say nothing . . . because in reality, without even being aware of it, they have deviated tragically from their course and from the goal established originally.

Shock 1 and shock 2 evoked by the teaching have the virtue of bringing about the initiation without which it is not only impossible to escape the maleficent circle of the confusion of tongues, but also impossible to reach the esoteric circles which alone can allow us the eventual possibility of evolution. These two shocks correspond to being-partkdolg-duties (conscious effort and voluntary suffering) and allow the speaker to avoid falling back into confusion and instead remain in the process of apprenticeship and evolution. All true art depends on the conscious introduction of the shock: "If, at the vital moment, the energies that are at work can enter into relations with the energies of a different order," Peter Brook writes,

> a change of quality is produced which can lead to intense artistic experiences and social transformations. But the process does not stop there. It continues to be nourished by higher energies. The consciousness rises to a superior scale which transcends art and can in turn lead to spiritual awakening—and eventually even to absolute purity, to the sacred. The sacred itself can be understood in terms of energies, but of a type that our instruments are not able to record.[51]

If the shocks are well placed or, in other words, if the frequency of vibrations is mastered, the speech then attains its goal without deviation, after the manner of the cosmic octave (the ray of creation):

As Ouspensky observes, the Law of Seven explains everything: "Everything anomalous, unexpected, and accidental disappeared, and an immense and strictly thought-out plan of the universe began to make its appearance."[52] We will not be surprised, then, at the prodigious strength of the golden number in classical constructions. In each case, it produces a sensation of harmony, signifying that "the psychological experience is linked to the mathematical description." As Peter Brook remarks, "Architecture has always observed and followed this marriage between sentiment and proportion, and at a more intuitive level, the painter and the sculptor correct and refine their work endlessly in order that finesse may shine forth from the gross matter, until the object becomes a sensitive mirror of the sentiment."

The same goes for everything we sense that aims to produce a particular effect, and poetry is also subject to this rule, as the director of the film *Meetings with Remarkable Men* (1979) remarks, enunciating a fundamental trait of what Daumal calls white poetry in his pertinent reflection on quality:

> The poet passes everything through the sieve of his thoughts. He pays attention to the suggestions of the *sound* and *rhythm,* which are somewhere far behind the bustling of the words that his conscious spirit proposes to him. Thus he creates a phrase that has a new force. The reader can then perceive the changing of his own sentiments along with the transformation of the energy via the impressions he receives. In all cases, there is a *difference of quality.* It is not the result of an accident, but of a process unique in its genre.[53]

This unique process—on which depends the quality itself, linked to the consciousness that characterizes the human experience—can be shown on the enneagram. The Law of Octaves, known to ancient and objective science and expressing the sequential order of a phenomenon, is perfectly expressed in the master symbol already mentioned; it is the perfect expression of the cosmic laws of the first order, which combine ingeniously in the nine-pointed circle.[54]

Here is how the representation of the octave on the enneagram should *apparently* be presented:

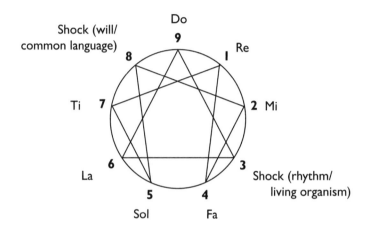

Later in the analysis, we will see that in fact the second shock is represented on the enneagram between *sol* and *la*.[55] We must remember, above all, that the enneagram is always in motion relative to the established order. Like the new organism that is the rhythm, it is alive. The points represent each stage of the process that is accomplished through additional shocks—which can themselves assume multiple realities, depending on the action that is executed. This fundamental symbol unites and integrates all knowledge relative to the law of the structure of the octave, which connects "all processes of the universe and, to one who knows the scales of the passage and the laws of the structure of the octave, it presents the possibility of an exact cognition of everything and every phenomenon in its essential nature and all of its interrelations with phenomena and things connected with it."[56] This ancient tool is the key to the universal language.[57]

Those who do not understand will be tempted to pass negative judgment easily on this apparently extremely complex system. Nevertheless, we must suspend hasty judgment, which will lead us into fatal error, and always remember that to progress along the path of the Fourth Way, we must force ourselves to understand everything. Gurdjieff was insistent on this point, which forms the very strength of such teaching. Otherwise, how can we explain why so many remarkable men, famous and less so, in all spheres of human activity and moreover in all corners of the world, have been and continue to be interested in good ideas?

This teaching applies to all human activities—artistic, social, and religious—because it nourishes them with water drawn directly from a pure source, feeding them energy and giving them a whole series of powers which—and herein lies the entire ambivalence of the system for some—serve the interests and goals of those who appeal to it. "This is the way things are," as Gurdjieff said. Thereafter, it falls to each of us to decide what we want. We can ignore (consciously or unconsciously), despise, condemn this idea. We can take up arms and babble more and more; but we cannot truly act, and we will spend all our life lamenting the fact that things go against us, that we have "bad luck," that it is chance, the fault of others, or even that it is God who has willed it thus. Yet it is none of these—at least, not as long as we submit ourselves unceasingly to the "accident." On the contrary, we must choose the true action that alone will permit us to do. The stakes are high, having to do with the very meaning of human life.

The Law of Octaves thus forms part of the complete process of the harmonious development of humans and our powers—"a transition of the note *do* through a series of successive tones to the *do* of the next octave." Heptaparaparshinokh implies and determines a harmony of being and language and of all phenomena. Knowing this law allows us to avoid the curved and subjective speech that misses its goal, that runs aground, that has nothing to say. Yet we must also truly perceive this law. Only the mastery of the shock permits us to attain our goal.

If the common language, whose absolute necessity Gurdjieff emphasized, performs the office of conciliation, like the cosmic octave in which the first shock corresponds to the will of the absolute, then the octave of speech is this new language, embodied by the word, the emanation of the absolute. The second shock (which can become the first in another octave) is perhaps dependent on techniques of conscious speech (just as organic life is dependent on the cosmic octave), such as the name, rhythm, and sound, the mastery of which is necessary for the speaker who wishes to attain his goal. In other words, the interval can be filled particularly by certain techniques inherent to speech, which, if mastered, allow the process of creation (or communication) to attain the premeditated result. This is what we will study next.

7

Techniques of Speech
and
Powers of the Logos

. . . How can one tell of silences with words? Only poetry can do that.

RENE DAUMAL, *MOUNT ANALOGUE*

Knowing the techniques of the magic word is the only means for activating our powers, because mastering these processes will allow us to fill the intervals of the octave, bringing about additional appropriate shocks. The main processes of the magic word obey the Law of Three fundamentally. The *word* is the affirmation allowing us to conjugate the "verb"—the power of creation offered to us—which is ineffective by itself and includes signifier and signified, and our harmony and mastery of these two confer real efficacy upon language. *Sound* is a passive force holding a message as a structure holds a windmill's blades. *Rhythm* is the conciliation that unites the living substance, creating the additional shock necessary for the regular continuation of the octave:[1]

104

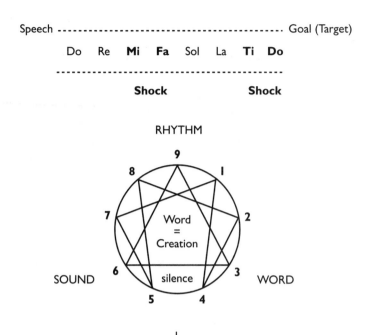

Let us remember that the origin of *poiesis* was an art of evocation, the invocation of spirits. The primary function of ecstatic poetry is therefore metaphysical: It exercises a magical action on the physical, emotional, and psychic planes and therefore, through a mechanism of threes, upon the spiritual plane. As Artaud explains: "True poetry . . . is metaphysical, and it is its metaphysical bearing, its degree of metaphysical efficacy, that give it its true value."[2] Daumal writes, "As with magic, poetry is black or white." And regarding "magical powers," shamanism clarifies a good number of points, as is shown in Stéphane Labat's marvelous book, *La poésie de l'extase et le pouvoir chamanique du langage:* "The shaman, placed at the center of the world, becomes physically conscious that everything is interconnected, and therefore that his least gesture, the least of his words coming from the spirit, from his very heart and that of the universe, can have a double repercussion: material and spiritual. This is the principle of power of the shaman's magical action.

"The word represents the power of creation offered to man. Language is not simply the reflection of thoughts; the sound that resonates at the center of the universe allows the poet-shaman to transcend all the techniques of ecstasy in order to participate actively in the universal movement. His prophetic message is at once the fruit of ecstatic experience and of vision. All poet-shamans use a magic of words and sounds, of rhythms and syllables, that has no need to be explained. . . . The poet of ecstasy receives . . . the silent knowledge of his double directly through his technique: the *word,* the *rhythm,* and the *sound.*"[3]

In chapter 5 we saw how adequation was possible between *words* and things, due to the conciliatory force known as consciousness—which, when it attains a high enough level, allows for an erasure of all the dualities that tend to crystallize in the human psyche. For this, how-ever, it is not the words that must be awakened, but the people who use them. In *Le Don des langues,* Jean Paulhan—an author engaged in the "path of writing,"[4] according to Jean-Yves Pouilloux—also attempts to resolve this question, suggesting a triangular relationship among the idea, the word, and the thing.

The idea arises principally from the intellectual center, and it cannot fill this distance, which has proved for some people to be a mass grave rather than a simple gap that we can jump over without falling into it and being swallowed and digested like a piece of dead meat. "Between the most similar things, appearances deceive most beautifully," writes Nietzsche, "for the smallest abyss is the hardest to bridge."[5]

Yet Paulhan's insight, although pertinent, cannot satisfy us. In the triad, however, we can find the poetic key: "The disciples of Hermes in the eighteenth century knew by the name 'gift of languages' a certain secret knowledge that permitted the voyager to speak immediately the language of the country he had just entered."[6] The signifying element, the word, is simultaneously poetic unity ("the profound words speak the essences," writes Bonnefoy) and psychic unity:"the ultimate unity recognizable by an individual [speaker] who knows how to neither read nor write—the viewpoint of Sapir and Jakobson—and knows not the acoustic and articulatory unity associated with a neuronal connection; laboratory experimentation of this has been performed without any possible doubt."[7] Moreover, the word is directly linked to the idea that people endeavor to express their thoughts by speech. Yet thoughts, connected to the intellectual center, are often confused and anarchic, because they are mechanical, swept along in this uncontrolled eddy of speech. The connection is very strong—we cannot say otherwise—but is insufficient when the adequation between the word and the thing must be reestablished: Union is possible only through the mediation of the consciousness, following the lines of knowledge and being.

In the first place, the idea often belongs to knowledge, whose content often remains abstract, resulting in the impossibility of *doing*. Because a relationship of equivalence is necessary between the word and the idea—or rather, between the word and the consciousness that circumscribes it—"An ideal language would therefore be one in which the word and the idea correspond perfectly."[8] This is exactly what Gurdjieff was proposing when he emphasized the absolute necessity for a new language following the lines of knowledge and being in order for this connection to take place. But how can Paulhan have approached this question with the totality of his being, when—although familiar with esotericism and Asian spirituality—he accused the system of "trickery"? Such a judgment can form only a barrier to understanding.[9] Language cannot be perceived solely as the projection of thought (as Paulhan believed),[10] but rather as the projection of thought inextricably connected to the body and to emotion. In other words, it can be perceived as the projection—no longer mechanical but conscious—of a block that links ideas, sensations, and feelings. Only at this price does adequation become possible. Paulhan, however, draws near to an essential truth, especially when he introduces the notion of law: "By law I mean, in the most ordinary yet most rigorous sense, the regular relationship that we are given to observe or to bring about between two facts."[11] Language—as Paulhan correctly believes—is indeed governed by laws: The inverse would radically contradict our hypothesis.

Further, these laws, as we have seen, are Triamazikamno and Heptaparaparshinokh, and not, as Paulhan believes, the "law of identity" and "counter-identity."[12] Although he writes, in a letter to Artaud dated 1931, that he is seeking "mathematical precision," and in a letter to Maurice Nadeau that his intent is "to outline, based on literature, a system of knowledge that is precise, rigorous—in short, scientific,"[13] the fact nevertheless remains that "the precision, the laws, the rigor" that he invoked unceasingly were perhaps not at the height of his aspirations. In Gurdjieff's teachings, which Paulhan criticized, everything corresponds to mathematical laws and follows Pythagorean logic with unparalleled rigor. Both emphasized the necessity of such a system of knowledge which transcended ordinary language, but only Gurdjieff understood perfectly that all was connected and that the question of language could not be dealt with separately from the question of the cosmic laws that rule the existence of all things in the universe—or, in other words, that the activities of people are inseparable from their levels of evolution. "It is very important to understand this division of man into seven categories," Ouspensky writes, "because it has applications in all the possible forms of study of human activity. It provides an instrument or a tool, powerful and precise in the hands of those who understand it, and it allows us to define manifestations which are impossible to define without it."[14]

If Saussure preferred *term* to *word,* thus allowing more easily for the possibility of integrating it into a system, the fact still remains that this linguist always denied the idea of evolution, however necessary for the development of every objective system. Literature offers us nothing more than what Paulhan calls a "machine of language." Because it is linked to human activity, it cannot be otherwise, and all we can do is observe that, like humans, this machinery is more controllable the more we master its system of functioning. "Making the word into an element of language, associating the idea with the word, hence the idea-word entity, the analyst-writer places emphasis on a mental space, the 'mental states,' as Valéry said regarding Bréal, whose functioning recalls that of a machine."[15] We are not reducing language to a simple mental organ, but rather to a three-centered organ. Only ordinary language arises exclusively from the psychic center (meaning many linguists are correct) or exclusively from the emotional center. It all depends, in fact, on the type of speaker as defined in chapter 4: Outside the circle of confusion, language—which is precise—allows for a precise study and takes its place in the heart of the totality of being, expressing its sacred union and radiance in a truly reciprocal and fruitful understanding.

In integrating the thing—that is, the world—into its idea-word relation, Paulhan finally made his great discovery: "After sixty-five years, I finally found what I was seeking—touching the language. . . ."[16] If seen in the light of the Gurdjieffian system, his discovery actually rests upon an "incomplete" and "erroneous" use of the triad, far from sufficient in that the proper use of the spoken word is based not solely on the Law of Three, but also on the Law of Seven. This said, *aliquid pro aliquo,* the triad, as Jean-Claude Coquet rightly notes, is ancient and leads us back to the viewpoints of Plato, Aristotle, the Stoics, and medieval scholars for whom the sign was a substitute for the thing.[17]

This tradition was revived in the late nineteenth century and popularized in the 1920s by the logician, mathematician, philosopher, and founder of American semiotics, Charles S. Peirce. He proposes "an ordinal organization of three categories, the third (the Interpreter) assuming the second (the Object) and the second being based on the first (the Representative),"[18] a proposition translated as *idea, thing, word* in Paulhan's language and as *consciousness, thing, word* in our own. These mark strongly the solidarity between the three terms: "In short," Paulhan writes, "everything takes place as if . . . the word were an object with three sides, one of which is made of words, a second of things, and a third of thoughts such that none of the three sides are sufficient by themselves but must in some way call upon the others, for they must step aside for one another."[19] But if "the face of the word which is made of things . . . corresponds to reality,"[20] it is less because it evokes reality and is its referent (as Paulhan believed) and more because this correspondence is the fruit of the conciliation operated by the consciousness, which—if it is sufficiently evolved—knows and feels the thing without contenting itself with "the idea that we form of this object."[21] This idea depends exclusively on the intellect, which, consequently, cannot be sufficient. In other words, the adequation does not in fact depend on the thing and the idea of the thing, but on the thing and the consciousness of the thing. Paulhan's project, Coquet notes, "was to find the return path to the unity of being and, finally, to have the most concrete possible experience of this being."[22]

Yet without precise knowledge of the fundamental Law of Triamazikamno, this unity, although undertaken pertinently, was doomed in advance to failure. Nevertheless, the conviction was there, Paulhan being convinced that words could "be contained by things" and by "singular things that it is urgent to say."[23] Likewise, in his justified denunciation of Jean-Paul Sartre—who, in condemning words, condemned "with them the entire language, of which they are the witnesses"[24]—Paulhan believes that in order to treat language correctly, we must "isolate the words." Sartre, whose "levity" Paulhan emphasizes, "judged the propriety of a word once he had integrated it into the discourse."[25] Paulhan inquires, "The thoughts, not the words, are what is profoundly different. . . . So why should we blame them?"[26] Because thoughts are linked to our intellectual center and, consequently, are "mechanical,"[27] it would be more correct to say, as Duits says, that "It is not the words, but the people that are dead." Surely, this is a more scandalous statement for the ordinary, separative consciousness—and yet, it is closer to reality. Without doubt, Sartre would have been even less accepting of this; he contented himself with "the modern conformist philosophers" in Pauwels's words—with the ordinary consciousness that is seen simply in psychological, lay, and primary terms as rejecting mechanically and ideologically the absolute consciousness, the transcendental *"I,"* even though it is the goal of every serious venture into the spiritual plane:

> . . . Phenomenology, or the science of existence, for the German philosopher Husserl, is based on what he calls the "experience of the transcendental *'I,'* accomplished and static"—that is, on an inner experience comparable to that of the yogi grappling with the Vedantic self or St. Paul wrestling with the inner man or that which Gurdjieff promised his disciples. Yet when Husserl's adapters took hold of this science, rejecting this experience of the transcendental *"I,"* of the absolute consciousness, then this science became an

instrument of confusion and disorder as proved by Sartrian exis-
tentialism, based on a phenomenology no longer of man but of the
fetus, a system whose most certain effect is to subject the intellect
increasingly to the maladies of the contemporary world.[28]

In fact, denying this transcendental consciousness brings us back
to "a pouring of the empty into the void," participating evermore in
the blindness, confusion, and general slumber. Sartre belongs to the
category of "universal Hasnamuss" represented by Lentrohamsanin in
Beelzebub's Tales to His Grandson: by denying this *"I,"* the great self, he
removes all possibility of inner evolution and, in a way, proclaims the
triumph of the ego, the false personality, and appearances—of *appearing,* to the detriment of *being.*

Here, it is worth recalling that Gurdjieff distinguished four states
of consciousness for a fully evolved human being. The ordinary human
being lives only in the first two and is often ignorant of the others or
else believes himself to possess them already.[29] He understands nothing
and can do nothing, but judges what he believes he knows about things
from the point of view of the inner states that are his own, which gives
him nothing but absurd, fallacious, and ouroboros conceptions! The
first thing to do is to realize our nullity, understanding why we are
nothing and why we can do nothing—in other words, understand that
we live in sleep, something that is repeated unceasingly in traditions
from Plato's allegories to the curtain of Maya, from the Buddhist "all
is illusion" to the true meaning of the Gospels, and includes, of course,
Gurdjieff's teachings, with the difference that these prove it completely,
while also giving us the "alarm clock" to awaken the sleepers.

We can illustrate these states of consciousness on the enneagram,
not taking into account the cosmic laws, but using as a basis the levels
defined by the table of 9 (see figure on page 112).[30]

The understanding of human life must take place unavoidably via
the understanding of the levels of consciousness possible for us, because
each level of consciousness defines a level of reality in which we move.
This is why, if there are four possible states of consciousness for a completely evolved human, the ordinary among us live only in the lower

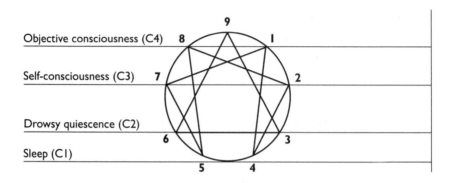

two, are ignorant of the two others, and judge the things of the lower states that are our own—which means that ordinary consciousness is dualistic, separative, mechanical, and above all, that it cannot produce anything but absurd conceptions, which it nevertheless judges to be pertinent and true. Further, if we speak to ordinary humans of superior states, they will invariably claim that they know of them and, what's more, possess them. People live in sleep (C1 and C2) and must first awaken (C3 and C4). In order to awaken, we must first truly realize that we are sleeping, and for this, we must understand it and not simply know it. This is the first stage of the human wish to evolve. Writes Georges de Maleville, "The admission of this 'waking sleep' is one of the most distressing observations that anyone can make about himself."[31] The effort of recapitulation is enough to make us realize that we are totally incapable of fully remembering all the moments of our journey:

> . . . It is rigorously impossible for those who observe themselves honestly to remember all of the actions they have nevertheless accomplished during a recent period of time, even if it is brief: an hour, a quarter of an hour. Thence, it is obvious that during the period of forgetting, those in question, even while acting and believing themselves to be awake in all ways, are thinking of other things, are dreaming—are sleeping—because dreaming and the passivity of the subject that accompanies it are the characteristics of sleep. This is waking sleep, and what we must do is recognize that all

people unknowingly spend the majority of their waking hours in this state.[32]

In order to evolve and get out of this waking sleep, we must have the will for it—for this, along with the consciousness, are two aspects of the same reality. Once again, we must clarify: Will is not an easy thing. It requires efforts that very few people have the strength to make. Yet if you ask people whether they wish to evolve, whether they believe they are evolving in their life, they will answer yes, even when in fact this is not the case, even when not only are they not evolving, but also they do not wish to, and indeed every day they work at breaking the machine a little more, putting themselves to sleep. This is because they live in the circle of confusion through the subjective states of consciousness that are their own—sleep (C1) and drowsy quiescence (C2), a state that some people continue to call lucid consciousness or normal consciousness, although in fact this state is a waking sleep or a relative consciousness that can only formulate truths that are likewise relative. Sleep is the passive and subjective state, populated by dreams, in which the ordinary among us spend half of life and in which we can do absolutely nothing but rest. The drowsy quiescence in which we spend the other half of our lives is the state in which we live, speak, and imagine that we are conscious and can know the absolute truth about things while having the impression of sharing it with others—and is also the state in which we take action, carry out our professional activities, talk, kill, procreate, and babble.

But all this is false. This ordinary, subjective, and separative consciousness is only just capable of sensing the difference between the body it inhabits and an exterior object: It tells me that I know I am myself and that this tree is something else because it is truly a tree and it is outside of me. This is a relative truth, because in the absolute, those who move in this state of consciousness see effectively the difference existing between themselves and the tree, but yet cannot really say why, because they do not know themselves any more than the tree can know itself. In other words, convinced of their own lucidity, they know nothing about anything and understand nothing, even if they insist the exact opposite with body, though not with soul. Consequently, they cannot evolve, because the main obstacle to ordinary consciousness (C1 and C2) is that it is convinced it is already on a higher level. It is difficult to look for something when you believe you already have it! In certain cases, certain experiences have the power of allowing those of us who live in C1 or C2 to perceive and feel C3 or C4 for a brief moment, which is enough for us to become aware of our true (inferior) level and then to do all in our power to gain lasting access to the higher levels, which are the state of self-consciousness (C3) and objective consciousness (C4).[33] These higher and objective states (sometimes identified as hallucinations by the separative consciousness of sleep or half sleep) are also known as states of ecstasy, enlightenment, or cosmic consciousness. Sometimes these terms are also used wrongly to refer to states that are in fact inferior. Reaching these higher levels, which are actually the only ones that are objectively normal, depends above all on what Ouspensky calls an "act of will"—in other words, "the frequency and duration of moments of self-consciousness depend on the control we have over ourselves."[34] As René Daumal writes, correctly, "awakening is not a state, but an action, and people are much more rarely awake than their words would have us believe. . . . The only immediate action we can accomplish is to wake up, to become conscious of ourselves."[35]

Those who attain the first of the higher levels finally become objective toward themselves and can know the truth about themselves—because they call to themselves and begin to be conscious of being conscious, thus becoming able to use their higher emotional centers[36] and gain access to the powers of which they were ignorant until now or which they considered supernatural, paranormal, or magical and which are simply the possibilities that human consciousness can offer. The fourth state concerns objective consciousness—rarely attained. According to Gurdjieff, we enter into contact with the real and objective world and are able to know the truth about everything, because we see the world as it really is (yatabutam). But this level of consciousness requires long work on the self and a profound inner transformation, the fruit of conscious effort and voluntary suffering—in other words, will and acceptance. The inferior and subjective states of consciousness belong to those who live in the circle of confusion, propagating word prostitution and producing black poetry. The higher states are the domain of white poetry and objective literature (speakers 4, 5, 6, and 7), in which nothing is random—in other words, speech signifies something precise and embodies things. Gurdjieff's students sought transcendental consciousness:

> The true consciousness, the consciousness to speak properly, we think, is that of the person who looks at this tree in the following manner: . . . I look at myself looking, I call to myself while I look, and in this difficult action—in which the object of my attention is not this tree but the very perception that I have of it, in which it is a matter of establishing my perception of this tree in relation to an *"I"* in me, compact and fixed, obtained through the *sacrifice* of all the elements of my person set in motion by the spectacle—my real consciousness begins to dawn, born of this effort that I make to call it. At the same time, this tree passes from relative existence into absolute existence. It delivers its real *being* to me. I no longer see this tree, I no longer examine it, I *know* it, we are born from each other.[37]

As an antithesis to this transcendental journey, in which the false *"I"*s are mortified, all debates between linguists—more or less sterile, because each one speaks his own language—lead us to what Benveniste calls "the human reality of dialogue," which is none other than the circle of the confusion of tongues, with its men of a thousand *"I"*s in the grip of a personality subject to the most maleficent exterior influences through their evolutionary forces. "Today's men," Gurdjieff said,

> . . . are conscious of the instability of their language up to a certain point. Each branch of science develops its own terminology, its own nomenclature, its own language. In the domain of philosophy, we attempt, before using a word, to explain in what sense it is to be taken. But despite all the efforts made to give words a permanent meaning, no one has accomplished anything thus far. Every writer believes he is in a position to develop his own vocabulary, change

that of his predecessors, and then contradict what he has himself established. In short, everyone adds his own contribution to the general confusion.[38]

The way of awakening requires sacrifice, voluntary suffering, without which there can be no dissipation of illusion and no rebirth: "Thus the entire world tells us, like doña Musique to the Viceroy, 'Do not prevent me from existing,' and it is in this asceticism that what we call commonly our conscience must be sacrificed to the state of consciousness, that we answer this loving prayer of the world, and that in answering it, we ourselves pass from illusory existence into real existence."[39]

To paraphrase Rabelais's saying, science of language without conscience is but the confusion of tongues (conscience obviously not being understood here or in Rabelais's maxim as what we call "moral conscience" in ordinary language).[40] Consciousness—which truly arises when the distinction is made between knowledge and being—is at the heart of the debate in which neither Descartes's *cogito ergo sum* nor Paulhan's opposing statement ("I think, therefore I am not") are authoritative. "I am conscious (of being conscious), therefore *I am* is the true reason for being": The holistic dimension of this makes it more acceptable, because being appeals to the thoughts but also to the sentiments and sensations. We have already spoken of this at length (but it is important to remind ourselves of it unceasingly).

The experience of the event ("lived experience of the thing spoken of," as Daumal puts it) is inseparable from the experience of language. At this price—and at this price alone, when these two experiences form part of the same level of consciousness and thus of the same reality—does it become possible to speak and to be included in the framework of one and the same language. Everything lies in the principle of relativity mentioned in Ouspensky's *In Search of the Miraculous: Fragments of an Unknown Teaching*. To attain unity—in other words, to merge the word, the thing, and the idea (here we continue to see consciousness)—is what Paulhan saw as being accomplished in the very act of speaking: "The man who speaks defines a reality whose secrets, key, and infrastructure he reveals to us, as if all the things in the world were made only in order to be said."[41] In fact, simply listening to a Pseudoanthrope, a Romantic, or a Savant talking (see chapter 6) is enough for us to know on what level of reality they exist. For those who have learned how to listen, a speaker's speech alone suffices to evaluate his degree of evolution and authenticity, for "we meet with being through the experience we have of it,"[42] as Jean-Claude Coquet concludes regarding Paulhan. The power of words therefore correlates to the power of people and the sincerity of their experiences, for "in a true poem, the words contain their things," writes Daumal, for whom poetry must above all else be experiential, involving the whole of the being, rather than simply intellectual and linked to knowledge.[43]

We cannot reproach Paulhan for having ignored this. To name a thing is to confer absolute existence upon it. Without a sufficient level of consciousness, the word does not incarnate the thing; it is only a pale phantom made of strings pulled by a simple machine. It has no power except that of inducing error and increasing confusion. This idea can be represented on the triad of the enneagram, which clearly shows how this adequation is possible according to the Law of Three:

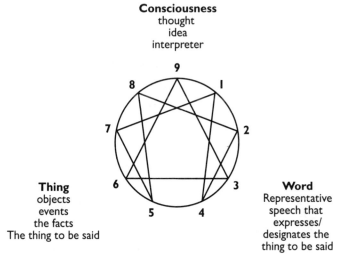

The word is therefore the first tool that actively works toward the proper use of the magic word (which is that of the new language), because, according to Triamazikamno, it incarnates the thing—it makes itself flesh (it is clear enough that this evangelical word does not include the body alone)—as long as the speaker has a sufficient level of consciousness. If the triad is complete, the word can suffice to fill one of the intervals of the octave of speech, with inadequacy being the result of deviation and therefore of curved speech. It thus allows two people of the same world to communicate and allows the writer to create. Yet its powers are not limited to this double function if we consider the shamanic approach: "Language is used by the poet-shaman not as a symbol or instrument of communication, but as a direct and effective technique of knowledge and power. Taking full responsibility for the mystery of himself, the shaman realizes that his language does not belong to him; the words are dictated to him by his eternal part, his double, and they have practical power over the world."[44]

The words are living and bear their own energy. Once again, as Charles Duits said, the people, not the words, are dead. Language "is not simply a representation of life, but an action upon the world."[45] It is not the pale caricature that some people imagine it to be. It takes part unceasingly in creating the things we claim to describe. The paradox simply points to semiconsciousness. The word arises from direct experience and designates as many levels of reality as there are levels of consciousness. It is the power that the white poet masters, the ball and chain that the black poet drags through the pain of the arbitrary. The one takes root in his essence, which is that of life, the other in his personality, in the imitation of his own reflection, in consideration and identification. The one integrates the word into movement, the other into rigidity. The one breathes life into things, the other breathes death. Poetry black, poetry white: The struggle of the magicians is a battle of words in which the winner is always the one who believes in life, because the other has for weapons only pale phantoms which are devoid of power. This is the terror of his situation.

The word of power requires a direct and physical apprehension of the reality that corresponds to experimental poetry as Daumal and Renéville defined it through the rigorous prism of efficacy. But the power is accessible only at the price of effort and suffering undertaken

in the framework of initiation, in the conscious sacrifice of the malig-
nant "*I*"s that inhabit and haunt us:

> The voice of divinity, of the spirit, murmurs the word in the heart
> of the shaman, the principle of universal harmony and the primor-
> dial chaos. The spirit of the ordinary man, in which the "*I*" rules as
> master, remains dead to this word, to the injunctions of the spirit
> and to impersonality. This sacred language effaces all individual
> perception and it is secret, because it is perceptible only by those
> who have known physically the pain of the initiation. Every secret
> passes through language, therefore every language, in its essence,
> holds a secret.[46]

But understanding this secret necessarily involves going through the
trials of initiation.

Beyond the notion of language, the word also has the singular
power of designation. For the shaman, to have power over things first
means knowing their names: According to Castaneda, "The names
must be used only to call for help in moments of great tension or
great difficulty, which are not lacking in the lives of those who seek
wisdom."[47] Castaneda also notes, "Words are formidably powerful and
important, and they are the magical property of those who possess
them."[48] "Before picking them, you must talk to the plants,"[49] declares
don Juan. In shamanism, speech goes far beyond the stage of communication, forming part of the very origin of poetry and magic, namely
invocation and incantation. Labat recalls:

> In Syria, magical formulas allow the overcoming of demons by means
> of their names, and thus allow us to fight the malignant influences
> of illness. In fact, for most sick people, being able to name their
> malady means already having made the first step toward healing.
> The name is also part of the power of creation: An unnamed thing
> does not exist. The designating vibration of the name is in essence a
> power that the lucid poet-shaman cannot neglect.[50]

The same is true for the cosmogony of the Dogon people, for whom each thing is the bearer of a word that must be deciphered. In fact, in Africa, where oral tradition is prevalent, the word is linked directly to its origins—in other words, to magic. "For the Dogons, we create the word in our own body and our own psyche, but in expressing ourselves, we act upon other bodies and upon other psyches. In the universe, every particle of matter contains a message destined for man; this is what the Dogon call the 'word of the world.' In naming things, the shaman learns from them, absorbs their essence, their word, their power."[51] According to the Fula people of the Sahara, "God has created nothing greater and more operative than the word."[52] Further, the Dogon sage is "he who knows the word" or "he who knows the world." Those who master words can master anything; but for this, we must first master ourselves.

"Language is born with the designation of the unknowable. The shaman, at the center of the universe and himself, can 'read' the world and predict the future from bird calls or animal footprints. Guided by silent knowledge, he knows that chance does not exist, that all is interconnected. Words have an extraordinary power to illuminate, to give form to inner knowledge. Once named, a thing is rejoined to its essence, to its primal state."[53] If symbols are arbitrary for some, it is because they are subject to the law of accident. For those who master the word in the perception of its essence, nothing is accidental, because the word links them to the world through the force of consciousness.

Those who have penetrated the esoteric circles of humanity know that speech is a serious thing with which we must not trifle. "I say unto you that every idle word that men shall speak, they shall give account thereof in the day of judgment. For by thy words thou shalt be justified, and by thy words thou shalt be condemned."[54] Names have extreme importance in the shaman's world—especially the shaman's own name, which he holds up as an identifying battle standard. But we must take care: The name also gives the illusion that we are one when we are in fact many. This is why the name must be worthy of itself in order to claim authenticity.

The shaman who has purified his perception knows the name of every plant, every animal, every element, every illness, every thing in the universe. "He knows the word which releases the elements, and can reverse the order of nature as he desires."[55] "Language," Labat writes, "a fundamental element of communication between beings, becomes a magical instrument after shamanic initiation, a new breath in the movement of the world, a penetration by the spirit into matter. The name confers upon a being that it dominates all the powers that being can imagine." "The Nagual Elias had first explained to don Juan that the sound of words and their meaning were infinitely important for hunters. They used the words like so many keys for opening everything that was closed."[56]

Certain names must not be pronounced, but only suggested—that is, with their invoking power. Don Juan tells Castaneda he must not pronounce the name "peyote." Later, Mescalito gives the seeker a name with which to summon him more easily. "Certain words are so powerful that it is mortally dangerous to pronounce them for those who are not prepared."[57] The same goes for the name of God, the essential name at the origin of all language. The shaman must be careful: In the forest, he must not pronounce the name of the tiger. Each one of us must verify his or her own words.

The word has no value unless it has been experienced, felt, understood, assimilated in all its variations (according to the scale of the seven categories), and it can truly be shared only through the power of common experience, often far beyond common expression and ordinary communication and toward the lines of knowledge and being in objective formulation and in the sacred spheres of personal evolution, which is the evolution of consciousness: "The ecstatic fire reforges the meaning of the words, eradicating their essence, their inner primordial power. The action of translating a thought is completed. The poetic text has a function of personal awakening in view of accessing the true poetry within ourselves. The poet-alchemist transmutes the material of words, converts the components of language, in order to attain the strangeness and infiniteness of sound, the sonorous gold."[58]

Separabis terram ab igne, subtile a spisso, suaviter, cum magno ingenio. (You will separate land from fire, thin from thick, sweetly, with great talent.)

The second fundamental power (after the magical power of *words* and names) is the mastery and the purity of *sound,* which determines the vibratory quality of the message inscribed upon the very heart of the speech. The generally accepted definition of speech is "a sound bearing a meaning." The sound is therefore the material structure that carries the meaning to its target. Sometimes, indeed, this structure is enough to convey the meaning without the support of words; it takes its own action and still bears the energy. A comparative and interdisciplinary approach of the great teachings and traditions (inherent to all truly effective research) and of shamanism and the esoteric experience, analyzed in close connection with music and oral poetry, shows us how and why sound can have a profound effect upon our consciousness and its states and levels. A true and real use of language exists in which the power of sound has a strong influence upon the oral and, more subtly, the written.

The art of the tone begins with the sacred sciences, which Gurdjieff mastered and the importance of which is emphasized in many testimonies. This is an account of a young medical student who rememberd a practical demonstration of Gurdjieff's during the 1920s. "While intoning the Lord's Prayer, Gurdjieff placed the student's hand against his chest. In a single breath, he chanted the entire text on one note. The young man reported having sensed something comparable to an electric current."[59] As we know, snake charmers use a primitive approach to objectivize sound and music. The sound can be heard because it can also be felt by the emotional center and can thus have a strong impact on the other centers— psychic and physical. The sound is a material that traverses the entire being. Objective sound, belonging to certain octaves, can produce psychic, psychological, or emotional effects and can also freeze water, kill a man, or break down walls, as in the Biblical legend of Jericho. In *Beelzebub's Tales to His Grandson,* Gurdjieff gives an astonishing example of the power of objective sound: An old dervish plays a repetitive series of notes on an ordinary grand piano harmonized according to a special system so that after a certain amount of time these notes cause a boil to appear on the leg of one of the listeners at the exact location indicated by the master. A new series of notes then causes the boil to disappear rapidly. Music is like magic, white or black, objective or subjective, divining and magical. It is like poetry, and as we can imagine easily, everything that applies to music applies to speech. In other words, a perfectly mastered voice would have had the same effect as the grand piano upon the boil. The beginning of Peter Brook's marvelous cinematographic adaptation of *Meetings with Remarkable Men* is another significant example: In the tournament of the Ashokhs (bards) devoted to improvisation in contests and songs, the winner is the poet who manages to produce the most powerful sound the force of which succeeds in shaking the mountains.[60] In *A Night of Serious Drinking*, René Daumal tells us that "After a few years of practice, the most moronic virtuoso gets to the point where he can shatter a crystal wineglass from a distance simply by emitting a note which corresponds exactly to the unstable equilibrium of the vitreous material."[61] All is matter, and matter acts upon matter. Sound has power over fire, water, air, and earth, over the elements, over all things that make up the universe.

"Thus sound retains its power over fire," the old man was proceeding when I started to listen again. "And over air through the voice, as you can tell from mine at this moment, or in a number of other ways. Over water, as you know from the work of the physicists Plateau, Savart, and Maurat and through the inquiries of Dr. Faustroll, the pataphysician, into liquid veins with special reference to their vertical flow from a hole opened up in a thin lining or wall. And over earth, by which I mean the solid element which Timaeus of Locri Epizephyrii said was composed of cubes, as I have already explained by the example of the vibrating plates; I would further instance the walls of Jericho if recourse to an authority of this sort were not in this day and age of dim luminaries more or less poohpoohed."[62]

Finally, in *A Night of Serious Drinking*, the sage Totochabo relates his ideas regarding the "viscosity of sound":

Sounds spread over surfaces, slide across polished floors, flow in gutters, pile up in corners, snap on ridges, fall like rain on mucous membranes, swarm on plexuses, flame up on body hair, and flutter on skin like warm air over summer fields. There are aerial battles where sound waves bounce back on themselves, start spinning and whirl between heaven and earth, like the indestructible regret of the suicide, who halfway down from the sixth floor all of a sudden no longer wants to die any more. There are words which do not reach their mark and roll up into roving balls, swollen with danger, like lightning does sometimes when it fails to find its target. There are words which freeze . . .[63]

There are full and living words, and empty and dead words.

Daumal, who was familiar with the philosophies of the East, knew that "beneath the perceptible form of sound is a silent essence. It is from this, this crucial point at which the kernel of the perceptible has yet to choose to be sound or light or something else, from this hinterland of nature where to see is to see sound and to hear is to hear suns, it is from this very essence that sound draws its power and its ordering force."[64] Writes Jean Biès, "No civilization has proclaimed the eminent dignity of the language born from the mouth of the gods more than that of India. From the renowned grammarians and metricians of Vak, Daumal learned to grasp the close correlation between sound and speech."[65] In *Les Pouvoirs de la parole,* Daumal's conclusions are crystallized, with immense significance.

Asian philosophies such as Hinduism and Buddhism also teach the powers of sound at the origin of the cosmos, its most famous usage being in the mantra Om—a pure sound symbolizing the universe in its entirety:

But he who contemplates the 3rd mantra of OM, i.e., views God as himself, becomes illuminated and obtains moksha. Just as the serpent relieved of its old skin becomes new again, so the yogi who worships the 3rd mantra, relieved of his mortal coil, of his sins and earthly weaknesses, and freed with his spiritual body to roam throughout God's Universe, enjoys the glory of the All-Pervading Omniscient Spirit, ever and evermore. The contemplation of the last mantra blesses him with moksha or immortality.[66]

Thus sound, along with word and rhythm, is one of the three techniques of the shamanic powers of language. During ecstatic rituals, the shaman uses sacramental plants to attain ecstasy and other levels of consciousness inaccessible to the ordinary consciousness. This is the moment when the shaman uses the power of speech and sound with the instrument of the voice to start acting upon his patient's psychology. Thus he can guide the patient into other worlds in order to locate his "problems" and heal him. In the Amazonian forest, shamans use sacred songs called *icaros;* the Huichol people use the songs of peyote; the Mazatec healer Maria Sabina used *nahualtcocatl,* the "language of the gods." In these special states of consciousness, sound can be seen literally as a material thing that conveys information.[67]

The same phenomenon is observable in trance states among certain Christian groups such as the Pentecostals with their *glossolalia*— unknown words that are full of meaning and that are revealed in a sonorous echo. In martial arts, the "kiai" is the cry with which the warrior paralyzes his adversary, because this sound produces a shock in the emotional center and, from there, in the mental and motor centers. This technique, often parodied and blindly mocked, is easily verifiable. The cry comes from the *hara,* several inches below the navel, where lies the *chi* (Chinese) or *ki* (Japanese)—the internal energy known to the Asians. A cry arising from the throat has no effect, but one that comes from the belly brings with it vibrations whose effect is incontestable for those who have felt it. The sound does not have to be loud to be effective. It all depends on the technique of delivery, which makes the sound either pass through a listener or imprint itself upon a listener's being and vibrate there. This technique is applicable broadly to all poetry and all music, but rare are the poets who know its powers.

Sound also has the power to bring about altered states of consciousness. We have scientific proof of this phenomenon, because sound has a profound effect on the brain—the center of gravity of the psychic center. Any religious context aside, this phenomenon is observable at rock and techno concerts, during which sound serves to unleash other states of consciousness and trance. Anthropologists have observed, especially in shamanic ceremonies, that the *rhythms* of the drum and the chant—following certain frequencies and applied over a certain length of time—lead to a response in the brain that tends to synchronize its electrical activity to these frequencies. Exterior sonorous stimulation therefore affects the nature of brain waves (and also the synchronization of the two cerebral hemispheres). The brain follows the frequencies that are presented to it with the aid of sound (a kind of frequency following reaction). Through these techniques, we can enter altered states of consciousness by means of simple sonorous stimulation. The different types of sounds (low, high, muffled, clear, deep, throaty, etc.) have a definite impact on our emotions, and can give rise to experiences that are truly profoundly mystical. A very high sound can become stressful quickly, even causing insanity in someone exposed to it for long enough. It is no accident that the Tibetans use horns and cymbals and the shamans drums and chants. Nor is it an accident that the sound of the beating of the human heart awakens the emotions, or that the songs of whales facilitate access to feelings of oceanic plenitude. In the same way, waves, wind, rain, storms, tempests, and so on make primordial sounds, charged with emotion: They are all part of the cosmic order.

Thanks to an ingenious assembly of sounds and rhythms, music is one of the greatest proofs of the powers of sound. Embodied by the musical octave, and therefore by the Law of Seven upon which Gurdjieff based all his theories as well as the functioning of his Institute for the Harmonic Development of Man, music is the art of perfection. According to Gurdjieff, however, only objective music is perfect, corresponding to the general properties of what he calls objective art—capable of unleashing precise emotions created intentionally and consciously by a creator.

Yet confusion still reigns, because we all expect generally that everybody will have the same reaction to works of subjective art when this is not so at all: "Everything depends on associations," according to Gurdjieff, and we can verify this idea easily. A funeral march will not necessarily evoke sad and solemn thoughts in everyone, because it depends on the context (associations) in which this music has been heard for the first time: "If on a day that a great misfortune happens to me I hear some lively tune for the first time this tune will evoke in me sad and oppressive thoughts for my whole life afterwards. And if on a day when I am particularly happy I hear a sad tune, this tune will always evoke happy thoughts. And so with everything else."[68] Subjective art is judged and sensed in a subjective manner, depending on the humor and ideas of the moment, whereas objective art cannot make an accidental impression. In the former case, the artist doesn't know what he is doing. For him, everything is accidental, haphazard (even if he believes he is infusing his work with something), and mechanical (as we can see!). For him, it creates itself, it thinks, it imagines, and so forth. As Gurdjieff says, this means that the artist "is in the power of ideas, thoughts, and moods which he himself does not understand and over which he has no control whatever."[69] In the case of the objective artist, everything is controlled. He introduces what he wants into his work, and "the action of his work upon men is absolutely definite," but we must remember, keeping in mind the difference in levels of being and therefore in the reception of the work, "I measure the merit of art by its consciousness," as Gurdjieff says. Music is a revealing example of what Gurdjieff called objective art.

Though the invention of music is attributed generally to Apollo, Cadmus, Orpheus, and Amphion among the Greeks or Thoth and Osiris among the Egyptians, historians of musical science give credit to Pythagoras, who invented a monochord in order to determine mathematically the relationships between sounds, and Lassus, the master of Pindar, who was the first to write about the theory of music in 540 BCE.[70] The Pythagoreans considered music—and the entire universe—to be the harmony of numbers and the cosmos, and that microcosm and macrocosm were constructed according to ideal proportional ratios producing a series of sounds. For Hermes Trismegistus, "music is nothing other than the application of an order that reigns in all things." Gurdjieff refers to Pythagorean ideas in *Beelzebub's Tales to His Grandson:* The Bukharan dervish Hadji-Asvats-Troov adapted Pythagoras's monochord for his own investigations into sound vibrations.[71] Christian tradition is inspired extensively by Pythagorean theories of music handed down by St. Augustine and Boethius. Here, the ternary rhythm, instead of binary rhythm, symbolizes perfection and three types of music are taken into consideration: the music of the world (cosmic), the music of man (soul–body), and instrumental music (which rules the use of instruments). Because the meter commands the order of the cosmos, the human order, and the instrumental order, music is the "art of attaining perfection."[72] And it is to this art (because it truly achieves its goal) that Gurdjieff, in agreement with Pythagorean and Hermetic thought, attributes the criteria of objectivity:

> Objective music is all based on inner octaves, and it can obtain not only definite psychological results, but also definite physical results. There can be such music as would freeze water. There can be such music as would kill a man instantaneously. The Biblical legend of the destruction of the walls of Jericho by music is precisely a tale of objective music. Plain music, no matter of what kind, will not destroy walls, but objective music indeed can do so. And it cannot only destroy, but it can also build up. In the legend of Orpheus there are hints of objective music, for Orpheus used to impart knowledge by music. Snake charmers' music in the East is an approach, however primitive, to objective music. Very often it is simply one note that is drawn out, rising and falling very little, but in this single note inner octaves are occurring all the time and melodies of inner octaves are inaudible to the ears but are felt by the emotional center. The snake hears this music—or, more strictly speaking, he feels it—and he obeys it. The same music, only a little more complicated, would have men obey.[73]

During the course of his investigation into man's "unexplored potentials," related in part in *Meetings with Remarkable Men,* Gurdjieff acquired the conviction that the essential characteristics inherent in certain cultures were preserved and revealed in their music. According to him, this music had the power to impart profound knowledge that words could not convey. For a seeker of the truth, music cannot be simple amusement or even a simple aesthetic exercise, transmitting merely the musician's subjectivity. Music is a sacred science at the very source of all knowledge. In *Meetings with Remarkable Men,* Gurdjieff reports a conversation with Vitvitskaïa, a remarkable woman who considered this science to be one of the greatest, because she knew the powers inherent in it.[74] Her words remained imprinted on his brain, and influenced his teaching objectively. This woman tells him that before truly understanding the interest of music, she would often state opinions regarding a given piece, depending on the mood and context of the moment, but always in an arbitrary, haphazard, and mechanical fashion, without a trace of sincerity or true understanding. Then she learned to play the piano and turned out to be gifted, and people saw in her a great deal of talent, as she had seen in others before. She then studied music theory, and, from the available books, learned all she could about this art. Her interest in the laws of harmony increased each day. Yet in these books, she found only perpetual and systematic repetition which always related to the same things but imparted no real interest: "[A]s to what music is and what effect it has on the psyche of people, nothing was said anywhere."[75]

She therefore abandoned reading, exploring the theory of music through her own thoughts. One day, however, out of boredom, she borrowed a book entitled *The World of Vibrations* in which she found the key she had been seeking for so long: "[T]he sounds of music are made up of certain vibrations which doubtless act upon the vibrations which are also in a man, and this is why a man likes or dislikes this or that music."[76] In order to test this idea, she intensified her experiments and research, to the detriment of her health. Only several years later did she return to her reflections on the powers of music as a consequence of explanations given by the "Monopsyche brethren" in Pamir and Afghanistan. Once again, however, her repeated experiments proved that she was not able to stimulate the same emotions in all listeners with a single piece of music. Until the day when she succeeded in this feat, but without knowing "the real cause of this phenomenon," her subsequent attempts at understanding all ended in failure and drove her to complete exhaustion and self-mutilation. Touched by her story and her perseverance in trying to understand, Gurdjieff in turn told her of an extraordinary phenomenon that he had witnessed the previous year: "I told her how thanks to a letter of introduction from a certain great man, Father Evlissi, who had been my teacher in childhood, I had been among the Essenes, most of whom are Jews, and that by means of very ancient Hebraic music and songs they had made plants grow in half an hour, and I described in detail how they had done this."[77]

After this exchange, Gurdjieff and Vitvitskaïa undertook further experiments. After she died, Gurdjieff continued until he found what he had been seeking since the beginning of his quest. Thanks to his exceptional abilities, he then reconstituted certain complex themes he had heard over the course of twenty years of investigation. These remembrances, sometimes nostalgic, formed part of the source of the music composed subsequently at the Avon priory in France, where he decided to transmit the great revelation—his teaching and his system. In close collaboration with Thomas Alexandrovich de Hartmann, an exceptional composer and musician whom he had met in 1916, he composed more than three hundred pieces for the piano in the space of two years (between 1925 and 1927), divided into four categories: pieces originating in folklore, dervish songs and dances, sacred hymns and prayers, and music for accompanying the movements.[78] Hartmann, who had played for Czar Nicholas II before meeting Gurdjieff, found Gurdjieff's teaching to be something new which transformed his being and his music. He remained closely connected with Gurdjieff and joined the Institute of the Avon priory in 1922. Until 1924, the two men's collaboration was focused on music to accompany the movements and dances taught by the master. Beginning in 1925, the composition of this objective music was developed in its full intensity. Hartmann relates:

> This music put me through very difficult, very trying moments. Sometimes Gurdjieff whistled or played a very complicated melody on the piano with one finger. The great moments generally took place at night in the great salon of the priory. From my room, when

I heard Gurdjieff begin to play, I would grab my sheet music and run downstairs. . . . While I listened, he had me scribble feverishly the complex movements of the melody. . . . When the melody was written completely, Gurdjieff tapped a rhythm on the side of the piano, and from this I could construct the basis for accompaniment and improvise the harmonies . . .[79]

It remains for the pianist himself to explore this music and to find in it the key to its interpretation; it remains for the listener to hear it and draw from it the knowledge that exists silently within the secret of sound. Peter Brook points out that the sonorous passage from one note to the next transforms the quality of the music: "When a sound reaches the high point of an octave, the first note is reproduced in order to begin a higher octave. The note is the same, but placed on another level, it generates a different feeling."[80]

Mastering objective music depends strictly on mathematical laws and obeys the golden number of architects. "The only objective music is based on exact knowledge of the mathematical laws that govern sonorous vibration and the relationship of sounds to one another."[81] In order to release a precise emotion in a listener without possible accident or chance, we must know these universal laws. The speaker who knows the golden number of speech has nothing more to learn. He possesses all the powers—and keeps them secret, offering these forces through sibylline fragments.

As we saw with Vitvitskaïa's discovery, one of the keys resides in the question of the vibrations with respect not only to musical laws but also to human and cosmic nature:

Like light, musical sound energy consists of a spectrum of pure vibrations that are harmonic. This primordial scale governs the structure of all musical sounds. Every note, vocal or instrumental, is a combination of these harmonics. . . . The harmonic series is reserved not only for music; it forms an integral part of creation and constitutes the nature of light, relativity, gravity, and heat. All wave energies manifesting in the body or in space take on the form of the harmonic series, the material universe being generated by the infinitely multiplied inner relationships of this series. The study of these apparently simple ratios can, in music and elsewhere, open the way to a contemplation of the origins and nature of things.[82]

This theory, fundamentally in line with Asian thought, shows how sound is at the origin of creation. "The physicist David Bohm goes so far as to suggest that creation is a harmony of energies that obeys harmonic theory."[83] This means, according to Hykes, that "the beginning of the universe, and therefore of life, was not the accidental event described generally by science, but rather the result of the conjunction of harmonious forces acting on an infinitely vast scale."[84] By this logic, music is a "harmonic movement of energies, and its laws, beyond their everyday application, are like waves of propagation," the harmonic series being "the source of melody, harmony, and rhythm."[85] According to Hykes, "the universality of harmonic sounds reveals extraordinary possibilities" whose development "could lead to that of a new sacred global music in the sense of what Gurdjieff called objective music." Further, this music, which Gurdjieff composed along with Thomas de Hartmann, embodies this law of vibrations and is "imprinted with a special quality that we can sense depending on the state in which we find ourselves when listening to it," bearing indisputable witness to the inner Work. According to Gurdjieff, "musical laws are perfectly symbolic of the structure and functioning of the inner life of man and creation."[86]

This music requires special attention, singular listening, which may offer certain people fuel for producing some few fragments of awakening. We must listen with our inner view, using our (higher) emotional center to capture the secrets that this music—crystallizing all cosmic laws—reveals to us. According to Hykes, these harmonics correspond to what Gurdjieff called the inner octaves, which explains their importance.[87] Yet the understanding of this phenomenon goes beyond strict intellectual demonstration and requires direct experience and an adequate teaching acquired in competent schools in order that we may integrate and use these laws in daily life for our harmonic development and accession to a higher level. Further, it was not by chance that Gurdjieff, in *Beelzebub's Tales to His Grandson,* insisted upon this law of vibrations inherent to his teaching. Sound—whose mystery he knew—is perhaps the source of all things.

Sound, whose magic quality depends on the levels of consciousness and at the same time on an action upon these levels, is the blood of language, the vehicle of the voice and the word, the path of rhythmic vibrations. Sound is wholly a part of the power of the word, speech, music, literature, and poetry—both oral and written—focusing on its resonances with the body, emotions, and ideas, and therefore, through a clear link, healing the being.

The objective sound lying within speech acts upon all the centers of man, due to the mediation carried out by another primordial element between sound and word: *rhythm,* which, in performing the task of conciliation, gives all its coherence and power to the techniques of the magic word.

Many are those who have not seen the importance of rhythm, the third fundamental power (along with the magic power of the word and the power of sound), yet it is present in everything. Each vibration, every energy, has its own cadence. Rhythm creates physical and poetic trances and has a fascinating contagious power. Dance, music, poetic speech: They all live the through rhythm, which is sacred when it merges with the universal laws at work in the rhythm of the universe itself and in cosmic forces.

In "Poetry Black, Poetry White," Daumal emphasizes its necessity, rhythm being a conciliatory force in that it works toward achieving a double operation which is impossible to conciliate by the intellectual or instinctive path. It allows the thing to be said not only to bend "the sounds of language to its breath" but also to compel them to "contain its images."[88] Hence the crucial importance, according to Daumal, of the "particular relation that exists between the various elements of the poet's machinery" and that allows this union, which would otherwise be impossible. Those who control their center master not only the rhythm, but everything. The growth of human power is in direct correlation to this self-knowledge.

But before attempting to define *objective rhythm*—which will be easily understood in light of all that has been said regarding the art and theory of numbers—it is particularly important to return to this notion of rhythm that is too elusive to use in a systematic and arbitrary manner, as is the case in ordinary exchanges. In fact, "this word is not clear to me," as Valéry writes in *Cahiers*. "I never use it. Because it is not a matter merely of giving a definition of something, we must regard most simply some of the phenomena from which the word *rhythm* proceeds. Regard them closely; isolate and name some general characteristics . . ."[89] Everyone can recognize simple rhythmic phenomena: a heartbeat, the ticking of a clock, breathing in and breathing out; the alternation of days and nights, the phases of the moon, the cycle of the seasons; playing a rhythm, dancing to music, chanting verse . . . or, indeed, writing in a "ternary rhythm." But as Valéry wrote, the word *rhythm* must "proceed," emerging into creation, imposing itself on the perception which reconstitutes it: "What rhythm!?" we exclaim. And yet this word is elusive and uncertain; it seems to escape all definition.

The words *rhyme* and *rhythm* have long been linked via a false etymology of *rhyme,* which was thought to originate, like rhythm, from the Latin *rythmus,* coming in turn from the Greek *ruthmos,* "regulated and measured movement" and, by analogy, "regular proportion" and "manner of being." This was thought to be abstracted from the verb *rein,* which means "to flow." Without confusing the two, Baudelaire, appeared sensible of a common, profound character when he wrote in his preface to the second edition of *Fleurs du mal* that "[r]hythm and rhyme answer to man's immortal need for monotony, symmetry, and surprise."[90]

Though it seems natural to characterize rhythm by the regular movement of the sea and the waves, Emile Benveniste's works[91] show that in the Greek, the word *rein* applies to the course of a river or stream and not to the rhythm of waves, which do not flow. Benveniste analyzes the different understandings of the word among various authors, including Leucippus, Democritus, Herodotus, Xenophon, and Plato. He concludes that *ruthmos* means "distinctive form, proportioned figure, disposition," "characteristic arrangement of parts into a whole," "particular manner of flowing," and, for Plato, "form of movement that the human body accomplishes in dance." These first meanings of *ruthmos* are far from the contemporary usage of the word *rhythm,* which results today from a series of extensions over a widening field of human activity: "Beyond human order, we project a rhythm into things and into events. A condition of this vast unification of man and nature under consideration of time, intervals, and similar cycles has been the use of the word itself, the generalization in the vocabulary of modern Western thought of the term *rhythm,* which, through Latin, came to us from Greek."[92]

The linguistic generalization of the use of the word is therefore the condition for the rhythmic unification of humans and nature. According to Benveniste, it is the use of language that models our way of thinking, imposing its rhythms upon the world. But what does it mean to impose its rhythms upon the world? In this statement, we can see easily the blind pretense of man subject to the cosmic rhythm, imagining that he is imposing his own rhythms. Yet this is not so, for subjective rhythm leads nowhere and only objective rhythm has a precise function within the functioning of the universe and therefore of us.

While rhythm is in itself obvious to practically everyone, the concept of rhythm is elusive and difficult to define in a theoretical manner. It is most often based on a more or less regular return to a constant point, whatever its nature may be, as mentioned regarding heartbeats, breathing, or the cycle of the seasons. This is therefore a matter of a primary experience in existential relation to the subject. For this reason, Henri Meschonnic adds the notion of subjectivity to the purely formal definitions of rhythm. The rhythm inscribes the voice of the subject in the poem, it is the "subjective organization of discourse." This idea of the relationship between rhythm and the body was mentioned earlier by Abbé Rousselot, who cites A. Spire in *Plaisir poétique et plaisir musculaire:* "The rhythm is the image of the entire man, body and soul, muscles and spirit, engraved in the speech."[93] In Meschonnic's poetics, the search for literary specificity is an aspect of the search for anthropological specificity. This search proceeds through a theorization of the concept of rhythm: "*[P]oetics,* through the necessity of the reciprocal implication between the *language,* the *history,* and the *subject,* is led to the search for a historic anthropology of language, and from there to recognizing rhythm as a major element."[94] Meschonnic's poetics are based on Benveniste's linguistics, but the notion of rhythm is placed at the center of his theory. In the late nineteenth century, rhythm was central to reflections upon language, especially for the symbolist poets and acoustic linguists who worked with Jean-Pierre Rousselot, author of *Principes de phonétique expérimentale (1897–1909)*.

In his study of the concept of rhythm, Benveniste shows that the "idea of regular repetition" is linked to Plato's philosophy, while the pre-Socratic philosophers used the term *rhythm* to describe dispositions or configurations without fixity or natural necessity, resulting from an arrangement forever subject to change.[95] Applied to literary discourse, this understanding of rhythm as a "distinctive form," a "characteristic arrangement of parts into a whole,"[96] provides an overture to an idea of specificity. Benveniste demonstrates that the Greek concept of rhythm is linked to ideas of form and proportion. It "designates the form in the instant it is assumed through that which is moving, mobile, whose form does not have organic consistency. . . . It is the improvised, momentary, modifiable form."[97] A great conciliator, rhythm therefore structures that which could be elusive: time, language, movement, informal matter, sounds. Benveniste concludes by insisting upon the highly cultural character of this notion, the rhythm in fact being a form bestowed outwardly: It does not in itself belong to the matter to which it is applied, but is in relation to the law of numbers and to "all that assumes a continuous activity divided by the meter into alternating periods."[98]

The connection with number is also mentioned by Claudel in his own definition of rhythm: "It consists of a measured impulse of the soul responding to a number, always the same, which obsesses us and draws us in."[99] The concept of number (a major notion in the theorization of literature in the poetic arts of the High Middle Ages and Renaissance) incorporates the concept of rhythm. During the Latin period, Cicero discussed rhythm in oratory prose, calling it "something analogous to the verse—that is to say, a sort of number,"[100] and Aristotle gave the same impression (still regarding oratory prose): "It is not a matter of rhythm in the strict sense of the word, but of something approaching it."[101] The rhetorician's viewpoint on rhythm is a metric one, because it develops the idea of a measured discourse. Cicero explains that "if, in prose, the words are grouped to form a verse, this is a defect, and yet we wish to recall the verse by their rhythmic cadence, their full and symmetric form."[102] The other character of rhythm for rhetoricians, connected with the theory of literarity, resides in its evocative function of a certain type of language (poetic and oratory). Cicero distinguishes a language without art, a language that is "ordinary" in its form:

> Among many traits, what essentially distinguishes the true orator from the man who does not command the practice of speech and does not know its rules is that the ignorant man delivers as many words as he can without art and measures sentences by his breathing, not by their principles. By contrast, the true orator encloses the thought in a framework of words which embrace it in a circuit of rhythm, simultaneously fixed and free.[103]

The notion of rhythm expressed by the idea of number is imprinted here upon the musical model, as Cicero writes, justifying the necessity for measuring discourse by the fact that "the instinct of the ear compels the delivery to have a musical cadence, which is impossible if there is no rhythm in this delivery. Now there is no rhythm in that which is uninterrupted."[104] In the same way, Aristotle believed that "all things are determined by the number, and the number applied to the form of elocution is the rhythm, of which the meters with their divisions form part."[105] In these rhetoricians' statements, we can clearly sense the influence of the logic of Pythagorean and Platonic numerism. For these rhetoricians, poetry is defined as a discourse that follows, in its verses, fixed metric patterns. Aristotle writes that "the language of prose must necessarily possess a rhythm but not a meter, for then it would be poetry."[106] The idea of rhythm inherited by the poetic arts of the Middle Ages and Renaissance in the form of a theory of number was an aesthetic concept of rhythm. The rhythmic marks are formal schemes generating aesthetic or psychological impressions without semantic implication. Moreover, in the case of an objective rhythm, answering by definition to the perfect knowledge of the mathematical laws at work in the universe (in line with what Gurdjieff said regarding art), the impressions evoked are always the same, created consciously and not by accident. Further, since the medieval era, the poetic arts have emphasized that the notion of rhythm (or number) is not only a question of syllable, but also is inseparable from phonic recurrence.

We now return to the question of the etymology of the words *rhythm* and *rhyme* first addressed by Benveniste. In his *Critique du rythme,* Meschonnic takes the counterposition to the rhetoricians' theories built around the concept of number. Indeed, he defines *rhythm* as "the sense of the unforeseeable," "the realization of that which, after the fact, will be called inner necessity, the inscription of a subject in its history."[107] It thus cannot be identified with the meter, whether it be a meter of verse or a meter of prose. Meschonnic diverges from Platonic theories of repetition and regularity, revived notably by Kristeva, according to whom repetition is the rhythmic principle par excellence: "This carving up and this repetition of sound elements, on the axis of time, is precisely *rhythm*."[108] Meschonnic's poetics is simultaneously a critique of the notion of rhythm and a theory of rhythm as a critical concept. The critique of the notion of rhythm aims essentially at a metaphysics of rhythm, making rhythm into a universal, a unifying concept, as in Plato's philosophy. Meschonnic compares this cosmic vision of rhythm to the perception of its historical character and its specificity: "One theory of rhythm in discourse will not necessarily have any relation to another theory of rhythm outside of discourse. Thus the meaning of the notion of rhythm in language could be only the particular realization of a universal, which assumes a universal rhythm or, rather, a universal notion of rhythm."[109] "Writing, in particular that of a poem, is a specific practice of rhythm only when it is a specific practice of a subject through social codifications."[110] For Meschonnic, subjectivity is at a maximum in poetry. A literary work is "a language that knows more about us than we know of ourselves."[111] The rhythm is plural depending on whether it is applied to music, biology, or linguistics. Meschonnic marks the distance between meter—fixed and measurable forms—and rhythm inseparable from the meaning of the subject and the historical nature of the poem. All the choices within a text (syntax, punctuation, etc.) therefore create the rhythm.

According to Paul Zumthor, "from within the rhythm a knowledge is born and is legitimated."[112] Many cultures, now vanished, built their idea of the world on repetition and parallelism—as their stories and oral poetry testify in the transient medium of the voice, such as in shamanic trance opening access to power. The linguistic work of the voice is defined and evaluated according to two parameters: modal and prosodic (prosodic by virtue of the rhythm of the poetic speech). Rhythm is meaning, untranslatable into language by other means. "The prosody of an oral poem refers to the prehistory of the spoken or sung text, to its prearticulatory genesis, the echo of which it interiorizes. For this reason, most performances, whatever the cultural context, begin with a nonvocal prelude—the beating of an object—not with dance, the preliminary musical measure. The frame is thereby exposed where voice is going to be deployed." In general terms, "the notion of rhythm is applied equally to neurophysiology, music, poetry, and history—all in one." Zumthor points to a "universal rhythmic human activity," characterized by techniques and aesthetics, in which "mathematics and music provide the only apparently effective language of analysis." But, he clarifies, "rhythms are no less diversely perceived, exploited, and connoted from culture to culture."[113]

> The very complex rhythmic impression that performance creates comes from the confluence of two series of factors: corporeal, therefore visual and tactile . . . and the vocal ones, therefore auditory. However, these last ones operate on two levels: first, that of the recurrences and the parallelisms . . . producer of rhythmic effects at the level of the constructed phrases . . . ; and second, that of the sonorous manipulations, even as immediately perceptible, in principle, in the ignorance of the language used. . . . The play of these diverse factors is projected into the proper space for the performance, engendering poetry there that is never the same. . . . Each performance thus creates its own rhythmic system.[114]

The drum utters true speech, exhaling the breath of the ancestors, Zumthor tells us:

> As source and mythical pattern for human discourse, the beating of drums accompanies in counterpoint the voice pronouncing phrases on which existence depends. It marks the base rhythm. . . . It is a constitutive part of the oral poetic "monument." . . . Percussion constitutes, structurally, a poetic language. . . . All cultures have created, while manipulating the acoustical elements of natural language, a secondary auditory level of language, some artifices of which put the rhythmical markings in order.[115]

Once tamed, the rhythms of speech inscribe the mark of a human order of the universe. Can this second level of rhythm be identified with the verse? If a text composed without proper rhythmic structure is chanted, it assumes the rhythm of the melody in performance. The performer's voice formalizes the text according to the concrete and immediate requirements of the music, dance, exclamation, or movement of the audience. The poetic structure of the rhythm, beyond the accentual, quantitative, or tonal elements of natural prosody, embraces the timbre of the sounds. In the texture of the message, every repetition of a phoneme initiates a rhythmic chain. Whether to break this chain or continue it is a decision that falls to the individual art of the poet. Of the multitude of possible sonorous echoes, most systems of versification have regularized and given value to one or two: alliteration and rhyme—in keeping with what Daumal calls, in the light of Hindu poetics, the "ornaments of sound." Again, their use must not be accidental or haphazard, but must be created to serve a single end of an aesthetic order. These tools, which give rhythm to the poem, must be mastered in order to serve entirely specific ends—without which they have no true and objective meaning. Writes Daumal, "The ornaments (*alamkara*) are to the body of poetry what bracelets, earrings, and so forth are to the human body. . . . Their function is to enhance poetry, and they are at the service of the knower."[116] In other words, they must serve "the moment of consciousness that the true work of art must evoke in whoever is gifted with an inner being and who has a measure for judging,"[117] which requires common experience, to generate certain feelings that belong to the poem. We will call them objective ornaments. "One and the same combination of sounds, for example, could be a defect or an ornament depending on whether it was accidental or desired." The defect in this case arises from the subjective ornament—accidental and mechanical by definition.[118]

In *Les Pouvoirs de la parole,* René Daumal provides a definition of *rhythm* in light of Hindu poetry:

> The Hindus have never had the absurd idea we have in the West of confusing rhythm and meter. If we do not hold fast to vocabulary, we will remember that in this study, rhythm has been described as an essential characteristic of the body of poetry. Rhythm is in fact inseparable from what have been called stylistic movements. These movements, with their innumerable varieties, are defined, as we have seen, by simultaneous ordinances of sounds and meanings determined by the attitude of the speaker—as in the corporeal analogy. Because the body of the poem is composed of sounds (furnished by the voice), images (furnished by the literal meanings that reside beneath the depicted meanings), concepts (depicted meanings), and emotions (suggested), the rhythm must result from the equilibrium and the composition of these various elements in motion. The meter, strictly speaking, is only the envelope (*chandas*) or the demeanor (*vrtti*) bestowed on the overall movement of the poetic material. Poetry is not unilinear; it is is an art of simultaneities in which materials subject to radically different laws (sounds of the voice, images, concepts, emotions) must be arranged with a common goal in view by the will of the poet. And it is in this that poetry has been made in analogy to life and the poems in man's image.[119]

It is rhythm, as Daumal also says in "Poetry Black, Poetry White," which has this power of unification and conciliation that is necessary for the poet and the poem, because it unites sound and meaning (images, concepts, and emotions). In other words, it unites sound and word into a living substance. This is what the word-rhythm-sound triad revealed to us at the beginning of this chapter. It represents what Daumal called the "body of the poem"—itself a conciliatory force between the "affective state of the poet" and the "affective state of the listener" ("manifestation of emotions, mental operations, and corporeal states").[120] In Hindu music there is also a conciliatory force directly connected to the poem: "When the head grasps the truth, it must try to make the two others hear this truth, so that man will understand. The rhythm is the primordial element of Oriental music, and the preeminence of rhythm gives the first place to the drums."[121] This rhythm—creating harmony, miming marvelously "all the multiplicity of life," as Daumal writes, its polarizing force striving for understanding—is, as we shall see, possible only at the price of an asceticism with which the white poet cannot dispense.[122]

We will define the word *rhythm*—"a vital element of music," as Jacques Dalcroze noted, as well as of poetic speech—according to the scale that the system proposes. In other words, we will apply the notions of evolution and relativity. We will simply distinguish subjective rhythms (men 1, 2, and 3) from objective rhythms (men 4, 5, 6, and 7), corresponding to the definitions proposed by Daumal: The rhythm of man 1 is mechanical, calculated from a vague impression or a ridiculous imitation, while man 2 produces an emotional rhythm, depending on his mood of the moment, which is equally subjective. The rhythm of man 3 is merely the fruit of the circumvolutions of his intellect, and like the two preceding ones, the rhythm he creates will only ever—except in cases of accident—have a destructive and separative effect, for it is bound to the ordinary consciousness, which is itself separative. The being who belongs to esoteric circles knows the rhythmic laws of the universe and uses them with awareness—as a conciliatory and unifying technique, as an additional shock to fill an interval when necessary, or in order to evoke consciously a specific impression or idea, for if the "poem is made in man's image," it is also made in the image of the universe, and consequently, it is also ruled by the same laws.

Corresponding to specific phases of operation, poetry comes about via the exercise of the voice inherent in every poem—which is not only a property of the vocabulary term but also, along with the meaning, the very definition of the word. The powers of the voice—in its phonological materiality—are more easily perceptible in oral performance, in the execution of the poem.[123] This is nothing new. We know that in the days of Homer—the archetypal poet—the bard's song had a magical effect on his audience: A religious silence took hold and he enchanted his observers, cheered them, or made them cry, depending on his own will. The bard knew objective art. Such is the primordial power of speech and music.

Originating from the Greek word *poïen* (to make, create), the objective poet creates a living work using a material that is language, like the alchemist who transforms gross matter into more subtle matter. He knows cosmic laws and applies them to his speech, the powers of which are obvious. The same fundamental principles that determine the efficacy of objective music, relating to the laws of vibrations and to fundamental cosmic laws, also apply to the voice that conveys information, and this is what constitutes the very essence of his powers, which can be qualified as Orphic. Moreover, he reaches a point—especially in states of mystical trance—where the distinction between speech, music, and dance disappears and the movement merges into a single primordial creative one, a single respiration, a breath that simultaneously traverses, surpasses, and silently resides in the body. What is breath if not life, voice, and speech? It is through this breath—*ruah* in Hebrew—that life is given, as Genesis tells us, and it is through this that it continues, ceases, and begins again. Breath and speech lend each other mutual assistance, the one supporting the emission of the other. There cannot be speech or, consequently, a voice without breath. The Hebrew term *ruah* is usually translated as "spirit." It corresponds to the Greek word *pneuma* and the Latin *spiritus*. These terms signify the breath coming out of the nostrils or mouth, and therefore the individual who has the voice and charges it with energy. While the term *ruah* means "spirit," it is also used to designate "speech," the breath-spirit of the Hebrew scriptures, which is the manifestation of the One, the single God, the creator God, the Word.

"In the beginning was the Word, and the Word was with God, and the Word was God," John relates in his Gospel. "In the beginning was a vibration . . . or, if you prefer, the Word," Gurdjieff said. The secret of the Word—closely connected with sonic power—resides in the esoteric doctrine that decompartmentalizes perception and transcends dualism to open up to the One—*"Et sicut omnes res fuerunt ab uno, mediatione unius, sic omnes res natae fuerunt ab hac una re, adaptatione."*[124] Biblical, Qur'anic, and Sanskrit sources all say the same thing, disregarding the apparent contradictions existing on the exoteric level. The word is the "healthy gold" of alchemical reason in which all the powers reside. Traditions are unanimous on this. The Gospel of John tells that the Word (speech) was made flesh in Christ—the Word of God—in order to make all things exist and to bring grace, truth, and salvation. As the symbol of the logos, language is the instrument of the divine intellect, activity, and will of creation: The world is the effect of divine speech, the word of life having been at the beginning. The powers of this speech go far beyond simple exchanges and allow us communication with the absolute by means of prayer and invocation—which, in order to be effective, also require knowledge of universal laws in order that we are served by them rather than serve them. Vedic texts also tell that in the beginning there was Brahma, and with him Vak, the creative Speech and the cosmic Breath. Islam calls the Word Kalimat Allah, Word of God or Founding Word. The quest for the lost word is that of the first revelation, because it is an invitation to drink at the source of all things. The rest is merely confusion and stagnation in the circle of illusion where Maya rules as master.

The white poet seeks the primordial word in order to become a creator and bearer of a word of luminous life for humankind: an awakening, divining, and magical word containing the spell of salvation. The question of the word plunges us into the heart of the poet's *becoming*, as Louis Pauwels expresses it:

This is what we wanted to become: responsible poets who have transcended inspiration in favor of knowledge, are free, and are not singers, but creators. We wanted to be God-speaking. We wanted to move toward where the word is made flesh. We began with Gurdjieff in search of knowledge, liberty, and unity. Our poetry can be nothing but this superior language which, expressing this knowledge, this liberty, and this unity, re-creates the things and the movements of human life in all their solemnity, in their heavenly meaning.[125]

Creating is part of what Gurdjieff called objective art, in which the creation of the poem takes place initially through the poet's creation (in the sense of evolution). There can be no creation without this fundamental and vital breath. Artaud writes, "The primordial forces let their echoes be heard in the spasmodic vibration of words, and the names that designate the secrets and forces designate them in the trajectory of these forces." The triad acts upon the spirit of the Word, in other words, upon the power of creation offered to us. Here and below, latently, there is the silence, the essence from which all speech draws its living energy and its powers.[126] This language, which might be called magical, acts upon the three centers of being: the physical center (carnal), the emotional center (related to feelings), and the psychic center (intellectual; center of thought). It is in this simultaneous action that its power and unity are manifested. This describes the entire metaphysical function of poetry. Poiesis was originally an art of evocation or of the invocation of spirits—"evocatory sorcery," according to Baudelaire. It is certainly white and black, but is also divining and magical or awakening. The primary function of ecstatic poetry is therefore metaphysical: It exerts a magical effect upon the three levels of being and consequently upon consciousness via a mechanism of threes. It transforms reality, restoring power to words.

If shamanic language acts upon the three centers of being, it is because it obeys the three "techniques" that are specific to it. It is the correct conjugation of these three fundamental elements (the mastery of these techniques)—*word, sound,* and *rhythm*—which allow the Word, the power of creation offered to us, to incarnate itself in something else, material or living, in order to act within it and play with the mechanicalness of the thing that is targeted. This fundamental law of speech is at work in the oral and, more subtly, in the written—in the very flesh of the text. "For the Word," Victor Hugo wrote, "is the Word, and the Word is God."

Speech is the primary means for physical communication among beings, as well as among worlds. A poem is a portal between different realities. Magical language is not fixed or rooted: "The word takes place before the action," Rimbaud said, though not for poet-hacks who, as Labat pointed out, "are afraid to change even a comma in their texts."[127] The shaman is a man of knowledge, conscious of the perpetual movement of the universe, a being for whom speech constitutes the primary instrument of power.

As we have seen, there are as many realities as there are levels of consciousness. It is all a question of perception. In burning the curtain that separates the *"I"* and the world, Charles Duits became aware of the close bond that connects them: the Word—that is, God—acting as the principle creator par excellence. "Suddenly I understood that we, the world and myself, were like two concentric circles, united by the same center, and that this center was the Word. Twenty-five years have passed since the revelation that made me the man who writes these lines."[128] Here, Duits alludes implicitly to his vision of Christ in 1943, in which the divine word was personified as in the first verse of John's Gospel. Christ is referred to as the Word of God, meaning that he is the Speech of God made flesh. The God-Word, the inspiring and creating power manifested in the artistic act, is predominant over all other manifestations of language. In his highly literary allegory "Imhotep," Duits expresses a fundamental experience with an unsurpassed poetics of substance, in a final attempt to write the unsayable, renewed and legitimized by peyote (the acting and conciliatory force):

> *The Word, separated from the We by a short interval,*
> *[was the supreme word.]*
> *It continued through a plain without borders overhanging the*
> *We. It added to the vertigo of altitude the vertigo of*
> *[expanse.]*
> *"Long ago, before there were men, We were!"*
> *Yes, they were! The splendor of the affirmation*

[destroyed every limit.]
It spoke the infinite expansion of Substance into
[eternity.]
The Gods, in the unceasingly widened circle of
Speech, formed a new circle; they floated, archipelagos
[of glory, in the glory of the Father.][129]

To destroy the separating membrane is, in a holistic logic, to suppress (or fill, from another point of view) this interval that separates the We of the word in the creative act itself, restoring to language the sensation of the One in the expression of its original plurality. The infinite Word extends beyond language and, via the We, renews the entire being value of the human, exploding the limits of description (the word-idea). Simply by speaking, the "splendor of the affirmation" legitimizes the entire salvational and unifying force of the substance, which, in breaking through these limits, works toward not only the liberation (moksha or satori) of the creation by the creator, but also, above all, the extension of creation via language, now purified and infused with profound meaning.

The heart (motor, action, or center) and the word (life) continually take part in creation, including artistic creation. God manifests in the creative act in general terms. He is pure creation, perpetual motion.

The word is at the heart of knowledge. Gurdjieff, who identified the Fourth Way as a form of "esoteric Christianity," knew this well. The Word is the enneagram, it is the principle, it is God. In Beelzebub's language, the *theomertmalogos* (the divine word that transforms) is the "emanations issuing from the Most Most Holy Sun Absolute," in other words, "Word-God."[130] Language is an emanation of God, and thus it has the power to create and transform everything existing. It is this conciliatory force (according to Beelzebub, "the Most Most Holy Theomertmalogos began to manifest itself in the quality of the third holy force of the sacred Triamazikamno") that generates the power of speech, which then has infinite range—though it does so only in cases where its application can be mastered and is perfectly conscious.

The primordial word—the only one that is valid in the proper use of the spoken word, because it is the language of power—appears to merge with the primordial sound and to bear in itself the mark of the divine fire, which it disseminates over all Creation as a brilliant radiance. To give power to his words, the new speaker must necessarily transcend the intellect, "literally and in all senses." The understanding of the mystery is to be sought elsewhere. The initiate searches the primordial word, the essential property of which is its power. "The word forged in the fire of silent knowledge, the word, farther than the passive ecstasy of sight, is animated with its own life: The dance, the trance, the active ecstasy of the power is for it alone."[131]

True prayer obeys this law because it joins word, sound, and rhythm—in the glorification of the Word—without which it would have no efficacy. Again, as Gurdjieff said, we must not ask the Lord to make it so that twice two is not four.[132] Then, because praying—a process for which, according to Abbé Henri Brémond, poetry is a pre-paratory teaching—is doing, prayer must be a conscious and voluntary action of speech and not a mechanical and insincere action, which amounts to doing nothing at all.

> The prayer of subjective man, that is, of man number one, number two, and number three, can give only subjective results, namely, self-consolation, self-suggestion, self-hypnosis. It cannot give objective results. . . . One must learn to pray, just as one must learn everything else. Whoever knows how to pray and is able to concentrate in the proper way, his prayer can give results. But it must be understood that there are different prayers and that their results are different. This is known even from ordinary divine service. But when we speak of prayer or of the results of prayer we always imply only one kind of prayer—petition, or we think that petition can be united with all other kinds of prayers. This of course is not true. Most prayers have nothing in common with petitions. I speak of ancient prayers; many of them are much older than Christianity. These prayers are, so to speak, recapitulations; by repeating them aloud or to himself a man endeavors to experience what is in them, their whole content, with his mind and feeling.[133]

Prayer, the true speech of power, requires us to be entirely present in ourselves and in what is pronounced, otherwise we could keep it up for ten days straight without producing the least result. Every word must be experienced intensely and felt by the whole being. It is the same for meditation. Having your rear placed on a cushion is not enough to bring about satori! "Simply sit," the Zen masters nevertheless say! But it is precisely this simplicity that we lack, and this prevents us from doing things correctly. (I just now caught myself writing "things" in the plural mechanically!) As all the masters say, it is truly "here and now, one thing at a time." There, I write, I speak, I pray . . . but if I do all three together, I am in fact doing nothing. As Taisen Deshimaru said with all the provocation and humor worthy of a Zen master, "Even when you are on the toilet, concentrate on the present action here and now; be present in what you are doing . . ."

But let us return to prayer. The important thing is therefore less the choice of words and more the manner in which these words are put into execution. To be effective, prayer must be freed from mechanical repetitions that join each word with the whole. The technique of *hesychasm* (from the Greek *hesychia:* "peace, silence, inner peace")—*philokalia,* also known as "prayer of the heart"—is a significant example that illustrates this idea.[134] This technique, known to the Orthodox monks of Athos (where Gurdjieff spent some time), can be viewed as the Christian mantra par excellence in that this prayer is based upon the contemplation and invocation of the name of Jesus in order to attain communion with God: "Lord Jesus Christ, have mercy upon me." If properly performed, preserving sensation in the whole body in order to connect to something higher, these words will bring about ecstasy. Gurdjieff, who evidently knew this technique and its powers of thought, explains:

> Take the ordinary "God have mercy upon me." What does it mean? A man is appealing to God. He should think a little, he should make a comparison and ask himself what God is and what he is. Then he is asking God to have *mercy* upon him. But for this God must first of all think of him, take notice of him. But is it worthwhile taking notice of him? What is there in him that is worth

thinking about? And who is to think about him? God himself. You see, all these thoughts and yet so many others should pass through his mind when he utters this simple prayer. And then it is precisely these thoughts which could do for him what he asks God to do. What can he be thinking of and what result can a prayer give if he merely repeats like a parrot: "God have mercy! God have mercy! God have mercy!" You know yourselves that this can give no result whatever.[135]

A form of hesychasm is also present in *Beelzebub's Tales to His Grandson*—"Holy God, Holy Firm, Holy Immortal, Have mercy on us"—expressing the hidden meaning of the holy forces (relating to Triamazikamno) and the longing to have a beneficent effect from them through our own individuality.[136] Ouspensky also mentions this prayer: "You know the prayer 'Holy God, Holy the Firm, Holy the Immortal'? This prayer comes from ancient knowledge. Holy God means the Absolute or All. Holy the Firm also means the Absolute or Nothing. Holy the Immortal signifies that which is between them, that is, the six notes of the ray of creation, with organic life. All three taken together make one. This is the coexistent and indivisible Trinity."[137]

In *Meetings with Remarkable Men*, Gurdjieff gives a concrete example of the efficacy of prayer. When drought and famine menaced the city of Kars, an astonishing event took place:

> When the archimandrite arrived in any town, the icon was carried from church to church, and the clergy, coming to meet it with banners, welcomed it with great solemnity. The day after the archimandrite arrived in Kars, the rumor spread that a special service for rain would be held before this icon, by all the clergy, at a place outside the town. . . . It was a day of particularly intense heat. . . . And then something occurred to which the explanations of contemporary people are absolutely inapplicable. Suddenly the sky became covered with clouds, and before the people had time to reach the town there was such a downpour that everyone was drenched to the skin.[138]

Another story shows the efficacy of speech through a similar but inverse operation against rain:[139] The shaman and his students were in a field, preparing *ayahuasca* (that soup of symbols with its visionary effect, made principally from two Amazonian plants), when a downpour occurred. As a young apprentice scrambled to shelter hastily, leaving the precious magical cauldron beneath the trees, the shaman smiled and intoned an icaro, a sacred Amazonian chant, and the clouds disappeared, along with the rain, making way for the sun—but only within the area desired by the shaman! The apprentice walked all around the field trying to understand this marvel: No, he was not dreaming. The shaman had succeeded, and with the swiftness of lightning! The cooking could now continue tranquilly, and the soup of salvation was, as foreseen, served for the dinner of the gods—the great banquet in the forest in which knowledge is shared.

To *pray,* which means "to say objectively," is not to ask, but to do. All the centers of being concentrate upon the same action with all the presence and attention necessary. Attaining our goal is in no way haphazard or accidental and in no way depends on the will of the absolute. We can obtain results only through ourselves, only if we know the cosmic laws and put to work all the will sufficient for arriving at our own ends. In other words, let us help, and the "heavens" will do the rest.

Through his mastery of speech, the objective speaker has the power to heal illnesses, because in fact he knows and masters the laws that permit it. "Arise," Jesus ordered a sick girl—and skeptical though the spectators were, she got up and walked.[140] Writes Labat, "All shamans become aware of the healing power of the word. Everything has speech, the sickness and the plant that heals it alike, the sick organ and the healthy organ alike. The shaman knows how to replace the evil speech with the good, with the poetic speech used in prayer, which associates the illness with the vast network of correspondences that pervade the cosmos, and in which the illness becomes a constitutive element,"[141] writes James Douglas Morrison, author of *An American Prayer,* "Words are lamentations that heal."[142] And it should be remembered that he who can heal can also kill, and he who knows how to build can also destroy. Poetry black, poetry white.

Language "contains a charge of energy which arises from the whole being and pervades the entire being. The force of the symbol permeates and intensifies its signs. It opens to the participation of one life."[143] And this participation must seek to awaken, to give man his inner liberty, but in order for this to be possible, the poet must tackle the climb up *Mount Analogue* after the fashion of René Daumal and Father Sogol. He must live poetry as asceticism. This alone will liberate him and may perhaps, by way of the poem, liberate others.

8

Writing

Spiritual Asceticism and the Technique of the Work

Remember yourself, always and everywhere.
G. I. GURDJIEFF

If the goal of objective literature is the awakening of readers, writing must first be a technique of awakening and consciousness for the author, otherwise there will be no evolution of saying, no advance in the level of the speaker: "There is a law according to which the quality of that which is perceived at the moment of transmission depends, as much for knowledge as for understanding on *the quality of the reference points constituted in him who speaks*."[1] The objective position we must take is better understood in view of the overly conventional distinction between the author and his text. As Jean Biès writes in *Les Grands Initiés du XXe siècle*, "Separating life and work distinctly . . . is not at all fitting for people involved in spiritual journeys whose lives and works are inseparable by the very reason of the correlation between what one *does* and what one *is*."[2] The book is a witness to the author whether or not he wants it to be.

"The speech reflects the soul of the speaker," writes Seneca.

It cannot be otherwise, because "what is well conceived is clearly expressed." For Boileau, this was like a lightning bolt striking subjective literature. We might ask, "Why do you say this to me?" The response: "Simply because this irritates you or because this unsettles you." This idea, which could not be any clearer, enrages those who cannot speak clearly and who write to say so. In other words, it enrages those who write to justify themselves, to say that it is not their fault but is instead the fault of language. They oppress language with their own weakness, their impotency. It is they who destroy literature, because all they do is project this impotency in order better to attempt—in vain—to destroy it. And if they remain powerless, malfunctioning, irritated machines inevitably—machines that write, to boot—then they will only aggravate the situation, transmitting this same mechanicalness to readers: a phantom wandering among empty pages.

In reference to Paulhan's work, Jean-Yves Pouilloux mentions, "that writing is found to be . . . the privileged space for an entirely fundamental spiritual adventure that brings existence itself into play."[3] Writing is an asceticism in which the writer's life is perpetually in play. It is a spiritual exercise, a technique of clairvoyance and consciousness transcending the narrow bounds of simple knowledge and books. It engages the poet's entire being, transforming him and crystallizing his refined substance. "A complete man can walk and talk. A head alone cannot even think,"[4] writes Daumal to Renéville.

Before discussing how this methodical asceticism is learned, let us remember, that for Gurdjieff, writing was the ultimate work beyond the mission, because it involved the transmission of his teachings. For him, writing was a religious act, a true exercise of spiritual awakening that worked to crystallize his consciousness in order that it might be used and shared by those aspiring to understand. He explained his literary project at length in the first chapter of *Beelzebub's Tales to His Grandson* and in the introduction to *Meetings with Remarkable Men:*

> Among other convictions formed in my common presence during my responsible, peculiarly composed life, there is one indubitable conviction that always and everywhere on earth, among people of every

degree of development and understanding and every form of manifestation of the factors which engender in their individuality all kinds of ideals, there is acquired the tendency, when beginning anything new, unfailingly to pronounce aloud or, if not aloud, at least mentally, that definite utterance understandable to every even quite illiterate person, which in different epochs has been formulated variously and in our day is formulated in the following words: "In the name of the Father and of the Son and in the name of the Holy Ghost. Amen."

That is why I now, also, setting forth on this venture quite new for me, namely, authorship, begin by pronouncing this utterance and moreover pronounce it not only aloud, but even very distinctly and with a full, as the ancient Toulousites defined it, "wholly-manifested-intonation" . . .[5]

Gurdjieff avoided and denounced "bon ton literary language," which generally serves only for word prostitution. Instead, he preferred an entirely singular form that intended, above all, to endow speech with a force able to reach the heart of the being.[6]

For Ouspensky, who relates Gurdjieff's words in the form of an instructive maieutics, writing was a method for testing the coherence of his ideas, an exercise intended to reestablish the equilibrium between the lines of knowledge and being and recreate the situation in which he found himself during his conversations with Gurdjieff. "Testimonies are abundant on Gurdjieff's extraordinary faculty for making good use of all questions in order to evoke that which could not be said, unseating the interlocutor, stopping him from all recourse to standard models of thought, and finally creating the conditions necessary for the direct transmission of a knowledge of being.[7] In his book *In Search of the Miraculous: Fragments of an Unknown Teaching,* Ouspensky conveyed most faithfully the character of this maieutics. An even more direct echo of it is found in the collection *Gurdjieff parle à ses élèves.*

This approach, although highly theoretical, energizes the reading. During it, readers find themselves situated, posing their questions through the voice of the author, because they occupy momentarily the place of a disciple.[8]

Guided writing as asceticism is inseparable from what Gurdjieff called the Work, because the two—each forming part of the other—are not an end, but a means, a necessary vector for evolution.

If, in his foreword to *A Night of Serious Drinking,* Daumal hands us the keys that allow for an authentic exchange in which speaker and listener can understand one another, then in "Poetry Black, Poetry White" he offers all the foundations for writing as a spiritual exercise, as a method of applied work in poetic expression. It is a programmatic reference text for every Apprentice Speaker—the luminous seed that inspires and nourishes the true and proper use of the spoken word. It must be understood, meditated upon, and applied, for it is this proper use in miniature, its very essence, its "flavor." Those who taste it are oriented irreversibly toward one ideal: "But if I was once a poet, I must certainly have been a black one, and if tomorrow I am to be a poet, I wish to be a white one." All the Work that the poet must accomplish is summarized magnificently in this text, which holds a unique position in the history of poetry. Everything is there for those who know how to read it. Concentrating our efforts in order to strive toward white poetry—which is addressed to everyone, not to the person who writes it—is the sole objective held by any author engaged in a path of wisdom. All the rest is mere subjective literature, blinding by definition. The poet is above all an alchemist whose supreme goal is less the art in itself and more the search for knowledge and truth. To accomplish the transmutation of being: Such is the Work the poet must carry out in his "laboratory."

"As with magic, poetry is black or white, depending on whether it serves the subhuman or the superhuman."[9] The black poet is a seeker of dreams; the white poet is a seeker of the truth. Therein lies the difference. The poetic gift of the former serves pride, imagination, falsehood, and laziness: "Whether schemer or visionary, the black poet lies to himself. . . . Black poetry is fertile in wonders like dreams and opium."[10] For the white poet, this gift serves superior ends: the evolution of being, understanding, and truth. In other words, the white poet (or rather, those who strive toward this whiteness, for in reality poetry is generally a mixture of white and black) seeks to destroy all that truly constitutes the properties of the black poet, whose egotistical desires are his single end. The black poet slides without effort like a machine, broken down on the "natural, subhuman downward slope," while the white poet goes against the current and "swims upstream like the trout who seeks to spawn in its birthplace."[11]

But how do we overcome the current? We do so in the effort of asceticism in which writing is undertaken as an exercise of awakening. René Daumal was the epitome of the writer transformed positively by Gurdjieff's teachings. He was the "archangel" who knew, unlike any other, how to apply the Work to writing, to the poetic power that—along with certain complementary exercises—forms part of the "integral education of man"—and he did so while gravely ill, no less. "This is truly a matter of asceticism," writes Jean Biès, "which leads the poet, like the sage from whom he differs little, to use the gift received for higher ends, fighting against pride, imagination, and fantasy. He frees himself from his nature, renouncing his so-called personality to operate in the interior of the consciousness, in the contemplation of all the senses—a denuding, a plunge into the light underlying habitual and egotistical activities."[12]

Writing allows these ideas to be tested, to be breathed into a phrasing that shocks the consciousness. It is part of the Work defined and taught by Gurdjieff in the sense that it seeks the awakening, the song of "immediate satori." To this end, all its activities are aimed toward the evolution of consciousness—"the rest being given additionally," as Gurdjieff said, because, as Daumal writes in "Pour approcher l'art poétique hindou," "before composing a poem, the poet must compose himself, dispose himself inwardly for being the best possible receptacle for the flavor (*rasa*)."[13] The stage preliminary to every journey is the accession of a sufficient level of consciousness, the only thing capable of making the poetic operation turn out well. In "Poetry Black, Poetry White," Daumal tells us, phrase by phrase, the proper use of this "being composition" that the white poet seeks and which itself forms part of the framework of other processes.[14]

The white poet is first invited to be silent in order that the central emotion (the seed, the thing to be said), which "seeks to express itself through my whole machine," may make its luminous speech heard. For though the seed is dark at first, silence will allow it to shine. Writing must therefore reconcile us initially, through a labor of attention and observation, to the silence necessary for the development of the being and the letter. This silence is the fundamental phase, alpha and omega at the same time, life, death, and rebirth in which the writer must always draw in the force of what he says. "Be silent," says the sage who tries to create conditions favorable for this development.

The habit of speaking to say nothing deprives us of a considerable amount of energy which might be economized effectively and then redistributed elsewhere. At group meetings, Ouspensky emphasized this fear of silence as a refusal to come face to face with ourselves, with our interior babbling: "I realized in this place that people feared silence more than anything else, that our tendency to talk arises from self-defense and is always based upon a reluctance to see something, a reluctance to confess something to oneself."[15] He added later, "I very soon saw that the struggle with the habit of talking, of speaking, in general, . . . more than is necessary, could become the center of gravity of work on oneself because this habit touched everything, penetrated everything, and was for many people the least noticed."[16]

Silence is the hardest form of fasting, because it requires hushing up something that rightly has a prominent position in our lives. Voluntary silence is "the most severe discipline to which a man could subject himself," and it is to this asceticism, this discipline, that the writer must subject himself. To write consciously is to stop all babbling (especially the innermost!) in order to recuperate energy in silence and channel it into a speech of power. Writes Daumal: "[S]ilence parts the shadows, the seed begins to glow, lighting, not lit. That is what you have to do. It is very difficult, but each little effort receives a little glimmer of light in reward. The thing-to-be-said then appears in its most intimate form, as an eternal certainty—a pinpoint of light containing the immensity of the desire for being." Writes Lanza del Vasto, "Hold your tongue. You must have many things to be silent about in order to have something to say."[17] Further, as Lao-tzu wrote, "He who knows does not speak; he who speaks does not know." This operation, however, first requires us to make a tabula rasa of our conditioning, whose noise resounds continually in our ears, preventing us from hearing this salvational silence. "I will not speak, I will not think at all,"[18] writes Rimbaud in "Sensation." Likewise he writes in "Alchimie du verbe": "I wrote silences, I wrote nights, I noted down the unutterable. I made giddiness stand still." He writes again in "Enfance," "I am master of the silence," and Daumal writes, "I am the seer of the night, the hearer of silence." This omnipresent silent essence that haunts *A Night of Serious Drinking* and *Mount Analogue* confers a true power upon the words, according to Pascal Boué, for, as another poet from the Ardennes— Herbert Juin—wrote, the "power of speech comes from silence."[19]

The poet must then clothe this luminous seed in the images that manifest it: "Here again, reviewing these images, we must reject and chain down those which would serve only easiness, lies, and pride—so many beauties we would like to show off. But once the order is established, we must let the seed itself choose the plant or animal in which it will clothe itself by giving it life."[20]

Then, thanks to the rigorous asceticism practiced by the worker of the word, a conciliatory force takes over, uniting it "in a single living substance," a ". . . verbal expression for which it is no longer a matter simply of internal work, but also of external science and know-how."[21] Because the luminous seed has its own respiration; "its breath takes possession of the expressive mechanisms by communicating its rhythm to them. . . . And as it bends the sounds of language to its breath, the thing-to-be-said also compels them to contain its images."[22] The importance of rhythm (the poet's rhythm, which is "the life of this new organism"),[23] with its unifying and conciliatory force, has already been emphasized—but this is accessible only insofar as the poet respects the lines of knowledge and being. In other words, what Daumal calls "the intelligence of the theory" must be in agreement with the practice. This is the only key to understanding: "Poetry is a means for helping our deficient reason to access the unveiled teaching of the truth."[24] This practice cannot take place without a great deal of conscious effort—the driving force of asceticism, as the Agni Purana, cited by Daumal, tells us: "It is difficult to become a man in this world; hence, it is difficult to attain consciousness; hence, it is difficult to become a poet; and hence, it is very difficult to attain creative power."[25]

Finally, the poet hunts down everything in the poem that does not serve the thing-to-be-said. He applies his method to his own words, overturning knowledge in the evolutionary spheres of being, for to write is also to correct our faults in order to save the "flavor which is the essence of the poem."[26] He struggles mercilessly against his overlong passages, his clumsiness, his imprecisions, and fully acknowledges their existence, conscious of being the only one responsible for them. "All that I produce is gray, salt-and-pepper, soiled, a mixture of light and darkness. . . . Few mistakes are purely technical. Almost all of them are my mistakes, and I cross out and correct with the joy we can have at cutting a gangrenous limb from our body." [27]

He observes himself and remembers himself, his *"I,"* and his words so that he may control all this machinery, whether it be physical, textual, or poetic. He works to transform gross matter into subtle matter, fighting negative emotions and thus fighting imagination and identification, for "we must sacrifice our suffering" if we wish truly to evolve. Writing can be part of this sacrifice—but it must not be legitimization, identification, imagination, a simple projection of the negative emotions. White poetry works to pulverize them, black poetry to foster them. René Daumal, a writer, white poet, and teacher, encouraged his "essential friend" Luc Dietrich to move in this direction: "He continually induced him to speak correctly, to free himself from the empty shells that encumbered his pages and his head."[28]

Here and now, I am writing: I hammer away at the fact that man is a machine, and now find myself falling into my own trap, my own mechanicalness. It is obvious, I am photographing it, I am recording it, and then, consciously, I pulverize its maleficent attributes, liberating myself and assuming this *"I"*—suppressing every little *"I"* that wants to take power. . . . And I write: action, doing which exists only in that fragile moment when *"I"* take the word, when truly *"I am."* Only in this moment, sacrificed, laid bare, the masks torn away by the unilateral action—integral, being–action—of the pen that is an extension of my arm, can I be objective toward myself. Only here can I truly correct myself—without seeking consoling excuses for my faults, breaking all my maleficent complicities with my self-love, my narcissistic flattery, and my perpetual need to justify to myself those faults that would have revealed my weaknesses and failings straightaway. All this exists in a movement that I remember unceasingly and at each moment, conscious of every action, beneath an attentive eye positioned just above myself.

Writing, as Daumal saw it, is therefore part of the Work—part of the application of Gurdjieff's ideas put to the test of understanding and evolution, of the development and continuation of research with the single goal of evolving. They can also be inscribed on the enneagram—proof of their good sense.[29] When we write, it is therefore necessary not to lose sight of fundamental cosmic laws or of all the points touched upon previously—namely, our mechanicalness, the function of the centers, the states of consciousness. This asceticism, practical by definition, must not lose sight of the object of this work and its goal, because the ultimate goal of the work—which is only a means and not an end in itself—coincides with the ultimate goal of the writer, of white poetry, and of objective literature. This means is self-observation and self-remembrance, along with the struggle against what Gurdjieff called "negative emotions."

But here we must remember that the Work, according to Ouspensky, begins with the study of the "exact language,"[30] which alone can assure a full and shared speech. This is the first stage of self-development, because it is a path toward mutual understanding, which alone can assure a constructive exchange. We must learn to speak in a clear and truly understandable manner, endowing our words with a true meaning that has been tested in order to be understood. Thus, in the logic of the new language, we speak of writers (speakers) 1, 2, and 3 when referring to those who—as black poets—scratch on paper like mechanical puppets, identifying themselves with their passions and their ideas, projecting their multiplicity and their falsehoods. By contrast, the white writers of the esoteric centers of humanity produce texts reflecting the unity and objectivity that characterize the being of those who write. I offer the target, a summary diagram in appendix 1 highlighting the proper use of the spoken word,[31] which, along with the enneagram, crystallizes the foundations of the system and can serve as an analytical basis for the development of this new language—an application of the concept relating to all things. Every word, every idea, every thing can be inscribed in this synthetic diagram, which in the blink of an eye—because of its seven concentric circles—allows for the task of evaluation necessary for the theory of relativity and evolution. The target, the compass of language, allows complete and objective meaning to be restored to words. It is the fundamental tool for those who seek to understand themselves and to begin together—because "one man alone can do nothing"—the inner work that will lead them to harmony, control, and objective consciousness.

Does a writer of the Fourth Way exist? Everything leads us to believe it, and even to prove it. Gurdjieff planted seeds that grew into marvelous trees of life, bearing "savory" fruits (in the Daumalian sense). Without a doubt, the man who Jean-Philippe de Tonnac calls the "archangel" represents the perfect archetype of such a writer—in his qualities as a pupil and teacher, in his profound understanding of the teachings, in his determination and obstinate rigor in searching without respite even through the hardest times. There are so many trials to overcome, intervals to fill, and shocks to apply in order not to deviate from the trajectory we set for ourselves voluntarily. Jean-Philippe de Tonnac notes the progression of the man who became a teacher: "René's speech simplified as the years went by. It went straight to its goal. The language no longer arose in the mouth to say nothing. Silence reclaimed its rights and was soon speech, active Speech."[32]

Before continuing, there is a question we must ask ourselves and that I wish to answer, here and now, once and for all: the question posed by the apparent ambivalence of the system for writers. Further, this question, raised by the words of certain people, is one that the writer must pose to himself: Does the Gurdjieff experience lead to the death of the writer's work? The answer, in my opinion, is to be found in the new language and in the idea of evolution and relativity. Because this experience pulverizes subjective creation, it opens a door to an immaculate whiteness, the keys to which René Daumal himself offered unceasingly.

Should we therefore believe Louis Pauwels when he states that "for certain writers, the Gurdjieff experience, which is a great temptation, has opened and risks opening again the way to illness, hospital beds, and the graveyard"?[33] And then there is René Zuber's warning: "I formally advise writers and aspiring writers not to frequent Gurdjieff. This will run the risk of a very bad outcome for their work."[34] These statements should be balanced by the counterexample of what is known as proof, contrasting them with the experiences of Ouspensky, Mansfield, Daumal, and Dietrich, to name only a few, not to mention Gurdjieff himself—although due to his role as inspirer, he occupies a separate place. Did these writers sacrifice their work to the teachings? In a way, perhaps, but Gurdjieff is held in contempt by only certain machines, suggestible to the utmost degree and spreading their mechanicalness to others and all the while holding on to a maleficent complicity. They strive not to point out the mote that is in their brother's eye (and plucking out the eye if need be), even when pointing out the mote becomes necessary.

Does the system kill creativity? Yes and no. Everything depends, once again, on how we define *creativity*. If it is a matter of imagination, phantasms, false dreams, subjective projections, and lies, then yes—the writer who fuels himself on these properties and who cannot or does not wish to detach himself from them must make a painful choice, the sacrifice necessary for evolution. Gurdjieff never condemned writing—far from it—or the many writers who crowded around his table. All these false claims only fuel our suggestibility, and that is why we must test them for ourselves (as Gurdjieff said), with all the sincerity appropriate in this kind of undertaking and, it must be added, without any reward. We must understand that only this will provide a real answer for those who make the necessary efforts. If Daumal renounced the black poetry of the "worlds without sun, lit by a hundred fantastic moons, populated by phantoms, decorated with mirages, and sometimes paved with good intentions,"[35] it was in order to turn toward what Gurdjieff called objective art and what Daumal called white poetry. With it the artist will not only understand the message he wishes to transmit, but also, above all, insure the proper transmission of his flavor, his essence, and release an objective and universal emotion. For Daumal, this orientation was transformed, as Jean-Philippe de Tonnac rightly notes, by "that will to measure the illuminating strength of a discourse by means of a spiritual practice which guarantees a merciless hunting down of lies. René thus did not become any less of a poet or writer in the hands of Gurdjieff's instructors. He simply chose to provide the public with the only propositions of which he had made himself the unrelenting experimenter."[36] It is as simple as that. The true difficulty comes from the fact that this experience presents us with an irreversible choice, a determining choice with regard to what we will become. The gravity of this choice is equal to that of the great question. This is why the Gurdjieff experience is by definition *transpoetic,* aimed simultaneously at the poem's essence (its flavor) and at the poet beyond the personality. This experience is intended to purify speech, to liberate it from all the factors of the highly contagious sleep that can afflict it.

Moreover, letting ourselves be trapped by anything points to a manifest weakness and lack of a certain slyness—the Fourth way being, we must remember, the way of the sly man. Gurdjieff's life bore witness to it to the highest degree. To be sly: Those who understand the profundity of this path will transcend all the dualisms that could weigh down their psyche. The greatest weakness that can be had by those who set out on the path of the Fourth Way—just as in the ordinary path of life, remember!—is a lack of slyness. Any weakness in this regard can be fatal, literally and in all other senses. Many are the traps awaiting us upon the path of knowledge. Only the spirit that is clever—though not wicked—has a chance of emerging from it "alive." Let those who can, understand.

The Fourth Way taught by Gurdjieff contrasts with traditional religious paths, which can lead to definite results but which remain forever insufficient, because they favor one part of the being to the detriment of another.[37] In what Gurdjieff calls the way of the *fakir,* evolution takes place with difficulty, painfully and very slowly, leading to a struggle against the physical body but not a development of emotion and intellect. Suffice it to say that the fakir cannot undertake any work of writing; he lacks the tools for it, preferring mere physical torture. The way of the monk is that of emotion, religious sentiment, faith, sacrifices, effusion, penitence, and an unceasing struggle against ourselves. Those who follow this acquire unity and "will over the emotions." Their fasts and prayers can instruct their writing, which then becomes more attentive and ascetic, developing in meditation and fervor. The way of the yogi is that of knowledge of the intellect. Adepts are conscious of their degree of development. This is generally the path that characterizes the best kind of ordinary writer, because it is limited to work upon intellectual activity. Still, there is the trap of falling into "fabrication."[38]

The traditional paths are the paths of sacrifice and are linked to "permanent forms"— religions—therefore demanding an act of faith. Each path corresponds to one of the three first types of humans on the scale of evolution. Due to their unilateral nature, these paths are insufficient for developing the being in its entirety.

Unlike the subjective paths, the Fourth Way combines, synthesizes, and transcends the traditional paths, requiring understanding and an integral and harmonic education of humans as a fundamental principle, which in itself guarantees the truth. Nothing should be done without understanding (except in the form of controlled experiments),[39] and therefore faith—a genuine obstacle to understanding—is not required. Following this way, we believe no one, not even our own teacher. "Don't believe what I tell you; try it out for yourself," Gurdjieff said to his students. A paradox may occur to us, which is in fact nothing of the kind. We may wonder, "Why follow someone whom I don't have to believe, and how is this even possible?" This should be seen as a prudent, conscious, attentive attitude, voluntary and directed toward awakening. It aims to prevent letting ourselves be "trapped" by our naïveté and suggestibility. Once again, it is a question of slyness. We must know ourselves, learn how to position ourselves correctly at the heart of our megalocosmos, thus know how the human machine works and become capable of governing it alone in order to be masters of ourselves. We must therefore sacrifice our suffering, those whirlwinds of thoughts, excuses, and lies that make it so difficult, in Rimbaud's words, "to grasp reality"—the reality that is already rough and coarse enough without the addition of our maleficent projections, which only further aggravate the situation.

The Fourth Way, the way of the sly man, performs simultaneous work on the three centers. It is a shortcut. The sly man knows a secret that the others do not: "How the 'sly man' learned this secret—it is not known. Perhaps he found it in some old books, perhaps he inherited it, perhaps he bought it, perhaps he stole it from someone. It makes no difference. The 'sly man' knows the secret and with its help outstrips the fakir, the monk, and the yogi."[40]

The enneagram, a formidable synthesis of this path, a speech of unitive life, always renewable and renewed, is the compass that guides us in the spheres of evolution. Those of the Fourth Way know how to achieve our goals and do so with our entire consciousness. All our movements are ruled by a goal and a necessity, part of the conditions for a clear discourse. The exactitude of our language guarantees us an exact approach to what is real. The ultimate goal of the Work is the pleasure that is an "attribute of paradise." It is essential to conquer pleasure and be capable of keeping it. "He who can do this has nothing more to learn," as Gurdjieff said to Ouspensky.

Further, the Fourth Way, Gurdjieff said, is the "way against nature, against God." How many stupid things—commentaries and declarations that could not be any more Hasnamussian—have been written about this statement, proving that it is not understood? As de Tonnac notes, "if the ordinary condition of man is sleep, the ways of awakening, whatever they may be, are against nature, and even . . . against God."[41] It follows pure logic. As Michel Random rightly says: "Taken literally, these words are hard to accept, because, by nature and God, Gurdjieff meant not what they are (ipseity) but what we imagine them to be."[42] "Where is God?" asked the poet Lanza, resistant to a teaching that apparently eliminated the questions of grace, Christian charity, and love. . . . When he confronted Gurdjieff, the latter retorted: "Your God is dirt." Jacques Baratier, who witnessed the scene, understood—unlike Lanza, who left the groups for good—that this pleasantry "was directed not against God or against the Christian poet, but was addressed to all those people endeavoring to hide their nonexistence behind theological discourse."[43] Moreover, when Gurdjieff declared that we must "go against God," in the sense that we must know the cosmic laws in order to make use of them and not be passively subject to action, which leads to accident, this was not, as some people believe, the master's Luciferian and diabolical side showing through. If we go against nature, it is because nature itself offers us this salvational possibility, because our possibilities of evolution form an integral part of Creation (though they are not necessary for organic life; herein lies the subtlety), and it would be foolish to deprive ourselves of them. Thus, when we read certain delirious statements, we can only condemn them and have an objective contempt for this type of universal Hasnamuss so well embodied by the likes of Whitall N. Perry, who not only understands nothing but also, if he is truly convinced of his subjective ideas, cannot and never will be able to do anything. "In order to situate Gurdjieff and his movement, the one and only question the seeker has to resolve is whether God is Omnipotent. If the answer is in the affirmative, then Gurdjieff and his hosts are doomed."[44]

Those who listen to Gurdjieff's words with the attention and sincerity required will understand the ignorance of those who dare to claim such inanities. Gurdjieff's demand is far too serious to be taken lightly. Those who call themselves Christians, Muslims, or Buddhists do nothing, at least nine-tenths of the time, but lie to themselves, to others, and to the cause they pretend to serve. They betray their words through their vain actions. According to Gurdjieff, only authenticity and sincerity are appropriate in this kind of undertaking: What counts is not to say you are Christian, Muslim, or Buddhist, but to be it, to truly become it. "To be a Christian," Gurdjieff said to Ouspensky, means "to live in accordance with Christ's precepts."[45] In light of this definition, as simple as it is true, we can see that very few of those who claim to be servants of God really are so. (How many of them might easily renounce their master's name overnight?) Further, in order to reach that sacrificial state in which words finally mean something, we must first spend a long time hounding out the lies. This alone can lead to the truth about ourselves and thence to the truth about the universe.

The writer who conceives of writing as asceticism—as an exercise of awakening—may proceed like the fakir, the monk, or the yogi, and may consequently sacrifice considerable time toward a goal that perhaps he will never attain. The traditional paths correspond to the first three types of people (and therefore to speakers, writers, or readers) who are dominated by physical things, by emotion, or by thought. Alternatively, the writer can take the path of the Fourth Way, striving to write with his body and emotions as much as with his intellect. More precisely, the writer must be conscious that he is writing; he must be conscious simultaneously of the action of writing and of the fact that this action is, from its origin, the fruit of the relationship between his intellectual center and his motor center before it senses the primordial and intellectual part of the emotional center. In writing, he must observe the functioning of his machine in order not to be duped by his mechanisms. The Work will allow him to escape from the state of hypnosis, lethargy, and sleep. Writing, among other things, can be the means for participating actively in awakening and liberation.

In order to write—a practical exercise—we must know the laws that rule us and the universe. In *Beelzebub's Tales to His Grandson*, Gurdjieff outlined what he called the five "being-obligolnian-strivings" that must be inherent to every fully evolved person and with which, for lack of anything better, we must work in order to attain "genuine conscience".[46]

1. To have in our ordinary being-existence everything satisfying and truly necessary for our planetary body.
2. To have a constant and unflagging instinctive need for self-perfection in the sense of being.
3. To consciously strive to know ever more concerning the laws of world creation and world maintenance.
4. To strive from the beginning of our existence to pay for our arising and our individuality as quickly as possible, in order afterward to be free to lighten as much as possible the sorrow of our common father.
5. To strive always to assist the most rapid perfecting of other

beings, both those similar to ourselves and those of other forms, up to the degree of the sacred "Martfotai," that is up to the degree of self-individuality.

These strivings—which involve altruism—go hand in hand with the being-partkdolg-duties (conscious effort and voluntary suffering) that are inseparable from objective writing.

We must work at our desk of awakening, here and now, in a total and conscious presence in the world, with our attention divided perfectly between the hand and the page it writes on. We must direct our attention, step back, plan out, then thrust our strength into the phrases, aim for the target, and "hit" it, sending our ball into the center of the net. The writer masters his energies, breathing them into the very body of the language, which in turn acquires many centers that work together to vibrate in the reader's consciousness. The entire being takes part in writing, aware that it "is only in the action of the moment," as René Daumal writes, "and that is why it is eternal."

Moreover, the objective writer does not stimulate his reader's emotional or intellectual centers (or motor or sexual centers) randomly, accidentally, or gratuitously. Instead, he does it consciously—and with Pythagorean precision—in order to bring about an appropriate and premeditated reaction, which must serve only his goal. It may be implicit, unconfessed, or hidden, but it serves his goal.

Let us take a revealing example. Though some people describe René Daumal as the least sentimental and least erotic writer, they can absolutely not apply such labels to Charles Duits, who, albeit from "outside the walls," was keenly interested in the teachings. Duits, author of *La Salive de l'éléphant,* came to believe pornography to be the only literary genre capable of capturing the reader's attention, because it was a circuitous means for leading him to ask himself other questions.

This example illustrates the profane powers of speech, because it acts directly upon the individual's sexual center via an action upon the mental and emotional centers. The goal remains an awakening to a grasping of consciousness—self-consciousness, simultaneous with a process connected to the powers of language. The writer must be sly, using his hypnotic powers to lead readers to his ends or, in other words, to help readers evolve in keeping with the fifth being–obligolnian–striving.

In *La Salive de l'éléphant*, Charles Duits seeks to awaken readers—which, as we have noted, is his principal concern—via the "force of fucking." Regarding obscenity, Henry Miller wrote: "Its intent is to awaken. The true nature of obscenity resides in the desire to convert." "[T]he lifting of the veil can be interpreted as the ultimate expression of the obscene: It is an attempt to spy on the secret processes of the universe." For Lucifer Ilje,[47] obscenity is a transparency. As Samuel Cramer writes in the book's preface:

> The originality of Duits's erotic tales lies in his confrontation of the crudest words with the most diaphanous images, with blasphemy and provocation beyond humor, with a certain degree of vehemence where necessary, and thereby renewing some of the secrets of sacred eroticism. It is no coincidence that the Great Suavity, the mysterious oil with which the characters in *La Salive de l'éléphant* coat their members before making love, is similar to the "large-grained greenish powder, with a very bitter flavor" mentioned in *Le Pays de l'éclairement*. Like adepts of peyote, the great Tchang ("an Asiatic cobra with the suppleness of flame, with perilous slowness, a smooth and sinuous emanation of hypnosis"), Rose (the erudite prostitute and "priestess of depravity"), and Lucifer Ilje ("Christ Phalliphorous") were able to explore the world of ecstasy—that Reality with a capital *R* that Duits spent his life seeking—for much longer than ordinary mortals are able to do. Lucifer Ilje's empire of fucking is in fact as large as Asia, Africa, and Paris put together, and the gods sport in the clouds that hang over it.[48]

Like all writers, Charles Duits struggled inexorably with the apparent powerlessness of language, with the difficulty of saying the essence of things with regard to describing his experiences with peyote, and also with conveying sensual pleasure and eroticism. Regarding the "great Tchang," a prostitute in whom the poet loses himself, the narrator ponders: "Before her, the writer that I am becomes excessively sensitive to the usury of words and the poverty of vocabulary. The adjectives I want to use—that I must use if I intend to speak clearly—lose their flavor. I seek vainly among them for those that my spirit shows to be both a correct and a living vocabulary."[49] How, indeed, can we describe sensuality without falling into clichés, into prefabricated words?

Duits excavates language, hollows it out and lays it bare, in order to observe its texture, its strength, its depth. In *La Salive,* between two pornographic scenes worthy of the Marquis de Sade's *La Philosophie dans le boudoir,* readers find themselves confronted with the writer's fundamental questions on writing and God. Above all, however, Duits's writing causes readers to question themselves along with the author, and to seek the proper word with him: "Tchang is sculptural, curvaceous, blooming, triumphant, sumptuous. No, she is vulcanian, pontifical. Opaque, tropical, voluminous. Oval. *Tchang is oval . . .* yes, the great Chinese woman finally fits happily with this description. But obviously, if I express myself this way, no one will understand me. Language is a blank slate on which is drawn only shadows. Precision is obtained by sacrificing intelligibility."[50]

It is indeed a question of language, its weaknesses and its strengths. The poet suggests words, steps back, moves forward again, retraces his steps—but always in order to advance. He makes mixtures on his palette so that he may paint. The word may be purely for itself, for its author, but Duits is conscious that the reader must "understand." And yet language, this blank slate, does not provide the transparency sought by the writer. Those shadows that are drawn in approximation are not the object that can be perceived through the perfect transparency of crystalline glass. This, Duits tells us, is why intelligibility must be sacrificed in order to achieve the essence. In other words, the transmission passes through another language which appeals to an understanding that is no longer intellectual but "of being." This is why the narrator in *La Salive* considers pornography to be "the only genre of literature that is still living, the only one that offers an author the opportunity to form an authentic relationship with the reader."[51] The writer seeks less to "exercise and influence" and more to "reach people, to truly act upon them." Writing is no longer solely descriptive, but is augmented by a material power. It is no longer merely the panache of the intellect, but implies the action of the emotional center and the physical center.

Charles Duits endeavors to restore the flavor to words in order to speak sensuality without falling into clichés and prefabricated words, into babbling and into the confusion of tongues. Pornography allows the powers of the word to be reactivated and thus to arouse the reader's attention in order to transmit fundamental truths to him—metaphysical truths. The reader is urged on constantly in ecstasy and existential questioning. Tantrism is accompanied with a "shortcut," that mysterious oil that breaks the physical barrier to the other world through a rapid and powerful elevation of the level of consciousness. The writing, infused with extraordinary powers capable of acting effectively upon the reader's consciousness, becomes effective through the simultaneous action of the three centers of being: "In the mental universe, we seek satisfaction that only life has the power to procure for us. We all do this to a greater or lesser degree—but we do not *know* it, and that is what is wrong. When masturbators ejaculate, their palace of mirages disappears. They have a handful of semen and an empty mind—that is, a clear mind. Therefore, we can reach them, speak to them. . . . This is what I do."[52]

This is a crude example, but it speaks to all the powers of the word. If the writer can make readers ejaculate, he can also instill in them other impulses, being impulses, moving toward an evolution of the consciousness and an expansion of the mind. This is what language can do; it is the very manifestation of the divine spirit in that it has the fundamental power to create. This is why it also obviously has the singular and infinitely powerful ability to stimulate the various centers of being, taking care not to focus on the intellectual center, but rather to watch over the harmony of all three. In order to achieve this, however, the center that we seek to excite mechanically must be stifled: "A writer who exercises an influence is one who stimulates his readers' mental activity—their cerebration, as I call it. He imagines that we do not think enough yet and believes that cerebration is a good thing and that the more we think hard . . . the more human we are. He assigns a value to the movement of the intellect. In fact, on the contrary, in order to know, in order to see what there is, we must know how to suspend this movement."[53]

Duits seeks not to influence readers—to incite them to live in the imaginary. On the contrary, his intent is that his words should have a beneficial action upon Reality, on all that is material or living in it. Pornography, for Duits, is a realistic and effective way of reaching his reader: "Suppose that my reader gets an erection.... He may then wonder how simple words can have such great power, and will gradually begin to ask himself real questions."[54] Pornography, a perfect illustration of the (profane) powers of the word, also provides the writer a margin of liberty, a literary space in which, between two sensual scenes, he can digress upon social, metaphysical, or political questions: "The pornographer is much less subject to the laws of composition than the ordinary novelist."[55] Moreover, substance is at the heart of true understanding: first, those "diabolical hashish candies" that the "great Tchang" offers the protagonist. But the ultimate aphrodisiac, the tantric object par excellence, is the Great Suavity—peyote oil—with which the curvaceous prostitute initiates the poet, flinging him into other levels of consciousness and thus into Reality. In a February 11, 1961, letter to Timothy Leary, Aldous Huxley mentioned the tantra, emphasizing "the infinite accumulation of rituals and magic words" in tantrism, the sexual yoga that allows us to find God by means of ordinary processes of life. Using a shortcut such as lysergic acid or peyote, the tantric experience takes on an infinite dimension rapidly: "It seems to me that one should use LSD and mushrooms in the framework of that fundamental Tantric idea of yoga, of total vigilance which leads to inward illumination of the everyday experience—which, obviously, becomes the world of miracles, of beauty and divine mystery when experience returns to being what it should never have ceased to be."[56]

Let us return to what Gurdjieff called being-partkdolg-duties, in relation to the writer's work.

"Doing," according to one definition by Gurdjieff, is "acting consciously and of our own will."[57] Writing is doing. The action corresponds to the same properties, to the same necessity for attention and presence in the world: remembering ourselves.

We should remember that according to Gurdjieff there are multiple states of consciousness: sleep, dozing (drowsy quiescence), the state of self-consciousness, and objective consciousness. The ordinary among us know only the first two states, because the third state is "the moment at which man is present in himself and his machine."[58] "There are moments," Gurdjieff adds, "when you are present in not only what you do, but in yourself while you are doing. You see at the same time the *'I'* and the *'here'* in *'I am here,'* the anger and the *'I'* who is angry. We can call this "remembering ourselves."[59] The objective, obviously, is always, at every moment, to be present in ourselves and to be less in passivity and more in action: "You must watch your machine while it is working."[60] After having become aware that we are divided and incapable of controlling our machine, which is subject to exterior influences, self-observation can begin—and this we repeat in all the moments that make up human activity. "If I say: 'I read a book,' and do not know that *'I'* am reading, that is one thing. But if I am conscious that *'I'* am reading, this is remembering myself."[61] In the same manner, the writer must be conscious that he is writing (just as the speaker must be conscious that he is speaking), all the while observing himself. This is, in fact, the first shock to apply to the octave in order not to deviate from the goal established originally. Remember what Daumal wrote: "The awakening is an act." Therefore, we must remember ourselves every minute, hold ourselves in this presence, awaken ourselves to our awakening, which then becomes more and more profound.

Writing can therefore function as remembering ourselves (once the writer has observed himself writing) in that the writer is conscious of writing—he is conscious that he writes. How can we write if we are absent from ourselves? The writer who forgets himself while writing does not know what he is doing or why he does it—even if he is convinced to the contrary. He is only transmitting his mechanicalness to the text and thence to readers. He produces only a mechanical text in which the vital breath necessary for white poetry does not circulate. Instead, an impulse of death circulates in it. Under these conditions, it is impossible for him to go against the current. He lets it carry him at random, like a piece of driftwood unable to return to land. He floats from one wave to the next without knowing where the current will take him, and finally, he drowns in the stagnant waters of his own indecision and laziness. By contrast, white poetry, the white work of alchemy, strives for the evolution of being via observation and self-remembrance in the act itself, trapping the mechanical flow of our thoughts in the very gesture of writing: "Our so-called thoughts are nothing more than formulas, all cribbed from a cheat sheet. What we call thoughts are not thoughts. We do not have thoughts; we have various labels, briefings, summaries, ramblings—but nothing but labels. . ."[62]

And if our thoughts are labels pasted abusively onto empty boxes, it is because these thoughts are mechanical—and because these labels proceed generally via speech, speech also can only be mechanical, which fully legitimizes the situation Gurdjieff describes: On physical, emotional, and intellectual planes alike, machinelike people skitter about and fidget in the circle of the confusion of tongues like so many hamsters in a cage, running on a wheel and unwittingly staying in the same place.[63] This agitation is due to memory: People have forgotten themselves, and they remember themselves only in rare moments, such as when they suffer from illness, in which case it is often too late. Further, writing—besides its capacity for testing ideas—is a remarkable technique for observing and remembering ourselves, the white poets seeking moksha or, as it is called in Zen, satori. "Without speech there is neither trace nor memory; the act of speech is deliverance."[64] This is why poetry must remember itself in order to evolve on the scale of types of speeches: Without memory, there can be no remembering, and without remembering, no objective writing. To remember ourselves is to become aware of our nullity, our powerlessness, our ignorance; it is to understand the role of each center that must act independently, depending on what action we wish to undertake. Michel Decant, supported by Daumal, notes that "to remember oneself is the sensation, the feeling, and the understanding of the meaning of a dynamic deficiency."[65] Consequently, this gaining of consciousness brings about the desire to fill this void . . . with life:

I am dead because I have no desire,
I have no desire because I believe that I possess,
I believe I possess because I do not try to give;
Trying to give, one sees that one has nothing,
Seeing that one has nothing, one tries to give oneself,
Trying to give oneself, one sees that one is nothing,
Seeing that one is nothing, one wishes to become,
Wishing to become, one lives.[66]

To remember ouselves, finally, is to fight simultaneously for and against ourselves. Writing reminds us of ourselves, of our presence, of all our being in its entirety; it serves to help us examine ourselves, observe ourselves, see inside ourselves, know ourselves; and finally, it aids in our *becoming.*

Again, we must be forever awake, maintaining the vigilance of what Madame de Salzmann called the "view from above," that impartial exterior eye which, from outside, watches every one of our actions that take place inside.

Those who wish to speak in an objective manner must truly live that silent asceticism in which suffering, answering to the will, allows us truly to evolve. The speaker must carry on a war against himself and against all things in order to reduce to nothing the crystallization of exterior influences—not in order to learn and know, but in order to become and be. To become, we must remember ourselves and engage in merciless combat against negative emotions (which are ordinarily dominant).

With great sarcastic blows, Daumal struck out against the laziness and lies of poets who were his contemporaries—propagators of word prostitution—reproaching them for

. . . an unfortunate tendency to speak many fine words, and to imagine that by writing poems or simply by talking about poetry and mysticism and by virtue of oration and rapture, they therefore have a "spiritual life"! How pitiful! . . . The misfortune of these poetico-mysticologists is that they have never glimpsed the reality of spiritual life. It is is pure imagination and babbling—for exciting people or putting them to sleep . . . the exact opposite of faith. And so people end up thinking that to write poems, you give up examining yourself, controlling yourself, following a discipline, and really working yourself to death.[67]

The Fourth Way is also the way of the warrior, and in order to "learn how to die"—learn how to be born—we must know not only how to fight ourselves but also how to truly want it.[68] We often say that someone "has nothing to say," which in fact means that he is not sincere—because speech exists only through that sincerity, that honesty that alone can encourage the true exchange, the understanding and confidence, that unites us. The black poet appeals to laziness, but the white poet appeals to the battle against our worst enemy: falsehood— precisely because these falsehoods generate imaginary suffering. This is why we must sacrifice them, hence the notion of voluntary suffering. Daumal the teacher said:

> Sacrifice your suffering, because almost all your suffering is imaginary, and in doing this, you will begin to understand what voluntary suffering is. So hunt out your imaginings as well as your inner babbling, your falsehoods and your mechanical associations, in order to try to learn about your sincerity. . . . To lie = to speak of something as if we know it when we do not know it. We lie not because we want to lie, but because the lie wishes it. Control your words; enter into your speech.[69]

Lying perverts the action of speech and encourages the deviation that causes every action to stray from its goal; lying empties the word of its living substance, thus generating more confusion and blindness, the main effect of which is to perpetuate the mechanicalness of the person who speaks, continually sliding down the subhuman slope. "In plain truth, lying is an accursed vice," as Montaigne wrote. "We are not men, nor have other ties upon one another but by our word. If we did but discover the horror and gravity of it, we should pursue it with fire and sword, and more justly than other crimes."[70] Jean-Yves Pouilloux's analysis clarifies this point:

> Lying, speech that does not respect or even falsifies deliberately the actualization of a speaking subject in its phrasing, breaks the tacit pact of mutual acknowledgment between beings and corrupts the contract that allows them to be together. There is nothing local or anecdotal in an individual lie; it is the whole of the exchange that it places in peril. Montaigne mentions this catastrophic corruption of speech elsewhere and it is worth quoting: "Our intelligence being by no other way communicable to one another but by a particular word, he who falsifies that betrays public society. It is the only way by which we communicate our thoughts and wills; it is the interpreter of the soul, and if it is wanting, we no longer know or have further tie upon one another; if it deceives us, it breaks all our correspondence, and dissolves all the ties of government."[71]

It is this lying that must be fought in order to save speech. This holy war, this manifesto of the writer at work, has never been better expressed than by René Daumal, who showed, in a text published in *Fontaine* magazine in 1946, how writing forms part of the Work leading to the great hunting down of lies and delving into the "unveiled secrets of the truth." Like no other, this text embodies the adventure of the writer on the Fourth Way and expresses admirably the ideal that the white poet seeks to attain. Speaking can be only the call to fight our negative emotions that block the path for us while inflating our ego—the call to fight the betrayer who gnaws at us from within and deceives us unceasingly, tricking our actions in which our words actively assist. "Arise, take up thy bed," says the master, conscious of the healing power of the word.

It is best to reproduce the entire text of "The Holy War," because it is one of those pure texts, free of any fault and shining with a thousand powers, containing everything writers must know, everything they must do in order to become people, analogous beings in line with vertical transcendence who have quenched their thirst at the source of all things. This is the sort of text we should quote without leaving anything out, the sort of text that we should remember continually as a flavor—in the sense of a direct perception of a state of being, a "moment of consciousness that the true work of art must incite," an objective emotion that takes place through the essence of a speech that is poetic by definition, perhaps a salvation for those who taste it. This flavor exists only "as far as it is tasted, through an act of communion," because we know it only by eating it, "it is this flavor that the power of suggestion of language has the duty of manifesting"—in other words, the "essence, the *self (atman)* of the poem."[72]

Campaigners for the crucifixion of masks, machines, and lies: Keep this text of René Daumal next to you, remember it, and meditate upon it until the "substantive marrow" of an immaculate whiteness is in your hands. The word is for the "archangel," the white poet, the climber of *Mount Analogue* who has sacrificed his babbling—surely the most difficult task for a writer—and found the right words for raising poetry to its highest degree of meaning and reality.

The Holy War

I am going to write a poem about war. Perhaps it will not be a real poem, but it will be about a real war.

It will not be a real poem, because if the real poet were here and if the news spread through the crowd that he was going to speak—then a great silence would fall; at the first glimpse, a heavy silence would swell up, a silence big with a thousand thunderbolts.

The poet would be visible; we would see him; seeing him, he would see us; and we would fade away into our own poor shadows, we would resent his being so real, we sickly ones, we troubled ones, we uneasy ones.

He would be here, full to bursting with the thousand thunderbolts of the multitude of enemies he contains—for he contains them, and satisfies them when he wishes—incandescent with pain and holy anger, yet as still as a man lighting a fuse, in the great silence he would open a little tap, the very small tap of the mill of words, and let flow a poem, such a poem that it would turn you green.

What I am going to make won't be a real, poetic, poet's poem for if the word *war* were used in a real poem—then war, the real war that the real poet speaks about, war without mercy, war without truce would break out for good in our inmost hearts.

For in a real poem words bear their own facts.

But neither will this be a philosophical discourse. For to be a philosopher, to love the truth more than oneself, one must have died to self-deception, one must have killed the treacherous smugness of dream and cozy fantasy. And that is the aim and the end of the war; and the war has hardly begun, there are still traitors to unmask.

Nor will it be a work of learning. For to be learned, to see and love things as they are, one must be oneself, and love to see oneself as one is. One must have broken the deceiving mirrors, one must have slain with a pitiless look the insinuating phantoms. And that is the aim and the end of the war, and the war has hardly begun; there are still masks to tear off.

Nor will it be an eager song. For enthusiasm is stable when the god stands up, when the enemies are no more than formless forces, when the clangor of war rings out deafeningly; and the war has hardly begun, we haven't yet thrown our bedding into the fire.

Nor will it be a magical invocation, for the magician prays to his god, "Do what I want," and he refuses to make war on his worst enemy, if the enemy pleases him; nor will it be a believer's prayer either, for at his best the believer prays "Do what you want," and for that he must put iron and fire into the entrails of his dearest enemy—which is the act of war, and the war has hardly begun.

This will be something of all that, some hope and effort towards all that, and it will also be something of a call to arms. A call that the play of echoes can send back to me, and that perhaps others will hear.

You can guess now of what kind of war I wish to speak.

Of other wars—of those one undergoes—I shall not speak. If I were to speak of them, it would be ordinary literature, a makeshift, a substitute, an excuse. Just as it has happened that I have used the word *terrible* when I didn't have gooseflesh. Just as I've used the expression "dying of hunger" when I hadn't reached the point of stealing from the food-stands. Just as I've spoken of madness before having tried to consider infinity through a keyhole. As I've spoken of death before my tongue has known the salt taste of the irreparable. As certain people speak of purity, who have always considered themselves superior to the domestic pig. As some speak of liberty, who adore and polish their chains; as some speak of love, who love nothing but their own shadows; or of sacrifice, who wouldn't for all the world cut off their littlest finger. Or of knowledge, who disguise themselves from their own eyes. Just as it is our great infirmity to talk in order to see nothing.

This would be a feeble substitute, like the old and sick speaking with relish of blows given and received by the young and strong.

Have I then the right to speak of this other war—the one which is not just undergone—when it has perhaps not yet irremediably taken fire in me? When I am still engaged only in skirmishes? Certainly, I rarely have the right. But "rarely the right" also means "sometimes the duty"—and above all, "the need," for I will never have too many allies.

I shall try to speak then of the holy war.

May it break out and continue without truce! Now and again it takes fire, but never for long. At the first small hint of victory, I flatter myself that I've won, and I play the part of the generous victor and come to terms with the enemy. There are traitors in the house, but they have the look of friends and it would be so unpleasant to unmask them! They have their place in the chimney corner, their armchairs and their slippers; they come in when I'm drowsy, offering me a compliment, or a funny or exciting story, or flowers and goodies—sometimes a fine hat with feathers. They speak in the first person, and it's my voice I think I'm hearing, my voice in which I'm speaking: "I am, I know . . . , I wish . . ." But it's all lies! Lies grafted on my flesh, abscesses screaming at me: "Don't slaughter us, we're of the same blood!"—pustules whining: "We are your greatest treasure, your only good feature; go on feeding us, it doesn't cost all that much!"

And there are so many of them; and they are charming, they are pathetic, they are arrogant, they practice blackmail, they band together . . . but they are barbarians who respect nothing—nothing that is true, I mean, because they cringe in front of everything else and are tied in knots with respect. It's thanks to their ideas that I wear my mask; they take possession of everything, including the keys to the costume wardrobe. They tell me: "We'll dress you; how could you ever present yourself properly in the great world without us?" But oh! It would be better to go naked as a grub!

The only weapon I have against these armies is a very tiny sword, so little you can hardly see it with the naked eye; though, true enough, it is sharp as a razor and quite deadly. But it is really so small that I lose it from one minute to the next. I never know where I stuck it last; and when I find it again, it seems too heavy to carry and too clumsy to wield—my deadly little sword.

Myself, I only know how to say a very few words, and they are more like squeaks; while *they* even know how to write. There's always one of them in my mouth, lying in wait for my words when I want to say something. He listens and keeps everything for himself, and speaks in my place using my words but in his own filthy accent. And it's thanks to him if anyone pays attention to me or thinks I'm intelligent. (But the ones who know aren't fooled; if only I could listen to the ones who know!)

These phantoms rob me of everything. And having done so, it's easy for them to make me feel sorry for them: "We protect you, we express you, we make the most of you, and you want to murder us! But you are just destroying yourself when you scold us, when you hit us cruelly on our sensitive noses—us, your good friends."

And an unclean pity with its tepid breath comes to weaken me. Light be against you, phantoms! If I turn on the lamp, you stop talking. When I open an eye, you disappear—because you are carved out of the void, painted grimaces of emptiness. Against you, war to the finish—without pity, without tolerance. There is only one right: the right to *be* more.

But now it's a different song. They have a feeling that they have been spotted; so they pretend to be conciliatory. "Of course, you're the master. But what's a master without servants? Keep us on in our lowly places; we promise to help you. Look here, for instance: suppose you want to write a poem. How could you do it without us?"

Yes, you rebels—some day I'll put you in your place. I'll make you bow under my yoke, I'll feed you hay and groom you every morning. But as long as you suck my blood and steal my words, it would be better by far never to write a poem!

A pretty kind of peace I'm offered: to close my eyes so as not to witness the crime, to run in circles from morning till night so as not to see death's always-open jaws; to consider myself victorious before even starting to struggle. A liar's peace! To settle down cozily with my cowardices, since everybody else does. Peace of the defeated! A little filth, a little drunkenness, a little blasphemy for a joke, a little masquerade made a virtue of, a little laziness and fantasy—even a lot, if one is gifted for it—a little of all that, surrounded by a whole confectioner's-shopful of beautiful words; that's the peace that is suggested. A traitor's peace! And to safeguard this shameful peace, one would do anything, one would make war on one's fellows; for there is an old, tried and true formula for preserving one's peace with oneself, which is always to accuse someone else. The peace of betrayal!

You know by now that I wish to speak of holy warfare.

He who has declared this war in himself is at peace with his fellows, and although his whole being is the field of the most violent battle, in his very innermost depths there reigns a peace that is more active than any war. And the more strongly this peace reigns in his innermost depths, in that central silence and solitude, the more violently rages the war against the turmoil of lies and numberless illusions.

In that vast silence obscured by battle-cries, hidden from the outside by the fleeing mirage of time, the eternal conqueror listens to the voices of other silences. Alone, having overcome the illusion of not being alone, he is no longer the only one to be alone. But I am separated from him by these ghost-armies which I have to annihilate. Oh, to be able one day to take my place in that citadel! On its ramparts, let me be torn limb from limb rather than allow the tumult to enter the royal chamber!

"But am I to kill?" asked Arjuna the warrior. "Am I to pay tribute to Caesar?" asks another. Kill, he is answered, if you are a killer. You have no choice. But if your hands are red with the blood of your enemies, see to it that not a drop splatter the royal chamber, where the motionless conqueror waits. Pay, he is answered, but see to it that Caesar gets not a single glimpse of the royal treasure.

And I, who have no other weapon, no other coin, in Caesar's world, than words—am I to speak?

I shall speak to call myself to the holy war. I shall speak to denounce the traitors whom I nourished. I shall speak so that my words may shame my actions, until the day comes when a peace armored in thunder reigns in the chamber of the eternal conqueror.

And because I have used the word *war*, and because this word *war* is no longer, today, simply a sound that educated people make with their mouths, but now has become a serious word heavy with meaning, it will be seen that I am speaking seriously and that these are not empty sounds that I am making with my mouth.[73]

————

To conclude and to try to rouse those whose ears are still switched off, let us recall what Gurdjieff said to Ouspensky: "If you understood everything you have written in your own book . . . I should come and bow down to you and beg you to teach me. But you do not understand either what you read or what you write."[74]

From this example of René Daumal's work, we can understand the power writing can have—when practiced under the right conditions. As a technique of observation and self-remembrance, it allows us to attain better mastery and better control over the human machine, to work on our understanding of the relationship among the centers and our understanding of what causes their strength and weakness. This is the holy war, this struggle against identification, consideration (the most maleficent form of identification, because it causes us to identify ourselves with others' opinions of us and consequently to disguise ourselves incessantly with masks),[75] imagination, falsehood, and babbling. In these terms, objective literature requires us to sacrifice our imaginary suffering; it needs this suffering in order to evolve and strive toward whiteness in the active work of the battle, and not in the simple passivity of observation. It permits the work of transforming gross matter into subtle matter—in other words, the alchemical work, the transmutation and harmonic development of the being and the text, the man and the poem. As Gurdijeff said:

> So you see that art is not merely a language but something much bigger. And if you connect what I have just said with what I said earlier about the different levels of man's being, you will understand what is said about art. Mechanical humanity consists of men number one, number two, and number three and they, of course, can have subjective art only. Objective art requires at least flashes of

objective consciousness; in order to understand these flashes properly and to make proper use of them a great inner unity is necessary and a great control of oneself.[76]

This apprenticeship of becoming, this asceticism, requires a great deal of effort and a persevering will that must continue over the long term to be effective: "Unlearning daydreaming and learning to think, unlearning philosophizing and learning to speak, these things can't be done in a single day."[77] Asceticism requires initially making a tabula rasa of all our values and of all that conditions us. Daumal writes to Paulhan: "First, one must make a clean slate of all these things [philosophy, metaphysics, tastes, beliefs], at least provisionally, which is not as easy as one might think. To do so intellectually is easy, certainly, but all that ideological apparatus clings to your body, to your heart."[78] Gurdjieff's *Beelzebub's Tales to His Grandson* has this goal: "to destroy, mercilessly, without any compromises whatsoever, in the mentation and feelings of the reader, the beliefs and views, by centuries rooted in him, about everything existing in the world." This is the moment when this Gurdjieff text can help us in this task of evacuation, preliminary to all attempts at reconstruction, and then with the birth "in the mentation and in the feelings of the reader, of a veritable, nonfantastic representation not of that illusory world which he now perceives, but of the world existing in reality."[79]

All that has been said since the beginning of this book is valuable only in that two fundamental factors—linked to understanding—intervene on all levels of this journey: sincerity and authenticity. Without these primary virtues, necessary for all real development and all true evolution, there can be no asceticism and therefore nothing to say, because objective speech exists only through this first impulse, which connects beings to one another.

Lying leads to individual and general confusion, because he who lies to himself is the first to be mistaken (tricked) and, inevitably, to miss out on the truth, which is contained entirely in the speech, bound into the duration and sincerity of the speaker at the moment when he speaks. If "life is real only then, when *'I am'*" (as the title of Gurdjieff's third book states), then life is also real only then, when I speak, here and now, in the mutual sharing of this "I," joining body, thoughts, and emotions with a conscious listener. "I can help another," Daumal stated, "or even communicate with another, only if 'I am'"[80]—in other words, only if I am conscious of being present through remembering myself, through being able to divide my attention at the very moment when I say *"I."* As Jean-Yves Pouilloux writes in "Le temps présent":

> The present I see is bound up with the duration (it being unimport-
> ant whether this is real or imaginary) that is necessary for me to
> assure myself of the continuity of my existence and the consistence
> of my person; and this binding is manifested in the moment when
> I take the word, when I actualize my presence in the world through
> the phrase that I speak. Perhaps one could go so far as to say that I
> have a presence only in the moment when I speak, and perhaps the
> same goes for everyone—if it is true, as I am forced to notice, that
> *"I"* does not designate me by rights, but only insofar as I have the
> current use of speech.[81]

This speech must also be bound up with what Pouilloux calls the "current present" (*I speak;* this is an observation), and not in the "topi-cal present" (*I am a man;* this is a value judgment), which in fact is evidence of our being asleep:

> If I arrive at an inkling of the truth—not general truth, but ade-
> quate for myself—then the only path that remains for me is to
> return from the second present to the first. This is difficult, because
> here attention must be paid to every moment, particularly to the
> beginning, that fragile point at which the observation of what is
> happening transforms imperceptibly into the formulation of the
> laws of the world, in which one gives up the things for the causes.
> An *"it's like"* (analogy) or a *"because of"* (causality) is enough for
> me to abandon the realm of facts and go adventuring in the order
> of reasons—that is, in the space of a discourse in which the second

present covers, absorbs, and effaces the first, substituting an imaginary world that is ordered and regulated according to my desire for order and harmony for the confusing universe without any intelligible law that my experience shows me.[82]

Is this not a marvelous definition of remembering ourselves? To remember ourselves is to exercise vigilance, to divide our attention in order to be conscious of two presents, evacuating the second one voluntarily in order that *"I"* may be situated completely—body, thoughts, emotions—in the first. This is the "current" word that carries us and connects us, that bears witness to our presence in the world and in ourselves, and it is always through it that the truth is expressed.

After sharpening his consciousness in the double task of writing—which serves to enable us to see our own interior and is simultaneously the "rediscovery" and the "conscious and voluntary application" of the proper use of the spoken word—the speaker must then transmit his consciousness in order that his word (conveying what Gurdjieff called "influence C") may be a word of life that lives through others. The means are many, as we will see in the following study of the multiple modes of transmission (we have already touched upon this idea with Ouspensky's maieutics): written, oral, and applied.

Writing that aspires to awaken people cannot be produced in primary and caterpillar sentimentality. There must be a tone capable of shaking the consciousness of the reader or listener. The tone par excellence, proved by most traditions, is that of blame. The other process—having a real effect on the listener-reader-spectator's consciousness—can be explained with the enneagram: It embodies the techniques of irony and sarcasm, the techniques of the way of blame which puts the target face to face with the terror of the situation, with the disgust reflected by our own condition as an unconscious slave and liar (the lot we all share), in hope of liberating us from this circle of the confusion of tongues.

PART THREE

The Esoteric Work

TRANSMISSION AND MAGIC

No verbal discipline can awaken the center of being, the only center from which intellectual, emotional, and motor activity can converge toward a single goal. But if the center of being, the consciousness, begins to shine, it will light all the languages with a new flame.

JEAN-PHILIPPE DE TONNAC

Give not that which is holy unto the dogs, neither cast ye your pearls before swine, lest they trample them under their feet, and turn again and rend you.

MATTHEW 7:6

9

The Way of Blame

The Poetics of Power and Passing on the Lamp

Deeming blame and praise
as equal in his view,
used to silence, happy with all things,
freed from space,
firm in his thoughts and sharing in my being,
that man is dear to my heart.

BHAGAVAD GITA

In order to awaken his disciple, the master often resorts to *blame* and to all the methods this word embraces: irony, satire, sarcasm, lampooning, black humor, and the art of "bad taste." How can a properly undertaken "objectively impartial criticism of the life of man" form part of a poetics that is useful and effective—having a real power of action, beyond its artistic qualities, upon the consciousness of the reader-listener-spectator (the target) via the psychic, emotional, and physical centers? How can this poetics of power allow the writer-

190

guide to change the author-reader relationship into a master-disciple relationship, with the goal of awakening and instructing?

The master instructs, creating conditions favorable for the some-times-violent gain of consciousness. He catches his disciple in the flagrant offense of lying, he shakes the machine to make its masks fall off, to cause a kind of short-circuit that will act as an "alarm clock." The speech of life is more easily imprinted in a situation in which the disciple is perturbed, where he receives a shock that will enable him to catch a glimpse of the truth about himself. The master breaks the mirror in which the disciple has seen unceasingly a distorted and backward image of himself that has nothing to do with what he truly is. The master is, to repeat the Zen saying, the finger pointing at the moon. Only an idiot looks at the finger, missing the essential element.

Though not well defined in literature, irony embraces a vast field of definitions and literary genres (including satire), encompassing a great number of viewpoints which are worth theorizing for a critical grasp that is not only new and original, but also pertinent. Satire, sarcasm, and the lampoon are genres that draw their power from the techniques of irony, forming part of the way of blame. The origins of this way might be traced to the seventh century BCE, with Archilochus, the first known satirical author. These genres, dominant in English and French literature, are still current, albeit weakened significantly by the prevailing mediocrity—and yet now they are more necessary than ever, because with irony, we touch the heart of true literature: that which teaches. Michel Waldberg writes, "To bewilder, baffle, and disorient are the paramount actions of the irony upon which we shall insist: a poetics of power that makes us see and undermines the consciousness with the goal of instructing."[1]

The way of blame—including all the genres mentioned above, especially satire—seeks to produce a critical display of the faults, vices, and lies observed in everyday reality, which we drag along behind us like a heavy, slimy ball and chain, making our destructive movements easy to trace. The convoluted path of blame is purposeful, always aimed at a certain goal that the initiator strives to attain—whatever may be the means.

There is no room for gratuitous or haphazard action; the comic who is closely connected with him always responds to an entirely specific impact. The target—for this involves a target—is embodied by a behavior, an idea, a theory, a personality, a group of people, or an institution.

The master of satire endeavors to restore order where chaos, absurdity, and stupidity reign. He avenges truth, imposes respect, and condemns traitors with all the rigor he possesses, and often enough he makes man's vanity visible by means of the laughter that works toward creating the tabula rasa. Humor is his utmost weapon, and many are the techniques he uses to strike his target. He uses derision, he exaggerates, he mimics, and he picks over vivacious faults and vices with a fine-toothed comb. He discredits, disqualifies, and reveals falsehoods and fatal weaknesses. This "gripping laughter," Michaux wrote, "gripping an infinitely absurd world from end to end," becomes the tremor of the being that topples all the illusory towers of the multiple "I"s. This laughter needs no sentimentality to be effective; it responds dryly to the unconscious farces of the machine-phantoms. It delivers objective contempt, the aggressiveness of which is proportional to the degree of stupidity. No pathos or larval passions are allowed in an approach that wishes to be sincere and detached; distance is required for criticizing mediocrity, for bringing the holy weapon to battle and shooting the slaves of farce. In order to wage this holy war against the enemy (which may be ourselves—in fact it is always ourselves at the start), the target must be in full view; this must be the case inevitably, because blame requires pointing out and even expanding its place of impact. Thus the master of blame corrects, rectifies, and reestablishes what was once devastated by blind imitation. He acts according to a double dynamic that is double by necessity: laughter intended to cause a reaction and the "lesson" that must emerge from the situation—reestablishing the truth by establishing, at the least, a will to change, a desire for evolution in order to escape the initial situation.

Gurdjieff, the master of sarcasm and satire, blew apart conventions not only in the master-disciple relationship, but also in the author-reader relationship. He shook up inattentive consciousnesses to rejuvenate them and prepare them for working on themselves. He was the unrivaled master of the way of blame, to the point that some have accused him of inhumanity—forgetting the similarities between his tradition and other traditions, all too hastily judging a teaching technique that came from a heritage whose efficacy requires no further proof.

Many great masters took this path, vanquishing vanity. Christ "came not to send peace, but the sword" (Matthew 10:34): "Give not that which is holy unto the dogs, neither cast ye your pearls before swine, lest they trample them under their feet, and turn again and rend you." When Christ ransacked the temple of Jerusalem, overturned tables, cast out the peddlers with a scourge of small cords, and told the Jews to destroy the temple so that he could rebuild it in three days (John 2:13–25), was this not an act of fearsome blame aimed at instructing people? Yet, as Waldberg points out, "nobody would dream of calling Christ inhuman." The popular imagination prefers to evoke the gentle Jesus, who, in fact, bears no resemblance to reality—he was much rougher than most would like to believe. When the Zen monk calls his disciple a "rice bag" and whips him with rods to lead him toward satori, is this not a striking example of this way of blame? In apprenticeship in martial arts, when the master insults his students and makes them start their exercise over a thousand times in order to lead them to more understanding, can he be said to be inhuman? Just as Milarepa did what his master Marpa told him to do, starting the same action many times because the goal had not been achieved, so Gurdjieff, with the same logic, had his students dig a gigantic hole, then told them to fill it again without giving an explanation. We can also consider the sarcastic reflections of the sorcerer don Juan toward his disciple Castaneda. The examples are many; ". . . to love the disciple," Michel Waldberg noted, "means not to console but to heal him. And the more serious the disease, the more violent the cure."[2]

Such is the nature of the way of blame, and this is a matter of a particular quality in the master, not of his alleged inhumanity. Making his disciple cry has no other goal, within the framework of authentic teaching, than to awaken him to his weaknesses, his faults, and his defects. Provocation has a power over the disciple's psyche, and nothing is "free" in such an approach: Everything is aimed to instruct. "He piled up the obstacles," Waldberg writes, "highlighted the difficulties, demanded much of those who wanted to follow him. He spewed out the lukewarm, and for this they never forgave him."[3]

The master also stirs up blame in another way (as a strange recurrence of things), but in this case, it would be more accurate to speak of subjective blame. As James Moore writes: "Singularly, Gurdjieff's first roles . . . were most closely reminiscent of the Qalandari dervish who, while secretly traversing the heart's fields of tranquillity, loves to invoke blame as a necessary counterpart of divine attention."[4] But "if an idiot treats me like an idiot, that does not affect me inwardly," the master said, all too aware of the real state of things. One of his students noted: "He has been accused, blamed for having been present and having been absent, for having helped and for having refrained from helping, for having spoken and for having remained silent whenever the most varied events—from desecration to taking the veil, from natural death to suicide, from bankruptcy to success—have marked the lives of any of his disciples."[5] The Gurdjieff mystery set imaginations going—lying machines projecting their most maleficent fantasies onto the smallest events without the least bit of verification and without the least objective rigor with regard to their validity. "In truth," Moore writes, "the most common accusations leveled against Gurdjieff arose from the most convincing refutations of the charges brought against him." On the other hand, it is harder to refute the fact that we are machines! Objective blame cannot be refuted, cannot be evaded, cannot be excused because it bears the colors of the truth; it alone is capable of lifting all the veils. No invention, confabulation, phantasm, or polemic can touch that which is profoundly untouchable.

Indeed, Gurdjieff was one of those enigmatic, provoking, and elusive characters, after the manner of Malamatiyah, those "people of blame," "Muslim mystics, bringing condemnation upon themselves from 'right-thinkers' and conformist minds by virtue of their eccentric behavior."[6] Michel Random also established a pertinent connection between Gurdjieff and Shams of Tabriz (the master of Rumi) after having explored various Sufi brotherhoods in Afghanistan, Iran, and Turkey:

Both are characterized by a teaching with abrupt and sometimes even extremely violent methods, with one difference: When Shams was offended, he did not hesitate to send someone from life to death, namely by uttering a word of malediction, giving forth a particular cry. No such manifestations are known on the part of Gurdjieff, though his rigor had no less redoubtable consequences. Both men aroused either the greatest veneration or the greatest hate.[7]

As St. John's Apocalypse says (3:16), "So then because thou art lukewarm, and neither cold nor hot, I will spue thee out of my mouth."

Beelzebub's Tales to His Grandson, that magnificent work containing some twelve hundred of the prickliest pages ever written, is a perfect example of this master-disciple relationship transferred to the author-reader relationship: satire incarnate, the highest achievement of the art of bad taste. Gurdjieff, intending "an objectively impartial criticism of the life of man," embodies this way of blame remarkably, the bad taste of which was saluted by André Breton in his preface to *L'Anthologie de l'humour noir,* because, as Waldberg so rightly notes, "the passing on of the lamp takes place in unexpected ways, for it is not enough to say; one must also make understood (in the sense of 'being') that which one wants to say."[8] This necessity corresponds to the conditions for a clear discourse set forth by René Daumal in *A Night of Serious Drinking* and "Poetry Black, Poetry White." The fundamental task of *Beelzebub's Tales to His Grandson* is to "to destroy mercilessly, without any compromises whatsoever in the mentation and feelings of the reader, the beliefs and views, rooted in him by centuries, about everything existing in the world."[9] The author-master never spoke or wrote to say nothing, unlike the ordinary man, who is a prisoner of the circle of the confusion of tongues and who, in the scathing words of Mullah Nassr Eddin, knows only how to "wrangle with pigs about the quality of oranges."[10] This famous line is illustrated admirably by Ionesco's famous play *The Bald Soprano* in which the characters lose themselves in vain babbling and confusion. As the narrator says in *A Night of Serious Drinking,* "You do not ask such questions when you are thirsty."[11]

Gurdjieff put his best aphorisms and his wisest and most perplexing commentaries in the mouth of the Persian master Mullah Nassr Eddin. His stories are funny and biting, metaphysical and troubling, perturbing and subversive. Though often embodying popular wisdom, the "incomparable" and "venerable" mullah generally takes on the madman's role, his apparently absurd logic overturning accepted ideas and subverting our ordinary conception of reality. He is the champion of bad taste, the grand master of the way of blame. His sentences are "always true and scathing," and they always hit right at the target's center.

Gurdjieff was a genius of insult and provocation, not hesitating to call his disciples—and even more so the Western intelligentsia—"absolute dirt," "dirt of dirtness of dirt," or even "dirt scum," always with the aim of helping our evolution by way of deliberate shocks in which insult and provocation took part actively. He was particularly opposed to those blind vultures who came to take advantage of the "crumbs of the feast" in order to play at being "fabricators of useless articles or utterances." "He would upturn you, he would unceremoniously shake the fleas off you. He was the absolute master of the way of blame, the most difficult path to understand, the most perilous path to follow."[12]

As with Diogenes or Rabelais, Gurdjieffian sarcasm has a single goal: to denounce human vanity and the vices that hinder our evolution. It was in this spirit that, at his Pantagruelian banquets toward the end of his life, Gurdjieff developed the "science of idiotism" with his famous "toasts to the idiots," a singular and extremely strange ritual on first examination. Conducted with brandy or vodka, his toasts were dedicated to the various categories of idiots who were present, and each idiot had to assign himself a rank in the hierarchy that Gurdjieff established.[13] This highly innovative teaching method was introduced by the master in 1922 and became a regular practice around 1940. The word *idiot* retained its pejorative sense, redoubled by its Greek root associated with individuality, meaning "I make my own." Notes James Moore, "Though idiocy was universal—God himself being the unique idiot . . . a subsidiary differentiation afforded a human typology at once poetic and profound."[14] There were twenty-one categories of idiot, twelve of which were "primitive." Among these, each student, guided by his intuition, had to give himself a ranking:[15]

1. Ordinary idiot
2. Super idiot (Alfred Orage)
3. Arch idiot (Dr. Stjoernval)
4. Hopeless idiot. "The distinction that reappears most often in texts is the one established between the subjectively hopeless idiot, who is conscious of his nullity and therefore a candidate for an honorable death, and the objectively hopeless idiot, mired in egotism and therefore doomed to die like a dog. (In Armenian, *merneel* refers to 'human death' and *satkeel* refers to 'animal death.')"[16]
5. Compassionate idiot (Solange Claustres)
6. Squirming idiot (Jessie Orage)
7. Square idiot
8. Round idiot (J. G. Bennett; also a suspicious idiot)
9. Zigzag idiot. "The zigzag is a perfect idiot who goes this way and that. He has many 'I's in his memory. He struggles against the dirt that he knows he is. . . . [I]f he acts on this, I admire him with all my presence! But the ordinary zigzag idiot, with five Fridays in the week, is the dirt of dirts."[17]
10. Enlightened idiot
11. Doubting idiot
12. Swaggering idiot
13. Born idiot
14. Patented idiot
15. Psychopathic idiot
16. Polyhedral idiot
17. Beginning of a spiritual hierarchy reflecting progressive gradations of objective reason:
18. The highest development a human being could reach (such as Gurdjieff achieved)
19. Level reserved for sons of God, such as Christ
20. Level reserved for sons of God
21. God himself (unique idiot)

Whereas categories 1 through 16 "each seemed to occupy one level of existence, being subdivided only on the behavioral plane," categories 17 through 20 represent various degrees of accomplishment and evolution, and "constituted a spiritual hierarchy, reflecting progressive gradations of objective reason." Solange Claustres offers some clarifications regarding the goal of the operation: "I observed that the name chosen would express what one thought of oneself. Sometimes Gurdjieff would give a name himself or change one that we had chosen. I noticed that these names would correspond to a trait in our character or else express the very depths of the person."[18]

The toasts to the idiots were abandoned immediately after Gurdjieff's death in 1949. Let us remember that idiots within a single category could be ordinary or not, designated subjectively or objectively, depending on their possibility of evolution: "One day, Gurdjieff said that we could square the circle or, conversely, circle the square where the edges are. The name change given by G. I. Gurdjieff was to indicate an inner passage to another level. This was therefore a matter of work on oneself, transforming one's being."[19] According to Gurdjieff, only Madame de Salzmann had "left idiocy." Moore tells us that "[w]ithout his decisive presence," it appeared that the toasting of the idiots "stood in danger of becoming a mere form without content." Although now abandoned, this historical ritual is no less an embodiment of the way of blame—only confirmed by the remark regarding the zigzag idiot. Moreover, its study attempting to link the ritual and the teachings remains a source of knowledge still awaiting exploration and understanding. Pointing to our gloomy depths, it forces us to realize our nullity in order to encourage a gaining of awareness leading to possible evolution.

Though there was undeniable disagreement over Gurdjieff's way of blame, many other writers have taken the path of satire and with it, the position of author-master: Villon, Marguerite of Navarre, Rabelais, Chateaubriand, Balzac, Baudelaire, Lautréamont, Rimbaud, Ionesco, Beckett, Artaud, Daumal, Michaux, Bloy, Bréton, Lecomte, Castaneda, Duits, and Waldberg, to name only a few. Let us muse over Rimbaud's *Letters of the Visionary:* "If old imbeciles had not found anything but the false meaning of the *I*, we would not have to sweep away those millions of skeletons which have everlastingly hoarded up the products of their one-eyed intellect, while claiming to be its authors!"[20] Further, Baudelaire, in his *Intimate Journals* as well as in the first lines of the *Fleurs du mal,* lamented the "signs of human perversity, alongside the most astonishing boasts of integrity, goodness, and charity and the most brazen declarations concerning progress and civilization." Elsewhere he defined his "romanticism" as "supernaturalism and irony."

This was not haphazard: Humanity being "indignant," the way of blame endeavors to make it recover its true liberty by way of a great gaining of awareness. According to Gurdjieff, we must first recognize our nullity before we begin all work on ourselves. But how to help us awaken from our sleep? "The supreme weapon in this duel of consciousness against sleep," Waldberg writes, "is humor, with its corollary, bad taste."[21] The tale appears to be the royal path of satire: Gurdjieff's *Beelzebub's Tales to His Grandson,* unique in its genre especially due to the distance he created between humanity and the reader, should not be approached as a didactic, theoretical text, but instead should be understood as "one of the most perfect expressions of an art form addressed not only to the mind but to the heart and the body too."[22] Only at the price of this "explosive effect," as Breton reminds us, can there be anything "genuinely comic." "Man is too attached to his own errors to enjoy having them pointed out to him."[23] That is why the master so often has to take the way of blame, in order to reconsider radically that which goes without saying.

Literature itself is not saved by blame. Far from it. For Gurdjieff, who considered it one of the highest disciplines, literature had deteriorated lamentably during the twentieth century into what he called harshly, in *Meetings with Remarkable Men,* "the development of word prostitution." Though the art of polemics has provided instruction for a number of major works, contemporary literature suffers from a lack of true writers who are capable of shaking the consciousness. The lampoon, although a genre closely connected to circumstances, appears to have lost a great deal of its popularity. This might be explained by the decline of moralizing ideologies, replaced through communication.

Meanwhile, the true initiates pass on the torch of blame, as we can see from reading such authors as Michel Waldberg. In *La Parole Putanisée*, published in 2002 (and an entirely contemporary work due not so much to its date of publication as to the authors it targets), he not only denounces the "deception of merchandise," but also refers to a lineage of true writers—namely, those for whom "writing is a question of life or death." We need only mention Rabelais, Montaigne, Rimbaud, Baudelaire, Mallarmé, Artaud, Breton, Bataille, Proust, Huxley, Beckett, Michaux, Daumal, Dietrich, Lecomte, Queneau, and Duits in order to see, along with Waldberg, the entire terror of the situation. "Polemics today have only little masters, jackanapeses of thought and style with sickly and limp pens."[24] This is an observation of something terrible made considerably weightier by the demographic density of the circle of the confusion of tongues. Michel Waldberg refers to Léon Bloy, recalling the "superior necessity of lampooning" that the author is obliged to use, given that the world he lives in is "ignobly futile and incidental, with a raging famine of absolute realities."

Unlike satire, lampooning requires no detachment, and it thrashes its target without any restraint. It puts impostors to the sword; it denounces, attacks, and crushes insignificant systems like vehicles in a car crusher. The engagement is total and resides in the very heart of the confusion denounced. Léon Bloy writes: "Every man who writes to say nothing is, in my eyes, a prostitute and a wretch, and this is why I am a lampooner."[25] This is precisely the way of blame that Michel Waldberg chose for criticizing an entire section of contemporary literature. He wrote to denounce those who write to say nothing and, consequently, those who speak to say nothing, pointing his finger, in Daumalian terms, at the fabricators of useless utterances. These—quite often "crumb pickers"—never cease propagating and are, it must be admitted, very numerous today. They swarm in the libraries like rats in the sewers. In his formidable projects of literary rat extermination, Michel Waldberg identifies his victims in the name of truth and without any hint of indulgence. The cadavers are many, and a great number of his dissected fabricators are—we cannot help but notice—familiar to us in that each day they corrupt the "box of images," which, in any case, is often only fascinating to those who are already dead.

A Night of Serious Drinking, just like *Beelzebub's Tales to His Grandson,* is an "objectively impartial criticism of the life of man" that leaves no room for the sentimentality and pseudo-humanism that have become so conventional. In his quest for the truth, Daumal tears apart the bizarre human psyche without the slightest compromise, making it into a work of art at the height of his understanding—an objective work of art tinted with an irony as ferocious as it is lyrical and drawing all its power from the teachings. Reading Daumal without knowing his master's teachings has the same result as reading Milton without having read the Bible—that is to say, no result at all, besides the probable appreciation of a certain verbal exquisiteness for which only Daumal held the secret. Like it or not, it can have no interpretation other than the Gurdjieffian interpretation—as is also the case for *Mount Analogue*—because the essential element is bound up with the supreme meaning aimed for by the author, the goal without which there is no true language. Further, like his master, René Daumal did not hesitate to thrash his contemporaries with devastating sentences in an attempt to open their eyes.

A Night of Serious Drinking necessarily evokes Gurdjieff's dinner parties. Many times, without a double meaning, Daumal mentions the substantive idiot. "Philosophy teaches how man thinks he thinks; but drinking shows how he really thinks."[26] Daumal is clear: These "brutes who resemble me like brothers," these "bipeds," this "mania for deforming words," these "incurables," these "fabricators" are all an allusion to the teachings. Daumal was truly a debunker with his succulent sarcasm, a machine-breaker, an evacuator of "crumb pickers" and false Savants ("scienters"). There are enough examples of the white poet's objective contempt for the "windmills of balderdash" and the "clarificators of clarifications." The goal of the initiators of blame is clearly defined by Roger Nimier in his introduction to *Mount Analogue:* "Naturally, the characters and circumstances in *Mount Analogue* are symbolic: *literature must be so if it is to be useful to man.* In this circumstance, it awakens doubly, because *all the sentences mean something.* This is due to

René Daumal's highly individual intelligence, and to what one might call his lyricism and irony."[27]

The way of blame must serve a precise goal and necessity: that of healing, removing us from the terrible and maleficent conditions of existence in which we become more and more bogged down each day, beginning, at the very least, by enumerating the defects, nervous tics, and pretenses that twitch away unceasingly in people's heads; by denouncing those things that nobody wants to denounce, because they are indubitably present in everyone. Courage and strength are required to denounce the great farce in the very face of the fabricators. Day after day, this masquerade is attended, orchestrated by robots who sell morals, and the air has become unbreathable for those who seek any kind of truth amid this jumble of lies. Taking up the legacy of Gurdjieff and Daumal, Waldberg tears back the veils and sets the record straight at the beginning of this millennium, locking up those who wiseacre in the train of mediocrity—and sending them off with a one-way ticket to the junk heap of the ages.

Objective blame thus combines genres in order to serve a common cause, exercising a subtle action upon the consciousness. Blame is the art of making people see mediocrity, and Gurdjieff was the absolute master of this game. We need only read *Beelzebub's Tales to His Grandson* to be sure of it. For a writer, to master blame is to be capable of establishing a master-disciple relationship by way of the author-reader relationship, and thus to act upon the consciousness. At this point, it becomes possible to speak of the way of blame as the poetics of power, with literature functioning as a remedy, both artistic and salvational. It is literature of awakening—literature that awakens in search of the source, seeking without respite to "pass on the torch." It also assists the breakdown of the personality, the social "I," the false "I," revealing the essence, the self, what we truly are. Blame, that subtle mask-ripper, is the greatest weapon against sleep and the mechanicalness that keeps people in illusion and error. It is readers' "alarm clock," the tool intended to yank us out of the circle of the confusion of tongues. This specific speech, embodied so masterfully and singularly in Gurdjieff's *Beelzebub's Tales to His Grandson,* is a "word of life" that has the "power to break through the thick walls of unconsciousness and indifference."[28] To master irony is to know how to show. It is simply to throw the full light of day upon what Gurdjieff called "the consequences of the crystallization of the maleficent properties of the organ Kundabuffer"—in other words, the singular traits of the strange human psyche, namely, an irresistible desire to be violent toward our fellow humans (war, and other aggressive manifestations, physical and mental) as well as egotism, envy, hatred, hypocrisy, contempt, vanity, pride, presumption, credulity (suggestibility), snobbery, the incapacity to think for oneself . . . the list is long.

Faced with the "stupefying intellectual rigidity of the privileged," Charles Duits wrote, "humorous affirmation is the only attitude possible."[29] Humor—which Daumal and Dietrich considered the "substitute for remembering oneself"[30]—in fact provides a magnified image of the machine, forcing us to laugh by the strength of its mockery. And yet humor is not always smiling. It can be black, tragic, or in bad taste when the norm it attacks is suffering, death, or, in more simple terms, the maleficent characteristics of the strange human psyche—all the things that make us blind and ignorant machines that must be put back on the path by means of the force of blame in order that we may achieve a higher level of consciousness and thus attain true freedom.

This poetics of blame also has some connection to film. Satire makes us see and shows: It causes readers or spectators to become aware of their nullity, their vices and his faults. Consider certain moments in Alan Ball's famous *American Beauty,* Jacques Tati's *Mon oncle,* or the films of Agnès Jaoui or Jean-Pierre Bacri. Everything is shown to be seen—us, at once naked and nothing, integrally exposed to ourselves—in order to unleash a being shock in the person-target (reader, listener, or viewer). A liberating grasping of consciousness may be born from our own reflection and in laughter—"the property of man," as Rabelais said—which is capable of ripping us out of sleep. Let it be understood, however: Laughter is not always shared, depending on whether or not we feel ourselves to be the target. It is hard to imagine a crumb picker, a fabricator, or a Savant, to use only these examples, laughing out loud while reading *Beelzebub's Tales to His Grandson*. Each will feel himself to be targeted, criticized, and humiliated and in his reading—like the great majority of those who have attempted adventures—will go no farther than the first few pages.

This way of blame—which takes oral paths as well as written—comprises all the traits of irony: the agents (subject-emitter-speaker and target), the processes, and the questioning of the norm. It can be represented in the triad upon which the issues and means for the approach are understood in light of the Law of Three:

Processes of blame
sarcasm, humor, laughter, etc.
detachment, signals, etc.

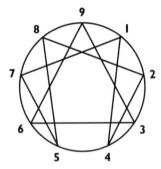

Target
("ironized," "blamed")
perhaps not a person:
values, groups, ideas,
objects, institutions,
knowledge, morals, opinion,
norms, questioning, etc.

Subject-Emitter
(Speaker; "blamer,"
"ironizer")
will to change
(denounce, correct)
things and establish
new norms

Our original triad of clear discourse can be seen here with the presence of agents (speaker and listener or target): The processes (techniques) work as a conciliatory force, because they allow for an effective blame, if possible. This schematization is the representation of a true poetics of power. The goal and the necessity for action are primordial and allow for the avoidance of gratuitous farce and simple moralizing blame, which are irrelevant.

This is the method for putting to work various processes, all with the single goal of shocking body, mind, and emotions all at once and, by way of this "being tremor," shocking the consciousness. Writing produces direct meanings but signifies a great deal indirectly. Irony plays on a double meaning of a fragment: one apparent, the other hidden and opposite. *Beelzebub's Tales to His Grandson* are garnished with these techniques, known as signals (the textual means of irony), especially the use of quotation marks, which generally surround the "language of the favorites"—ordinary men not taken charge of by the author. Everything must be redefined, and language in itself is an efficacious process. Among the signals—these techniques—are found the outlines of known styles, especially those connected with amplification, comparison, the staging of ridicule, excess, devaluing, quotations, and situations taken out of context. We should note that *Beelzebub's Tales to His Grandson* leaves no room for what Gurdjieff calls the "morals of good taste," and consequently, direct aggression is obviously appropriate—unlike with those who seek to get around obstacles by means of courtesy; decency; convention; social, moral, or cultural norms; or any other Hasnamussian properties. The master of blame knocks down the obstacle, accuses and denounces without wiseacring for the greater good of those who aspire to elevation. And the collaborators in this area of seeking were initially targets who were hit and had the strength to recover and understand why they had been targets prior to becoming, in some cases, masters of blame in their turn. Remember: The enneagram is always in motion.

For provocation, the master uses cries, blows, insults, and skillful assault as well as paradoxes (the koan), contradictions, repetitions, exclamations, and "apparently pointless responses or outright refusal to respond," as Waldberg writes—always with the goal of making people see reality not as it is commonly seen, but as it really is. "What is necessary," Gurdjieff said to Ouspensky, "is conscience. We do not teach morality. We teach how to find conscience. People are not pleased when we say this. They say that we have no love. Simply because we do not encourage weakness and hypocrisy but, on the contrary, take off all masks."[31]

This is why some authors desirous of "shaking the consciousness" have recourse to this instructive technique, which is as devastating as it is salvational, because blame is perhaps the ultimate defense against human stupidity. This is why Gurdjieff required and legitimized certain specific processes in order to reach his target (goal), namely reproach (from the Latin *blastemare,* "to reproach"), judgment, accusation, anathema, attacks, jeering, taunting, derision, mockery, jokes, gibes, digs, barbs, black humor, bad taste, sarcasm, condemnation, criticism, discouragement, reprimand, and even, in some cases, violent fustigation and vituperation, chastisement, and verbal flagellation—always with the goal of awakening the target.

As for *love,* there is nothing more subjective and deceiving, and this word is the source of a great deal of confusion. Those who have reproached Gurdjieff for his lack of love have understood nothing. In order to satisfy their subjectivity, let us simply remember the master's words: "The highest goal, and the very meaning of human life, is to strive for the good of our fellow man, which is possible only through renouncing ourselves." Gurdjieff devoted his life to seeking, teaching, transmitting his ideas, and creating conditions favorable for our harmonic development. Who else can boast of having done as much? Random notes that only for Gurdjieff and Shams (a few others could be mentioned) does the word *love* "not suggest any sentimental connotation. It is associated with properties resulting from the sacred nature of all things, from their faculties as emanations from the Creator, and therefore from the creative movement that manifests all things at once in being and nonbeing. Thus it is a human and divine love, a love of an objective character."[32] What Gurdjieff is reproached for, in fact, is that his ideas "destroy the humanist ideas that we have always fostered, no matter how pessimistic we may be. The fact is that we have not heard the lesson of the masters."[33] Who, indeed, would not have reacted upon hearing Gurdjieff say, entirely in earnest, that "men are not men," that we can do nothing, that we are machines, that we must realize their entire nullity? There is no truth that does not hurt—and Gurdjieff knew this, making honesty the principal technique of his Work.

> . . . Whomever I should meet, for business, commerce or any other
> purpose, whether an old or new acquaintance and whatever his social
> standing might be, I had to discover immediately his "most sensitive

corn" and press it rather hard. . . . Thanks to this principle, which turned out to be miracle-working for me, I, besides having always and everywhere an abundance of material for my chief aim, that is, for my regeneration, also, thanks only to it, so affected everyone who met me, that he himself, without any effort on my part whatsoever, as if with great satisfaction and complete readiness, took off his mask presented to him with great solemnity by his papa and mama.[34]

"Without the liberty to blame," there can certainly be no "fawning praise," as Beaumarchais said, but what's more, if we are sincere with ourselves, there can be no hope of escaping from the growing illusion in which we are cloistered from birth. Blame teaches humility properly, for by lifting the masks beneath which we hide, it shows us that we are nothing. Every true way of blame is an "objectively impartial criticism of the life of man;" otherwise it is not a true way.

Thus we can speak of books of power—books that exercise a real force over readers, who become disciples in their turn. In order truly to act as a book master, the author must establish this sincere relationship in the actual phase of writing. He then becomes the initiator of another mode of consciousness. Readers must take the role of initiates, of those to whom the teachings are dispensed. From the attentive reading of the text, a new flame must be born at the very depths of themselves, a new force ready to face life while following the path of wisdom.

Reading is then no longer passive and mechanical, but active, and it becomes real teaching. All great texts are either like this or they are not. And in the rare cases where they are like this, it is because they have been inspired, because they have been the work of an author pervaded by forces at a certain moment, a receptive author who listened for the "mouth of shadows," the demonic consciousness ready to catch all the signals on the other side of the mirror.

Seekers of the truth know how to decipher the symbols—or at least, they use them, for knowledge resides silently in myths and symbols: words of life intentionally veiled.

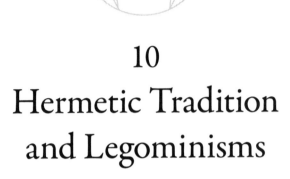

10

Hermetic Tradition
and Legominisms

Myths, Symbols, and Truth

*Wheresoever we have spoken plainly, there we have spoken
nothing, but where we have used riddles and figures, there we
have hidden the truth.*

ROSARIUM PHILOSOPHORUM

*". . . And then, like him, you must, by a sedulous lecture and
frequent meditation, break the bone and suck out the marrow . . ."*

RABELAIS, *GARGANTUA AND PANTAGRUEL*

The passing on of the torch often takes place through the acquisition
of a word that is obscure to the ordinary among us, but is filled with
knowledge for those who know how to grasp its meaning. By definition,
esotericism is a doctrine that must not be vulgarized and is intended
only for groups of initiates and not for the masses or the greater public
(which is *exotericism*).

In his book *Les Grands Initiés,* which has become cult material, Édouard Schuré retraces the secret history of religions, conjur-
ing up those great initiates—or "envoys from above," as Gurdjieff
said—whose teachings constitute the core of esoteric doctrine.
Rama, Krishna, Hermes, Moses, Orpheus, Pythagoras, Plato, and
Jesus (and there is great temptation to add Gurdjieff to the list)
bring us a fundamental message from which we can draw the secret
laws of the universe, even if we must often transcend literal and exoteric meaning, which leads only to dualism, in order to understand
their teachings as One: "Only the certainty of the immortal soul
can become a solid basis for earthly life—and only the understanding of the great religions, through a return to their common source
of inspiration, can secure the brotherhood of the peoples and the
future of humanity."[1] All these religions contain a word of power
capable of freeing us from the heavy chains of our ordinary condition. The goal of esotericism—there has been enough insistence on
this point—is nothing other than the evolution of being. The very
essence of esoteric truth, according to Schuré, cannot be expressed
"in a more striking and more luminous manner" than in these lines
from Frédéric Amiel:

> Each sphere of being tends toward a higher sphere and already has
> revelations and presentiments of it. The ideal under all its forms is
> the anticipation and the prophetic vision of that existence, higher
> than his own, toward which every being perpetually aspires. And
> this higher and more dignified existence is more inward in char-
> acter, more spiritual. Just as volcanoes reveal to us the secrets of
> the interior of the globe, so enthusiasm and ecstasy are the passing
> explosions of this inner world of the soul, and human life is but
> the preparation and means of approach to this spiritual life. The
> degrees of initiation are innumerable. Watch, then, disciple of life,
> watch and labor toward the development of the angel within thee!
> For the divine odyssey is but a series of more and more ethereal
> metamorphoses in which each form, the result of what goes before,
> is the condition of those that follow. The divine life is a series of

successive deaths in which the mind throws off its imperfections and its symbols and yields to the growing attraction of the ineffable center of gravitation, the sun of intelligence and love.[2]

But this evolution within the various higher spheres of being is accessible only with great effort, through long years of study and apprenticeship. We must begin by first deciphering the truths left by the ancients at the heart of a language considered cryptic.

Besides meditating, Hermes himself studied medicine, architecture, sacred music, the various sciences of his era, and the most ancient hieroglyphs. "Will I one day be permitted to breathe the rose of Isis and see the light of Osiris?" he asked during his apprenticeship, and he was answered: "That does not depend on us. The truth does not give itself. One finds it in oneself, or else one does not find it."[3] The master or the school can only create the conditions of awakening, for only the will of the seeker can determine his progression along the scale of truth. The secret, if it is obtained, must necessarily remain under the law of mystery, and so the hierophant said to the new initiate: "Complete knowledge cannot be revealed except to our brothers who have gone through the same trials we have. One must measure the truth according to the intellect, veil it from the weak whom it would drive mad, hide it from the malicious who could grasp only fragments of it, from which they would make weapons of destruction. Enclose it in your heart, and may it speak through your work."[4] When the adept finally became a priest of Osiris, he was required to make an absolute promise: "But before leaving, he promised solemnly, by a formidable oath, to keep absolutely silent regarding the secrets of the temple. He must never betray to anyone what he had seen or learned or reveal the doctrine of Osiris except *under the triple veil of mythological symbols or mysteries.*"[5]

Thus the Hermetic tradition was born, and thus it continued through centuries and initiations, leaving the traces of past revelations in myths and symbols. It was thus that the Caucasian master G. I. Gurdjieff proceeded in the twentieth century. After a lengthy initiation, he never divulged his teaching initially except to restricted groups of students motivated by the quest, who then had to guard the secret.

Later, before his death, he gave orders for the publication of his writings. *Beelzebub's Tales to His Grandson* are part of the Hermetic tradition in that the objective truth in them must be deciphered. Each reading is a new experience, forever a fresh source of knowledge. This is because this work, in particular, is a *legominism*—an initiatory mode of transmitting the truth, "one of the means existing there of transmitting from generation to generation information about certain events of long-past ages, through just those three-brained beings who are thought worthy to be and who are called initiates."[6] We should note that the Work as a whole is a full-fledged legominism, after the manner of chapter 26 of *Beelzebub's Tales to His Grandson:* The Legominism concerning the Deliberations of the Very Saintly Ashiata Shiemash under the Title "The Terror of the Situation." In this sense, *Beelzebub's Tales to His Grandson* must be decoded using the proper tools. Gurdjieff, as was his tendency, took care to explain what he meant by *initiate:*

> In former times on the planet Earth, this word was always used in only one sense, and the three-brained beings there who were called initiates were those who had acquired in their presences almost equal objective data which could be sensed by other beings.
>
> But during the last two centuries this word has come to be used in two senses: In one sense it is used for the same purpose as before, referring to those beings that are so named who became initiates thanks to their personal conscious labors and intentional sufferings, and thereby, as I have already told you, they acquire in themselves objective merits which can be sensed by other beings irrespective of brain system, and which also evoke in others trust and respect.
>
> In the other sense, those beings call each other by this name who belong to those that are called criminal gangs, which, in the said period, have greatly multiplied and whose members have as their chief aim to steal from those around them only essence values. Under the pretense of following supernatural or mystic sciences, these criminal gangs are really occupied, and very successfully, with this kind of plunder.
>
> And so, any and every genuine member of such a gang there is

called an initiate. . . . Well then, my boy, *Legominism* is the name given to the successive transmission of information about long-past events which have occurred on the planet Earth from initiates to initiates of the first kind, that is from really meritorious beings, who have themselves received their information from similar meritorious beings."[7]

Initiates should therefore be understood in Schuré's sense: beings who have already reached a high level of development and are not beginners. The knowledge, in fact, is not hidden, but it will not fall randomly into a machine's hands. The will alone can allow the sincere seeker of truth to gain access to the philosopher's stone. "Knock, and it shall be opened unto you," as the parable says. Knowledge is material, Gurdjieff tells us. People make considerable efforts to obtain futile things, and yet they want knowledge to be given to them freely. But we must pay—literally and in all senses, sacrificing something. "From the sweat of thy brow shalt thou earn thy bread"; such is the true meaning of this biblical parable. There is nothing that is fundamentally hidden or inaccessible; the will of the seeker alone will permit him to access knowledge and truth, which indeed are often revealed beneath intentional "lies."

This is how *Beelzebub's Tales to His Grandson* operates, even more singularly than Gurdjieff's other writings. If a book is generally published to be read, this does not mean it is published to be understood. Rare, in fact, are those who nourish themselves with the "substantive marrow." The main obstacle to the study of this text is simply its style. It is complex and difficult to access—so much so that idle readers soon find themselves discouraged by its long sentences, interminable digressions, and the characteristic avalanche of neologisms created for the occasion. *Beelzebub's Tales to His Grandson,* although written in Russian, preserves its essential powers in translation, because the task was accomplished directly by the master's students.* And if the style appears "repulsive" to some people, this is because, according to Michel

---

*[This applies to the English and French translations. —*Trans.*]

Waldberg, "we are not accustomed to it, for it runs counter to all the fashions and all the researches outside of which the iron rule holds that there is no possible salvation for a writer."[8] Another reason is simply that Gurdjieff encrypted his text intentionally while writing it in order to divulge its essence only to those worthy of it. The language of *Beelzebub's Tales to His Grandson* is not a language by default—that is to say, the result of some difficulty of writing or conforming to good taste—but a language chosen and rendered consciously as difficult to access by the very will of its author. From this ascetic experience arises a language that is original and formidably effective—on the level of its action on the various centers of being. Readers who make the effort necessary to penetrate this singular cosmology will be beginning the Work, because they will have already initiated unconsciously a struggle against themselves, against their laziness and passivity. To read *Beelzebub's Tales to His Grandson* is itself an asceticism for those who do so sincerely. Those who have approached its reading will know of the strange power that emanates from this book.

Charles Duits, for whom *Beelzebub's Tales to His Grandson* was nightly bedtime reading, underscores pertinently some essential traits recorded by Michel Waldberg as well as recorded throughout the pages of Duits's own writings. He emphasizes "the great qualities of the introduction," "in its own right one of the most striking works of its era," while the "apparently forbidding" main text belongs, as its title alone indicates, "to one of the best-known of literary genres: the genre of Montesquieu's *Lettres persanes* and Voltaire's *L'Ingénu*."[9] Although highly singular in its form, *Beelzebub's Tales to His Grandson* belongs to a "classic" genre amid truly traditional perspectives. "Beneath the humorous surface of the fable," Duits notes, "we again meet the doctrine of illusion, of Maya, of the famous sleep about which all the masters speak, a sleep which must be broken and from which the sleeper must awaken."[10] Duits continues:

> Having said this, it must also be said that no matter how apparently strange, baroque and even preposterous is the form adopted by Gurdjieff . . . it too belongs to a very old tradition, that of

the *Thousand and One Nights*. It seems to me very important to underline this point, because it is indisputable that only a reader capable of taking a childish pleasure from listening to stories can appreciate such a work. The gravest problems are at issue, yet Beelzebub is addressing a child, his grandson Hassein, and he narrates the cosmic adventure in the oriental style, that is to say, according to a certain rhythm which has admittedly become quite foreign to the modern Western mind. It is obvious that Homer's listeners enjoyed hearing the same epithets and the same phrases repeated again and again. The same goes for the Sultan listening to Scheherazade, and certainly too for the troubadours' listeners as they learned, for the thousandth time, that Charlemagne had a "flowing beard."[11]

These repetitions, which are intolerable to excessively intellectualized readers, function as a kind of hammering indispensable for the transmission of certain truths. Also, in a tale as long as Beelzebub's, they function as a memory exercise for following the thread of the text, rendered obscure by its singularly succulent style. To write in keeping with this ancient tradition in the twentieth century was to raise a barrier for many readers conditioned by their own era who no longer had the virtuous patience needed to appreciate such words, which are instructive not merely for their lengthiness and the effort required to listen to them and not only for the active and entirely conscious reading required of them, but also through a being presence that today's readers do not know how to foster. The breath that animates this masterpiece of esotericism maintains its remarkable intensity throughout, carrying readers to a land of magnificent richness:

> The process in question—as anyone soon realizes who has the patience to read a work like the *Tales*—in fact has a very special quality. Certainly a fearsome dragon stands on the threshold of such a book, a dragon which can only be called boredom. But whoever crosses the threshold discovers little by little that the repetitions and so on produce an altogether different effect. They take

hold of the reader, create an "atmosphere"; he wants to go further, and like Hassein he asks for more . . .[12]

Readers are appealed to by the reading; they find themselves returning again and again to these tales, which ruthlessly point them toward their own reflection. They thus come to understand that they themselves are part of the terror of the situation, that they are equally guilty of the terrible confusion in which they are pitifully entangled. Yet it is in this painful face-to-face encounter with themselves that they move forward into life as into their reading, freeing themselves of the many masks that would otherwise immobilize and degrade them. Page by page, they draw the power necessary for continuing their reading, as sweet as it is painful:

> I have mentioned the *Iliad* and the *Thousand and One Nights;* in many ways the *Tales* are also reminiscent of Rabelais, who, like Gurdjieff, takes his time and presents the modern reader with what is at first a hard surface to penetrate, but eventually gains a lasting hold on him. One returns to these books again and again, reading a page, or a chapter, stopping and then starting again, so that their quintessence penetrates without being noticed.[13]

Moreover, this singular form serves for the "objectively impartial criticism of the life of man" put forward by Gurdjieff. Duits continues:

> Having said this, we can now tackle the modern and even ultra-modern aspect of the book, Gurdjieff's great comic innovation, an invention which to my mind makes him one of the literary geniuses of the century, and from which he draws an infinite variety of effects whose humor is sometimes disquieting. The entire book is written in a pseudo-scientific jargon whose cumulative effect—but with Gurdjieff all effects are cumulative—is in my opinion utterly irresistible.
>
> In some respects *Beelzebub's Tales to His Grandson* is nothing other than a marvelously extended satire on modern science

or, to be more precise, on the scientific mind. Certainly, Gurdjieff sees the extraordinary vanity of scholars as one of the most perfect illustrations of universal folly. This vanity goes hand in hand with pedantry and is manifested principally in the continual use of a Greco-Latin jargon which enables the pundits to conceal the ordinariness of what they are saying, exactly like Molière's doctors, and to impose on everyone's credulity. Thus *saliakooriapa* is used for "water," *teskooano* for "telescope," etc. I must add straight away that this jargon also has another totally serious purpose: There is in Gurdjieff a "verbal kabbalah" which calls for an extremely meticulous and careful examination.[14]

Listening to the venerable Mullah Nassr Eddin, the satirical aspect of *Beelzebub's Tales to His Grandson* is obvious and leaves no doubt concerning the severe criticism of Savants who know only how to fabricate what are often merely pale fictions. "A flea exists in the World just for one thing—that when it sneezes, that deluge should occur with the description of which our learned beings love so much to busy themselves."[15]

Gurdjieff's literary art in *Beelzebub's Tales to His Grandson* is an art of creating distance between readers and humanity to the point that readers come to acquire distance from themselves—and so much so that they recognize certain characteristic and fundamentally maleficent traits in their "strange psyche." It thus becomes possible for them to act. With Gurdjieff, Duits notes, "the process is radicalized to the utmost." The master leads us to reconsider all things, to make a tabula rasa of our ideas concerning everything. As to the reflections that arise from the reading of this magnificent text, let us return to the words of Charles Duits, who points to one of the essential traits of this extraordinary legominism:

> . . . He has begun to consider mankind from outside, and from much further outside than when he slipped into the skin of Montesquieu's Persians or Voltaire's Ingénu. It is our whole language, and hence our whole world, which loses its familiarity, and no longer just various manners, customs, laws and conventions. Like Montesquieu,

and like Voltaire, Gurdjieff interposes a distance between the reader and mankind. But here the process is radicalized to the utmost. It is not our society which is made foreign, but the whole Earth, its history and geography, the most common and ordinary things. One is quite surprised to learn that human beings also practice *Elmooarno* (make love) and at the end of their lives undergo *Rascooarno* (die).

Thus the book is presented in the form of a comic ethnology—which takes the wind out of many sails. Just as ethnologists enjoy larding their writings with words borrowed from the peoples they study, so Gurdjieff manages to thoroughly "exoticize" us, so that our lives and our most everyday activities display their underlying structure. Life could be different: things are not simply "as they are."

And of course other fields are involved, as well as ethnology. Through this infinitely simple and infinitely effective process, Gurdjieff perfidiously incites us to ask questions: first, of course, to question the authority of science. But also—and even more disconcerting—to question the very reality of its findings. Everything is affected—physics, chemistry, biology. For it goes without saying that Gurdjieff is not satisfied only to substitute words of his own devising for those we use in everyday life. Generalizing the process, he replaces our entire science with another, and our "laws of nature"—as we call them—with a whole other system, described, of course, in a pompous, rebarbative language. Never mind the value of this system for the moment. The important thing here is once again the disorienting and "diabolic" effect, for in "explaining" all phenomena by laws unknown to Earth science, Gurdjieff insinuates a fundamental doubt. Is Einstein right? But what is there in Einstein which is not in the law of Triamazikamno or of Heptaparaparshinokh? Perhaps we do obtain some results, but not because we know the laws, rather because we have glimpsed certain aspects of much more general laws which we do not know. To tell the truth, here one tends to forget that the *Tales* are, after all, a work of fiction. Thoroughly bewildered, we are ready to admit that the sun gives neither heat nor light, that the moon is a nascent planet, not a dead one, and so on. Without realizing it we reach the point of taking Gurdjieff at his word, so that we have to make a certain effort to wake up, to understand the game we have just been taken in by, and also to see that in life we are perhaps taken in by just such a game.

I hasten to add that Gurdjieff's "laws" are definitely not as fantastic as one might think, and that his cosmology may be less absurd than it seems. For the moment, though, this is not what matters: the important thing is to see the process through which Gurdjieff, so to speak, disabuses his reader, forces him to question what he never questions and—last but not least—makes him grasp at first hand what it is that produces that dismal mechanization of thought which lies at the root of so many of our troubles.[16]

Thus, Gurdjieff captures readers' attention, making them place their finger upon the blind mechanisms that drive every one of their actions. Initially, he stimulates an active reading—requiring conscious effort and some suffering—without which it would be impossible to understand any part of this singular mythology. With these, however, a door may open that leads to infinite hope. Those who have passed through it know this well. *Beelzebub's Tales to His Grandson* directs a word of power capable of transforming the whole life of readers. Here we touch upon the primordial forces of language, the remarkable powers of full and active speech. And among all the powers put into action by Gurdjieff's writing, it is first and foremost this mythological writing that strikes us full in the face, making us turn around, falter, fall over backward—and finally, making us see things the right way round.

According to Gurdjieff, objective knowledge is transmitted especially well through myths and symbols—true legominisms, crucibles of all wisdom—thanks to which the truth is passed on to those who know how to decipher it, offering salvational keys to those who know how to use them, words of life for those who want to live.

Breaking past linguistic, temporal, and disciplinary barriers, the study of myth (from the Latin *mythus* and the Greek *muthos*, "tale, fable") is entirely a part of the truth-seeker's path. Literature, which arises from a double movement, has been nurtured by myths since its beginning, either giving meaning to the text or generating new myths. This mythological womb, this gigantic crucible of creation, shows that the myth can save us the trouble of other critical approaches relative to its interpretation, including certain esoteric approaches. Herein, perhaps, lies the ultimate key.

The true myth surpasses the general scope of the myth in that it is rooted in a depth of meaning that transcends distortion, collective amplification, and literary tradition, yet its real value—real because it is instructive for us—remains forever intact. The myth goes beyond legend, beyond the mere constructions of the mind, confabulation, gratuitous invention, and utopia. It tends more toward allegorical and symbolic representation, itself ruled—according to the conditions for a clear discourse that René Daumal assumes in his foreword to *A Night of Serious Drinking*—by a goal (that of liberating us) and a precise necessity aimed to instruct by means of a common language. A myth is not simply a story devoid of meaning; it speaks the truth behind appearances and it stores knowledge in the form of symbols, as in, for example, the visionary knowledge contained in the myths of the earliest peoples. If a myth's meaning cannot be read directly, the myth is still living; it has resonances, connotations, an answer concerning what is confronted—but its true interpretation, just like that of the symbol, depends clearly, in light of the teaching, on the level of consciousness of those who endeavor to interpret it: ". . . [O]bjective knowledge, the idea of unity included, belongs to objective consciousness. The forms which express this knowledge when perceived by subjective consciousness are inevitably distorted and, instead of truth, they create more and more delusions."[17] This is so because objective consciousness is unitive, whereas ordinary or subjective consciousness is separative.

Myth is a source of inexhaustible wisdom, offering a cipher of understanding that, for a worthwhile and real use, requires the most concrete keys possible. But where to find them? This is the question that each reader must answer for himself.

True, transcendent myths pose questions that we encounter eternally. Our metaphysical preoccupations relate incessantly to the same existential problems of the origins and the end—revolving around the central questions of *how* and *why*. Who and what are we? Where do we come from? Where are we going? Why and how?

Gurdjieff's teachings and literary works give singular answers to these problematic principles, emphasizing what makes the myth important, namely its symbolic value, which reveals its profound meaning that is able to provide us with concrete information regarding the meaning of human life.

"Realizing the imperfection and weakness of ordinary language the people who have possessed objective knowledge have tried to express the idea of unity in 'myths,' in 'symbols,' and in particular 'verbal formulas' which, having been transmitted without alteration, have carried on the idea from one school to another, often from one epoch to another."[18] These forms—traversing history in all their original purity—are effectively "such forms as would insure its proper perception by others and avoid in its transmission the possibility of distortion and corruption."[19]

> It has already been said that the higher psychic centers work in man's higher states of consciousness: the "higher emotional" and the "higher mental." The aim of "myths" and "symbols" was to reach man's higher centers, to transmit to him ideas inaccessible to the intellect and to transmit them in such forms as would exclude the possibility of false interpretations. "Myths" were destined for the higher emotional center; "symbols" for the higher thinking center. By virtue of this all attempts to understand or explain "myths" and "symbols" with the mind, or the formulas and the expressions which give a summary of their content, are doomed beforehand to failure. It is always possible to understand anything but only with the appropriate center.[20]

Objective knowledge is unity—realized by symbols—and can therefore be transmitted only by myth, which can be understood only by a simultaneous action of certain human centers transcending reason.

Gurdjieff's childhood tales confirm this idea: Listening to the stories his father told him, such as the *Thousand and One Nights* and especially the tale of Gilgamesh, he gained the ability to "comprehend the incomprehensible."[21] He relates that around 1913, he read a magazine article "in which it was said that there had been found among the ruins of Babylon some tablets with inscriptions which scholars were certain were no less than four thousand years old."[22] These inscriptions were none other than the legend of the hero Gilgamesh in a form almost identical to the story his father told. This discovery caused a "grasping of consciousness," an "inner excitement" for Gurdjieff that was instrumental in his destiny, especially with the idea that this legend could be handed down orally over thousands of years by generations of storytellers and poets without being altered in form: "After this occurrence, when the beneficent result of the impressions formed in my childhood from the narratives of my father finally became clear to me—a result that crystallized in me a spiritualizing factor enabling me to comprehend that which usually appears incomprehensible—I often regretted having begun too late to give the legends of antiquity the immense significance that I now understand they really have."[23]

The interest of Russians, Europeans, and Americans in mythology during the 1920s and 1930s (the period during which Gurdjieff wrote) was the result of several determining factors which today offer various possible readings of the myth: the archaeological and anthropological explorations of ancient cultures in the late nineteenth and early twentieth centuries, especially in Mesopotamia and Egypt; the publication of Frazer's *Golden Bough;* the synthetic mythology used in theosophical literature (Blavatsky's *Secret Doctrine*); the interest in myths exploring the psyche (Freud's *Interpretation of Dreams,* Jung's *Psychology of the Unconscious*). As a tale, the myth therefore lends itself to multiple interpretations, depending on methods of approach, cultural context, and history. Gurdjieff's case, significant from many viewpoints, transcends the conventional readings of the myth, referring to it allusively, as with psychoanalytical, psychological, structural, or socio-historical approaches, giving it a new and innovative dimension. These various approaches and influences were expressed in literary forms by modern writers such as Bely, T. S. Elliot, Joyce, and Yeats.

Gurdjieff's own writings also echo these issues. His major work,

Beelzebub's Tales to His Grandson, corresponds precisely to the various accepted definitions of the myth while at the same time transcending them in that this text is not only a singular work, truly unique in the history of literature and spirituality, but also and above all, a true myth in itself, incorporating and subverting many other myths, among them the biblical myths of Creation, the Fall, Redemption, and Revelation; the myth of Atlantis; the myth of the supremacy of classical Greece with its scientific and philosophical accomplishments; the traditional teachings of Buddha, Moses, Jesus, and Muhammad and the occult and esoteric myths connected with these teachings; and the myths of progress, including Enlightenment, industrialization, Marxism, and Darwinian evolution.[24] Along with his other writings, *Meetings with Remarkable Men* creates the myth of his own life in a form (autobiography) similar to the myth created by Blavatsky for her own personal history. This should be listened to rather than read, if we wish to hear its marvelous echoes. The Gurdjieff case therefore includes the myth of this singular person himself and his cosmogonic and cosmological myth—itself composed of a multitude of underlying submyths (that of the organ Kundabuffer, the philosopher's stone, the myth of the universal language) as well as references to other known myths.

Gurdjieff's myth, in light of the definition given by Mircea Eliade in *Aspect du mythe,* thus recounts a "sacred history" and "relates an event which took place in primordial times, the fabulous times of the beginning." The myth is distinguished by its narrative form, to which it owes a great part of its power of action upon the consciousness of its reader. For Lévi-Strauss, "myths have no author, they are transmitted orally, they live in an anonymous tradition." The transmission therefore takes X number of collective paths, as is again confirmed by the *Beelzebub's Tales to His Grandson,* the crystallization of teachings rooted in oral tradition and synthesized by Gurdjieff. Via this mythic tale on a universal scale, a form common to all great traditions, Gurdjieff gets to the heart of his discoveries—that is, the meaning of human life—all the while fostering and generating the myth simultaneously as his fiction engenders and dynamizes the myth. In *Mythocritique,* Pierre Brunel defines the myth as "a signifier of the most fluctuating things. . . . Myths are true stories responding to a need for explanation or understanding of reality. . . . The myth offers an explanation of the world . . . of the cosmos."[25] Brunel agrees with Eliade, who writes in *Aspect du mythe* that "the myth provides models for human conduct, and thereby confers meaning and value upon existence."[26] Literature must also do this if it is to be useful to us. This is precisely the fundamental task that Gurdjieff imposes with his myth, which is addressed to the totality of humankind. As Charles Duits notes, "the myth is the truth on condition that the myth is good, and Gurdjieff's is splendid."[27]

As Simone Fraisse suggests, if, in the symbolic tale, "men decipher a meaning that stares back at them," it seems clear that if the means put into action are truly effective, this meaning can also connect them with an original and primordial form of knowledge. Gurdjieff's myth is cosmogonic and cosmological, embracing and transcending all the conventional readings of myth. It is hardly surprising, then, that the entirety of his work is entitled *All and Everything* and aims, in keeping with alchemical discipline, for the transmutation of being by means of the evolution of consciousness. Myth—the organization of fictional material assembled from fundamental elements—not only gives meaning to history, but also and above all and under certain previously mentioned conditions, crystallizes the meaning of human life for which it is the depository and guarantor. It not only contains this primal answer, but also offers those who know how to read it the means for achieving their ultimate goal.

In the case of Gurdjieff and from a purely critical point of view, the mythological element is reactivated in the very flesh of the literary text, giving it life and meaning following an esoteric method tested and proved in itself. The mythological element, the image, and the subject receive a singular semantic illumination here while taking part in the foundation and then the theorization of the myth under various aspects. The myth presents the primary base material (subject), which is consciousness or, from another viewpoint, the person itself, along with the structuring function (pattern) that is the quest or situation in which this person is located.

The same is true in the case of René Daumal, for whom the crystallization of the visionary and ascetic experience takes place through entirely singular modes of writing, as Pascal Boué so admirably notes:

> The dreamlike structure of the story in *A Night of Serious Drinking* and the literary processes of sleep and awakening constitute a passage into this mythical writing, exploring Nerval's second life. The use of myths and symbols completes the liberation from all prosaicism and didacticism. This is a matter of revealing, triggering the awakening, but not of teaching—simply indicating a path by means of signs. The use of allegory, analogy, geometric symbolism, and the relativity of space, for example, especially in *Mount Analogue,* allows an escape from what might have been, without the irony Daumal manifests with regard to writing, a strict philosophical treatise.[28]

The writing of myth is part of the recovery of the proper use of the spoken word, the lost word that endures silently in the archetypal symbols and visions of humanity, for as Adam Watts writes in his essay "Zen Buddhism," "every positive declaration concerning ultimate things must be made in the evocative form of a myth or a poem." This, as his essays show, was the exact path chosen by René Daumal. As with Gurdjieff, mythic writing in Daumal's tales breaks down all the barriers, whether they are cultural, linguistic, or philosophical. At the very beginning of *Mount Analogue,* he explains—parodying Eliade's definition of the myth—"my story begins with some unfamiliar handwriting on an envelope." Known myths are told to generate the myth anew. Daumal knew that myths, through their subtle action upon the emotional center, were a means for transmitting a truth: "'[T]hey are as true,' one of [the guides] told us, 'as your own fairy stories and scientific theories.'"[29]

Indeed, these "fabulous tales of the times of the beginning" embody the prodigious application of the powers of speech: Pascal Boué writes, "The myth appears as the model of the active, living, authentic word itself, a full word in contrast with the word that freezes or the arbitrary, relative, prosaic, or empty word. The poetic word is therefore absolutely a mythic and symbolic word."[30] And this word draws its power from a silent asceticism, which works toward the recentering of the being by means of a communion with the source: "The importance of the not-said determines an undertaking of word purification and, to use a medical term, a sort of proximal writing—that is, close to the root or the center, endeavoring to rediscover the original, mythic power of the word. This writing therefore uses symbol and myth very specifically in a sort of writing between the lines."[31] For Daumal, mythic speech and poetic speech combine to access that primordial speech that is the very essence of the proper use that has been lost to mechanical humanity but whose functioning, which gives white poetry all its efficacy and power, has never been forgotten by the initiates.

"I did not speak of the mountain," the author of *Mount Analogue* wrote, "but through the mountain. With this mountain, as with language, I spoke of another mountain, which is the way uniting earth and heaven, and I spoke not to resign myself, but to exhort myself." [32]

In this logic of opening and connection, by means of the holistic myth of the game, let us now revisit all existing myths, whatever form, definition, and properties they may conceal. This singular, syncretic, and holistic approach to studying myths not only renews certain operative and practical theoretical bases (designing new structures), but also, in light of an original, primordial, and pertinent poetics, allows us to envisage and broaden all sciences and religions with new perspectives of research—transcending the common horizontal line that is drawn habitually, extending into the infinite, and moving toward the ultimate goal of all seekers: the meaning of human life.

"The symbols that were used to transmit ideas belonging to objective knowledge included diagrams of the fundamental laws of the universe," Gurdjieff said, "and they not only transmitted the knowledge itself but showed also the way to it."[33] Further, because we are an image (a microcosm) of the universe, through studying ourselves, we will arrive at the understanding of these cosmic laws that are at work everywhere. "Know thyself," in this sense, is an objective aphorism, like those engraved on the Emerald Tablet. As in all approaches aiming toward work on ourselves, will is necessary for understanding:

The transmission of the meaning of symbols to a man who has not reached an understanding of them in himself is impossible. This sounds like a paradox, but the meaning of a symbol and the disclosure of its essence can only be given to, and can only be understood by, one who, so to speak, already knows what is comprised in this symbol. And then a symbol becomes for him a synthesis of his knowledge and serves him for the expression and transmission of his knowledge just as it served the man who constructed it.[34]

Due to this, it is imperative to transcend the dualities that form barriers to understanding. Thus, Gurdjieff notes, "the understanding of duality in oneself begins with the realization of mechanicalness and the realization of the difference between what is mechanical and what is conscious. This understanding must be preceded by the destruction of the self-deceit in which a man lives who considers even his most mechanical actions to be volitional and conscious and himself to be single and whole."[35] Thus, the understanding of symbols is impossible for someone who has not embarked on this holy war so resolutely proclaimed by René Daumal under the impulse of his masters, a war requiring a total investment of the being—and not one that is partial or dualistic. The symbol summoning the "reader's" active participation will never be interpreted fully; "it can only be experienced, in the same way, for instance, as the idea of self-knowledge must be experienced."[36]

The same goes for a system of symbols as already discussed: the Law of Octaves according to which every completed process is a transition of the note *do* through a series of successive tones to the *do* of the next octave. The complete cycle of a process is in fact constituted, as a whole, by ten levels: the seven fundamental tones (expressing the Law of Seven), the two additional shocks (or intervals), and the *do* of the next octave. "The last, the tenth, step," Gurdjieff explains, "is the end of the preceding and the beginning of the next cycle. In this way the Law of Octaves and the process of development it expresses include the numbers 1 to 10. At this point, we come to what may be termed the *symbolism of numbers*."[37] Gurdjieff distinguished various methods of symbolism, together offering a "complicated but more perfect method": numbers, geometric figures, letters, and words (the Kabbalah, for example), but also a "symbology of magic," one of alchemy and one of astrology, as well as the system of the tarot that, according to Gurdjieff, "unites them into one whole."[38]

But these systems of symbols can easily lead us into error, especially when we attempt to interpret them with ordinary language in only a single sense. It is even possible to interpret the symbol as something exactly opposite its true meaning. "The truth," said Gurdjieff, "is again veiled by an outer covering of lies, and to discover it requires immense efforts of negation in which the idea of the symbol itself is lost."[39]

> At the same time the right understanding of symbols cannot lead to dispute. It deepens knowledge, and it cannot remain theoretical because it intensifies the striving towards real results, towards the union of knowledge and being, that is, to Great Doing. Pure knowledge cannot be transmitted, but by being expressed in symbols it is covered by them as by a veil, although at the same time for those who desire and who know how to look this veil becomes transparent.[40]

Gurdjieff also speaks of a "symbolism of speech" that is rarely understood, because it requires a certain level of development, which in turn requires corresponding efforts. Yet we should note that for most "favorites," this higher state of development has already been achieved. This is what Gurdjieff points to elsewhere as the basic lie that impedes all evolution:

> On hearing things which are new for him, instead of making efforts to understand them, a man begins to dispute them, or refute them, maintaining against them an opinion which he considers to be right and which as a rule has no relation whatever to them. In this way he loses all chance of acquiring anything new. To be able to understand speech when it becomes symbolical it is essential to have learned before and to know already how to listen.[41]

Listening is a science, and those who do not master this science are condemned to ever-increasing confusion and error. Once again, nobody can make the necessary efforts for each of us: "All that another can do is to give an individual the impetus to work and from this point of view, symbolism, properly perceived, plays the part of an impetus of this kind for our knowledge."

The same goes for the master symbol of the Fourth Way: The enneagram represents the purest form of the symbol as well as the most significant, the most complete, the most profound, and the most useful in that it expresses the two fundamental cosmic laws, the Law of Three and the Law of Seven.[42] It contains nine elements, nine points, the summation of seven tones (the eighth being a repetition of the first), and two intervals. Therefore, it is a perfect expression of the Law of Octaves. As we saw in the chapter on the Law of Seven, the shocks are positioned, in conformity with the cosmic octave, between *mi* and *fa* and *ti* and *do,* but if we take into account the lateral octaves and the triad, the second shock will appear on the enneagram between *sol* and *la,* which, in appearance alone, seems to contradict the Law of Octaves.[43]

In fact, 3 and 6 correspond to the two shocks, whereas 9 informs us in what way the intervals are to be filled, in that, as Gurdjieff explains, "any phenomenon which is able to act reciprocally with a phenomenon similar to it sounds as the note *do* in a corresponding octave. Therefore, *do* can emerge from its circle and enter into orderly correlation with another circle, that is, play that role in another cycle which, in the cycle under consideration, is played by the 'shocks' filling the 'intervals' in the octave."[44] In other words, the points of the triad appear to inform us of the nature of the shocks to be applied, which seems to be confirmed by this statement:[45] "The apparent placing of the interval in its wrong place itself shows to those who are able to read the symbol what kind of 'shock' is required for the passage of *si* [*ti*] to *do*."[46] Because the shock between *sol* and *la* is not necessary for the progression of the octave, it in fact indicates valuable information for us regarding the nature of the shock to be applied in order to pass to the *do* of the next octave without deviating from the original trajectory.

Moreover, if the enneagram is the master symbol that is drawn repeatedly, this is because it contains all the secrets of the universe. Everything can be explained through it, and those of the Fourth way know how to take advantage of it: "The understanding of this symbol and the ability to make use of it give man very great power. It is perpetual motion and it is also the philosopher's stone of the alchemists."[47]

This, as Paul Valéry writes, is because "[m]yth is the name of all that exists and subsists only in having the word as its cause," which is so valuable to it. It is the very memory of the esoteric word and therefore, naturally, that of the most ancient truths. It is what reconciles the seeker of the truth—the decipherer-pioneer—to a form of knowledge which, by definition, he is seeking.

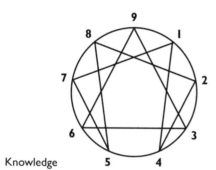

Myths and Symbols

Schuré writes:

> As for us, we poor lost children, who believe that the ideal is the only reality and the only truth in the midst of a changing and fleeting world, who believe in the sanction and fulfillment of its promises both in the history of humanity and in future life, who know that this sanction is necessary, that it is the reward of human brotherhood as the reason of the universe and the logic of God, for we who have this conviction, there is only one side to take: We must affirm this truth without fear and as strongly as possible; we must

throw ourselves, for it and with it, into the arena of action, into that chaotic fray. By way of individual meditation and initiation, we must try to penetrate into the temple of immutable ideas, there to arm ourselves with infrangible principles.[48]

Another practice is related to this secret search for knowledge: chemical ecstasy—popular among the earliest peoples, but more discreet in industrialized civilizations with regard to its "religious" usage. Timothy Leary tried to popularize it despite the reservations of Aldous Huxley, Gordon Wasson, and others who knew that such experiences— the ambivalence of which needs no further proof—were absolutely not to be recommended for everyone. At the heart of many mysteries, myths, and initiations such as the rites of Eleusis, the philosophical substance is a true myth, a chemical initiation to the other world in this world. The initiates have not forgotten its use or the interest that these kinds of fundamental experiences—"elicited mysticism" for James, "experimental metaphysics" for Daumal, "applied mysticism" for Huxley, "scientific yoga" for Leary—can hold for those whose quest is the meaning of human life.

11
The Psychedelic Powers of the Word

Language and Modified States of Consciousness

A special vocabulary is needed for describing all the characteristics of a divining substance and the qualities of radically new states of consciousness.

GORDON WASSON

In the quest for the proper use of the spoken word, few seekers have remarked upon the importance of the ecstatic experience and of modified states of consciousness. Yet there are numerous strong connections joining language and its powers to these types of experiences in which shamanic knowledge predominates.[1] Poetry is divining and magical and, like magic, black or white. In this "savage" approach to consciousness, where mystery reigns as king of the profane, magic reigns as queen for the initiate. Often enough, in order to say, know, or do, we must no longer look (with the eyes) but see (with the entire being) and

231

understand what we have seen. Such is the nature of modified states of consciousness. In the great vortex of ecstasy, only the well-informed consciousness will find its truth amid the racket of sounds, the hammering of words, and the rapidity of rhythms.

Parallel to the great ethnobotanical discoveries begun by various scientists in the early twentieth century, which held crucial interest for the progress of psychedelic research, others began an experimental search for the knowledge that would secretly reveal the foundations of a teaching that had, until then, remained unknown to Westerners.

Shamanic knowledge, ancestral among the earliest peoples, was opened little by little to an atrophied West in search of spiritual experiences. Thus, the knowledge of medicinal plants in relation to the inner journey and the practice of introspection became more and more widespread, especially in the 1960s and 1970s. Apart from notorious extreme behaviors and all manner of excesses brought about simply by the ignorance of the users, numerous testimonies have supplied the quest for consciousness with evidence for the existence of "techniques of applied mysticism" that can, in just a few hours, lead us to see degrees of reality previously invisible to ordinary perception.

René Daumal's experiences, although extremely dangerous, are highly significant in this regard. In 1922, at his school in Reims, a group began to form in the eighth grade class. It was organized by four boys—Roger Gilbert-Lecomte, Robert Meyrat, Roger Vaillant, and René Daumal—obsessed by existential questions and inspired by the texts of censured poets. The four Phrères,* as they called themselves, assumed poetic nicknames and lived on the fringes of the bourgeois reality of the times. They began to experiment with the substances most easily available to them, such as carbon tetrachloride and ether, welding their friendship in the fire of experience.

Nevertheless, their approach to intoxicants was never on the same order as modern usage, especially regarding narcotics, which are now generally used recreationally or as a consequence of social malaise. The

---

*[An altered spelling of the French *frères,* "brothers." —*Trans.*]

young men's quest was solely metaphysical, and their goal was to attain an ultimate form of understanding. In 1924, the small group, then in the equivalent of eleventh grade, smoked opium with an opiomaniac bibliophile.[2] They founded an ephemeral literary magazine, *Apollo,* and developed a sort of philosophical doctrine which they called *simplism,* endeavoring to reconcile a certain degree of childhood nostalgia and a revolt against the rational exercises of thought and language. There were doubtless also some influences from the Dada and surrealist movements. Here is the definition Daumal gave to another student, Maurice Henry, in order to satisfy his curiosity: "Simplists. No meaning to seek in the word. Perhaps, however, there is some analogy to the state of childhood we seek—a state in which everything is simple and easy. Evident: evasion—evidently . . . that which voids before me = to evade it. The facility for which we strive is what the theologians call grace. . . . It is for this slithering on our backs toward a swirling of souls that we love the surrealists—just like opium."[3] Daumal—who would later revise his opinion on these points—explained to his correspondent a month later how to access this inner simplification advocated by the group: "First seek the most unconsciousness state possible, for example putting your intellect to sleep. (Opium and other drugs are the proper means for achieving this; but this is the answer to another of your questions, which must be discussed at greater length.)"[4]

If drugs played a predominant role for the group that would found *Le Grand Jeu,* this aspect of their quest has been thought of as minor by some specialists in the area, considering that "when *Le Grand Jeu* appeared in 1928, it had already . . . passed out of its experimental phase."[5] The group's dispersion halted all collective activity, and drug use then corresponded to the differing motivations of the individuals: Daumal very soon stopped his "toxic" experiments, trying in vain to persuade Roger Gilbert-Lecomte to do the same, while Roger Vaillant remained hooked on opium, cocaine, and heroin until the end of his life, though his work never crystallized his experiences. Gilbert-Lecomte's work, by contrast, explored unceasingly the question of the relationship between drugs and literary creation. Meyrat, for his part, never wrote anything.

Be that as it may, these experiences nurtured the doctrines developed in *Le Grand Jeu,* which were organized into three major themes: the process of rationalism, the search for the "absolute word," and the rediscovery of the religious fact in its pure state. Language was to recover its original power and poetry its value as a spiritual exercise through seeking to experiment with the "notion of souls, salvation, and initiation," if only in passing—as Rimbaud recommended in his *Letters of the Visionary*— through experimenting with "all forms of love, suffering, and folly" and through the famous "derangement of all the senses." In these limited experiences and this "experimental metaphysics,"and haunted by the idea of death, Daumal and Lecomte sought a total annihilation of consciousness, a violent alteration that might perhaps contain some ultimate truth of human existence.[6] This had nothing to do with any kind of hedonistic search for artificial paradises, as has been the case for numerous writers and addicts since the age of Romanticism. Instead, this working upon the consciousness was a quest for the profound meaning of human life, as William James had done a few years previously.

In issue 4 of *Le Grand Jeu,* René Daumal explains how the inhalation of carbon tetrachloride (used to kill and preserve insects)[7] allowed him to move from fairly banal sensations into metaphysical clarity: "At a certain moment, the rhythm became so rapid that I could no longer follow it, and suddenly I recognized the truth I had always known; I woke up to this truth. With an obviousness, a clarity of which I cannot convey the least idea, so unknown is this character of certainty or absolute necessity to normal human thought, I understood the appalling meaning of this visual and sonorous movement, despairing at its simplicity and its obviousness."[8] At the beginning of the experience, there was the auditory hallucination of the noise of a motor and the perception of phosphenes arranging themselves into geometric figures, moving "according to a strict but geometrically absurd law," while the noise, along with the accelerated rhythm of the blood in his arteries, forced him to pronounce an unpronounceable word, *"temgouf temgouf drr . . ."*[9] At this moment, the "absurd obviousness" took the form of a truth that revealed to him, with a determining certainty (for him, the "archetype of precision"), the fact that something else truly existed beyond the appearances of ordinary consciousness:

The only part of this experience that can still be thought and formulated in my ordinary state is this—though they'll have my head off for it: I had the certainty of the existence of something else, something beyond, another world or a kind of knowledge; and, at this moment, I knew directly, I perceived this beyond reality itself. It is important to repeat that in this new state, I perceived and understood the ordinary state very well, the one being contained in the other, as the waking person understands dreams, and not the other way round. This irreversible relationship proved the superiority (on the scale of reality or consciousness) of the second state over the first.[10]

As he writes in 1943, Daumal knew that testimonies existed of similar experiences during which the consciousness opened to other levels of reality or, rather, to "a single and same reality"[11]—a fundamental nuance! We are reminded of Pascal, "of the revelation of the divine being in the Bhagavad Gita, of the visions of Ezekiel and St. John of Patmos, of the Tibetan Book of the Dead . . ."[12]

This almost primordial experience—close to the state of death, according to Daumal—should not require the use of drugs. He was convinced that drugs were only a shortcut, allowing us to alter our consciousness more rapidly and in a particularly radiant manner. This is why the magazine did not further insist on the use of intoxicants; Daumal was convinced that the use of drugs was, ultimately and paradoxically, a hindrance to this quest for consciousness: "This is why the possibility for man of such an experience as that of which I speak is entirely contradictory to a taste for intoxicants."[13] Conscious of the existence of a fundamental reality, Daumal was certain that other, non-chemical paths could also allow us to achieve these different levels of consciousness—with much less risk to our health. Fascinated by the sacred texts of India (due to René Guénon's discovery), this idea was confirmed for him in his initiation to Asian doctrines. As for Roger Gilbert-Lecomte, heroin ruled him, although his addiction was not devoid of an individual consciousness that led him to a remarkable literary production—divergent, however, from Daumal's approach.[14]

All too conscious of the danger of his chemical experiments and parallel to his studies of Sanskrit and ancient Indian texts, Daumal continued to seek the truth that obsessed him so greatly. It was in this way that he encountered Alexandre de Salzmann, who ultimately showed him the door into the meaningful and salvational world he had sought all along: "See, here is an open door—narrow and hard to access, but a door—and it is the only one for you."[15] This decisive step, this great turnaround, took place at the end of 1930, giving him "hope and a reason for living": At the age of twenty-two, René Daumal encountered Mr. Gurdjieff and the teaching of the strange and *charismatic*—in the most etymological sense of the word, having a "unique gift conferred by divine grace." And though the door was (and fundamentally is) narrow, Daumal had all the qualities necessary for passing through it.

Although, after his meeting with Alexandre de Salzmann, Daumal gave up the chemical experiments he had undertaken for *Le Grand Jeu,* he still preserved a "determining memory" of them in his quest for consciousness. His experience with carbon tetrachloride had left him with the conviction of the existence of something else, which he would unceasingly pursue until his death.

He had penetrated into the fundamental and superior reality shared by all great mystics and visionaries: He had *seen,* and, like Jacob after his battle with the angel and just like all those who venture into the ambivalent spheres of chemical ecstasy, he was destined forever to bear the mark of this encounter. As those of us who risk it must know, the conviction that results from this seeing drives us to regain this higher state of consciousness permanently, through a spiritual work whose goal and scope we have been able to perceive briefly through experimentation. As Jean-Yves Pouilloux wrote, those who have had "the experience of an unforeseen, startling upsurge, of the present in the present . . . have had the privilege of sustaining a rip in the continuous fabric of their days, experiencing a rupture like a jump from one level to another, and through this rupture, sensing the brilliance of the glory of the world, albeit briefly. But also, they have had the patience and disposition to welcome it, to receive it, gather it, and bear witness to it."[16]

William James (1842–1910), a philosopher and psychologist, was the first seeker to become interested in the effects of certain substances upon the brain and upon elicited mysticism. At Harvard, he began the tradition of research on altered states of mind (founding the psychology department there) and shocked the academic community with his experiments with peyote and nitrous oxide (laughing gas). In *On the Varieties of Religious Experience*, he showed how certain drugs allowed us to access important levels of intelligence, obliterated by the narrowness of the conditioned spirit: ". . . drunkenness expands, unites, and says yes. It is in fact the great exciter of the YES function in man. It brings its votary from the chill periphery of things to the radiant core. It makes him for the moment one with truth."[17]

James was one of the first to demonstrate that certain substances such as nitrous oxide and ether, with which he experimented himself, "stimulate the mystical consciousness in an extraordinary degree," and was one of the first to believe that although "This truth fades out . . . at the moment of coming to . . . the sense of a profound meaning having been there persists . . ." This ecstasy approaches "a genuine metaphysical revelation."[18] His conclusions on states of consciousness are precursors by several decades of the reflections that would be developed in the 1960s: "Our normal waking consciousness . . . is but one special type of consciousness, whilst all about it, parted from it by the filmiest of screens, there lie potential forms of consciousness entirely different. We may go through life without suspecting their existence; but apply the requisite stimulus, and at a touch they are there in all their completeness."[19] It was no coincidence that James was one of the main authors read by Timothy Leary in the 1960s at the advice of Frank Baron! Nor is it surprising that James, in *The Will to Believe* (1897), invites readers to travel with him as he relates his experiences with nitrous oxide:

> I strongly urge others to repeat the experiment, which with pure gas is short and harmless enough. The effects will of course vary with the individual, just as they vary in the same individual from time to time. . . . With me, as with every other person of whom I have

heard, the keynote of the experience is the tremendously exciting sense of an intense metaphysical illumination. Truth lies open to the view in depth beneath depth of almost blinding evidence.[20]

There are so many accounts telling of this plunging into the layers of our reality that together they satisfy the criteria of objectivity and authenticity. What is important in approaching these testimonies is that we always evaluate the degree of truth that emerges from them while seeking ever more to understand what truly takes place. "We must take care not to let the words run away, for some would surely slip on the newly cleared paths,"[21] writes Philippe Jaccottet in *La Promenade sous les arbres,* examining the visions described by the poet Georges Russell. Further, as Jean-Yves Pouilloux writes, "For in the writing itself, it is a matter of a deliberate and vigilant exercise of reticence—a fascinating term evoking a limit between speech and silence, a restraint that still gives way to the necessity to say, that speaks while being silent."[22]

The comparative approach is an effective tool, because it allows us to form connections, to build bridges between the varieties of experience, which permits us to derive easily verifiable constants through experimentation. We have mentioned James and Daumal, but we can also include Aldous Huxley, Henri Michaux, Charles Duits, Alan Watts, and Timothy Leary, to name only a few of those whose rigorous studies provide further proof of the validity of these kinds of experiences. Moreover, it is no accident that these substances lay at the heart of the mysteries of ancient rituals such as those of Eleusis, in which the adepts, like Plato, drank the famous *kykeon,* thanks to which they saw God.

These testimonies, easily verifiable in light of experience, prove the legitimacy of this means of express access to knowledge—though again, we must have the disposition—the requisite abilities for receiving this enlightening brilliance. Gurdjieff himself told Ouspensky of the potential value of this experimental research:

There are schools which make use of narcotics in the right way. People in these schools take them for self-study; in order to take a look ahead, to know their possibilities better, to see beforehand, "in advance," what can be attained later on as the result of prolonged work. When a man sees this and is convinced that what he has learned theoretically really exists, he then works consciously, he knows where he is going. Sometimes this is the easiest way of being convinced of the real existence of those possibilities which man often suspects in himself. There is a special chemistry relating to this. There are particular substances for each function. Each function can either be strengthened or weakened, awakened or put to sleep. But to do this a great knowledge of the human machine and of this special chemistry is necessary. In all those schools which make use of this method experiments are carried out only when they are really necessary and only under the direction of experienced and competent men who can foresee all results and adopt measures against possible undesirable consequences.[23]

While advising against the dangers of uncontrolled use, Gurdjieff maintained the distinction between transcendental experiences induced by drugs and those brought about by work. Many times, he mentioned his own version of the scientific method and practice, speaking of a special chemistry that could be used for maneuvering the human machine. For his part, Ouspensky described his own study of narcotics in his *New Model of the Universe* (1931), in a chapter entitled Experimental Mysticism. Although he does not state what substance(s) he used, his biographer, James Webb, believes he used hashish and nitrous oxide.[24] Ouspensky also mentions his interest in achieving other states of consciousness before abandoning his experiments, concluding that although they were useful, he found himself facing "the impossibility of conveying the impressions of the living world in the language of the dead."[25]

Even if Gurdjieff appears to state many justified reservations regarding narcotics, the fact remains that with well-mastered use, a "little pill" can act as a philosophical substance and thus as a shortcut, because the Fourth Way, we must not forget, is the way of the sly man in which the ends justify the means:

But on the fourth way knowledge is still more exact and perfect. A man who follows the fourth way knows quite definitely what substances he needs for his aims and he knows that these substances can be produced within the body by a month of physical suffering, by a week of emotional strain, or by a day of mental exercises—and also, that they can be introduced into the organism from without if it is known how to do it. And so, instead of spending a whole day in exercises like the yogi, a week in prayer like the monk, or a month in self-torture like the fakir, he simply prepares and swallows a little pill which contains all the substances he wants and, in this way, without loss of time, he obtains the required results.[26]

Along the path of mystical experience, many apply themselves to the way of the shortcut. Charles Duits legitimizes the well-mastered use of unlimiters in order to liberate ourselves from what prevents us from seeing: "In order to heal, we have the right and indeed the duty to resort to all imaginable subterfuges. . . . The object of all asceticism is to bring about an enlightenment and to draw the spirit out of its cosmic sleep. From this perspective—absolutely different from that of the West, as we can see—we cannot *a priori* consider the man guilty who uses unlimiters of consciousness, as long as awakening is the goal of his research."[27] What is legitimate here is the will to experiment with other levels of consciousness that permit or facilitate an access to a new understanding, a new perception of what is real, a new perception of others and of ourselves, as well as an access to the hidden possibilities of man and to elevation and, as Michael Camus calls it, the "vertical growth of consciousness." This spiritual approach is also justified by Alan Watts, who defends the use of unlimiters, proclaiming that "those who want to study the mind of man must have the right to use them." But these are only ambivalent tools and are in no way an end in themselves. It is absurd to confuse the moon with the finger that points to it.

Michel Waldberg gives some fundamental clarifications concerning what Gurdjieff meant by *narcotics*—a word belonging more to Ouspensky's language than that of Gurdjieff: "There are substances that yogis take to induce certain states. Might these not, in certain cases, be narcotics?" To the student's question, the master responded: "In many cases these substances are those which you call *narcotics* . . ."[28] implying the use of other substances that allow for a rapid access to knowledge, as Waldberg confirms: "These narcotics could be for example the *iboga* of the Africans, the peyote of the Indians, substances that Charles Duits would have called 'illuminators of consciousness' or, to paraphrase the disparaging nature of the accepted terminology, 'lucidogens.'"[29] Waldberg might have added ayahuasca, *Psilocybe* mushrooms, *olioluqui, Salvia divinorum,* and even LSD—in other words, the substances known as *psychedelic* ("revealing the mind") and *entheogenic* ("generating the divine in oneself"), modifying the consciousness in order to make it receptive to other levels of reality in which the divine presence lies:

> I do not becomes something else when I eat the bitter stuff; I become myself. The black period is black precisely because I fear losing myself. It ends when I discover that the opposite occurs. I do not lose myself; I lose my limitations. Sometimes the loss is dramatic: if I believe that these limitations (aberrant convictions, scientific or philosophical or conformist ideas) are my personality. It is sublime if I understand that I am in my innermost heart the Tao, God, the One without a second, the Void, the Brahman, Tathagata—and all the intermediary states of consciousness and the infrahuman states as well.[30]

We are the victim of considerations, identifications, and acquired knowledge, which dampen the essence (our own, our truth) and inflate the personality (not our own)[31] putting the whole being out of balance. The true *"I"*—which can grow only from our essence—is smothered and annihilated by the other little *"I"*s (the fruit of education, culture, and imitation). A substance, then, can be used to make the clear distinction between essence and personality and to sense the fragmentation and dissolution of the *"I"*s:

> There exists a possibility of experimental verification of the relation of personality to essence. In Eastern schools, ways and

means are known by the help of the possibiliy of separating man's personality from his essence. For this purpose, they sometimes use hypnosis, sometimes special narcotics, sometimes certain kinds of exercises. . . . Certain narcotics have the property of putting the personality to sleep without affecting essence, and for a certain time after taking this narcotic, a man's personality disappears, as it were, and only his essence remains.[32]

Thus investigators find their child's view relieved (for a while, at least) of the dross that makes up their personality, their social mask, the fruit of the exterior influences that have formatted them over the years. Initiated to the joys of mescaline, Aldous Huxley writes in *The Doors of Perception*: "I was seeing what Adam had seen on the morning of his creation—the miracle, moment by moment, of naked existence."[33] Also, it appears equally clear that some people, after having ingested an unlimiter of consciousness, reveal themselves to be completely empty—or, alternatively, that they turn out to be fully developed, which is quite rare, considering that "the development of essence depends on work on oneself." Ouspensky adds, "Essence has more chances of development in men who live nearer to nature in difficult conditions of constant struggle and danger."[34] These are exactly the conditions in which a shaman exists. He lives in mountains and forests and communicates with spirits by ingesting the sacramental plants mentioned here. As a master of ecstasy (he is the perfect archetype of it), the shaman has the competence that allows him to guide those who go adventuring in the spheres of their inner world.

The psychedelic experience involves a clear experiential distinction between knowing and feeling (knowledge and understanding), but also between seeing and looking. "We rarely see what we look at. Man is a personality full of prejudices. There are two kinds of prejudices: One kind comes from the essence, the other comes from the personality. Man knows nothing; he lives under authority, he accepts all influences and believes in them. We know nothing."[35] We are blinded by our prejudices, passions, and desires. We are content to look at things passively, but we do not see them. We think and imagine, but we see nothing. Yet objective speech—drawing its force from the essence—is a matter of seeing, not of looking, because it sees farther than the eye.

Lucidogenic substances therefore allow us to see what we only look at habitually; they allow us to "feel," as Charles Duits writes, "that which we ordinarily only know." A true conciliatory force, these substances, in addition to breaking down our conditioning, allow us brilliant access to higher levels of consciousness, rebalancing what Ouspensky called "the lines of knowledge and being."[36] Indeed, the philosophical substance, that honest mirror, allows us to pull back the masks that ordinarily cover our face, facilitating the hunting of lies and revealing to those who ingest it, those things that we do our best to hide or ignore habitually. In a chapter entitled Hasnamuss (let those who can, understand), Charles Duits writes:

> . . . Peyote not only gave me the power to see myself as I truly was; it not only delivered me from insidious and almost involuntary complacencies—from that light, impalpable, but impenetrable mask that we put on instinctively every day when we come face to face with our reflection; a mask that allows us to believe that we are a little of what we want to be all the same; that despite everything, things are not so bad; that we are not truly at risk of becoming the horrible clowns that in fact we already are and became long ago. . . . Peyote gave me not only the power to see, but also the courage to see.[37]

We should note that many experimenters do not actually explain the inner mechanism set in motion by the absorption of lucidogens. For some, the knowledge resulting from it is inner knowledge, generated by the brain, while for others, especially for Mexican and Amazonian shamans, this knowledge comes from outside, from the plant itself, which conveys the information. If this is a difficult distinction to tackle, it is nevertheless obvious that the receptivity produced during the experience is facilitated by the expansion of consciousness. Yet in light of the teachings, especially the functioning of the centers, it is possible to gain a somewhat greater understanding of the phenomenon. According to Gurdjieff, mystical ecstasy is brought about when the investigator accesses the higher centers, however briefly.[38] In fact, the higher centers (unlike the lower centers) are fully developed within us and yet are inaccessible by ordinary means. Due to them, however, the powers hidden within us can be developed. Hence the necessity for a proper use of the lower centers, which alone—in correlation with a powerful elevation of our level of consciousness—will allow access to the higher emotional and intellectual centers. But if only work on ourselves permits us to attain a sufficient, durable, and stable degree of mastery, then these mystical and visionary states—the consequence, as Gurdjieff teaches us, of "a temporary connection with a higher center"—may manifest for brief moments through particular narcotics.[39]

If the lower centers are malfunctioning or if we make improper use of them or if the higher centers are inaccessible to us, it is because we are overrun by negative thoughts, sensations, and emotions that we have not managed to control—and this is because we do not remember ourselves, because everything in us is mechanical. Each center must be restored to its proper task in order for it to be effective, and this must take place without loss of energy. But we should note that in order to function correctly, they must also be fed by a particular "combustible substance," known as hydrogen. "What is necessary to understand, and what the table of hydrogens helps us to grasp," Gurdjieff declares, "is the idea of the complete materiality of all the psychic, intellectual, emotional, volitional, and other inner processes, including the most exalted poetic inspirations, religious ecstasies, and mystical revelations."[40]

The table of hydrogens helps us to understand that all reactions are material, originating from matter—from the "foods" (including the staples of air and received impressions) that enter the organism, which obviously must be transformed subtly through an appropriate (alchemical) work. Religious psychedelic ecstasies are an example of this and are marvelous and highly unique because they arise spontaneously and rapidly after the absorption of a very specialized food ("particular narcotics," as Gurdjieff said). Is there, then, a relationship (and if so, what kind) between the effect produced by the combustion of hydrogen 6 and 12 (fueling the higher centers) and the effect produced by the absorption of what the shamans call the "food of the gods"?

We have already mentioned the various states of consciousness accessible to us. The higher levels correspond naturally to the use of the higher centers. In other words, active substances can allow those of us who live in the state of sleep or drowsy quiescence to access momentarily ("relative glimmerings of consciousness") the state of self-consciousness or objective consciousness in order to perceive and feel its reality. It is also obvious that those of us who live in the state of self-remembering will gain a much greater benefit from this type of experience than those who live under the influence of ordinary, separative consciousness. It is a question of predisposition, but for those who live in the state of objective consciousness, the highest state accessible to us, no chemical is necessary, because they continuously see reality as it truly is.

Speech, just like sacred medicine, forms the basis of the shamanic path in that it permits us not only to see but also to do. Ethnobotany, the science that studies man as a function of his relationship to the plants around him, offers us new paths of reflection, explaining our relationship to language from a new angle that reconsiders all human evolution in a single movement. It now appears clear that the greatest power of the shaman, that master of ecstasy, resides in his mastery of the magic word stimulated by the ingestion of modifiers of consciousness.

For the shaman, language produces reality, our world being made of language. Terence McKenna, in his revolutionary endeavor to rethink human evolution, shows how plants have been able to influence the development of humans and animals.[41] He explains why farming and the domestication of animals as livestock were a great step forward in our cultural evolution: It was at this moment, according to him, that we were able to come into contact with the *Psilocybe* mushroom, which grows on and around dung. He supports the idea that "mutation-causing, psychoactive chemical compounds in the early human diet directly influenced the rapid reorganization of the brain's information-processing capacities."[42] Further, because "thinking about human evolution ultimately means thinking about the evolution of human consciousness," he supports the thesis that psychedelic plants "may well have synergized the emergence of language and religion."[43]

Studies undertaken by Fischer have shown that weak doses of psilocybin can improve certain types of mental performance while making the investigator more aware of the real world. McKenna distinguishes three degrees of effects of psilocybin: improvement of visual acuity, increase of sexual excitation, and, at higher doses, "certainly . . . religious concerns would be at the forefront of the tribe's consciousness, simply because of the power and strangeness of the experience itself."[44] Because "the psilocybin intoxication is a rapture whose breadth and depth is the despair of prose," it is entirely clear to McKenna that shamanic ecstasy, characterized by its "boundary-dissolving qualities," played a crucial role in the evolution of human consciousness, which, according to him, can be attributed to "psilocybin's remarkable property of stimulating the language-forming capacity of the brain." Indeed, "[i]ts power is so extraordinary that psilocybin can be considered the catalyst to the human development of language."[45] In response to the neo-Darwinist objection, McKenna states that "the presence of psilocybin in the hominid diet changed the parameters of the process of natural selection by changing the behavioral patterns upon which that selection was operating," and that "the augmentation of visual acuity, language use, and ritual activity through the use of psilocybin represented new behaviors."[46]

Be that as it may, it is undeniable that the unlimiters of consciousness, as Charles Duits calls them, have a real impact upon linguistic activity in that they strongly stimulate the emergence of speech. If, according to McKenna's theories, "psilocybin inclusion in the diet shifted the parameters of human behavior in favor of patterns of activity that promoted increased language," resulting in "more vocabulary and an expanded memory capacity,"[47] then it seems obvious that the birth of poetry, literature, and all the arts came about ultimately through the fantastic encounter between humans and the magic mushroom—a primordial plant, the "umbilical cord linking us to the feminine spirit of the planet," and thence, inevitably, to poetry. Rich in behavioral and evolutionary consequences, the mushroom, in its dynamic relationship to the human being, propelled us toward higher cultural levels developing parallel to self-reflection.[48]

This in no way means that this level of consciousness is inherent in all people, but it must be observed that the experience in itself leads to a gaining of consciousness which, in order to be preserved and maintained, requires rigorous and well-directed work on ourselves. This being said, the experience allows us to observe this action in ourselves in order to endeavor to understand its subtle mechanisms. Terence McKenna writes,

> Of course, imagining these higher states of self-reflection is not easy. For when we seek to do this we are acting as if we expect language to somehow encompass that which is, at present, beyond language, or translinguistic. Psilocybin, the hallucinogen unique to mushrooms, is an effective tool in this situation. Psilocybin's main synergistic effect seems ultimately to be in the domain of language. It excites vocalization; it empowers articulation; it transmutes language into something that is visibly beheld. It could have had an impact on the sudden emergence of consciousness and language use in early humans. We literally may have eaten our way to higher consciousness.[49]

If we espouse this hypothesis, then speaking means evoking and repeating the primordial act of eating the sacred medicine. Ethnobotanists insist upon the role of the human brain in the accomplishment of this process, pinpointing precisely the relevant area of activity, which, in Gurdjieffian terms, is located in the center of gravity of the intellectual center: "Our capacity for cognitive and linguistic activity is related to the size and organization of the human brain. . . . The most recently evolved areas of the human brain, Broca's area and the neocortex, are devoted to the control of symbol and language processing."[50] It thus appears that these are the areas of the brain that have allowed for the emergence of language and culture. Yet McKenna adds, "our linguistic abilities must have evolved in response to enormous evolutionary pressures," though we do not know the nature of these pressures. According to him, it is this "immense power to manipulate symbols and language" that "gives us our unique position in the natural world."[51] This is obvious, in that speech and consciousness, inextricably linked, are solely the property of humans. Thus it seems logical that the plants known as psychoactive must have been the catalysts "for everything about us that distinguishes us from other higher primates, for all the mental functions that we associate with humanness,"[52] with the primary position being held by language, "the most unique of human activities," and the catalyst for poetic and literary activity.

Under the influence of an unlimiter, we have the incontrovertible impression that language possesses an objectified and visible dimension that is ordinarily hidden from our awareness. Under such conditions, language is seen and beheld just as we would ordinarily see our homes and normal surroundings. In fact, during the experience of the altered state, our ordinary cultural environment is recognized correctly as the bass drone in the ongoing linguistic business of objectifying the imagination. In other words, the collectively designed cultural environment in which we all live is the objectification of our collective linguistic intent.

> Our language-forming ability may have become active through the mutagenic influence of hallucinogens working directly on organelles that are concerned with the processing and generation of signals. These neural substructures are found in various portions of the brain, such as Broca's area, that govern speech formation. In other words, opening the valve that limits consciousness forces utterance, almost as if the word is a concretion of meaning previously felt but left unarticulated. This active impulse to speak, the "going forth of the word," is sensed and described in the cosmogonies of many peoples.

Psilocybin specifically activates the areas of the brain concerned with processing signals. *A common occurrence with psilocybin intoxication is spontaneous outbursts of poetry* and other vocal activity such as speaking in tongues, though in a manner distinct from ordinary glossolalia. In cultures with a tradition of mushroom use, these phenomenons have given rise to the notion of discourse with spirit doctors and supernatural allies. Researchers familiar with the territory agree that psilocybin has a profoundly catalytic effect on the linguistic impulse.[53]

Here we are touching upon the higher powers of speech—spontaneous creations, outbursts of poetry and suprahuman communications—which are part of the knowledge of the shamans and "sorcerers" who, through years of rigorous education, have become highly perceptive of these phenomena, which elude the subjective consciousness. In his essay "The Mushrooms of Language," Henry Munn points to the direct links existing between the states of ecstasy and language: "Language is an ecstatic activity of signification. Intoxicated by the mushrooms, the fluency, the ease, the aptness of expression one becomes capable of are such that one is astounded by the words that issue forth from the contact of the intention of articulation with the matter of experience. . . . The spontaneity they liberate is not only perceptual, but linguistic . . . For the shaman, it is as if existence were uttering itself through him."[54]

In the 1920s, the Polish writer S. I. Witkiewicz, who attributed crucial importance to verbal creation, showed how peyote (he was one of the first people in Europe to experiment with it, or, at least, one of the first to give an account of doing so) acts upon the actual creation of words and also intervenes in the structure of sentences themselves: ". . . [I]t must also be remarked that peyote, perhaps by reason of the desire one has to capture with words that which cannot be captured, creates conceptual neologisms that belong to it alone and twists sentences in order to adapt their constructions to the frightening dimensions of its bizarrification . . ."[55] Peyote also gives those who ingest it a desire to create "new combinations of meanings." Witkiewicz distinguishes three categories of objects in his visions: dead objects, moving objects, and living creatures. Regarding this last category, he distinguishes the "real" living creatures from the "fantastical" living creatures, which "discourage any attempt at description." This is the moment when peyote intervenes: when those who wish to describe find themselves facing the limits of language. Peyote does not break through these limits; it simply shows that they do not exist, that they are hallucinations of the ordinary consciousness, that they are illusory, a mirage of tradition and the history of language.

The lucidogen—as it is called by Charles Duits, who created other neologisms for describing his experience with the sacred cactus—shows that life is present in everything, including speech, and he proves it. Sometimes, peyote leads us to the signifiers that escape us, always in order better to embrace the signified. Witkiewicz, pushing the phenomenon to the extreme limits of the senses and the sensible, insists:

> I must draw attention to the fact that under the influence of peyote, one wants to make up neologisms. One of my friends, the most normal man in the world where language is concerned, in a state of trance and powerless to come to grips with the strangeness of these visions which defied all combinations of normal words, described them thus: *"Pajtrakaly symforove i kondjioul v trykrentnykh pordeliansach."* I devised many formulas of this type on the night when I went to bed besieged by visions. I remember only this one. There is therefore nothing surprising in the fact that I, who have such inclinations even under normal conditions, should sometimes be driven to create some fancy word in order to attempt to disentangle and sort out the infernal vortex of creatures that unfurled upon me all night long from the depths of the ancient world of peyote.[56]

Here, we cannot help but remember René Daumal's experience, reported in "Le souvenir déterminant": Under the influence of carbon tetrachloride, he pronounced with difficulty: "approximately: *temgouf temgouf drr* . . ." Henry Munn makes a similar remark after having taken part in shamanic rituals: "The mushroom session of language creates the words for phenomena without name."[57] Sacred plants (and some other substances) are *neologens,* meaning they produce or generate neologisms from the attempts made at description by the subjects who consume them. This new word, this neologism created by circumstance, appears to be suited for this linguistic reality. We now have a word to designate this particular phenomenon pushing us against the limits of language, which in fact are revealed to be illusory.

Beyond this specific case, what is it that prevents us from creating new words whenever it appears necessary? Witkiewicz, speaking of language and life, defends the writer's right to take liberties with the rules and invent new words. "Although certain professors insist on clinging to their own tripe," he writes, "language is a living thing, even if it has always been considered a mummy, even if it has been thought impermissible to change anything in it. We can only imagine what literature, poetry, and even this accursed and beloved life would look like otherwise."[58] Peyote not only incites us to this, but also, more forcefully, exercising a mysterious magnetic attraction toward a sort of supreme meaning beyond language and shaking up conventional signifiers and beings alike, peyote acts directly upon the heart of speech within the body of language. In this sense, it takes part actively and favorably in the creation of the being, the new and infinitely renewed human who, after a death that is more than symbolic, is reborn to new life. It is also very clear, in light of this example, that psilocybin alone does not explain everything, and that all lucidogenic substances work toward this same opening, this same outpouring of speech. McKenna writes:

> Languages appear invisible to the people who speak them, yet they create the fabric of reality for their users. The problem of mistaking language for reality in the everyday world is only too well known. Plant use is an example of a complex language of chemical and social interactions. Yet most of us are unaware of the effects of plants on ourselves and our reality, partly because we have forgotten that plants have always mediated the human cultural relationship to the world at large.[59]

The approach depending on the level of the speakers—the concept of relativity—confirms the idea that languages create the fabric of reality. For those who are part of mechanical humanity, reality will not have the same consistency and the same meaning as for someone who is a member of esoteric circles because the use of speech reflects the perception we have of ourselves and of the universe and because, consequently, not all people can live on the same level of reality. Subjective perception and consciousness has subjective speech, and therefore subjective reality. It cannot be otherwise.

Consider, by contrast, the healing powers of speech, the perfect archetype of which is represented by Jesus' "arise, take up thy bed." Likewise, when the shaman chants or beats his drum, he knows what he is doing and why he is doing it: in order to heal, for the shamanic paroxysm is the mastery of the powers of speech acting upon all the centers of being. "The psychoanalyst listens, whereas the shaman speaks," Lévi-Strauss notes.

Among the Huichol Indians, the *mara'akame,* the priest-shaman, often performs two closely linked functions: He is the singer and the healer. In order to become an expert in sacred things, a master of mystical ecstasy, the future shaman must be initiated to the powers possessed by speech: "Before receiving their official consecration, the future priest-shamans must have assisted the mara'akame in the mythological songs and evocations that take place during the feasts."[60] Sounds are of essential, invocatory importance, as is confirmed by the *curandero,* who "cracks the joints of his fingers now and again to imitate the crackling of flames (*shushuweri*)—that is to say, *Tatewari,* prince of the curanderos—and in order to invoke his aid."[61] The songs learned during peyote-induced ecstasy have the principal virtue of healing—besides being remarkable instruments of knowledge. The Indians speak little, but "well"; they do not babble, but weigh every word, which goes right to the heart and the body. It is no coincidence that the mara'akame are also known as "those who know how to speak."

Ayahuasca sessions led by Amazonian healers are also accompanied by curing songs—icaros—that convey a healing energy: "At this point the old woman begins to sing. Hers is no ordinary song, but an *icaro,* a magical curing song that in our intoxicated and ecstatic state seems more like a tropical reef fish or an animated silk scarf of many colors than a vocal performance. The song is a visible manifestation of power, enfolding us and making us secure."[62]

The experience induced by ayahuasca is particularly rich on the visionary plane, and the visions are greatly influenced by sounds, especially vocal sounds. Icaros have a double aspect, auditory and visual, allowing the shaman to pilot these visions. These sacred chants not only embody the cultural treasures and knowledge of South American shamans, but also bear witness, above all, to the highest point of the magical powers of speech. The experience is as auditory as it is visual. Speech, whose field of action is much higher than that of the eye, penetrates the patient, revealing the illness and eradicating it from the body. The key to its efficacy certainly comes, in great measure, from its vibratory force. We may remember how, in chapter 41 of *Beelzebub's Tales to His Grandson,* the dervish Hadji-Asvatz-Troov made a boil appear on the leg of Hadji-Bogga-Eddin by striking certain keys on his piano. Before his demonstration, he had written some words on a piece of paper that he put in an envelope and hung on a hook. The piece of paper read: "On each of you, from the vibrations issuing from the grand piano, there must be formed on the left leg an inch below the knee and half an inch to the left of the middle of the leg what is called a 'boil.'"[63] We also know the importance vibrations held for Gurdjieff. There is no such thing as chance!

The shaman who masters icaros uses a language that allows him to communicate with the human, vegetable, and animal worlds as well as the world of spirits. Indeed, this is the breath; the alpha and omega; the vital, consubstantial force of the voice releasing all its vibratory power, connecting the world of the dead with that of the living. Pascal Lacombe writes:

> The quality of a shaman is linked directly to his repertoire. . . . This appropriation takes place through incorporation outside of any cognitive process. Reason and simple thought form obstacles to the mastery of an icaro, which, being the voice, the fundamental vibration, the pure energy of a spiritual entity, cannot undergo analysis. The icaro penetrates the shaman in his body, and he releases it with his breath. The shaman is the crucible in which the transmutation of spiritual energy takes place, the instrument chosen by the spirit for revealing itself in sonorous form. It is the shaman's task to master his corporeal and spiritual instrument, to keep it as clear and well harmonized as possible in order that the melody may unfurl in its most limpid form.

> By trial and error, repeated attempts, and studied complicities, the
> shaman and his new icaro entwine and come apart again until they
> unite, in a complex and respectful combination. . . . In the icaros, it
> is not the words that heal; what is important is the vibratory melody,
> the rhythm, the breath, and the tonality combined.[64]

In fact, the therapeutic effect is not linked specifically to the meaning of what is spoken, because the icaro always remains effective, even
if the patient does not understand the meaning of the song. Everything
is in the vibrations (as Gurdjieff has shown us), but it should be noted
that these vibrations are contained in a speech of power whose richness
and efficacy depend on the ensemble of elements that constitute it and
give it life.

We should note, furthermore, that sacred chants can be written or
materialized in paintings, tapestries, or carpets, as is confirmed in various cultures and locations. Among the Shipibo Indians, for example, this
writing takes the form of simple or complex geometric motifs, which the
initiate can decipher in a single glance, reading an icaro in them. Along
the same lines, Ouspensky learned many things from Gurdjieff concerning the making of carpets, which according to the master represented one
of the most ancient forms of art.[65] Gurdjieff explained to him how, in this
remarkable craft, "all the work is done to the accompaniment of music
and singing," and "each locality has its own special tune, its own special
songs and dances connected with carpet making from time immemo-
rial." During this discussion, Ouspensky had an idea that appears highly
relevant in connection with Amerindian art: "And as he told me this the
thought flashed across my mind that perhaps the design and coloring of
the carpets are connected with the music, are its expression in line and
color; that perhaps carpets are records of this music, the notes by which
the tunes could be reproduced. There was nothing strange in this idea
to me as I could often 'see' music in the form of a complicated design."[66]
Ouspensky, it seems, had seen correctly.

Finally, to return to the arising of the healing word in the ecstatic experience, we should explore the highly significant case of the Mazatec

healer Maria Sabina, the "sage of the saint children," who claimed to lend her voice to the spirit of the mushrooms: "All my language," she said, "is in the Book that was given to me. I am she who reads, the interpreter. That is my privilege. Although the Language is not the same for different cases. If I'm curing a sick person, I use one type of language. If the only aim in taking the little things is to encounter God, then I use another Language."[67] Sabina's language, although in the first person, is impersonal in that the one who speaks is always the mushroom. It says:

> *I am a woman who was born alone, says*
> *I am a woman who fell out by herself, says*
> *Because your Book exists, says*
> *Your Book of Wisdom, says*
> *Your sacred Language, says . . .*[68]

With her incantatory songs, Maria Sabina was a true poet whose work was very similar to certain contemporary oral "performances." She was "the body that receives the language" of the saint children, the body possessed by *teonanacatl*—the "flesh of the gods." Once again, here we see a paroxysm of the shamanic practice in which the shaman's body becomes the instrument of spirits. "The Mazatecs say that the mushrooms speak. . . . No mushroom speaks, that is a primitive anthropomorphization of the natural, only man speaks, but he who eats these mushrooms, if he is a man of language, becomes endowed with an inspired capacity to speak."[69] His voice is accompanied by magnificent gestures; his hands clap at each "verse," accompanying the trance:

> *I am a daylight woman*
> *I am a Moon woman, says*
> *I am a Morning Star woman*
> *I am a God Star woman . . .*

The shaman, a mediator between the world of the dead and the world of the living, a "doctor of the word," allows the mushroom to make itself understood. "The ignorant could never sing like the wise," Maria Sabina said. "The saint children dictate to me, I am the interpreter. The Book appears and there I begin to read. I read without stammering. The Book doesn't always appear because I keep in memory what is written in it."[70] She attributes a true magical power to language, a power she used to cure illness, as the story of Perfecto illustrates. An orphan child, he was near death when Sabina endeavored to heal him: "I took the children and began to work. In the trance I found out that Perfecto's spirit had been frightened. His spirit had been trapped by a malevolent being. [. . .] I let myself be carried away by the Language that sprang from me, and though Perfecto didn't take the little mushrooms, my words made him get up and succeed in standing. . . . In the course of the vigil, the sick one got to his feet, because the Language gave him strength."

Sabina had created a very specific poetic language, incomprehensible even to the inhabitants of her village, Huautla de Jiménez. Fernando Benitez writes:

> This same esoteric language was used by Asiatic shamans and Mexican healers, and priests called it *nahualtocatl,* the language of divinity. What Maria Sabina created was not exactly an esoteric language, but rather a poetic language in which the incessant repetition of psalm and litany followed a series of often obscure metaphors, with those liberties and idiomatic word games that are common among great poets, and with the mention of unknown plants and animals, which increased the already considerable difficulties of the tonal Mazatec language.[71]

It is interesting to note this dimension of speech specific to shamans, this inspired, active, healing speech. "It is not I who speak," Heraclitus said, "it is the word." The receptiveness brought about by an increased level of consciousness allows us not only to understand other voices, but also, above all, to express them in their entire magical substance. "Language is an ecstatic activity of signification. Intoxicated by the mushrooms, the fluency, the ease, the aptness of expression one becomes capable of are such that one is astounded by the words that issue forth from the contact of the intention of articulation with the matter of experience. . . . The spontaneity they liberate is not only perceptual, but linguistic, the spontaneity of speech, of fervent, lucid discourse, of the logos in activity."[72]

The shamanic paroxysm is therefore the mastery of the word, the mastery of the sacred songs very often inspired by the powers that live in plants—which instruct us, making us receptive to phenomena that escape the ordinary consciousness. The shaman becomes a channel through which subtle energies can pass. Because of the mystic intoxication, he becomes the instrument for spirits that express themselves through him. Hence the word *tzo*—"says"—which punctuates the phrases of the Mazatec shaman in her communication with the "little growing things": "Says, says, says. It is said. I say. Who says! We say, man says, language says, being and existence say."[73] "The inspired man," writes the Mexican poet Octavio Paz in an essay on Breton, "the man who speaks the truth, says nothing that is his own: Through his mouth, it is the language that speaks."[74]

The language thus regains its primordial power, its creative force and Orphic value, which determine all true poetry, for, as Duits writes, poetry—which is born in the visionary experience—is nothing other than "the language of the gods." There is nothing phantasmagoric, hallucinated, or illusory about this speech. "[W]ords are materializations of consciousness; language is a privileged vehicle of our relation to reality," writes Munn. Because poetry carries the world, it is the language of power, a tool in the service of knowledge and action. The incantatory repetition of names, for example, an idea we have already touched upon in our discussion of prayer, acts upon the heart of the being. "The shaman has a conception of *poesis* in its original sense as an action: words themselves are medicine."[75] The words—used in their sacred dimension—work toward the transmutation of being, the healing of the spirit, our development, but in order for it be effective, the magic word must be born from a direct confrontation with the experience, because experience alone is a safe reserve for truth. Knowledge is not enough; only those who have eaten are in a position to understand, only those who have heard and seen are in a position to say. If speech goes farther than the eye, it is because it has the power of doing. "Though the psychedelic experience produced by the mushrooms is of heightened perceptivity," Munn writes, "the *I say* is of privileged importance to the *I see*."[76] Psychedelic speech is speech of power, revealing the spirit.

The magician and diviner poets have no goal other than to wake us up, to draw us out of our cosmic sleep. Words in their hands awaken us and remind us of the shamanic function of poetry, which is in essence transpersonal and transcultural because it has the ultimate power to connect us to other degrees of reality using the power of a common and universal language that is significant and salvational. It is through saying that the shaman enunciates the truth. Again, we must have a consciousness capable of capturing its salvational signs, secret words that light only under silent suns.

"Being is only in the action of the moment," René Daumal writes, "and that is why it is eternal." Ecstasy reconciles us to this presence in the world—an active and conscious presence which is that of speech, embracing all eternity, extending into the absolute. Those who are here and now are eternal and can perceive reality as it truly is: "If, by chance, there were a rip in my leaden sky through which color, freshness, and density would come to give my presence all its brilliance," Jean-Yves Pouilloux writes, "then I would (or will) be able to see fallacious images substituted with the youth of truth, a present in all its plenitude, such as I see the being of things accomplished there."[77] Victor Hugo had already noted in his preface to the *Odes* (1822): "Beneath the real world, there exists an ideal world, which shows itself resplendent to the eyes of those who have been accustomed by deep meditation to see, in things, more than the things."[78]

In order to see without resorting to chemicals, we must exercise objective thought, the view from above spoken of by Jeanne de Salzmann, the "free view, that which sees," "placed above me," without which "I cannot know that I exist."[79] "When Madame de Salzmann was asked what the courses consisted of, she generally answered that they consisted of movements."[80]

If a fundamental reality exists, then many other paths exist that allow access to it. Some of these are dangerous and require a great deal of time; others are much faster and constitute shortcuts. The trance calls up the movement and the movement calls up the trance. The psychedelic influence brings about the movement in order to encourage the expression or become its vector, but for its part, movement—in gesture, but also in speech—brings about the trance, aligns the centers of being, and opens the way to modified states of consciousness. The best known examples are the dances of Amerindian and Siberian shamans and those of whirling dervishes who acquire consciousness through imitation of the universal movement. The sacred dances taught by Gurdjieff—paroxysms of self-remembrance—may have been second-hand, but they contain a content and a radical transformation of which only the master held the absolute secret.

"You need a knowledge that is not book knowledge," Madame de Salzmann said. "At this point, your head can be informed by reading books in which you recognize your experiences. What is needed is direct perception."[81]

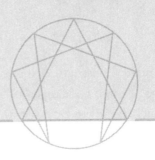

12

Movement in the Creative Process

From the Dance to the Word

Writing or dance, this is the domain of metamorphosis.
DOMINIQUE DUPUY

"What you cannot find in your body, you will not find anywhere else," an Asian saying goes. This is because the body is the crucible of all the revelations that are needed for sounding its depths, for understanding every layer, down to the heart of the being, where the subtlest energies lie. "The knowledge of the body," Daumal states in his study on Spinoza, "is a necessary part and the indispensable beginning of all knowledge."[1] In separating body from spirit, the ordinary consciousness makes a grave error, for it ignores the support necessary for all real evolution—and even when it does consider it, it pays no attention to human conditioning, to what makes this very support mechanical: "It is, in fact, a great functional disorder that veils the perception of this original energy; a disorder made up of multiple tensions, complex automatisms which are themselves linked to the deepest conditioned reflexes. Our postures, our gestures, our attitudes, which are always the same and are our own, determine us. They are ultimately what we are, even though they are an imaginary identity in the distorting mirror of our mind."[2] The same goes for ordinary, conditioned speech, the prisoner of multiple automatisms.

But in language, the logos takes shape through the proper gesture, in the controlled movement that leads to the harmony of being and man, to the true stability of the self, and to the authenticity of the creative act via self-consciousness and sensations—via the state of "presence." If they are deciphered and correctly applied, certain appropriate techniques known as movements or sacred dances and taught by the master Gurdjieff allow us to liberate ourselves from blinding automatisms and to gain access to a perfect knowledge of ourselves that is beneficial for being and for its manifestations in which all creative processes take place. "Know thyself, and thou shalt know the universe and the gods," reads the inscription on the temple of Delphi.

Gurdjieff also wanted to be remembered, above all, as a master of the dance. "... Thanks to this branch alone," he wrote, "which survived from the period of the Babylonian learned beings, a very limited number of three-brained beings there now have the possibility, by means of certain conscious labors, to decipher and learn the information hidden in it and useful for their own Being."[3] Notes James Moore, the great biographer of Gurdjieff, "Some gifted students were effectively transformed, deciphering with their bodies the 'universal language' of postures, gestures, and movement."[4] This apprenticeship of gestures is passed on only within a school and requires all the will and conditions that characterize those of the Fourth Way, beginning with a total respect for the lines of knowledge and being. We should note that all book knowledge is powerless when we are faced with movements; only experience—the necessity for which Gurdjieff never ceased to emphasize—can provide a real response regarding the process of evolution. "This discipline," writes Marthe de Gaigneron, "will in fact permit us to experiment through the body in movement with all its functional mechanisms and, above all, to awaken our latent capacities corresponding to an unexplored side of our nature."[5]

For the master of the dance, the art of movement was a lifelong subject of experimental research. In his preliminary quest, Gurdjieff gained access to a mysterious monastery named Sarmoun; nobody has succeeded in finding any trace of it. There, in the company of Prince Lubovedsky, he attended the sacred dances of the "great priestesses" and lessons taught in the "women's court." There, he gathered a great deal of information that fueled his teachings: "Everyone in the monastery knows the alphabet of these postures and when, in the evening in the main hall of the temple, the priestesses perform the dances indicated for the ritual of that day, the brethren may read in these dances one or another truth which men have placed there thousands of years before."[6]

"Reading," "alphabets," "truths," "deciphering": This science is nothing other than a coded language that possesses intrinsic powers. The reading of it requires the total engagement of the being. It is a language of words and a language of gestures invoking Orpheus and Shiva in the very act of presence. "These dances," Gurdjieff relates, "correspond precisely to our books. Just as is now done on paper, so, once, certain information about long past events was recorded in dances and transmitted from century to century to people of subsequent generations. And these dances are called sacred."[7] The body is a living letter always in motion, opening up the cosmic alphabet to let pour forth a word that bears the memory of the world. "The principle of these movements," writes Solange Claustres, "is that they emerge as a text in which each gesture and its succession represent words and phrases, like characters in a book to decipher. G. I. Gurdjieff never explained to us the meanings of the positions, nor did Madame de Salzmann, but the strictness required in order not to distort them, however slightly, was similar to learning how to write."[8] Likewise, Marthe de Gaigneron writes: "It is a new alphabet for deciphering a new language, a type of direct knowledge which permits us to sense our mechanicalness in the body and at the same time to prepare to receive other currents of energy which can no longer be accessed. New attitudes proceeding from a different inner order confront an entire repertoire of solidly rooted automatic reactions."[9]

Once again, we cannot give knowledge and truth: It is possible to create favorable conditions for this quest, but it is for each of us alone to discover it in him- or herself, thanks to and for him- or herself. "The material and the indications are given to the students, but only they can make the effort of being present, in contact with themselves, with a concentrated attention for the proper execution of these movements. No one can make this effort in their place."[10] In fact, this effort, emphasized repeatedly, is a crucial and necessary aspect of the Work, an essential characteristic of the movement—the "musical notation of the body":[11]

> Another aspect concerns the quality of effort, the in-depth action that we must have in the movements when they are exercised under certain perfectly controlled conditions. When difficulties that appear insurmountable have been overcome, the state changes. Fatigue and obstacles vanish. We can now say that the effort has a true transforming quality. The sentiment becomes more confident, the thought clearer, the body lighter. And once, the experience has ended, the body preserves its traces. It is no longer the same. It is as if it has been baptized, initiated. This is a beneficent state. A new horizon opens to the quest.[12]

The movement arises concretely from the alchemical operation, because it has the quality of transforming: "Transformation through movement: Find permanence in this art of the moment, find the interior, the within, in this outward, exterior action."[13]

Around 1914, in St. Petersburg, Gurdjieff announced the creation of *The Struggle of the Magicians,* a performance piece of dances with music composed by Gurdjieff to accompany the dances. In 1919, in collaboration with Jeanne de Salzmann, a dancer and student of Jacques Dalcroze, he presented the movements at the opera in Tbilisi. In December 1923, he gave a performance at the Theater of the Champs-Élysées. This spectacle was later presented in the United States (New York, Philadelphia, Chicago, and Boston). Fifteen days before his death (October 29, 1949), he composed the last of the movements, no. 39, at the Salle Pleyel with his students, as if applying the finishing touches to his teachings before departing. Afterward, thanks especially to the exceptional qualities of

Madame de Salzmann and some other direct students, the alphabet gave forth yet more new poems, new fruits that others would be able to eat, before there passed, from one hand to the next, the magical words that constitute the secret and reveal all the meanings.

Testimonies concerning the character and power of the sacred dances are numerous—but only testimonies remain, for the most part offering only mystery and incomprehension to the uninitiated. The most direct is perhaps the session of movements, fragments of which we can see in Peter Brook's film *Meetings with Remarkable Men* (1979)—a valuable and rare film, brilliantly orchestrated and directed. In fact, the scenes of dances were taken from the dozens of archival films shot in Paris by various groups collaborating under the direction of Madame Jeanne de Salzmann. These archives are a work of immense value that, unlike Brook's film, can be seen only under certain conditions, which involve a personal invitation.

These dances are called sacred in that "through precise gestures, they transmit and preserve laws and universal truths."[14] When Ouspensky asked his teacher about *The Struggle of the Magicians,* Gurdjieff replied:

Imagine that in the study of the movements of the heavenly bodies, let us say the planets of the solar system, a special mechanism is constructed to give a visual representation of the laws of these movements and to remind us of them. In this mechanism, each planet, which is represented by a sphere of appropriate size, is placed at a certain distance from a central sphere representing the sun. The mechanism is set in motion, and all the spheres begin to rotate and move along prescribed paths, reproducing in a visual form the laws that govern the movements of the planets. This mechanism reminds us of all we know about the solar system. There is something like this in the rhythm of certain dances. In the strictly defined movements and combinations of the dancers, certain laws reproduced visually are intelligible to those who know them. Such dances are called sacred dances.[15]

Here, the notion of the group gains all its meaning from the fact that it is impossible to go about such asceticism in solitude: "The difficulty in memorizing and realizing these movements beyond all the automatisms to which our bodies are accustomed, the concentration necessary for arriving at a group harmony, and the energy that must be put to work for the execution of movements develop a power of 'voluntary attention' and lead us to 'let go.'"[16]

Writes Solange Claustres, "These movements are composed from several progressions of positions, asymmetrical attitudes, rhythms, meters, and words, all before being executed simultaneously in a very strict fashion. . . . There are various series: hieratic postures, geometric figures, prayers, dances, dervishes—whirlers, wrestlers, strikers. Many exercises contain words."[17] Only rigor will lead to a concrete result under the direction of an instructor who reveals the faults, the muscular tensions, and the absences. The movements—exceptional in their variety and richness—have no connection to ordinary gymnastics; they have a real power of action upon the being and the organism at the very depths of its constitution, as one former student of Gurdjieff relates: "Executed in their complete composition, these exercises led to a change in the circulation of the blood, the respiratory rhythm, and the oxygenation of the brain. Keeping all of these in synchronicity and in motion brings about a lucid state, a state of conscious presence, and creates a more real relationship to oneself."[18] "Our body then develops a different energy, nourished by the impulses of our emotions and our mind, creating unity and harmony among all our centers, independently from exterior impulses. New possibilities open before us; our awakening and our 'inner journey' gain meaning."[19] Moreover, besides the study of Gurdjieff's teachings, there are a multitude of preparatory movements and preliminary exercises designed to prepare us for the dances. Because these dances are practiced ritually at seminars, the Work also involves its share of daily suffering, of conscious efforts achieved only in ongoing life, each day, in every second, with an appropriate exercise in each case. The movements are simultaneously a paroxysm—one of teaching—and a passage toward other levels of evolution and reality.[20]

These dances—bearing no resemblance to any other known

form—open other levels of reality that are inaccessible to the ordinary consciousness and allow us to enter into harmonic resonance with the universal forces at work in the cosmos and us alike. Marked by a striking beauty, these dances are magnificent not because they were composed based on aesthetic principles but because they emanate the splendor of the truth and the meaning of life. The Sufis know this. Although Gurdjieff studied a great variety of sacred dances in highly diverse cultures, the fact remains that those he passed on are a unique synthesis, the fruit of his own personal research whose application blends harmoniously with the music specially composed for the occasion. This music itself enjoys a harmonious syncretism made possible in the light of the greatest inner discipline. Such is the case for everything that makes up the teachings. Everything is connected, and the movements are part of this mysterious union of centers and ideas. Each of the movements is associated with a mental exercise and develops a particular faculty. Each educates and aligns the body, the intellect, and the emotions, allowing the three centers to merge into a single body, to fuse into a single *"I,"* a single movement raising the consciousness up to One in order finally to be able to say, *"I am."*

Jeanne de Salzmann says, "These movements permit us to move from one center of gravity to another. It is the change that creates the state. What is important is the gesture, the movement, and not the attitudes."[21] Placing the body in certain precisely codified positions following a chosen tempo allows us to set in motion certain energies in the body in order to diffuse the forces throughout all of the being. "Each position attracts a precise energy, in a precise direction, with a precise goal. From this point of view, one could say that the movements constitute a language,"[22] Josée de Salzmann writes. They constitute a universal language that all of us, by our human nature, can decipher and understand in order to serve our own development and goals. "Like scales on a piano for loosening and controlling the fingers," Solange Claustres notes, "or like intellectual or physical training yielding a desired result, after a long period of practice, these exercises become a different way of sensing and living."[23]

Moreover, it is no coincidence that certain dances follow the pattern of the enneagram according to fundamental cosmic laws: The same laws and the same goals are in play, and the gestures follow the esoteric map of the universe in which each planet has its place and is ruled by a precise energy. Ouspensky recalls: "On the floor of the hall where the exercises took place a large enneagram was drawn and the pupils who took part in the exercises stood on the spots marked by the numbers 1 to 9. Then they began to move in the direction of the numbers of the period in a very interesting movement, turning round one another at the points of meeting, that is, at the points where the lines intersect in the enneagram."[24] Solange Claustres relates the properties of the master of the dance: "You make the movement of the cosmos in the sky; the planets and the stars shift in space, advancing or retrograding, trajectories invisible at first sight."[25] Gurdjieff even said that without studying the movements, it would be almost impossible to understand the master symbol of the Fourth Way: "It is possible to experience the enneagram by movement. . . . The *rhythm* itself of these movements would suggest the necessary ideas and maintain the necessary tension; without them it is not possible to feel what is most important."[26] And in order to "feel what is most important," we must know how to get away from books.

It is no accident that the movements attracted certain great writers—those, we can safely say, who wished to attempt a new approach at writing. "Dance, like poetry, can tell silence," writes dancer and choreographer Dominique Dupuy. "Words are not enough; poetic speech or gestures are needed. They can say something, which is different from talking about something."[27] In an account from the autumn of 1922, Katherine Mansfield shared her strong impression:

Each night, about fifty people meet at the salon. There is music, and at present, they are working on a prodigious, very ancient collective Assyrian dance. Words fail me for giving a description of it. *I must say that these dances have led me to a completely different conception of writing.* I am speaking of very ancient Oriental dances. One of them lasts about seven minutes and contains the entire life of a woman, truly everything. Nothing is missing. I have benefited from it. I have learned more from it about a woman's life than from any novel or poem. How strange it is: There is enough room in this dance for Flaubert's *Coeur simple* and for Princess Marya . . .[28]

The writer Rom Landau also alludes to a session he attended, on the one hand speaking a great deal to the difficulty and complexity of the work, and on the other to its effect on the ordinary, false, social self that dissolved, as if in a psychedelic experience, by the force and power of ecstasy:

> I have practiced certain movements . . . I know what efforts they require. They are the result of a kind of crucifixion of the being. Imagine making contradictory movements with all your limbs at once. This is already very difficult, and requires a certain mastery of the body. Imagine, at the same time, applying yourself to an extremely complicated mental calculation in order to regulate these movements, which goes against your habituation to ordinary arithmetic (a calculation in which one plus one make three, two plus two make five, three plus three make seven, with additions and subtractions in revolving bases). . . . Imagine, finally, that in this same moment all your faculties of sentiment must be fixed upon a given topic, the emotional value of which must be perceived in depth (say, for example, within yourself, "My God, have mercy," and feel what you say)—and you will have a concise overview of the "work" to which these dances bear witness, accompanied by a music in which every note is to be interpreted in reference to the highest religious traditions, as a symbol of one of the many situations of the being in the cosmos. We left these sessions shattered, and strangely cleansed of our ordinary "I"s.[29]

Progressively, always following the rhythm of the sacred music, including footsteps, arms, legs, head, directions, flexions, eyes, memory, breath, and speech . . . thus the mind can let go and subtly connect with the body in order to open the being to the finest emotions. The movement unmasks the "traitors" living within us and dismantles inwardly the mechanics of flesh and bone in order to reharmonize them so that we may open our own eyes and walk with our own feet toward a higher consciousness.

In a lecture in Mexico in 1936, Antonin Artaud reported a conversation he had with Alexandre de Salzmann about theater—not only as a technique for transcendence and awakening, but above all as a means for accessing a "lost language": "His answer was that poetry, true poetry and not the poetry of poets, holds the secret of this language, and that certain sacred dances come closer than any other language to the secret of this poetry."[30]

Writes Marthe de Gaigneron,

> There are dances that in their development recall the laws that rule the secret movements of the stars and of men and are in fact the living symbols of them. If one can submit one's entire being to them, making one's body as supple as possible, one can also renew and nourish oneself at this source of life through this. The dance then acquires an entirely different meaning, man himself becomes the instrument of a universal energy held for an instant in a body through an entirely different glory.[31]

The movements give those who practice them the ability to move themselves on a higher plane, "with body, sentiment, and thought in mutual equilibrium," as de Tonnac writes, "to retranscribe the movement or ballet of the stars, to suggest symbolically the great forces that rule the movement of the universe."[32] De Tonnac also suggests that they tend toward generating a full and "charged" speech in the speaker. The dancer becomes a Pygmalion of being and of cosmic laws: He or she is able to understand the hermetic substance through a writing of the body, joining it harmonically to the mind and the emotions for an evolution of consciousness and an overall development of humans. Thus the body, the crucible of a mysterious energy that animates us and all our manifestations, becomes the workshop allowing us to pass from sensation to writing, then from writing to sensation, whether it be pictorial, musical, or literary.

In a marvelous text that crystallizes his experience, René Daumal shows how the body—itself composed of the motor, instinctive, and sexual centers—is not only a place of construction of the being, but also, above all, an infinite field for investigation and experience relayed between speech and writing, between gesture and word, movement and expression.[33] The body becomes "the rotating plate of the relationship to the world" that articulates our relationship to the real, the visible, and the invisible through the mastered medium of ancestral techniques—because movement, "the only form of existence common to the various aspects of the individual being," is part of not only the integral education of man, but also of the creative process, in that "all movement is subject to a speed (tempo), a cadence, and a rhythm." Further, we must not forget, without rhythm there is no conciliation, no true life. This lived science, requiring attention and determination, allows for true education by way of dance and music via what Gurdjieff called objective art—writes Daumal, "[a]rts not in the sense of satisfactions of the digestive, emotive, or intellectual orders of which we ordinarily know, but arts in the sense of superior know-how, superior knowing-how-to-make-ourselves, in the sense whereby music, for the Greeks, enveloped all culture, in the sense that poetry is creation and self-development."[34]

The consciousness establishes rhythmic links between body and expression, restoring to the creative process its original and primordial power. The art of movement allows us to tear off the masks with which the human machine disguises itself in turn: "Every minute you see a little more clearly all that is mechanism, death, sleep, cowardice, posture, vanity, babbling in the various functions of your being." Yet there is no despondency in this regenerating and purifying approach, no fatalism, for on the dancer's horizon, the light of life glimmers: "But you will not be overcome by despair," Daumal adds, "for you will see an open way, a means for aiming yourself toward the flickering glow, weak and bare, gleaming in you with eclipses; to reanimate this little flame, to feed it, to make it grow and last and shoot forth upon the free path that it is to illuminate." Thus the student learns how to walk all over again, and the writer who made the simple gesture of writing with difficulty and unconsciousness "is suddenly illuminated by joy and fluency,"[35] showing that he has finally truly performed the action of writing with his entire consciousness, balancing his hand, head, and heart, rather than making the physical pretense of writing or painting.

Initiated to the movements by the Salzmanns, Daumal experienced this rebalancing of the being, feeling its unifying and vivifying effects:

> You know what real contact with oneself can mean: joy when it rises up at the moment when it is no longer a simple tempo, but a rhythm living within you. You will discover treasures and garbage in your heart. You will watch your brain working, your theories sewn with white thread, the mildewed libraries encumbering the highest room, and at this moment perhaps an eye will open inside your head and will chase out of it the babbling parrots . . .[36]

Movement, sometimes including speech, leads to the discovery of ourselves and the proper word via the rhythm that links body and creation inextricably. "Writing is corporeal," writes Michel Camus, "it does not deceive; it mercilessly embodies our state of consciousness of the moment. . . . Writing is an operative path only if it engages us entirely, body and soul, with the greatest possible accuracy possible unceasingly questioned."[37] This consciousness of being, implying the sudden fluency of the body, extends into all the actions of life, including the consciously directed creative process: "[M]ore clarity, more justice, and more accuracy will be established in your gestures, your works, your leisure time, and your daily relations."[38] Thus even the immobility (the "absolute mode of movement") of the writer at his desk becomes active and conscious, articulating the passage from the idea to the form of the work, from the language of the body to the body of the language, and from the writing of the sensation to the sensation of the writing.

The human-creator—thus encountering "an often unexpected aspect of himself"—can effectively use his energy in all its forms and serve his goal in the total equilibrium of the centers not only because he knows how to do this, but also because he wants to do this. "Thus," Daumal concludes, "step by step, man can arrive at weighing what he is worth; what he can do; to command with a proper economy the resources, reserves, transformations, and uses of his energy—under all the aspects in which it manifests itself—for the best possible output; to move himself, body, sentiment, and thought in mutual equilibrium, toward his goal, namely that which he wants to do; and to do it, to love doing it, and to want what he does."[39]

The tool and territory of writing that abolishes barriers between world and being, between reality and fiction, between the invisible and the visible, between the sayable and the unsayable, the body is "that true temple of God, the receptacle and transformer of all the energies that pass through it."[40] It is the artist's studio, the alchemical laboratory, the human athanor presiding over the real accomplishment of all evolution of being and over every sincere and authentic creative process. What more, then, can be said about an experience that by definition appears to be language beyond language?

Nothing remains but to act, to remember ourselves, to engage in the harmony of things and being, to form ourselves with the power of experience, and to dare to seek this absolute, in order to *become* and recover the primordial word intact in the crucible of revelations, the primordial speech that has never ceased living and shines in the hearts of all with a thousand lights.

The Dance Within

The Dance is God within Our Body.

Dominique Dupuy

The dance within is the supremacy and triumph of the truth.

It observes itself from outside, but can truly see itself only from inside, where the flame burns that lights and nourishes head, body, and heart with a thousand lights and a thousand forces.

It is a salvational fire bringing about transmutation. From the great massacring of our fears and lies, our mechanisms, and our many "I"s a new energy is born, a rare and necessary staple for the harmonic development of the being. In an alchemy without fantasy, what was dense becomes subtle, and the newborn finds the nourishing nectar at the very heart of his body.

The first step is perhaps the hardest to take. To go up or down, that is the question. But the arms reaching toward the earth, then toward the sky indicate the trajectory that each of us must accomplish in order to touch the hand of another, and to help us, here and now, to sit by the roadside before climbing, just this once, on the march upward.

On the Great Circle there is the impression of a narrow path, the mark of a silent speech that examines and sees.

Feeling in the left hand and right brain, wisdom in the right hand and left brain. Arms folded and heart in the middle, as open to knowledge as the gold leaf that covers jars of lead.

The consciousness spreads itself out to the cosmos and extends into the infinite, a clean breath guided by the stars. A new body grows in this creative chaos and cries *"I am"* before being initiated to a higher level in which death is transcended momentarily.

The joy of Arjuna on his battlefield cannot be imagined; it lives in the action of the movement that brings about being. Thus we must march, head high, along the path not of having, but of giving. We must give in order to become—not to become gods, but simply to become people. And how great is the task, how wide the distance that separates us from wisdom! What must we do? Must we imitate, like an ape, the jeremiads of Job? No, for we must act in order that the joy may shine forth, present as an eternal springtime.

"By performing action without attachment," Krishna said in the Bhagavad Gita, "man attains the Supreme."

Thus, after a great salvational effort, a soul may begin and spread its magic throughout the world.

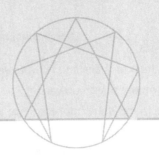

Word Lost,
Word Regained,
Word Present

How do we speak the power of language?

In rereading *A Night of Serious Drinking*, especially Totochabo's final speech, we note that the end of the speech, the text on the "power of words," clearly shows two essential and opposite notions: first, that a hollow use of language generates the confusion of tongues in which reality is perceived in reverse, in which people kill each other in the name of love. In this mechanical circle of humanity, literature and art in general can serve only to "sharpen the crows' beaks" (as Gurdjieff put it) and, at worst, to foster the suggestibility—that is, the meniality—of the masses. These are the gloomiest consequences of this Babelization of speech, but this also shows the second notion: that a clear discourse such as Totochabo's can have a profound effect upon the consciousness of the listener (target), perhaps leading him along the path of true freedom: "We all got up, for there were *several pressing things for each one of us to do*. There were *many things to be done towards the business of living*."[1]

For Daumal, the first thing to do was to recover this lost word, this word of life and hope that he had found in Gurdjieff's teachings. And

274

this magic word whose proper use is to be regained is nothing other than that new language that came from Caucasian regions. Because the system reconciles us and things, speech is reinvested with its nominative and primordial force, its Orphic powers that alone are capable of waking the dead. The teaching is this conciliatory speech; the gold alchemists have forever sought the transforming, essential speech justified by the experience of the thing said that will irreversibly change the course of existence for those who take the time to listen to it.

All the keys—including those that open the magic word—can be found in our evolution, which is the evolution of our consciousness, for the powerlessness of words is the consequence of the powerlessness of men and vice versa. "No verbal discipline can awaken the center of being," writes Jean-Philippe de Tonnac, "the only center from which intellectual, emotional, and motor activity can converge upon a single goal. But if the center of being, the consciousness, is set alight, it will enlighten all the languages with a new flame."[2] To help it to light, we must work on the alignment of the centers. As Madame de Salzmann said, above all else, we need "a relationship between head and body. The one must not be stronger than the other. They must be of equal strength. Then the sentiment will emerge."[3]

The first thing to do in order to begin studying ourselves and learning to speak—or rather, to become speaker 4, 5, 6, or 7—is to restore the true meanings to words in a logic that takes account of the variations and gradations specific to things, applying rigorously the principle of relativity. Thus objective categorization becomes the fundamental instrument of all analysis. We have seen a revealing example of this new language with the division of the words *man* and *speaker* into seven distinct categories. Every study must pass through this universal prism in order to be understood, because this new language is "the universal language that men sometimes attempt to discover or invent." Ouspensky explains:

> The expression *universal language* or *philosophical language* must not be taken in a metaphorical sense; this language is universal in the same sense that mathematical symbols are universal. Moreover,

it contains in itself all the interpretations that men are capable of formulating. The few words of this language that have just been explained already give the possibility of thinking and speaking with a greater precision than ordinary language allows, even if we use one of the scientific or philosophical terminologies or nomenclatures.[4]

It then becomes possible to speak of *psychology,* which acquires many definitions:[5] "Psychology is the study of the principles, laws, and facts relative to the possible evolution of man," and it must be understood that "due to appropriate methods and correct efforts, man may acquire control over the consciousness and may become conscious of himself"—in other words, "psychology is the study of the self," and therefore, at the start, "the study of lies," because "lies fill up our entire life." Finally, psychology is "the study of a new language," bearing in mind the principle of relativity. It thus becomes possible, thanks to this valuable tool and with all the precision required for mutual understanding and exchange, truly to define notions that usually escape us.

Speech is at the origin of all things—"in the beginning was the Word"—and all things have their origin in speech. Its powers require no more demonstration; it is enough to reflect upon them in order to be convinced of them. It is enough to understand fully that it is speech—and nothing else—that connects beings to one another and that it is through speech that all hierarchies are established, revelations transmitted (even if they are transmitted through a veiled speech), judgments pronounced, and teachings passed on.

Moreover, if the magic word has the power to build and awaken (white poetry), it also has the power, on its dark, Luciferian side (black poetry), to enslave and destroy. The great dictators gained power initially through words before seizing it with weapons. The power of hypnotism passes, above all, through the gaze and the word. The oratory art is also an art of war, and in this domain each of us must choose a side. Those who choose consciously choose well: The sly among us know that this battle is one we must begin by fighting against ourselves. Speech is an art and a source of life, but also a science containing all the secrets and mysteries of the human condition. Those who master it will liberate themselves, but those who ignore it will enslave themselves to it, putting themselves in the service of exterior influences. To control this objective, science must reach into the secret of life, for life itself rests upon speech and takes place through it. It is at once the beginning and the end, the signifying breath that brings existence to its highest degree. Observation alone is enough to verify and vindicate these statements.

Writes Ravi Ravindra, "[t]he Rig Veda says that we are children of heaven and earth. Perhaps we have forgotten our link with heaven. To allow this energy to descend into the body is to allow heaven to descend to earth. This is the incarnation of the word."[6] As Madame de Salzmann says: "Transformation is not a change of energy. You cannot change the higher energy. You can allow it to find a place in yourself. This is very difficult. It requires a great deal."[7] "Your body," she adds, "is not yours alone. You must work in order to reconnect what is higher to what is lower. That is the goal of human existence."[8]

Mount Analogue exists just as Father Sogol existed, and it is in this ascent that the logos recovers its primordial properties, for the only valid myth is the true myth, likewise the symbol that serves it. The sacred mountain, the place of power and elevation, invites the transcendence of the *"I"* and the being. Words rise up in the silence, in the momentum of the ascent, and in the growth of consciousness, forming themselves into a speech of power.

In order to help his ascent and to give a correct and rectilinear direction to his speech, the speaker has a fundamental tool at his disposal, a living and moving master symbol capable of opening all doors: the enneagram. Only that which can be placed upon it will be understood perfectly and, what's more, will be right. For the rest, more work is needed with the single goal of achieving a perfect understanding and, objectively, a masterful and effective speech that must not lack precision. The speaker of the Fourth Way possesses the philosopher's stone that paves the way to transformations.

Along the path of writing, only super-efforts, motivated by what Gurdjieff called the "impulse of persistence"[9] allow us to surmount the difficulties and pitfalls on the path in order finally to achieve the goal.

As for those who seek, they shall find: "Knock, and it shall be opened unto you," as the objective parable says. We have already touched upon René Daumal's hope for the existence of a superior humanity that alone can lead us (triple in our constitution and septuple in our evolution) out of sleep and mechanicalness. But where do we find it? Where do we begin? What to we do? Such are the questions the seeker will ask himself when he becomes conscious of the existence of a narrow door. Before trying to pass through it, body and soul, he must locate it, feel it out, catch a glimpse of the light that glimmers through the keyhole in order to nourish himself from it and give himself the power to pass across that which separates him from true life.

Daumal provided another element of response to these existential questions:

> It is difficult to question everything if one has not seen or has not even heard tell of an open way, however hard, however narrow it may be, in search of a real answer. But it seems, in the miraculous logic of life, that every true search will find help from outside, an indication of the path that is needed; not a vehicle that will transport one without fatigue, in which one can rest and let oneself be driven, but a precise finger always pointing to the most direct path, and also the roughest one, in a region in which, in order to advance, everyone can rely only on his own effort.[10]

Advocates of the least effort, experts at laziness, are condemned to remain stuck in their dismal state and to prefer—when their condition titillates them a little, or when the fear of death is too present in their sickened spirits—to live in the illusion of a belief, in the consolation of a caterpillary philosophy that exists only for robots ruled by the current social norm: conformity. The construction of being requires active and conscious participation in a rigorous and truly effective work, as Daumal discovered with the movements taught by Gurdjieff and as he said, always so remarkably, in prose that bore the powerful touch of the white poet:

> If I have spoken of a miraculous logic of life, it is because, at a moment when the necessity for it is so alive for all of us, I have seen at work a method of education in the exact sense of the word that is capable of indicating to everyone, child or adult, the most correct direction in which to seek. This direction is shown not only to indicate, but through an incessant call to the consciousness and the presence of the entire individual, by means of exercises, conditions, and experiences appropriate to each of us, to incite each of us to march forth, bloom, and mature on the path along which each of us travels alone in the solitude of a single presence. This is the place where we can all communicate.[11]

This place, this conscious and unique presence, is the act of speech itself beyond appearances—perhaps the only instant in which "I speak, therefore I am." When I say *"I am,"* I remember myself, I feel the unity of all things and affirm my existence in relation to the cosmic order.

Magical and divining poetry, awakening poetry: "Only the awakened poet knows that the living are of the same essence as the dead," writes Michel Camus. In cleansing the doors of perception, the speaker also purifies his speech, placing under a microscope the real things that are words. This yoga of writing is part of the silent asceticism working for the harmonic development of the whole man and the path of One.

Purified perception changes our view of art in general. Sometimes we even become artists ourselves, transcribing our visions onto canvas if we are not able to do so with words. Yet the evolution of consciousness, which is the evolution of perception, of the *"I"* and of the spirit, also changes our view of literature: Criticism is sharpened, refined to denounce cases where the merchandise is described falsely. The demand grows and is manifested by a greater desire for sincerity and authenticity. The objective writer denounces powerless language and word prostitution, words suffused with lies by sick machines. He exalts the high, awakening voice, the letter of power that leads the being to understand, silences the babbling, and, above all, takes up the path of universal language voluntarily because his quest is the quest of the magic word. The sacramental experience—during which colors, smells, and sounds answer—manifests itself with noble and notable secondary effects upon writing, reading, and the manner in which we glimpse communication between various living beings. Acting upon our consciousness to make it evolve, sacred plants act upon speech. They reduce the use of ordinary language to nothing in order to help rebirth writers to true poetry— that is, to the objective word. The true work of art is transmuted lead, the gold of merit that enlightens and liberates, raising the "place of the word, a necessary expression for the development of thought, of that which is analyzed through self-observation."[12]

The speech of power is not disguised in artifice. It seeks only to find the proper word, to hit its target at the center, head-on, with all its force. Jean-Yves Pouilloux refers to the "familiar letter" beloved by certain authors: "It is because it does not take on a preestablished form to approach that which is fugitive and informal by nature. It is because it engages in a giving and receiving of speech where, in the exchange, the truth of the relationship comes into play as does, therefore, the possible modification of being through speech."[13]

Writing must be a path of awakening, a call to conversion, a place "in which a presence is felt, namely the experienced incarnation in which the word, thought, and thing of the world intertwine in the instant of a coincidence—a mystic, sacred instant *par excellence*."[14] Those poets who seek the immaculate word, the philosopher's speech, will find it present in themselves, in the remembering of their essence, their self—in other words, at the source of all things, in the silence of their being. It is in this silence that the healing speech germinates and to this silence that it returns, finally to be incarnated. Meister Eckhart spoke of the essence of a third speech, neither said nor thought, for as Michel Camus writes, "we must rediscover the meaning of listening, of the inaudible or unheard murmuring of the source."[15] We must rediscover it in order finally to understand what is said to us. As Madame de Salzmann said, "beneath the movement, another movement is hidden," so, beneath this speech, perhaps another speech is hidden (just as "beneath the sensory aspect of the sound, a silent essence is hidden"), which we must discover in order to heal ourselves simply by saying it, perhaps even without pronouncing it. "All is koan," as Zen masters often say.

There is speech that fabricates and speech that transforms; the speaker who babbles and the speaker who elevates. There is the liar and the master, the desirous and the detached, poetry black, poetry white. Objective speech, full and living, is a gesture and an action, a movement—sonorous, silent, written, pictorial, or gestural—bearing a meaning that serves for the evolution of consciousness, a magic word of sorcerers and diviners.

The particular case of Gurdjieff's teachings, far from being an exception even if they borrow extensively from other systems, fall under what we might call the fourth speech, a holistic speech addressing the intellect through books, emotion through music, and the body through movements. In fact, however, each form acts upon the entire being, albeit with certain specificities unique to each respective one, bringing about a real change and a radical transformation of the level of consciousness.

White poetry connects tongues to the esoteric fire of a single circle. It opposes the dividing of being and unity, chaos and harmony, and brings solution to dissolution, thus piercing into the sibylline secrets of knowledge. The world in reverse is finally set the right way, and speech is placed back on its feet to step toward the target, to break the lying mirrors and proclaim the unity of the "I." In this reconciliation with the world and words, in this battle against illusion and the divided human, the opener of the reborn word relearns, little by little, how to speak in order to say.

We seek to become the analogous people climbing up the superhuman slope of harmonic development, the tireless and conscious workers who devote themselves to reaching the salvational summit of knowledge in order to make our speech as white as the snow of those peaks above.

Sufficient Unto
the Level Is
the Evil Thereof

Don't believe what I tell you; try it out for yourself.

G. I. GURDJIEFF

To move forward along the path of the Fourth Way requires us to get through what may appear at first sight to be confession of ignorance and intolerance, which may then discredit the message studied as *sectarianism* and *fanaticism*. These two words throw blame objectively upon things that have these properties.

This observation is true in almost all cases, except—and we should absolutely not view this as the crystallization of these maleficent properties—in matters of certain teachings. It is perfectly understandable and logical, for those who claim neither God nor master, that this type of teaching should appear sectarian in the sense that it claims to hold absolute truth. Yet this conventional idea arises in the psyche only if those interested go too fast, reading works in which the reflection is too advanced for them while, for readers who proceed step by step, regulated by the duty and necessity to move forward only when they have understood perfectly and integrated into their entire being what they have read—for those who respect the different levels of apprenticeship and thus the different stages of evolution—for those alone, all will appear as an obvious truth that will be impossible to question as long as they are truly conscious of what they are doing and are truly sincere and authentic with themselves.

This truth, paradoxical though it may appear (once again, "all is koan," says the Zen master), and linked inextricably to what Gurdjieff calls the "taste for understanding," resides precisely in the transcending of affirmation. That which is essential, in fact, resides in the quality of being that manifests at least as much in anxiety (the quest) as in certainty (grasping). Doubting the theories is not at all compatible with the Work—quite the contrary. When Gurdjieff announced certain propositions (or revelations) in an ostensibly dogmatic fashion, he did so in the way of a Zen master—in order to provoke and unleash a reaction. In other words, he put forward a challenge that every person had to face for him- or herself and to which everyone had to try to respond in order to try to understand even more the very meaning of his or her existence.

This is also the reason why true knowledge can be transmitted only very sparingly, often only in circles of initiates belonging to a school. If this tradition is not respected, there is a risk of those who are interested being struck by the lightning bolt of the revelation of the way. Thus we must advance along the way of true awakening supported by real things that we have acquired and properly integrated and understanding the need to be silent—not to speak, write, paint, or even make films except in order to serve the single goal worth fighting for: the evolution of consciousness. All the rest is mere babbling and confusion, chance and accident, illusion and vanity—the lot of humanity, sleeping and ignorant.

Finally, in keeping with the epigraph, which indicates that we must experiment with everything and verify all for ourselves, I quote a magnificent echo of this, the wise words of Father Giovanni in *Meetings with Remarkable Men*, G. I. Gurdjieff's second series— an echo whose profound meditation challenges the consciousness, elevating it to the invigorating splendor of the meaning of human life, to its authentic value and its true price: "Yes, professor, knowledge and understanding are quite different. Only understanding can lead to being, whereas knowledge is but a passing presence in it. New knowledge displaces the old and the result is, as it were, a pouring from the empty into the void. . . . One must strive to understand; this alone can lead to our Lord God."[1]

Diagrams of Jakobson's Schematic

The Proper Use of the Magic Word Relative to the Enneagram, the Target, and the Seven Centers of the Three-Level Human Factory

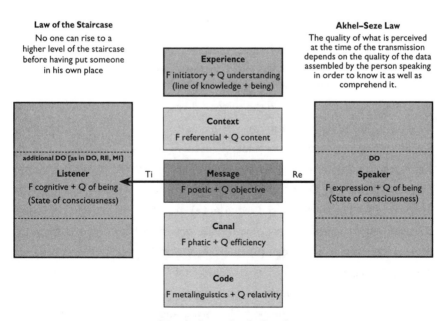

Law of the Staircase
No one can rise to a
higher level of the staircase
before having put someone
in his own place

Akhel–Seze Law
The quality of what is perceived
at the time of the transmission
depends on the quality of the data
assembled by the person speaking
in order to know it as well as
comprehend it.

Experience
F initiatory + Q understanding
(line of knowledge + being)

Context
F referential + Q content

additional DO [as in DO, RE, MI]
Listener
F cognitive + Q of being
(State of consciousness)

Ti

Message
F poetic + Q objective

Re

DO
Speaker
F expression + Q of being
(State of consciousness)

Canal
F phatic + Q efficiency

Code
F metalinguistics + Q relativity

Operating Instructions for Speech
Communication and language functions based on the *Initiatory Path:
My Path Toward Understanding and Evolution*. Pierre Bonnasse

Diagram of the proper use of the magic word in accordance with the enneagram

Development of the Consciousness of the Speaker upon the Master Symbol

According to a logic inherent in the system, there are seven degrees of reading for the Powers of Speech diagram—in this there are seven levels of speakers (writers/poets) and listeners (readers), each word being itself seen according to the principle of relativity and thus divided into seven categories (seven types of "powers"). Only the new language (9)—a common language (corresponding to a common shared experience), the absolute necessity of which Gurdjieff emphasized—can act as a conciliatory force between a speaker (3) who has a goal and a listener (6), the target able to receive the speech, or the target in general. This is why exact discourse is necessary for all conscious work and is the starting point for all operations. The enneagram is always in motion, which explains the possible permutations and choices adapted to additional shocks for every possible situation—the success of which (achieving the goal for which we aim) depends on the Law of Heptaparaparshinokh.

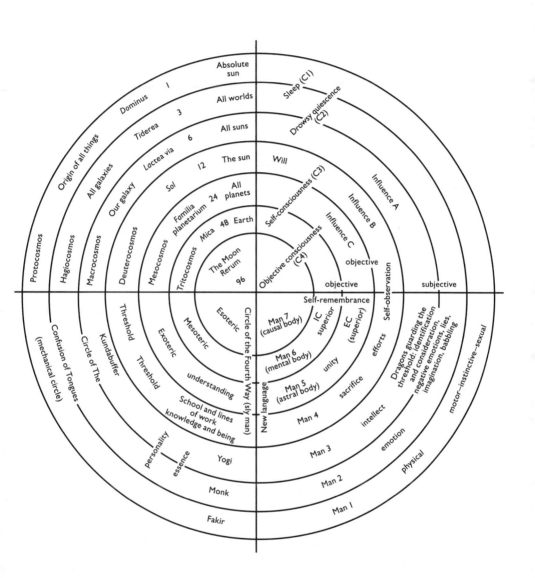

The target (the principle of relativity)

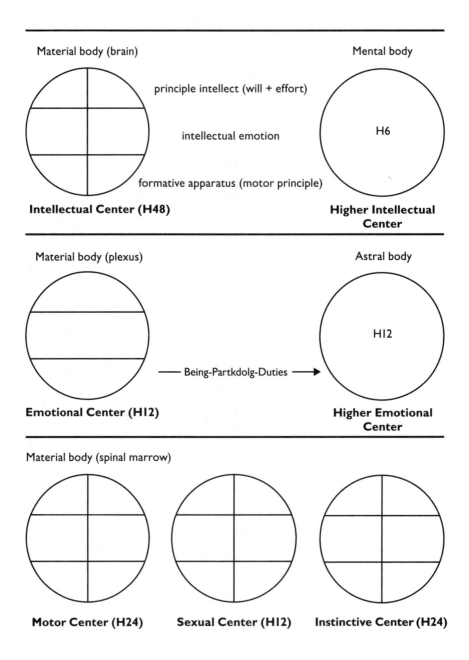

*Complete diagram of the seven centers of
the three-level human factory*

The Centers of
the Human Being

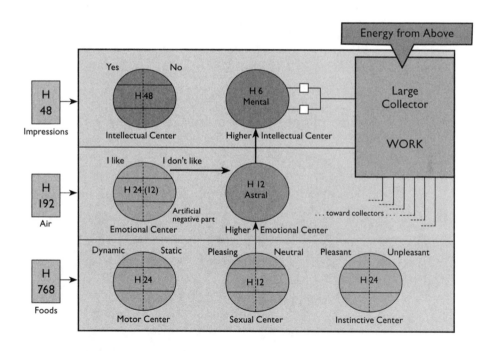

All the work performed by the centers and collectors

The Intellectual Center

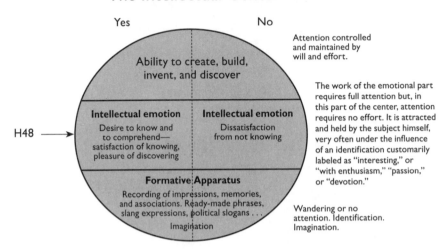

Yes   No

Attention controlled
and maintained by
will and effort.

Ability to create, build,
invent, and discover

The work of the emotional part
requires full attention but, in
this part of the center, attention
requires no effort. It is attracted
and held by the subject himself,
very often under the influence
of an identification customarily
labeled as "interesting," or
"with enthusiasm," "passion,"
or "devotion."

H48 →

Intellectual emotion

Desire to know and
to comprehend—
satisfaction of knowing,
pleasure of discovering

Intellectual emotion

Dissatisfaction
from not knowing

Formative Apparatus

Recording of impressions, memories,
and associations. Ready-made phrases,
slang expressions, political slogans . . .

Imagination

Wandering or no
attention. Identification.
Imagination.

Function of thought (intellectual) includes all mental processes (perception
of impressions, formation of representations and concepts, reasoning,
comparison, affirmation, negation, word formation, speech, imagination . . .)

The Higher Intellectual Center

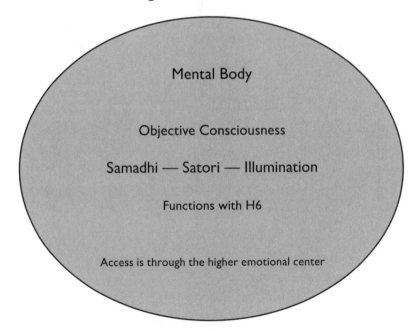

Mental Body

Objective Consciousness

Samadhi — Satori — Illumination

Functions with H6

Access is through the higher emotional center

The Emotional Center

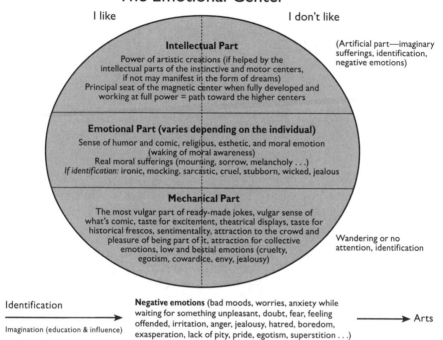

I like | I don't like

Intellectual Part
Power of artistic creations (if helped by the intellectual parts of the instinctive and motor centers, if not may manifest in the form of dreams)
Principal seat of the magnetic center when fully developed and working at full power = path toward the higher centers

(Artificial part—imaginary sufferings, identification, negative emotions)

Emotional Part (varies depending on the individual)
Sense of humor and comic, religious, esthetic, and moral emotion (waking of moral awareness)
Real moral sufferings (mourning, sorrow, melancholy . . .)
If identification: ironic, mocking, sarcastic, cruel, stubborn, wicked, jealous

Mechanical Part
The most vulgar part of ready-made jokes, vulgar sense of what's comic, taste for excitement, theatrical displays, taste for historical frescos, sentimentality, attraction to the crowd and pleasure of being part of it, attraction for collective emotions, low and bestial emotions (cruelty, egotism, cowardice, envy, jealousy)

Wandering or no attention, identification

Identification
→
Imagination (education & influence)

Negative emotions (bad moods, worries, anxiety while waiting for something unpleasant, doubt, fear, feeling offended, irritation, anger, jealousy, hatred, boredom, exasperation, lack of pity, pride, egotism, superstition . . .)

→ Arts

The Higher Emotional Center

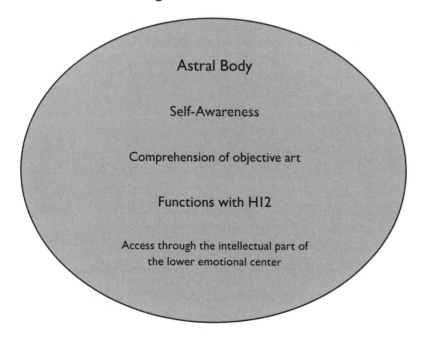

Astral Body

Self-Awareness

Comprehension of objective art

Functions with H12

Access through the intellectual part of the lower emotional center

The Instinctive Center

Agreeable   Disagreeable

Intellectual Part

Very large and substantial contact with state
of one's self-awareness, permitting the collection of
much data on the operation and possibilities of the
machine. Center governing the work of the body.

Emotional Part

Physical emotions: pleasant and unpleasant physical sensations.

Pains or unpleasant sensation (disagreeable flavor or odor) and physical
pleasures (agreeable flavors and odors)

Mechanical Part

Habitual sensations serving as the base for the other sensations.
Physical pains. Reflexes (laughter, yawning).
Physical memories (memories of tastes, odors, pains = internal reflexes).
Internal work of the body (physiology): digestion and food assimilations, breathing,
blood circulation, work of internal organs, construction of new cells,
elimination of wastes, labor of glands of internal secretion.
Five senses: sight, hearing, smell, taste, touch + sense of weight,
temperature, dryness, humidity . . . (indifferent sensations
neither agreeable or disagreeable)

All the instinctive functions
(4 kinds) without exception
are innate, no learning period
is required to lose them.

The Motor Center

Dynamic (movement)   Static (rest)

Intellectual Part

A very important and advantageous instrument.
Physical work and invention. Ability of some actors to
imitate at will the voice, intonations, and gestures of other
people (on the higher levels, the power of imitation is connected
to the work of the intellectual part of the emotional center).

Emotional Part

Pleasure of movement, love of sports and games (it should, normally, derive from
this part of the motor center, but, when identification and other emotions are
mixed up with it, this is rarely the case and most of the time, love of sports is
located in the motor part of the intellectual center or emotional center).

Mechanical Part

All the automatic movements labeled instinctive in ordinary
language (catching a falling object without thinking). Mimetism,
ability to imitate all the exterior movements:
walking, writing, speaking, eating, and
the memories they leave.

None of the motor functions are
innate. They all must be learned like
a child learns to walk, or someone
learning to write or draw.

The Sexual Center

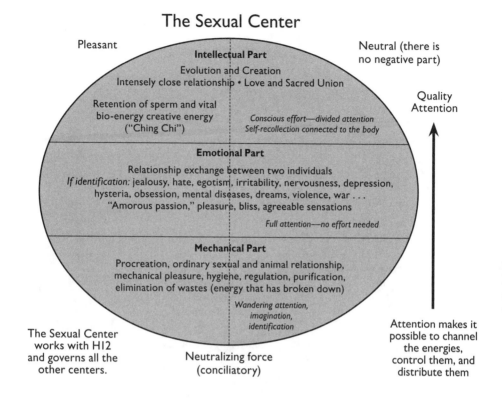

Pleasant

Neutral (there is no negative part)

Quality Attention

Intellectual Part

Evolution and Creation
Intensely close relationship • Love and Sacred Union

Retention of sperm and vital
bio-energy creative energy
("Ching Chi")

*Conscious effort—divided attention
Self-recollection connected to the body*

Emotional Part

Relationship exchange between two individuals
If identification: jealousy, hate, egotism, irritability, nervousness, depression,
hysteria, obsession, mental diseases, dreams, violence, war . . .
"Amorous passion," pleasure, bliss, agreeable sensations

Full attention—no effort needed

Mechanical Part

Procreation, ordinary sexual and animal relationship,
mechanical pleasure, hygiene, regulation, purification,
elimination of wastes (energy that has broken down)

*Wandering attention,
imagination,
identification*

The Sexual Center
works with HI2
and governs all the
other centers.

Neutralizing force
(conciliatory)

Attention makes it
possible to channel
the energies,
control them, and
distribute them

Essence and Personality

Personality	Essence
That which is acquired, That which is not his, What is not	That which is innate, That which is his, What is
Lie	Truth
Persona, the multiple masks, multiple egos, "false personality and identification," useful personality	Essentia, being
	Influence C
Influences A & B	The centers, in other words, their functions, their strong suits, and their gaps belong to essence. The development of essence is the fruit of work upon oneself. The being from which the higher body may grow.
Their content, which is to say everything acquired by a center, derives from the personality, if identification exists, the center works with the mechanical portion.	
Me I Ego Parasite Impostor Marionette	I am Self Original Face Buddha Nature Kingdom of Heaven

The Circles of Humanity

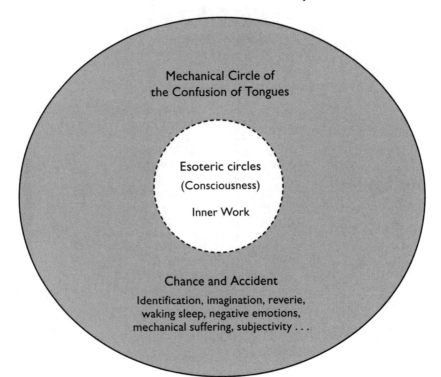

Mechanical Circle of
the Confusion of Tongues

Esoteric circles

(Consciousness)

Inner Work

Chance and Accident

Identification, imagination, reverie,
waking sleep, negative emotions,
mechanical suffering, subjectivity . . .

Gurdjieff, Pupils, and Colleagues

"Awakening is not a state, but an action, and people are much more rarely awake than their words attempt to make one believe."

—*René Daumal, 1934*

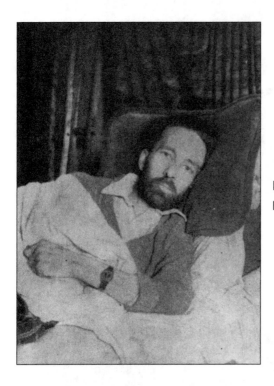

René Daumal, three days
before his death.

"I don't want to die without having understood why I lived."
— *René Daumal,* Mount Analogue

*"I shall speak to call myself to the holy war. I shall speak to denounce the traitors
whom I nourished. I shall speak so that my words may shame my actions, until the
day comes when a peace armored in thunder reigns in the chamber of the eternal
conqueror."*

— *René Daumal, "The Holy War."*
Photo by Luc Dietrich, May 19, 1944,
published in Cahiers du Sud *no. 332,*
and used with the kind permission
of Cahiers du Sud.

René Daumal (farthest back),
posing for the photographer.

Charles Duits (used with the kind
permission of Juste-Emmanuel
Duits).

*"It is not the words that are dead,
but the people."*

—*Charles Duits*

le 23 août

Mon cher Lebeau,

Je regrette que vous ne m'ayez pas apporté de
nouvelles plus détaillées — ce n'est pas votre faute—
Il est vrai que je n'ai rien à vous dire que vous
ne sachiez : nous allons tout mettre en œuvre
pour revenir à Paris en octobre. Il est très
probable que nous devrons pour cela repasser
par Marseille. D'ici, n'étant pas en contact avec
un centre important, c'est trop difficile et long.
Ci-joint les 4 ex. de La guerre sainte dont j'ai
peu disposer. Et une photo qui est destinée à
ma mère.
Nous avons hâte de vous retrouver tous. À
cet automne donc. À vous, et à tous les nôtres,
notre amitié

René Daumal

Letter from René
Daumal to Lebeau.

Portrait of Alexandre de Salzmann,
"Father Sogol."

*"See, here is an open door; narrow and
hard to access, but a door, and it is the
only one for you."*
                    —*Alexandre de Salzmann*

Jeanne de Salzmann.

Thomas de Hartmann, photographed
by Joseph Sima.

Alexandre and Jeanne de Salzmann.

G. I. Gurdjieff.

"There is a law according to which the quality of that which is perceived at the moment of transmission depends, as much for knowledge as for understanding, on the quality of the reference points constituted in him who speaks."
—*G. I. Gurdjieff*

P. D. Ouspensky.

". . . I had the inner conviction that something had already changed for me, and that now everything would take a different path."
—*P. D. Ouspensky*

G. I. Gurdjieff.

"For a precise study, a precise language is necessary."
—*G. I. Gurdjieff*

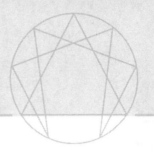

Notes

PREFACE TO THE AMERICAN EDITION

1. On this subject, read Aldous Huxley's excellent book, *The Perennial Philosophy* (New York: Harper & brothers publishers; 3rd edition, 1944).
2. René Daumal, *Correspondance III* (Paris: Gallimard, 1996), 227.
3. Aphorism no. 14, inscribed on the vellum of the Study House at the Avon Priory.
4. G. I. Gurdjieff, *Beelzebub's Tales to His Grandson* (New York: A. Dutton, 1973), chapter 39.
5. P. D. Ouspensky, *In Search of the Miraculous: Fragments of an Unknown Teaching* (London: Routledge and Kegan Paul, 1950), 20.
6. See the works of Roman Jakobson.
7. These ideas are then developed in the work.
8. See "Jakobson's Schematic" in appendix 1.
9. G. I. Gurdjieff, *Meetings with Remarkable Men* (New York: E. P. Dutton, 1963), 306. See the example of Brother Akhel and Sister Seze.
10. G. I. Gurdjieff, *Meetings with Remarkable Men,* 306.
11. W. P. Patterson, *Gurdjieff et les femmes de la cordée* (Paris: Éditions de la Table Ronde, 2005), 74.
12. See the golden number in architecture, for example. See also the enneagrammatic construction of *Beelzebub's Tales to His Grandson* (in the sense that the very poetics obey certain laws that the author qualifies as "objective" and "cosmic" in that, according to him, they define the functioning of all things) and its capacity to act upon the whole of man. On this subject, see Keith Buzzel's remarkable work, *Perspectives on Beelzebub's Tales* (Salt Lake City: Fifth Press, 2005). The relationship between subjective art and objective art is developed amply in the first part of *The Magic Language of the Fourth Way.*
13. Antonin Artaud, "Le Pèse-Nerfs," in *Œuvres complètes* (Paris: Gallimard, 2004), 164.
14. P. D. Ouspensky, *In Search of the Miraculous: Fragments of an Unknown Teaching,*

111–12 and P. D. Ouspensky, *L'homme et son évolution possible* (Paris: L'Originel, 1999), 55–61. See also G. I. Gurdjieff, "Pour une étude exacte, un langage exact est nécessaire," in *Gurdjieff parle à ses élèves* (Monaco: Éditions du Rocher, 1995), 84–102; *Beelzebub's Tales to His Grandson,* 1150–55. See also Henri Thomasson, *Batailles pour le présent: journal d'une expérience, 1947–1967* (Lyon: Etudes et recherches psychologiques, 1974), 13–14.

15. P. D. Ouspensky, *In Search of the Miraculous: Fragments of an Unknown Teaching,* 95.

16. G. I. Gurdjieff, *Gurdjieff parle à ses élèves,* 87.

17. René Daumal, *Correspondance III,* 101.

18. Ibid., 102.

19. P. D. Ouspensky, *In Search of the Miraculous: Fragments of an Unknown Teaching,* 158. See the diagram of the centers in the appendices.

20. I Kings 7:13–14.

21. Jean Chevalier and Alain Gheerbrant, *Dictionnaire des symboles* (Paris: Robert Laffont, 1982), 506.

22. Luke 11:9–10.

23. René Daumal, *Correspondance III,* 50.

24. Pierre Bonnasse, *Dans la nuit d'Aghtamar* (Paris: Éditions Éoliennes, 2007).

25. Jean-Yves Pouilloux, in Alexandre Hollan, *Je suis ce que je vois, Notes sur la peinture et le dessin, 1979–1996* (Cognac: Le temps qu'il fait, 1997).

PREFACE TO THE FIRST EDITION

1 Jean Biès, *René Daumal* (Paris: Pierre Seghers éditeur, 1967), 9.

2. Ibid., 25.

3. Michel Waldberg, *Gurdjieff hors les murs* (Paris: La Différence, 2001), 228.

4. René Daumal, *Mount Analogue,* trans. Roger Shattuck (Boston: Shambhala, 1992), 26.

5. Jean-Philippe de Tonnac, *René Daumal, l'archange* (Paris: Grasset, 1998), and James Moore, *Gurdjieff, anatomie d'un mythe* (Paris: Seuil, 1999).

6. Matthew 7:7.

7. G. I. Gurdjieff, *Beelzebub's Tales to His Grandson: An Objectively Impartial Criticism of the Life of Man* (New York: A. Dutton, New York, 1950), vol. 1, 361.

INTRODUCTION: THE ENNEAGRAM, MASTER SYMBOL OF THE FOURTH WAY

1. G. I. Gurdjieff, *Beelzebub's Tales to His Grandson,* vol. 2, 86.

2. Nicolas Tereshchenko, *Gurdjieff et la Quattrième Voie* (Paris: Guy Trédaniel, 1991), 251.

3. Ibid., 254.

4. P. D. Ouspensky, *In Search of the Miraculous: Fragments of an Unknown Teaching*, 294.

5. René Daumal, *A Night of Serious Drinking*, trans. David Coward and E. A. Lovatt (Boulder: Shambhala, 1979), 1.

6. Ibid.

7. René Daumal, "Poetry Black, Poetry White."

8. René Daumal, *A Night of Serious Drinking*, 73.

9. Jean-Philippe de Tonnac, *René Daumal, l'archange*, 201.

CHAPTER 1. THE MAN–MACHINE
AND THE CIRCLE OF THE CONFUSION OF TONGUES

1. René Daumal, *A Night of Serious Drinking*, 16. This quote is the origin of this text's [French] title, emphasizing the foundation of this text on the ideas of René Daumal and, via Daumal, those of Gurdjieff.

2. P. D. Ouspensky, *In Search of the Miraculous: Fragments of an Unknown Teaching*, 18.

3. René Daumal, *A Night of Serious Drinking*, 99.

4. Ibid.

5. Ibid., 100.

6. Ibid., 101.

7. Ibid., 103.

8. Ibid., 103–4.

9. P. D. Ouspensky, *In Search of the Miraculous: Fragments of an Unknown Teaching*, 18.

10. Ibid., 21.

11. René Daumal, *A Night of Serious Drinking*, 15. This first chapter is intentionally brief, calling readers at the very beginning to recognize and consider their "drowsy quiescence." The idea of sleep will be developed throughout this text, because speech, requiring a certain lucidity, is very closely connected with it.

12. Ibid., 16. We will study the possibilities of evolution in chapter 4.

CHAPTER 2.
NECESSARY DIGRESSIONS ON ART

1. P. D. Ouspensky, *In Search of the Miraculous: Fragments of an Unknown Teaching*, 26.

2. Ibid. Regarding the different levels, see chapter 3.

3. Ibid.

4. René Daumal, *A Night of Serious Drinking*, 44.

5. Ibid.

6. G. I. Gurdjieff, *Beelzebub's Tales to His Grandson,* vol. 2, 106.

7. Ibid., 105.

8. Ibid., 103.

9. René Daumal, *A Night of Serious Drinking,* 44.

10. Ibid., 48.

11. Ibid., 52.

12. Ibid., 46–47.

13. Ibid., 49.

14. Ibid.

15. G. I. Gurdjieff, *Beelzebub's Tales to His Grandson,* vol. 2, 92–96.

16. Ibid., 91.

17. Peter Brook, in G. I. Gurdjieff, *Dossiers H. Gurdjieff* (Paris: L'Âge d'Homme, 1993), 83.

18. Georges de Maleville, *Élements pour une possible évolution intérieure* (Paris: Institut pour le Développement Harmonique de l'Homme, 2004), 32.

19. Ibid.

20. Ibid., 33. Regarding identification and consideration, see the work cited previously, in which these phenomena are clearly explained and proved.

21. P. D. Ouspensky, *In Search of the Miraculous: Fragments of an Unknown Teaching,* 26–27.

22. We will return to the subject of centers in chapter 4.

23. See chapter 4.

24. Charles Duits, *Le Pays de l'éclairement* (L'Isle-sur-la-Sorgue: Le Bois d'Orion, 1994), 83–84.

25. Ibid.

26. Aldous Huxley, *The Doors of Perception* (New York: Harper and Row, 1963).

27. Charles Duits, *Le Pays de l'éclairement,* 84.

28. Aldous Huxley, *The Doors of Perception.*

29. Antonin Artaud, *Van Gogh le suicidé de la société* (Paris: Gallimard, 2001), 41.

30. Aldous Huxley, *The Doors of Perception.*

31. Charles Duits, *Le Pays de l'éclairement,* 84. Antonin Artaud, *Van Gogh le suicidé de la société,* 47: "Van Gogh thought it was necessary to know how to deduce the myth from the most matter-of-fact things in life. . . . Reality is terribly superior to all history, all legend, all divinity, all that is surreal. It is enough to have genius to know how to interpret it." To "have genius," or better, to *learn* how to do it . . .

32. Ibid., 85.

33. Antonin Artaud, *Van Gogh le suicidé de la société,* 53.

34. Charles Duits, *Le Pays de l'éclairement,* 87.

35. Aldous Huxley, *The Doors of Perception.*

36. G. I. Gurdjieff, *Beelzebub's Tales to His Grandson,* vol. 2, 112.

37. P. D. Ouspensky, *In Search of the Miraculous: Fragments of an Unknown Teaching,* 27.

38. Charles Duits, *Le Pays de l'éclairement,* 145.

39. Ibid.

40. Ibid., 146.

41. Ibid., 148.

42. Aldous Huxley, *The Doors of Perception.*

43. G. I. Gurdjieff, *Beelzebub's Tales to His Grandson,* vol. 1, 308–11.

44. Ibid., vol. 2, 112.

45. Nicolas Tereshchenko, *Au-delà de la Quattrième Voie* (Paris: Guy Trédaniel, 1996), 233.

46. Jean-Yves Leloup, *L'Icône, Une école du regard* (Paris: Pommier-Fayard, 2000), 6–7.

47. Ibid.

48. Ibid., 11.

49. For more on legominism, see chapter 10.

50. Regarding music, see chapter 7 on the power of sound.

51. Peter Brook, in G. I. Gurdjieff, *Dossiers H. Gurdjieff,* 84.

CHAPTER 3.
THE PROPAGATION OF "WORD PROSTITUTION"

1. G. I. Gurdjieff, *Meetings with Remarkable Men,* translated by A. R. Orage (New York: E. P. Dutton, 1963), 8.

2. Ibid., 8–9.

3. This idea will be the subject of chapter 5.

4. G. I. Gurdjieff, *Meetings with Remarkable Men,* 9.

5. René Daumal, *A Night of Serious Drinking,* 52.

6. Ibid., 64.

7. Ibid., 74. See chapter 4.

8. Ibid., 79.

9. Ibid., 84.

10. Ibid., 87.

11. P. D. Ouspensky, *In Search of the Miraculous: Fragments of an Unknown Teaching,* 144.

12. G. I. Gurdjieff, *Meetings with Remarkable Men,* 9.

13. Georges de Maleville, *Éléments pour une possible évolution du bonheur,* 27–28.

14. G. I. Gurdjieff, *Meetings with Remarkable Men,* 9.

15. See chapter 7, sound.

16. G. I. Gurdjieff, *Meetings with Remarkable Men,* 10.

17. Ibid.

18. Ibid., 12.

19. Michel Waldberg, *La Parole putanisée* (Paris: La Différence, 2002), 19.

CHAPTER 4.
EVOLUTION AND THE PRINCIPLE OF RELATIVITY

1. René Daumal, *A Night of Serious Drinking,* 104.

2. Ibid.

3. Ibid., 104–5.

4. See the diagram of the centers of man in the appendices.

5. The Law of Three will be discussed in depth in chapter 5.

6. Please refer to Ouspensky's explanation for an understanding of the role of hydrogens.

7. René Daumal, *A Night of Serious Drinking,* 104–5.

8. Ibid., 106; italics are mine.

9. For a complete and detailed diagram of the centers, see the appendices.

10. René Daumal, *A Night of Serious Drinking,* 109.

11. Ibid., 107.

12. Ibid., 108.

13. P. D. Ouspensky, *In Search of the Miraculous: Fragments of an Unknown Teaching,* 57.

14. Ibid.

15. René Daumal, *A Night of Serious Drinking,* 108.

16. Ibid., 109.

17. P. D. Ouspensky, *In Search of the Miraculous: Fragments of an Unknown Teaching,* 5.

18. René Daumal, *A Night of Serious Drinking,* 109.

19. René Daumal, *Mount Analogue,* 30.

20. Ibid., 35.

21. Ibid.

22. Ibid.

23. René Daumal, *A Night of Serious Drinking,* 110.

24. Ibid., 111.

25. G. I. Gurdjieff, *Beelzebub's Tales to His Grandson,* vol. 1, 378.

26. René Daumal, *A Night of Serious Drinking,* 111.

27. Ibid.

28. G. I. Gurdjieff, *Beelzebub's Tales to His Grandson.*

29. Jean-Yves Pouilloux, "Le Temps présent," in *l'Inactuel,* no. 12 (2004).

30. Louis Pauwels, *Monsieur Gurdjieff* (Paris: Albin Michel, 1996), 387.

31. P. D. Ouspensky, *In Search of the Miraculous: Fragments of an Unknown Teaching*, 57.

32. Ibid., 58.

33. Ibid., 57.

34. Ibid., 58.

35. Ibid.

36. Ibid., 64.

37. Ibid., 68.

38. Ibid., 68–69.

39. Ibid., 69.

40. Ibid., 70. See also "Pour une étude exacte, un langage exact est nécessaire," in G. I. Gurdjieff, *Gurdjieff parle à ses élèves*.

41. Ibid.

42. Ibid., 70–71.

43. Ibid., 73. There is nothing shocking about this hierarchy: The West generally distinguishes people in terms of "having" (exterior wealth), the East in terms of "being"—in other words, in terms of inner wealth, the fruit of work on the self. Montaigne noted: "Plutarch says somewhere that he does not find so great a difference betwixt beast and beast as he does betwixt man and man. . . . I could enhance Plutarch willingly, and say that there is more difference betwixt such and such a man than there is betwixt such a man and such a beast." *The Essays of Michel de Montaigne* (chapter 42).

44. The subsequent chapters of this text develop this idea, which reveals itself to be a law.

45. See the diagram of the target in appendix 1, illustrating the circles of humanity.

46. A word invented by Charles Duits to describe the ordinary man. See Charles Duits, *Le Pays de l'éclairement*.

47. P. D. Ouspensky, *In Search of the Miraculous: Fragments of an Unknown Teaching*, 73.

48. See chapter 10.

49. Matthew 12:37. We will return to this in chapter 8.

50. Luke 6:41.

51. P. D. Ouspensky, *L'Homme et son évolution possible* (Paris: L'Originel, 1999), 60.

52. René Daumal, foreword to *Contre-ciel* (Paris: Poésie/Gallimard, 1990).

53. See the diagram of the synthesis in appendix 1.

54. René Daumal, *A Night of Serious Drinking*, 16.

CHAPTER 5.
REFLECTIONS IN LIGHT OF THE LAW OF TRIAMAZIKAMNO

1. The Law of Three is also found in other traditional systems.

2. Charles Duits, *Le Pays de l'éclairement*, 93.

3. Ibid.

4. Ibid., 95.

5. We will return later to the crucial importance of what Daumal calls "common experience," a necessary condition for all real exchange between a speaker and a listener.

6. Charles Duits, *Le Pays de l'éclairement*, 96.

7. Ibid., 135–38.

8. Ibid., 153.

9. See chapter 4, evolution.

10. Charles Duits, *Le Pays de l'éclairement*, 153.

11. Ibid., 155–56.

12. Ibid., 156.

13. Ibid., 165

14. Charles Duits, *La Salive de l'éléphant* (Paris: Losfeld/Blanche, 1999), 50; italics are mine. Daumal says exactly the same thing.

15. "Some are already dead," notes Gurdjieff. Some are "broken machines" and are not repairable. P. D. Ouspensky, *In Search of the Miraculous: Fragments of an Unknown Teaching*.

16. Michel Waldberg, *Gurdjieff hors les murs*, 130.

17. Charles Duits, *Le Pays de l'éclairement*, 209.

18. Rimbaud, *Œuvres complètes* (Paris: Gallimard, 1972), 251.

19. René Daumal, "Poetry Black, Poetry White," in *The Powers of the Word: Selected Essays and Notes 1927–1943*, edited and translated by Mark Polizzotti (San Francisco: City Lights, 1991).

20. René Daumal, *A Night of Serious Drinking*, 1.

21. René Daumal, "Poetry Black, Poetry White." Verbal expression is the meaning that is conveyed.

22. P. D. Ouspensky, *In Search of the Miraculous: Fragments of an Unknown Teaching*, 77.

23. Ibid., 78.

24. René Daumal, "Poetry Black, Poetry White."

25. René Daumal, *A Night of Serious Drinking*, 16–17; italics are mine.

26. René Daumal, "Poetry Black, Poetry White."

27. On the powers of thought, see Gurdjieff's thoughts in *Meetings with Remarkable Men*, 192, because this is what Father Sogol says in René Daumal, *Mount Analogue*, 88. See also P. D. Ouspensky, *In Search of the Miraculous: Fragments of an Unknown Teaching*.

28. René Daumal, "Poetry Black, Poetry White."

29. René Daumal, *A Night of Serious Drinking*, 17; italics are mine.

30. René Daumal, "Poetry Black, Poetry White." See the last chapter of this book, on movements.

31. Ibid. Should this unique Sun—with a capital S—be equated explicitly with the

"sun absolute" of Gurdjieff? This connection says a great deal about the ultimate goal of all true poetry that is by definition "white."

32. René Daumal, "Poetry Black, Poetry White."

33. Ibid., 192.

34. Charles Duits, *Le Pays de l'éclairement,* 61.

35. Ibid., 155.

36. René Daumal, *A Night of Serious Drinking,* 1; italics are mine.

37. G. I. Gurdjieff, *Meetings with Remarkable Men,* 241.

38. René Daumal, *A Night of Serious Drinking,* 1–2.

39. G. I. Gurdjieff, *Meetings with Remarkable Men,* 39.

40. On the subject of the Bhagavad Gita, Daumal wrote in *Le Grand Jeu* (spring 1929): "I always find each one of my discoveries shortly after I have made it in some verse of one of the Upanishads or the Bhagavad Gita that I have not noticed before. This induces me necessarily to trust in these words, in the single word from which they proceed, and in the mystic tradition that ensues from them."

41. Michel Camus, "Paradigme de la transpoésie," in *l'Arbre* (1999).

42. Louis Pauwels, *Monsieur Gurdjieff,* 387.

43. Ibid., 388.

44. P. D. Ouspensky, *In Search of the Miraculous: Fragments of an Unknown Teaching,* 20.

45. Michel Waldberg, *Gurdjieff: An Approach to His Ideas,* translated by Steve Cox (London: Routledge and Kegan Paul, 1981), 2. See chapter 9 of this text on the way of blame, which is also a sophisticated method for transmitting a truth, consequently forming part of the magic powers of speech even when we are silent.

46. Elaborated in the next chapter.

47. René Daumal, *A Night of Serious Drinking,* 2.

48. See the target illustrations in appendix 1.

49. L. Jenny, *Poétique,* no. 27 (1976): 262.

50. See chapter 7—the relationship Paulhan establishes among word, thing, and idea, which is called consciousness here.

51. Louis Pauwels, *Monsieur Gurdjieff,* 388–89.

52. These are the five propositions set forth by Rolland de Renéville and René Daumal in *Chaque fois que l'aube parait* and repeated in *Les Pouvoirs de la parole.* The notion that the consciousness must be "that of the absolute" confirms the idea that the sun referred to earlier by Daumal may well be the "Sun Absolute" mentioned by Gurdjieff in *Beelzebub's Tales to His Grandson* (vol. 1, 52) in which "our lord sovereign endlessness has the fundamental place of his dwelling."

53. G. I. Gurdjieff, *Beelzebub's Tales to His Grandson,* vol. 1, 137.

54. Ibid., vol. 2, 343.

CHAPTER 6. REFLECTIONS IN
LIGHT OF THE LAW OF HEPTAPARAPARSHINOKH,
OR HOW TO REACH YOUR TARGET (GOAL)

1. This chapter is simply a hypothesis, a mere attempt at understanding, which may turn out to be right or wrong. The statements in the chapter and notes do not claim to hold any absolute truth. Also, it is difficult to summarize this law of seven in one chapter; it is much more complex than the law of three. Those serious seekers can apply themselves by exploring Heptaparaparshinokh with the tools at their disposal.

2. Peter Brook, "Une autre dimension: la qualité." In G. I. Gurdjieff, *Dossiers H. Gurdjieff* (Paris: L'Âge d'Homme, 1993); italics are mine.

3. P. D. Ouspensky, *In Search of the Miraculous: Fragments of an Unknown Teaching*, 122.

4. See the next chapter, on sound.

5. P. D. Ouspensky, *In Search of the Miraculous: Fragments of an Unknown Teaching*, 125.

6. Ibid., 126–27.

7. Ibid., 127.

8. Peter Brook, "Une autre dimension: la qualité," 81.

9. P. D. Ouspensky, *In Search of the Miraculous: Fragments of an Unknown Teaching*, 128–29.

10. Ibid., 129.

11. Ibid.; italics are mine.

12. Ibid., 127–28.

13. G. I. Gurdjieff, *Beelzebub's Tales to His Grandson*, vol. 2, 342.

14. P. D. Ouspensky, *In Search of the Miraculous: Fragments of an Unknown Teaching*, 129.

15. Jean Chevalier and Alain Gheerbrant, *Dictionnaire des Symboles*, 716.

16. René Daumal, "Poetry Black, Poetry White."

17. Ibid., 189.

18. Ibid.

19. Ibid.

20. Ibid.

21. P. D. Ouspensky, *In Search of the Miraculous: Fragments of an Unknown Teaching*, 129.

22. Michel Waldberg, *Gurdjieff hors les murs*, 171.

23. Peter Brook, "Une autre dimension: la qualité," 82.

24. P. D. Ouspensky, *In Search of the Miraculous: Fragments of an Unknown Teaching*, 129–30.

25. Ibid., 130.

26. Ibid.

27. Ibid., 131.

28. Peter Brook, "Une autre dimension: la qualité," 82; italics are mine.

29. P. D. Ouspensky, *In Search of the Miraculous: Fragments of an Unknown Teaching*, 131.

30. Ibid., 132.

31. Ibid.

32. Ibid.

33. Ibid., 133.

34. Ibid., 132–33.

35. Paul Diel, *Psychologie de la motivation* (Paris: Payot, 1991), 6; italics are mine.

36. Ibid., 7.

37. Ibid., 46.

38. P. D. Ouspensky, *In Search of the Miraculous: Fragments of an Unknown Teaching*, 133.

39. Ibid., 134.

40. Ibid.; italics are mine.

41. Ibid.

42. Ibid., 135. Note that the cosmic descending octaves are creative and the cosmic ascending octaves are evolutionary. In other words, "the line of evolution is opposed to the line of creation." The serious reader will also be interested in the relationships of each octave to the others. Ouspensky gives an interesting illustration of this with the metaphor of the tree: The trunk represents the fundamental octaves and the branches the subordinate ones. See also the functioning of the "inner vibrations," 135.

43. See the cosmological diagram of the target in appendix 1.

44. See chapter 7, Techniques of Speech and Powers of the Logos, for more explanations regarding this "additional shock."

45. P. D. Ouspensky, *In Search of the Miraculous: Fragments of an Unknown Teaching*, 138.

46. Ibid. Note that "any note of any octave may at the same time be any note of any other octave passing through it"—from P. D. Ouspensky, *In Search of the Miraculous: Fragments of an Unknown Teaching*, 139.

47. René Daumal, "Poetry Black, Poetry White."

48. P. D. Ouspensky, *In Search of the Miraculous: Fragments of an Unknown Teaching*, 139.

49. Ibid.

50. Ibid.

51. Peter Brook, "Une autre dimension: la qualité," 82.

52. P. D. Ouspensky, *In Search of the Miraculous: Fragments of an Unknown Teaching*, 140. Any who wish to study this more deeply should refer to the law of seven in the transformation of food in the three-story human factory, or universe in minia-

ture (*In Search of the Miraculous: Fragments of an Unknown Teaching,* 182ff.). Of further interest is the fundamental role of the "lateral octave." This law of seven contains all the numbers from 1 to 10 and explains the symbolism of numbers.

53. Peter Brook, "Une autre dimension: la qualité," 81; italics are mine.

54. By "sequential order," we should understand the decimal series obtained by calculating the numeric value of each ninth: $1/_7 = 0.142857\ldots, 2/_7 = 0.285714\ldots, 3/_7 = 0.428571\ldots, 4/_7 = 0.571428\ldots, 5/_7 = 0.714285\ldots, 6/_7 = 0.857142\ldots, 7/_7 = 0.999999.\ldots$ Examining the numbers, we may observe that they obey a sequential order that is always the same. This symbol is therefore the arithmetical illustration of *premum mobile,* perpetual motion, which has remained secret since the dawn of time and was only revealed for initiatory purposes. This series of numbers also indicates to us that the enneagram acquires its full meaning only if we abandon our static and peripheral reading for a dynamic reading that follows the movements within the figure. Gurdjieff choreographed numerous "movements" (among the 39 of the final series) in which the dancers had to arrange themselves in columns according to these mathematical series (see chapter 12).

According to certain interpretations—which often neglect to cite their sources, claiming sacred symbolism for something they do not understand at all—the enneagram defines nine personality types on the psychological plane, each one formed by our defense mechanisms when faced with exterior aggression starting at birth. It must be made clear, however, that Gurdjieff never mentioned this possibility, and that in any case, this idea has nothing to do with the fundamental cosmic laws that are the law of three and the law of seven and that by definition constitute the enneagram and the essence of its interpretation. Let the reader beware!

55. See chapter 10 on this subject.

56. P. D. Ouspensky, *In Search of the Miraculous: Fragments of an Unknown Teaching,* 285.

57. We will return to the enneagram throughout our studies, continually attempting to explain the phenomena connected to the powers of speech.

CHAPTER 7.
TECHNIQUES OF SPEECH AND POWERS OF THE LOGOS

1. Techniques of the magic word according to the Law of Three. Is each technique itself ruled by a triad? It is important to note that the triad is always in motion and that in certain cases (in lateral octaves), the word or the sound will perform the office of conciliation. This idea applies to both the oral and the written.

2. Antonin Artaud, *Le Théâtre et son double* (Paris: Gallimard, 1964).

3. Stéphane Labat, *La Poésie de l'extase et le pouvoir chamanique du langage* (Paris:

Maisonneuve et Larose, 1997), 329; italics are mine. On ecstasy and altered states of consciousness, see chapter 11.

4. From Jean-Yves Pouilloux, "Paulhan, le défaut de la littérature," in *Yale French Studies,* no. 106 (2004): "At the heart of Paulhan's adventure, there endures a paradox, or rather an inner and unpretentious immoderation, consisting of maintaining the ambition of achieving the sacred by purely profane means, which we might, in mystic terms, call 'the path of writing.' It is made up of this: To get to what is real, we must wait, in writing, for the moment of reversal in which contrary things become equivalent, the coincidence of opposites."

5. Friedrich Nietzsche, *Ainsi parlait Zarathoustra,* Bouquins II, 455–56.

6. Jean Paulhan, *Le Don des langues* (1964–1967), *Oeuvres complètes,* vol. 3 (Paris: Tchou, 1970), 422. I did not discover this text by Paulhan until I was well into the writing of this book, but far from undermining my thesis, it allowed me to explore new ideas and allowed me to confirm my initial notion of the triad (thing-consciousness-word) while critiquing Paulhan's.

7. Jean-Claude Coquet, "Jean Paulhan et langage," in *Colloque de Cerisy-la-Salle* (Paris: Gallimard, 1999), 168. The discussion of Paulhan's ideas is based essentially on this article, which I used as a source of reflection for this paragraph. I have followed Coquet's analytical path in interpreting and commenting on Paulhan with the tools that have allowed me to shape the proper use of the spoken word from the beginning of this book.

8. Ibid., 169.

9. Louis Pauwels, *Monsieur Gurdjieff,* 107–8. After having a discussion with Paulhan about the esoteric schools and their masters, Pauwels received a card from him showing Picasso's *Still Life with Antique Head,* on the back of which Paulhan wrote: "My dear friend, there are some very fine words in the Upanishads on this matter: 'Do not linger where you have found.' And a no less obvious fact: Those who linger will always end up being tricked—whether it be Gurdjieff or the most miserable little medium in the area . . . " Though this remark is certainly true for many masters, it is perfectly clear that, setting aside any ambiguities regarding Gurdjieff (if indeed there are any), he cannot have been a trickster. This partially veiled accusation of Paulhan is unacceptable if we understand that Gurdjieff devoted his life to seeking and transmitting knowledge. Even after two very serious automobile accidents, he continued to teach, although his health was greatly weakened, at least for a while. How could Gurdjieff be called a trickster? Even while lying enfeebled on his hospital bed, he continued to raise his glass to "the health of the idiots" in order to awaken his students and continually sacrificed his time and his health in order to come to the aid of these "nullities" who were striving to become themselves. Gurdjieff was honest about the goal he had set himself, and

the writing of his "legominism," which took place during a very definite period, is the material proof of it. What kind of trickster would have written twelve hundred unparalleled pages (not to mention his other two "series")? What kind of trickster would have offered such a teaching? Those who consider Gurdjieff a trickster, con-man, or charlatan are mistaken, and in being wrong, they trick themselves. The situation reverses and stops the Kundabuffer in its steps, pulverizing the malefi-cent properties that have crystallized in their critiques. "Every ear for itself," as Daumal said. Now we must reflect . . .

10. Jean Paulhan, *Oeuvres complètes,* vol. 3, 375.

11. Jean Paulhan, *Oeuvres complètes,* vol. 2, *Clef de la poésie* (Paris: Tchou, 1970), 243.

12. Jean Paulhan, *Oeuvres complètes,* vol. 3, *Le Don des langues,* 405–6.

13. Ibid., 289.

14. P. D. Ouspensky, *L'Homme et son évolution possible* (Paris: L'Originel, 1999), 60.

15. Jean-Claude Coquet, "Jean Paulhan et langage," 174.

16. Ibid., cited by Jean-Claude Coquet.

17. Ibid., 175.

18. Ibid.

19. Jean Paulhan, *Oeuvres complètes,* vol. 3, *Le Don des langues,* 379.

20. Jean-Claude Coquet, "Jean Paulhan et langage," 176.

21. Jean Paulhan, *Oeuvres complètes,* vol. 3, *Le Don des langues,* 387.

22. Jean-Claude Coquet, "Jean Paulhan et langage," 177.

23. Jean Paulhan, *Oeuvres complètes,* vol. 2, *L'Expérience du proverbe,* 124.

24. Jean-Claude Coquet, "Jean Paulhan et langage," 178.

25. Ibid.

26. Jean Paulhan, *Oeuvres complètes,* vol. 2, *Petite préface à toute critique,* cited by Jean-Claude Coquet, "Jean Paulhan et langage," 179.

27. See the issue of mechanical thoughts, consequences of those who have forgotten themselves, in the following chapter.

28. Louis Pauwels, *Monsieur Gurdjieff,* 146.

29. Here I perform the synthesis of what Ouspensky relates on this subject in *In Search of the Miraculous: Fragments of an Unknown Teaching* and *L'Homme et son évolution possible* (Paris: L'Originel, 1999).

30. The states of consciousness. We will return to this in chapter 12.

31. Georges de Maleville, *Élements pour une possible évolution intérieure,* 17.

32. Ibid. For a more detailed demonstration of this phenomenon, refer to Georges de Maleville's work.

33. See chapter 11 on this subject.

34. P. D. Ouspensky, *L'Homme et son évolution possible,* 43.

35. René Daumal, "La mort spirituelle," in G. I. Gurdjieff, *Dossiers H. Gurdjieff,* 341.

36. We will return to this later.

37. Louis Pauwels, *Monsieur Gurdjieff,* 70.

38. G. I. Gurdjieff, *Gurdjieff parle à ses élèves,* 85–86.

39. Louis Pauwels, *Monsieur Gurdjieff,* 70.

40. Ibid., 145–46: "This is how Rabelais's words should be understood: 'Science without conscience is but the ruin of the soul' is so often interpreted in the unfortunate lay and primary sense: science without moral conscience. . . . This is absolutely not a matter of moral conscience for Rabelais, who is here expressing an initiatory truth, and not an everyday truth. This refers to higher consciousness—that is to say, accession to the fixed and transcendent *me,* the great *"I"* hidden by the multiple little *"I"*s of individuality subject to what Gurdjieff calls 'mechanicalness.' This is the consciousness revealed by inner experience, the object of the initiatory path itself."

41. Jean Paulhan, *Le Don des langues, Oeuvres complètes,* vol. 3, 421 and 376.

42. Jean-Claude Coquet, "Jean Paulhan et langage," 183.

43. See the next chapter.

44. Stéphane Labat, *La Poésie de l'extase et le pouvoir chamanique du langage,* 332.

45. Ibid.

46. Ibid., 337.

47. Carlos Castaneda, *L'Herbe du diable et la petite fumée* (Paris: Christian Bourgois, 1985), 61. Wisdom here should be understood in the sense of knowledge.

48. Carlos Castaneda, *La Force du Silence* (Paris: Gallimard, 1987), 92.

49. Carlos Castaneda, *Voir, les enseignements d'un sorcier Yaqui* (Paris: Gallimard, 1973), 124.

50. Stéphane Labat, *La Poésie de l'extase et le pouvoir chamanique du langage,* 341.

51. Ibid.

52. Cited by Anne Stamm, *La parole est un monde* (Paris: Seuil, 1999), 123.

53. Stéphane Labat, *La Poésie de l'extase et le pouvoir chamanique du langage.*

54. Matthew 12:36–37.

55. Antonin Artaud, *Le Moine, Oeuvres complètes,* vol. 6 (Paris: Gallimard, 1982).

56. Carlos Castaneda, *La Force du Silence,* 239.

57. Stéphane Labat, *La Poésie de l'extase et le pouvoir chamanique du langage,* 344.

58. Ibid., 330.

59. David Hykes, in G. I. Gurdjieff, *Dossiers H. Gurdjieff,* 137.

60. G. I. Gurdjieff, *Meetings with Remarkable Men,* 32. We should also note the purity of the sound produced by the *ney,* the reed instrument with which the Dervishes compete. This ancient instrument causes a strong sense of unity and elevation, a mystic breath that is easily perceptible to those who listen to it, especially to those who hear it.

61. René Daumal, *A Night of Serious Drinking,* 10.

62. Ibid., 12.

63. Ibid., 18–19.

64. Ibid., 12–13.

65. Jean Biès, *René Daumal,* 53.

66. From *The Mandukyopanishat Being the Exposition of OM, the Great Sacred Name of the Supreme Being in the Vedas.* In Aldous Huxley, *Moksha* (New York: Stonehill, 1977).

67. These ideas (the relationship among sound, music, and shamanism) will be expanded in chapter 11.

68. P. D. Ouspensky, *In Search of the Miraculous: Fragments of an Unknown Teaching,* 296.

69. Ibid.

70. Jean Chevalier and Alain Gheerbrant, *Dictionnaire des symboles,* 655.

71. We will return to this in chapter 11.

72. Jean Chevalier and Alain Gheerbrant, *Dictionnaire des symboles,* 655.

73. P. D. Ouspensky, *In Search of the Miraculous: Fragments of an Unknown Teaching,* 297.

74. G. I. Gurdjieff, *Meetings with Remarkable Men,* 129–33.

75. Ibid., 130.

76. Ibid., 131.

77. Ibid., 133.

78. Laurence Rosenthal, "La musique de Gurdjieff," in G. I. Gurdjieff, *Dossiers H. Gurdjieff,* 151–52.

79. Thomas de Hartmann, *Notre vie avec Monsieur Gurdjieff* (Monaco: Éditions du Rocher, 2003), 300.

80. Peter Brook, "Une autre dimension: la qualité," 81.

81. Laurence Rosenthal, "La musique de Gurdjieff," in G. I. Gurdjieff, *Dossiers H. Gurdjieff,* 146.

82. David Hykes, in G. I. Gurdjieff, *Dossiers H. Gurdjieff,* 137.

83. Ibid.

84. Ibid., 138.

85. Ibid.

86. Ibid.

87. Harmonics is a vast and complex subject, and an entire book—written by a specialist—would be required to address it with the necessary rigor. We therefore advise the cautious reader—in addition to persevering in studying the system—to explore this question, referring to the work of David Hykes, who offers the guidance necessary for further understanding.

88. René Daumal, *A Night of Serious Drinking.*

89. Paul Valéry, *Cahiers 1894–1914*, édition intégrale (Paris: Gallimard, 1974).

90. Charles Baudelaire, *Œuvres Complètes* (Paris: Gallimard, 1975), 182.

91. Emile Benveniste, "La Notion de rythme dans son expression linguistique." In *Problèmes de linguistique générale 1 (1951).*

92. Ibid.

93. Adré Spire, *Plaisir poétique et plaisir musculaire* (Paris: Corti, 1949).

94. Henri Meschonnic, *Les États de la poétique* (Paris: PUF, 1985), 8; italics are mine.

95. Emile Benveniste, "La Notion de rythme dans son expression linguistique," 333.

96. Ibid., 330.

97. Ibid., 333.

98. Ibid., 335.

99. Claudel, "Réflexions sur la poésie," in *Idées* (Paris: Gallimard, 1953).

100. Cicero, "De l'orateur," vol. 3, 173, translated by Edmond Courbaud and Henri Bornecque, (Paris: Les Belles Lettres, 1956): 70.

101. Aristotle, *Rhétorique,* translated by Charles-Émile Ruelle, edited by Patricia Vanhemellryck (Paris: Le Livre de Poche, 1991), 322.

102. Cicero, "De l'orateur," 71.

103. Ibid.

104. Ibid., 185–86, 76.

105. Aristotle, *Rhétorique,* 322.

106. Ibid.

107. Henri Meschonnic, *Critique du rythme* (Lagrasse: Verdier, 1982), 85.

108. Julia Kristeva, *Polylogue* (Paris: Seuil, 1977), 449.

109. Henri Meschonnic, *Critique du rythme,* 76.

110. Ibid., 85.

111. Ibid., 87.

112. Paul Zumthor, *Oral Poetry: An Introduction, Theory and History of Literature,* vol. 70, translated by Kathryn Murphy-Judy (Minneapolis: University of Minnesota Press, 1990), 112.

113. Ibid., 131.

114. Ibid., 132.

115. Ibid., 134–35.

116. René Daumal, *Les Pouvoirs de la parole,* 64.

117. Ibid., 50.

118. Ibid. René Daumal also mentions the "ornaments of meaning," which in order to be valid must also be opposed to chance and accident: "The analysis of these ornaments is often very exact and conforms to the general laws of meaning. An *alam-*

kara is not used haphazardly; it corresponds to a particular psychological operation, a certain attitude, and a certain distance the speaker maintains with respect
to language." Metaphors, contrast, comparison, synecdoche, and paradox belong in
this category; see page 66.

119. Ibid., 70–71.

120. Ibid., 73.

121. Jean-Philippe de Tonnac, *René Daumal, l'archange,* 179.

122. See the following chapter.

123. Here we will not discuss oral poetry, which would require a more profound study.
I simply establish a connection that is revealing, in my view, because it embodies
the setting of speech into action: through the illocutory force of the voice, oral language has a "moral" effect, a force of persuasion that acts authoritatively. The oral
has its own powers of action, which also must be mastered in a total apprenticeship. We will discuss these chapters in chapter 11, covering the psychedelic powers
of speech of which the shaman is the great specialist. For certain oral poets, the
word must be spoken in order to exist; it must take part in a verbal dance that
alone can prove its action and its existence.

124. Anon., *The Emerald Tablet of Hermes* (Whitefish, MT: Kessinger Publishing,
2004).

125. Louis Pauwels, *Monsieur Gurdjieff,* 390–91.

126. The notion of silence will be developed in the next chapter.

127. Stéphane Labat, *La Poésie de l'extase et le pouvoir chamanique du langage,* 330.

128. Charles Duits, *La Vie, le fard de Dieu* (L'Isle-sur-la-Sorgue: Le Bois d'Orion,
1994), 23.

129. Charles Duits, *Le Pays de l'éclairement,* 191.

130. G. I. Gurdjieff, *Beelzebub's Tales to His Grandson,* vol. 2, 348–52. See also G. I.
Gurdjieff, *Gurdjieff parle à ses élèves,* 253.

131. Stéphane Labat, *La Poésie de l'extase et le pouvoir chamanique du langage,* 331.

132. Ouspensky reports a highly interesting conversation in *In Search of the Miraculous:
Fragments of an Unknown Teaching* (94–95), which I consider an important point
of reflection that goes against ordinary and conventionally accepted ideas:

> When G. went to Moscow, our permanent group met without him. There
> remain in my memory several talks in our group which were connected
> with what we had recently heard from G. We had many talks about the
> idea of miracles, and, about the fact that the Absolute cannot manifest its
> will in our world and that this will manifests itself only in the form of
> mechanical laws and it cannot manifest itself by violating these laws. I do
> not remember which of us was first to remember a well-known, though not

very respectful school story, in which we at once saw an illustration of this law. The story is about an over-aged student of a seminary who, at a final examination, does not understand the idea of God's omnipotence. "Well, give me an example of something that the Lord cannot do," said the examining bishop. "It won't take long to do that, your Eminence," answered the seminarist. "Everyone knows that the Lord himself cannot beat the ace of trumps with the ordinary deuce." Nothing could be more clear. There was more sense in this silly story than in a thousand theological treatises. The laws of a game amount to the essence of the game. A violation of these laws would destroy the entire game. The Absolute can as little interfere in our life and substitute other results in the place of the natural results of causes created by us or created accidentally as he can beat the ace of trumps with the deuce. Turgenev wrote somewhere that all ordinary prayers can be reduced to one: "Lord, make it so that twice two be not four." This is the same thing as the ace of trumps of the seminarist.

133. P. D. Ouspensky, *In Search of the Miraculous: Fragments of an Unknown Teaching,* 300.

134. See Biès, Leloup, and Goettmann for more on *hesychasm.*

135. P. D. Ouspensky, *In Search of the Miraculous: Fragments of an Unknown Teaching,* 301–2. "The Christian church is—a school concerning which people have forgotten that it is a school" (page 302): Gurdjieff discusses the origins of the Christian church, which, according to him, was not invented by the fathers of the church, but was taken from "Egypt, only not from the Egypt that we know, but from one which we do not know. . . . Only small bits of it survived in historical times . . . preserved in secret and so well that we do not even know where." In fact, prehistoric Egypt was Christian long before Christ in that its religion was based on the same principles as those of Christianity.

136. G. I. Gurdjieff, *Beelzebub's Tales to His Grandson,* vol. 2, 344.

137. P. D. Ouspensky, *In Search of the Miraculous: Fragments of an Unknown Teaching,* 132.

138. G. I. Gurdjieff, *Meetings with Remarkable Men,* 81–82.

139. Recounted by Pascal Lacombe in the presence of the shaman don Francisco Montes Shuna at a conference on shamanism in Paris, March 2004.

140. Mark 5:41–43.

141. Stéphane Labat, *La Poésie de l'extase et le pouvoir chamanique du langage,* 343.

142. James Douglas Morrison, *Arden Lointain,* 111. See also Maria Sabina on sacred mushrooms in chapter 11.

143. Jean Chevalier and Alain Gheerbrant, *Dictionnaire des symboles,* 561.

CHAPTER 8. WRITING: SPIRITUAL ASCETICISM AND THE TECHNIQUE OF THE WORK

1. G. I. Gurdjieff, *Meetings with Remarkable Men;* italics are mine.

2. Jean Biès, *Les Grands Initiés du XXe siècle* (Paris: Lebaud, 1998).

3. Jean-Yves Pouilloux, "Paulhan, le défaut de la literature."

4. Letter from March 3, 1932.

5. G. I. Gurdjieff, *Beelzebub's Tales to His Grandson,* vol. 1, 3.

6. The processes set forth (intended to act upon the reader) in *Beelzebub's Tales to His Grandson* will be examined in chapter 10, especially in light of Charles Duits's reflections.

7. P. D. Ouspensky, in G. I. Gurdjieff, *Dossiers H. Gurdjieff,* 293.

8. In chapter 9 we will see how the author-reader relationship can become a master-disciple relationship.

9. René Daumal, "Poetry Black, Poetry White."

10. Ibid.

11. Ibid.

12. Jean Biès, *René Daumal,* 54.

13. René Daumal, *Les Pouvoirs de la parole.* Esssais et notes II (1935–1944), Gallimard, 1981 (1972).

14. See the enneagram of the synthesis in appendix 1.

15. P. D. Ouspensky, *In Search of the Miraculous: Fragments of an Unknown Teaching,* 272.

16. Ibid., 356.

17. Cited by Jean-Philippe de Tonnac, *René Daumal, l'archange,* 243.

18. Rimbaud, "Sensation."

19. Pascal Boué, in René Daumal, *Dossiers H. René Daumal.*

20. René Daumal, "Poetry Black, Poetry White."

21. Ibid.

22. Ibid.

23. Ibid.

24. René Daumal, *Les Pouvoirs de la parole,* 71.

25. Ibid., 72.

26. Ibid., 67.

27. René Daumal, "Poetry Black, Poetry White."

28. Jean-Philippe de Tonnac, *René Daumal, l'archange,* 263.

29. See the enneagram of the synthesis. Here I revise the enneagram of language in light of the scheme of poetic operation proposed by Daumal according to Hindu theory (see Aldous Huxley, *The Doors of Perception*), and attempt to give it a fixed form. This is the "body of the poem," which reconciles the "affective state of the poet" and that of the listener. Thus the "flavor" is transmitted.

30. P. D. Ouspensky, *L'Homme et son évolution possible*, 75.

31. See appendix 1.

32. Jean-Philippe de Tonnac, *René Daumal, l'archange*, 243.

33. Louis Pauwells, *Monsieur Gurdjieff* (Paris: Seuil, 1954; Paris: Albin Michel, 1996).

34. René Zuber, *Qui êtes-vous, Monsieur Gurdjieff?* (Paris: Éditions Éoliennes).

35. René Daumal, "Poetry Black, Poetry White."

36. René Zuber, *Qui êtes-vous, Monsieur Gurdjieff?* (Paris: Éditions Éoliennes), 222.

37. See P. D. Ouspensky, *In Search of the Miraculous: Fragments of an Unknown Teaching.*

38. It is extremely difficult not to fall into this trap, a major cause of deviation. Surmounting it requires a presence, a factor of effective remembrance permitting us to give words their true weight.

39. See chapter 11.

40. P. D. Ouspensky, *In Search of the Miraculous: Fragments of an Unknown Teaching*, 50. We will discuss this again in chapter 11.

41. Jean-Philippe de Tonnac, *René Daumal, l'archange*, 227.

42. Michel Random, in G. I. Gurdjieff, *Dossiers H. Gurdjieff*, 174.

43. Ideas cited and proposed by Jean-Philippe Tonnac, *René Daumal, l'archange*, 275–76.

44. Whitall N. Perry, *Gurdjieff in the Light of Tradition* (Ghent, N.Y.: Sophia Perennis, 2001), 96.

45. P. D. Ouspensky, *In Search of the Miraculous: Fragments of an Unknown Teaching*, 74.

46. G. I. Gurdjieff, *Beelzebub's Tales to His Grandson*, vol. 1, 386.

47. Lucifer Ilje is a character in Charles Duits' book, *La Salive de l'éléphant*.

48. Charles Duits, *La Salive de l'éléphant*.

49. Ibid., 19.

50. Ibid.

51. Ibid., 49.

52. Ibid., 50.

53. Ibid., 51.

54. Ibid., 52.

55. Ibid., 55.

56. Aldous Huxley, *Moksha*, 328–29. We will return in depth in chapter 11 to these substances that modify the consciousness.

57. G. I. Gurdjieff, *Gurdjieff parle à ses élèves*, 95.

58. Ibid., 109.

59. Ibid.

60. Ibid.

61. Ibid., 111.

62. Ibid.

63. In chapter 11 we will see how psychedelic substances can break this circular conditioning and make us understand the luminous word, the seed that desires to express itself throughout the whole machine.

64. Michel Decant, "Conscience et mécanicité," in G. I. Gurdjieff, *Dossiers H. Gurdjieff,* 233.

65. Ibid., 234.

66. René Daumal, cited by Michel Decant, "Conscience et mécanicité."

67. "Lettre du 11 août 1942 à un ami," cited in Jean-Philippe de Tonnac, *René Daumal, l'archange,* 208.

68. Herein lies the efficacy of blame, generating an increase in awareness. This idea will be expanded in chapter 11.

69. René Daumal to Geneviève Lief, cited in Tonnac, Jean-Philippe de Tonnac, *René Daumal, l'archange,* 273.

70. Montaigne, *Essays,* I, IX, 36, cited by Jean-Yves Pouilloux in "Le temps présent," *L'Inactuel,* no. 12 (2004).

71. Ibid. *Intelligence* means mutual understanding. "[I]f it is wanting" is meant both in the sense of language failing us and perhaps in the sense of it "betraying" us (II, XVIII, 666–67).

72. Jean-Philippe de Tonnac, *René Daumal, l'archange,* 207.

73. René Daumal, "The Holy War," translated by D. M. Dooling, in *Parabola* 7, no. 4 (1982). Originally written in spring 1940.

74. P. D. Ouspensky, *In Search of the Miraculous: Fragments of an Unknown Teaching,* 20.

75. On the phenomenon of identification and consideration, see Georges de Maleville, *Élements pour une possible évolution intérieure,* in which these characteristic traits of the human psyche are very clearly developed and explained.

76. P. D. Ouspensky, *In Search of the Miraculous: Fragments of an Unknown Teaching,* 297–98.

77. René Daumal, foreword to *Contre-ciel.*

78. Cited in Jean-Philippe de Tonnac, *René Daumal, l'archange,* 238.

79. The purpose of the third series of G. I. Gurdjieff's works, *Life Is Real Only Then, when "I Am"* (New York: Viking Arkana, 1991), v.

80. Cited in Jean-Philippe de Tonnac, *René Daumal, l'archange,* 284.

81. Jean-Yves Pouilloux, "Le Temps present."

82. Ibid.

CHAPTER 9. THE WAY OF BLAME

1. Michel Waldberg, *Gurdjieff hors les murs.*

2. Ibid., 18. The issue is addressed admirably in this work, which is remarkable

in many ways. I refer to it often in this chapter as well as in the following one, intending to offer new elements in response. Further, if Waldberg presents a theoretical approach in *Gurdjieff hors les murs,* he moves masterfully into practice in *La Parole Putanisée*—a perfect illustration of the lampooning and satirical spirit of which Gurdjieff was so fond.

3. Ibid., 22. Many striking examples can be found in the numerous testimonies of former students. Gurdjieff once said to a famous novelist: "It would be a thousand times better for you to wash the floor just once the way it ought to be done than to write twenty books." Some people abandoned Gurdjieff after having been violently lambasted. This kind of trial was the test with which the master would evaluate his disciples as well as people he was meeting for the first time.

4. James Moore, *Gurdjieff,* 217.

5. Ibid., 389.

6. Jean Biès, *Les Grands Initiés,* 92.

7. Michel Random, "Les hommes du blâme et la Quattrième Voie," in G. I Gurdjieff, *Dossiers H. Gurdjieff,* 172. "The Malamati came into being in the nineteenth century around Nishapur in Khorassan. They were also known as the 'people of blame,' because they exhibited an apparent contempt for all rules and did not hesitate to violate religious or social taboos, whatever they might be. . . . It has been understood that the rule of these various orders consisted of concealing their meritorious actions and spiritual grandeur beneath contentious appearances precisely in order to avoid receiving praise." See Michel Random, page 173. It should be noted that during the famous "toasts to the idiots" (see next paragraph), Gurdjieff systematically prohibited anyone from raising their glass "to the master's health," and severely chastised those who ventured it. He refused all praise, even from his students.

8. Michel Waldberg, *Gurdjieff hors les murs,* 206.

9. G. I. Gurdjieff, *Meetings with Remarkable Men,* introduction.

10. G. I. Gurdjieff, *Beelzebub's Tales to His Grandson,* vol. 1, 15.

11. René Daumal, *A Night of Serious Drinking,* 5.

12. Michel Waldberg, *Gurdjieff hors les murs,* 14.

13. On the toasts to the idiots, refer especially to J. G. Bennett, Solange Claustres, J. Moore, M. Waldberg, Christian Bouchet, Rina Hands, and Beth McCorkle.

14. James Moore, *Gurdjieff,* 400.

15. By way of example, I mention a few well-known names connected with the various categories. These examples, drawn from the context of the epoch, have merely historical value today. I also offer a few clarifications concerning some of the categories, according to the information at my disposal.

16. Explanation from James Moore, *Gurdjieff,* 401.

17. Ibid.

18. Solange Claustres, *La Prise de conscience et G. I. Gurdjieff* (Utrecht: Éditions Eurêka, 2003), 39.

19. Ibid.

20. Letter to Paul Démeny, May 15, 1871, Rimbaud, *Œuvres complètes*. Cited in Michel Waldberg, *Gurdjieff: An Approach to His Ideas*, 6.

21. Michel Waldberg, *Gurdjieff: An Approach to his Ideas*, 7–8.

22. Ibid., 9.

23. Ibid., 10.

24. Michel Waldberg, *La Parole putanisée*, 77.

25. Léon Bloy, cited by Michel Waldberg in *La Parole putanisée*, 78.

26. René Daumal, *A Night of Serious Drinking*, 59.

27. Italics are mine.

28. Michel Waldberg, *Gurdjieff hors les murs*, 61–62.

29. Charles Duits, *La Vie le fard de Dieu*, 307.

30. Jean-Philippe de Tonnac, *René Daumal, l'archange*, 254.

31. P. D. Ouspensky, *In Search of the Miraculous: Fragments of an Unknown Teaching*, 157.

32. Michel Random, in G. I. Gurdjieff, *Dossiers H. Gurdjieff*, 178.

33. Michel Waldberg, *Gurdjieff: An Approach to His Ideas*, 5.

34. G. I. Gurdjieff, *Life Is Real Only Then, When "I Am,"* 44, 51.

CHAPTER 10.
HERMETIC TRADITION AND LEGOMINISMS

1. Édouard Schuré, *Les Grands Initiés* (Paris: Perrin, 1960), 8.

2. Frédéric Amiel, *Amiel's Journal: The Journal Intime of Henri-Frederic Amiel,* translated by Mrs. Humphrey Ward; cited in Édouard Schuré, *Les Grands Initiés,* 24.

3. Édouard Schuré, *Les Grands Initiés,* 150.

4. Ibid., 161.

5. Ibid., 163; italics are mine.

6. G. I. Gurdjieff, *Beelzebub's Tales to His Grandson,* vol. 1, 349.

7. Ibid., 350–51.

8. Michel Waldberg, *Gurdjieff: An Approach to His Ideas,* 18.

9. Charles Duits, cited in Michel Waldberg, *Gurdjieff: An Approach to His Ideas,* 20.

10. Ibid., 20–21.

11. Ibid., 21.

12. Ibid., 21–22.

13. Ibid., 22.

14. Ibid.

15. G. I. Gurdjieff, *Beelzebub's Tales to His Grandson,* vol. 1, 351.

16. Charles Duits, cited in Michel Waldberg, *Gurdjieff: An Approach to His Ideas,* 23–24.

17. P. D. Ouspensky, *In Search of the Miraculous: Fragments of an Unknown Teaching,* 279.

18. Ibid.

19. Ibid., 278–79.

20. Ibid., 279–80.

21. G. I. Gurdjieff, *Meetings with Remarkable Men,* 34.

22. G. I. Gurdjieff, *Meetings with Remarkable Men.*

23. Ibid., 36.

24. We should also understand the biblical myth in Gurdjieff's teachings as an esoteric lesson from which we can draw a portion of the knowledge of universal laws.

25. Pierre Brunel, *Mythocritique. Theorie et parcours* (Paris: Presses universitaires de France, Ecriture, 1992).

26. Mircea Eliade, *Myth and Reality* (New York: Harper Torchbooks, 1968).

27. Charles Duits, *La Vie le fard de Dieu* (L'Isle-sur-la-Sorgue: Le Bois d'Orion, 1994).

28. Pascal Boué, "La parole proximale de René Daumal ou les pouvoirs du silence," in *Dossiers H. René Daumal,* 118.

29. René Daumal, *Mount Analogue,* 131.

30. Pascal Boué, "La parole proximale de René Daumal ou les pouvoirs du silence," in *Dossiers H. René Daumal,* 124.

31. Ibid.

32. P. D. Ouspensky, *In Search of the Miraculous: Fragments of an Unknown Teaching,* 280.

33. René Daumal, *Le Mont analogue—roman d'aventures alpines, noneuclidiennes et symboliquement authentiques* (Paris: Gallimard, L'imaginaire, 1981 [1952]).

34. Ibid., 281.

35. Ibid., 281–82.

36. Ibid., 282.

37. Ibid., 283.

38. Concerning the tarot, I advise readers who wish to study this more deeply to refer to the works of Nicolas Tereshchenko, especially *Les Trésors du tarot: accès aux mystères du cosmos* (Paris: Guy Trédaniel, 1986).

39. P. D. Ouspensky, *In Search of the Miraculous: Fragments of an Unknown Teaching,* 284.

40. Ibid.

41. Ibid.

42. See Ouspensky for the detailed and "technical" description of this symbol first revealed by Gurdjieff.

43. See the enneagram of the synthesis in appendix 1 concerning the placement of the intervals. I refer to Ouspensky regarding the "lateral octaves." To expound upon this point would lead us into overlong digressions. Furthermore, the rigorous understanding and application of this law requires a much more profound study, which will not fit within the framework of this book, its main subject being the powers of speech.

44. P. D. Ouspensky, *In Search of the Miraculous: Fragments of an Unknown Teaching,* 290.

45. A hypothesis to be tested.

46. P. D. Ouspensky, *In Search of the Miraculous: Fragments of an Unknown Teaching,* 291.

47. Ibid., 294.

48. Édouard Schuré, *Les Grands Initiés,* 28.

CHAPTER 11. THE PSYCHEDELIC POWERS OF THE WORD

1. This chapter develops a few ideas already touched upon in "La littérature enthéogène et les pouvoirs psychédéliques de la parole," in Pierre Bonnasse, *Les Voix de l'extase, l'expérience des plantes sacrées en literature* (Paris: Éditions Trouble-fête, 2005).

2. In September 1924, Roger Gilbert-Lecomte announced to René Maublanc that he was going to study philosophy, and he sent Maublanc some poems including "Rêve opiacé" and "Les tablettes d'un visionnaire," in which he attempted to "convey [his] hallucinations without literary artifice, or choice." Roger Gilbert-Lecomte, *Correspondance,* preface and notes by Pierre Minet (Paris: Gallimard, 1971), 39–40.

3. René Daumal, *Correspondance,* vol. 1, edited and annotated by H. J. Maxwell (Paris: Gallimard, 1992), 116, letter dated June 8, 1926.

4. Ibid., 121.

5. Michel Random, *Le Grand Jeu* (Paris: Denoël, 1970), 102.

6. "I was in love with my death," wrote Daumal, with a particularly mystical measure of affection. Many examples are found in his work testifying to this fascination for the "mastery of fear, the mastery of the end" that always haunted him.

7. CCl_4 dangerously modifies the composition of the blood through a radical destruction of red blood cells and an increase in white blood cells. This results in irreversible anemia, a factor in the development of tuberculosis.

8. René Daumal, "L'Asphyxie et l'Évidence absurde," in *Le Grand Jeu,* no. 4. Text reproduced in *l'Évidence absurde* (1930) and in René Daumal, *l'Évidence absurde, essais et notes, I (1926–1934),* edited by Claude Rugafiori (Paris: Gallimard, 1972), 53.

9. See S. I. Witkiewicz for a similar experience.

10. René Daumal, "Le souvenir déterminant," in *Les Pouvoirs de la parole, essais et notes, II (1935–1943)* (Paris: Gallimard, 1972), 114. We will return to this idea, which is central to my subject matter.

11. Ibid., 119.

12. Ibid., 120. We will have occasion to return to this later.

13. Ibid., 55.

14. He died of tetanus in 1943, the result of a heroin injection. His work, which remains highly interesting, does not fit with the logic of our studies, even though Lecomte made allusions to mystical experiences. Thus we will abstain from any attempt to analyze his texts (relating to opiates), instead sticking to Daumal's work, which is more in line with our topic. See Jean-Philippe Tonnac for the differences between Daumal and Lecomte.

15. René Daumal, *Les Pouvoirs de la parole*, 120.

16. Jean-Yves Pouilloux, "Le Temps present."

17. William James, *The Varieties of Religious Experience: A Study in Human Nature* (New York: Modern Library, 1902), lectures 16 and 17.

18. Ibid.

19. Ibid. See the second part of the chapter on "union with the divine."

20. William James, "The Subjective Effects of Nitrous Oxide," in *Mind* 7 (1882).

21. Philippe Jaccottet, *La Promenade sous les arbres* (La Bibliothèque des arts, 1996), 39.

22. Jean-Yves Pouilloux, "Paulhan, le défaut de la literature."

23. P. D. Ouspensky, *In Search of the Miraculous: Fragments of an Unknown Teaching*, 8.

24. James Webb, *The Harmonious Circle: The Lives and Work of G. I. Gurdjieff, P. D. Ouspensky, and Their Followers* (New York: Putnam, 1980), 112.

25. P. D. Ouspensky, *A New Model of the Universe* (New York: Vintage Books, 1971), 274–304.

26. P. D. Ouspensky, *In Search of the Miraculous: Fragments of an Unknown Teaching*, 50–51.

27. Charles Duits, *La Vie le fard de Dieu*.

28. P. D. Ouspensky, *In Search of the Miraculous: Fragments of an Unknown Teaching*, 8.

29. Michel Waldberg, *Gurdjieff hors les murs*, 141.

30. Charles Duits, "Dieu vert Ciguri," in *La Conscience démonique* (L'Isle-sur-la-Sorgue: Le Bois d'Orion, 1994).

31. P. D. Ouspensky, *In Search of the Miraculous: Fragments of an Unknown Teaching*, 161. "*Not his own* means what has come from outside, what he has learned or reflects, all traces of exterior impressions left in the memory and in the sensations, all words and movements that have been learned, all feelings created by imitation—all this is not his own, all this is personality. . . . A small child has no personality yet. He

is what he really is. He is essence. His desires, tastes, likes, and dislikes express his being such as it is."

32. Ibid., 162.

33. Aldous Huxley, *The Doors of Perception*.

34. P. D. Ouspensky, *In Search of the Miraculous: Fragments of an Unknown Teaching*, 162.

35. G. I Gurdjieff, *Gurdjieff parle à ses élèves*.

36. P. D. Ouspensky, *In Search of the Miraculous: Fragments of an Unknown Teaching*.

37. Charles Duits, *Le Pays de l'éclairement*, 78.

38. P. D. Ouspensky, *In Search of the Miraculous: Fragments of an Unknown Teaching*, 195. See the schematic illustration of the centers in the appendices.

39. Ibid.

40. Ibid., 197. It would take too long to discuss thoroughly the role and constitution of hydrogens. I merely allude to it here in order to clarify my point (to show the material nature of all processes), and I advise the reader who wishes to explore this topic to refer to Ouspensky's work, *In Search of the Miraculous: Fragments of an Unknown Teaching*, which contains an excellent introduction to this part of the teaching.

41. Terence McKenna, *Food of the Gods: The Search for the Original Tree of Knowledge* (New York: Bantam Books, 1992), 20.

42. Ibid., 24.

43. Ibid. The idea that psychoactive plants may have been behind the flourishing of religious beliefs was also supported particularly by Weston La Barre and Gordon Wasson.

44. Ibid., 26.

45. Ibid.

46. Ibid., 27.

47. Ibid., 27–28.

48. Ibid., 41.

49. Ibid., 42.

50. Ibid., 48. Henry Munn, also noted in "The Mushrooms of Language," in *Hallucinogens and Shamanism,* edited by Michael J. Harner (New York: Oxford University Press, 1973), that the influence of the mushroom on language is not unique to the Mazatecs, but is a universal reality shared by all experimenters: ". . . [B]etween the experiences of individuals with differing social inherences, the common characteristic would be discourse, for judging by their effect the chemical constituents of the mushrooms have some connection with the linguistic centers of the brain."

51. Ibid., 49.

52. Ibid., 52.

53. Ibid., 52–53; italics are mine.

54. Henry Munn, "The Mushrooms of Language."

55. S. I. Witkiewicz, "Le peyotl," in *Les Narcotiques suivi des Âmes mal lavées* (Lusanne: L'Âge d'Homme, 1980).

56. Ibid., 70–71.

57. Henry Munn, "The Mushrooms of Language."

58. S. I. Witkiewicz, "Le peyotl," 64.

59. Terence McKenna, *Food of the Gods*, 15.

60. Marino Benzi, *Les Derniers Adorateurs du peyotl: croyances, coutumes et mythes des Indiens Huichol* (Paris: Gallimard, 1972), 140.

61. Ibid., 145.

62. Terence McKenna, *Food of the Gods*, 11.

63. G. I. Gurdjieff, *Beelzebub's Tales to His Grandson*, vol. 3, 84.

64. Pascal Lacombe, "Icaros: des outils chamaniques," in *Les Voix d'Extase, l'expérience des plantes sacrées en littérature* (Paris: Trouble-fête, 2005).

65. P. D. Ouspensky, *In Search of the Miraculous: Fragments of an Unknown Teaching*, 35.

66. Ibid.

67. Maria Sabina, *Selections*, edited by Jerome Rothenberg (Berkeley, Calif.: University of California Press, 2003), 38.

68. Ibid., 38–39.

69. Henry Munn, "The Mushrooms of Language."

70. Maria Sabina, *Selections*, edited by Jerome Rothenberg (Berkeley, Calif.: University of California Press, 2003).

71. Fernando Benitez, *Les Champignons hallucinants* (Paris: Éditions du Lézard, 1995), 43; italics are mine.

72. Henry Munn, "The Mushrooms of Language."

73. Ibid.

74. Octavio Paz, *Le labyrinthe de la solitude,* seguido de "Critique de la pyramide." (Paris: Gallimard, 1972).

75. Henry Munn, "The Mushrooms of Language."

76. Ibid.

77. Jean-Yves Pouilloux, "Le temps present."

78. Victor Hugo, *Odes et ballades* (Paris: Gallimard, 1980 [1822]).

79. Jeanne de Salzmann, in *Dossiers H. Gurdjieff.*

80. Jean-Philippe de Tonnac, *René Daumal, l'archange,* 218.

81. Madame de Salzmann in Ravi Ravindra, *Un cœur sans limite, le travail avec Jeanne de Salzmann* (Halifax, Nova Scotia: Shaila Press, 2002), 33. Dominique Dupuy also notes in *Dossiers H. Daumal,* on René Daumal, page 263: "The reading and approach of thought acquires its true resonance only when it reaches a given point,

confirming something that we have ourselves researched and experimented, something we have glimpsed, perceived, lived through."

CHAPTER 12.
MOVEMENT IN THE CREATIVE PROCESS

1. René Daumal, *l'Évidence absurde*.

2. Marthe de Gaigneron, "Danses Sacrées," in *Dossiers H. Gurdjieff*, 154.

3. G. I. Gurdjieff, *Beelzebub's Tales to His Grandson*, vol. 2, 109.

4. James Moore, *Gurdjieff*, 52.

5. Marthe de Gaigneron, "Danses Sacrées," 155.

6. G. I. Gurdjieff, *Meetings with Remarkable Men*, 162.

7. Ibid., 162–63.

8. Solange Claustres, *La Prise de conscience et G. I. Gurdjieff*, 102.

9. Marthe de Gaigneron, "Danses Sacrées," 156.

10. Solange Claustres, *La Prise de conscience et G. I. Gurdjieff*, 115.

11. Pierre Schaeffer, *Dossiers H. Gurdjieff*.

12. Pauline de Dampierre, "Les Mouvements," in *Dossiers H. Gurdjieff*, 131.

13. Dominique Dupuy, "D'Orphée à Civa, la danse pour 'ceux qui ont un coeur,'" in *Dossiers H. Daumal*, 260–63.

14. Extract from a lecture given through the Institut pour le Développement Harmonique de l'Homme [Institute for the Harmonic Development of Man], Georges de Maleville, *Élements pour une possible évolution intérieure*, 70.

15. P. D. Ouspensky, *In Search of the Miraculous: Fragments of an Unknown Teaching*, 16.

16. Georges de Maleville, *Élements pour une possible évolution intérieure*, 70.

17. Solange Claustres, *La Prise de conscience et G. I. Gurdjieff*, 101. James Moore (*Gurdjieff*, 398) defines seven categories of dances created by Gurdjieff, thanks to which the harmonic development of man and the transmission of esoteric knowledge is accomplished: 1. Rhythms (harmonic, plastic and occupational); 2. Six preliminary exercises or "Obligatories"; 3. Ritual exercises and medical gymnastics; 4. Women's dances; 5. Men's ethnic dances (dervish and Tibetan); 6. Sacred temple dances and tableaux; 7. The thirty-nine movements of Gurdjieff's last, partly enneagrammatic, series.

18. Ibid., 102.

19. Georges de Maleville, *Élements pour une possible évolution intérieure*, 70.

20. Jean-Philippe de Tonnac writes (on page 233 of his book on Daumal): "In the instructor's hands, the student goes through a profound substantial mutation, generating a new vision of the world. Thermodynamics explain to us how, under the effects of a certain temperature, the structure of a body itself can be overturned

partially or completely, ice can change into water or water into vapor. The exercises that occurred sought to modify this 'temperature,' and our sorcerer's apprentices worked on the same transformation with the instructor's aid."

21. Jeanne de Salzmann, *Gurdjieff International Review* (spring 2002). Movements are a valuable aid for attaining "direct perception." As Salzmann emphasizes (in Ravi Ravindra, *Un cœur sans limite, le travail avec Jeanne de Salzmann,* 10): "The movements will help you. In the movements, the important thing is not the postures but the impulse, the energy, from one posture to the next. And nobody can teach this; you must observe it in yourself."

22. Josée de Salzmann, "Le Maître de Danse," *Magazine littéraire,* no. 131 (December 1977).

23. Solange Claustres, *La Prise de conscience et G. I. Gurdjieff,* 119.

24. P. D. Ouspensky, *In Search of the Miraculous: Fragments of an Unknown Teaching,* 294–95.

25. Solange Claustres, *La Prise de conscience et G. I. Gurdjieff,* 106.

26. P. D. Ouspensky, *In Search of the Miraculous: Fragments of an Unknown Teaching,* 295; italics are mine.

27. René Daumal, *Dossiers H. René Daumal.*

28. Katherine Mansfield, cited in *Dossiers H. Gurdjieff,* 319–20; italics are mine.

29. Rom Landau, *God Is My Adventure: A Book on Modern Mystics, Masters and Teachers* (London: Ivor Nicholson and Watson, 1935).

30. Antonin Artaud, "Le théâtre d'après guerre à Paris," VIII, 181–82; René Daumal, *Dossiers H. René Daumal,* 225.

31. Marthe de Gaigneron, "Danses Sacrées," 157.

32. Jean-Philippe de Tonnac, *René Daumal, l'archange,* 232.

33. René Daumal, "Le mouvement dans l'éducation intégrale de l'homme," in *l'Évidence absurde,* 276–80. See also Daumal's letter to Paulhan from August 16, 1934, in which he points to the "constant miracles" that the movements procured for him (René Daumal, *Dossiers H., René Daumal,* 290). All the quotes in this paragraph are from Daumal, except where otherwise noted.

34. Rene Daumal, *L'Evidence absurde. Essais et notes I* (1926–1934) (Paris: Gallimard, 1981 [1972]).

35. Ibid.

36. Ibid.

37. Michel Camus in *Dossiers H. Gurdjieff.*

38. René Daumal, *L'Evidence absurde. Essais et notes I* (1926–1934) (Paris: Gallimard, 1981 [1972]).

39. Ibid.

40. Marthe de Gaigneron, "Danses Sacrées," 156.

CONCLUSION:
WORD LOST, WORD REGAINED, WORD PRESENT

1. René Daumal, *A Night of Serious Drinking,* 113; italics are mine.
2. Jean-Philippe de Tonnac, *René Daumal, l'archange,* 187.
3. Madame de Salzmann in Ravi Ravindra, *Un cœur sans limite, le travail avec Jeanne de Salzmann,* 34.
4. P. D. Ouspensky, *In Search of the Miraculous: Fragments of an Unknown Teaching* (London: Routledge and Kegan Paul, 1950), 61.
5. Ibid.
6. Ravi Ravindra, *Un cœur sans limite, le travail avec Jeanne de Salzmann,* 41.
7. Ibid.
8. Ibid., 55.
9. G. I. Gurdjieff, *Life Is Real Only Then, when "I Am,"* 44.
10. René Daumal, *A Night of Serious Drinking,* 277.
11. Ibid., 277–78.
12. Solange Claustres, *La Prise de conscience et G. I. Gurdjieff,* 136.
13. Jean-Yves Pouilloux, "Paulhan, le défaut de la literature."
14. Ibid.
15. Michel Camus, in Michel Random, *La Pensée transdisciplinaire et le reel* (Paris: Éditions Dervy, 1996), 148.

AFTERWORD:
SUFFICIENT UNTO THE LEVEL IS THE EVIL THEREOF

1. The words of Father Giovanni, G. I. Gurdjieff, *Meetings with Remarkable Men,* 242.

Bibliography

Anonymous. *The Emerald Tablet of Hermes*. Whitefish, MT: Kessinger Publishing, 2004.

Appelbaum, David. *Voice*. Albany: State University of New York Press, 1990.

Artaud, Antonin. *Van Gogh le suicidé de la societé*. Paris: Gallimard, 2001.

Baudelaire, Charles. *Intimate Journals*. Translated by Christopher Isherwood, San Francisco: City Lights Books, 1983.

Bennett, John Godolphin. *L'Énigme Gurdjieff*. Geneva: Georg, 1996.

———. *Gurdjieff, artisan d'un monde nouveau*. Paris: Le Courrier du livre, 1977.

———. *Des idiots à Paris—Quelques mois avec Monsieur Gurdjieff*. Geneva: Georg, 1993.

Benzi, Marino. *Les Derniers Adorateurs du peyotl: croyances, coutumes et mythes des Indiens Huichols*. Paris: Gallimard, 1972.

Biès, Jean. *Athos. La montagne transfigurée*. Paris: Les Deux Océans, 1997.

———. "G. I. Gurdjieff. Promesses d'une parole." In *Question de*, no. 50 (1982).

———. *Les Grands Initiés du XXᵉ siècle*. Paris: Philippe Lebaud, 1998.

———. *Littérature française et pensée hindoue. Des origines à 1950*. Paris: C. Klincksieck, 1992.

———. *René Daumal*. Paris: Pierre Seghers, 1967.

———. "René Daumal: chamanisme et alchimie." In *Dossiers H. René Daumal*. Paris: L'Âge d'Homme, 1993.

Bonnasse, Pierre. *Dans la nuit d'Aghtamar*. Paris: Editions Eoliennes, 2007.

———. *Les Voix de l'Extase, l'expérience des plantes sacrées en littérature*. Paris: Trouble-fête, 2005.

Bouchet, Christian. *Gurdjieff, Qui suis-je?* Puiseaux: Éditions Pardès, 2001.

Boue, Pascal. "La parole proximale de René Daumal ou les pouvoirs du silence." In *Dossiers H. René Daumal*. Paris: L'Âge d'Homme, 1993.

Brook, Peter. "Une autre dimension: la qualitée." In Bruno de Panafieu, *G. I. Gurdjieff.* Paris: L'Âge d'Homme, 1993.

Camus, Michel. "De la conscience du corps au corps de la conscience." In Bruno de Panafieu, *L'Enjeu du Grand Jeu.* Aiglemont: Mont Analogue, 1994.

———. *G. I. Gurdjieff.* Paris: L'Âge d'Homme, 1993.

———. "Le grand tournant de 1930." In *Dossiers H. René Daumal.* Paris: L'Âge d'Homme, 1993.

Castaneda, Carlos. *La Force du Silence.* Paris: Gallimard, 1987, 92.

———. *L'Herbe du diable et la petite fume.* Paris: Christian Bourgois, 1985.

———. *Voir, les enseignements d'un sorcier Yaqui.* Paris: Gallimard, 1973.

Chevalier, Jean, and Alain Gheerbrant. *Dictionnaire des symboles.* Paris: Robert Laffont, 1982.

Claustres, Solange. *La Prise de conscience et G. I. Gurdjieff.* Utrecht: Éditions Eureka, 2003.

Coquet, Jean-Claude. "Jean Paulhan et le langage." In *Colloque de Cerisy-la-Salle.* Paris: Gallimard, 1999.

Dampierre, Pauline de. "Les Mouvements." In Bruno de Panafieu, *G. I. Gurdjieff.* Paris: L'Âge d'Homme, 1993.

Daumal, René. *Chaque fois que l'aube paraît. Essais et notes 1.* Paris: Gallimard, 1953.

———. *Contre-ciel.* Paris: Poésie/Gallimard, 1990.

———. *Correspondance I, Correspondance 1915–1928.* Paris: Gallimard, Cahiers de la Nouvelle revue Française, 1992.

———. *Correspondance II, Correspondance 1929—1932.* Paris: Gallimard, Cahiers de la Nouvelle revue Française, 1993.

———. *Correspondance III, Correspondance 1933–1944.* Paris: Gallimard, Cahiers de la Nouvelle revue Française, November 1996.

———. *L'Évidence absurde. Essais et notes I (1926–1934).* Paris: Gallimard, 1981.

———. "The Holy War." Translated by D. M. Dooling. In *Parabola* 7, no. 4 (1982).

———. "Inedits." In *Dossiers H. René Daumal.* Paris: L'Âge d'Homme, 1993.

———. *Je ne parle jamais pour ne rien dire (Lettres à Artür Harfaux).* Amiens: Éditions Le Nyctalope, 1994.

———. *Mount Analogue: A Novel of Symbolically Authentic Non-Euclidean Adventures in Mountain Climbing.* Translated by Roger Shattuck. Boston: Shambhala, 1992.

———. *A Night of Serious Drinking.* Translated by David Coward and E. A. Lovatt. Boulder: Shambhala, 1979.

———. "Poetry Black, Poetry White." In *The Powers of the Word: Selected Essays and Notes 1927–1943.* Edited and translated by Mark Polizzotti. San Francisco: City Lights Books, 1991.

————. *Les Pouvoirs de la parole. Essais et notes II (1935–1944)*. Paris: Gallimard, 1981.

————. *Tu t'es toujours trompé*. Edited and introduced by Jack Daumal. Paris: Mercure de France, 1969.

Daumal, Véra. "Le littérature à propos de Gurdjieff et de René Daumal." In *Nouvelle Revue Française*, (1954).

Driscoll, J. Walter. *Gurdjieff, an Annotated Bibliography*. New York: Garland Publishing, 1985.

Duits, Charles. *André Breton a-t-il dit passé*. Paris: Maurice Nadeau, 1991.

————. *La Conscience démonique*. L'Isle-sur-la-Sorgue: Le bois d'Orion, 1994.

————. *Le Pays de l'éclairement*. L'Isle-sur-la-Sorgue: Le bois d'Orion, 1994.

————. "Remarques sur *Les Récits de Belzébuth*." In Michel Waldberg, *Gurdjieff hors les murs*. Paris: La Différence, 2001.

————. *La Salive de l'éléphant*. Paris: Losfeld/Blanche, 1999.

————. *La Vie, le fard de Dieu, Journal 1968/1971*. L'Isle-sur-la-Sorgue: Le bois d'Orion, 1994.

Francois, Bruno. "René Daumal, du grand jeu à Gurdjieff." In "Dossier Gurdjieff," *Magazine littéraire* (1977).

Gaigneron, Marthe de. "Danses sacrées." In Bruno de Panafieu, *G. I. Gurdjieff*. Paris: L'Âge d'Homme, 1993.

Gurdjieff, G. I. *Beelzebub's Tales to His Grandson: An Objectively Impartial Criticism of the Life of Man,* three vols. New York: A. Dutton, 1950.

————. *Gurdjieff parle à ses élèves*. Monaco: Éditions du Rocher, 1995.

————. *Life Is Real Only Then, When "I Am."* New York: Viking Arkana, 1991.

————. *Meetings with Remarkable Men*. Translated by A. R. Orage. New York: E. P. Dutton, 1963.

Hartmann, Thomas, and Olga Hartmann. *Notre vie avec Monsieur Gurdjieff*. Monaco: Éditions du Rocher, 2003 .

Huxley, Aldous. *The Doors of Perception* and *Heaven and Hell*. New York: Perennial Classics, 2004 .

————. *Moksha. Expériences visionnaires et psychédéliques*. Paris: Éditions du Lézard, 1998.

————. *The Perennial Philosophy*. New York: Harper & Brothers, 3rd edition, 1944.

James, William. *The Varieties of Religious Experience: A Study in Human Nature*. New York: Modern Library, 1902.

Labat, Stéphane. *La Poésie de l'extase et le pouvoir chamanique du langage*. Paris: Maisonneuve et Larose, 1997.

Lannes, Henriette. *Retour à maintenant*. Lyon: Tournadieu, 2003.

Leloup, Jean-Yves. *Écrits sur l'Hésychasme*. Paris: Albin Michel, 1990.

————. *L'Icône, une école du regard*. Paris: Pommier-Fayard, 2000.

Maleville, Georges de. *Éléments pour une possible évolution intérieure*. Paris: Institut pour le Développement Harmonique de l'Homme, 2004.

McKenna, Terence, *Food of the Gods: The Search for the Original Tree of Knowledge. A Radical History of Plants, Drugs, and Human Evolution*. New York: Bantam Books, 1992.

Mansfield, Katherine. *Lettres*. Paris: Stock, 1985.

Montaigne. *Essays of Michel de Montaigne*. Translated by Charles Cotton, edited by William Carew Hazlitt. n.l.: n.p., 1877.

Moore, James. *Gurdjieff, anatomie d'un mythe*. Paris: Seuil, 1999.

————. "Gurdjieff, the Man and the Literature." In *Gurdjieff International Review* 2, no. 1 (1998).

————. *Gurdjieff and Mansfield*. London: Routledge and Kegan Paul, 1980.

Mouravieff, Boris. *Gnôsis: étude et commentaires sur la tradition ésotérique de l'orthodoxie orientale*, three volumes. Boudry, Switzerland: Éditions de la Baconnière, 1996.

Munn, Henry. "The Mushrooms of Language." In *Hallucinogens and Shamanism*. Edited by Michael J. Harner. New York: Oxford University Press, 1973.

Needleman, Jacob. *À la recherche du christianisme perdu*. Paris: Albin Michel, 1990.

Negrier, Patrick. *Gurdjieff, maître spirituel*. Paris: L'Originel, 2005.

Ouspensky, P. D. *L'Homme et son évolution possible*. Paris: L'Originel, 1999.

————. *In Search of the Miraculous: Fragments of an Unknown Teaching*. London: Routledge and Kegan Paul, 1950.

————. *Un nouveau modéle de l'Univers*. Paris: Stock, 1996.

Panafieu, Bruno de. *G. I. Gurdjieff*. Paris: L'Âge d'Homme, 1993.

Paulhan, Jean. *Œuvres complètes*, five volumes. Paris: Tchou, 1970.

Pauwels, Louis. *Monsieur Gurdjieff*. Paris: Albin Michel, 1996.

Peters, Fritz. *Une enfance avec Gurdjieff*. Monaco: Éditions du Rocher, 1996.

Plato. "Cratyle ou De la rectitude des mots." In *Œuvres complètes 1*. Paris: Gallimard, 1950.

Pouilloux, Jean-Yves. "Le Temps présent." In *L'Inactuel*, no. 12 (2004).

————. *Montaigne, l'éveil de la pensée*. Paris: Honore Champion, 1995.

————. "Paulhan, le défaut de la littérature," In *Yale French Studies*, no. 106 (2004).

————. *Rabelais: Rire est le propre de l'homme*. Paris: Gallimard, 1993.

Random, Michel. *Le Grand Jeu*, two volumes. Paris: Éditions Denoël, 1970.

————. "Les Hommes du blâme et la Quattrième Voie." In Bruno de Panafieu, *Georges Ivanovitch Gurdjieff*. Paris: L'Âge d'Homme, 1993.

————. *Les Puissances du dedans, Luc Dietrich, Lanza del Vasto, René Daumal, Gurdjieff*. Paris: Denoël, 1966.

Ravindra, Ravi. *Un cœur sans limite, le travail avec Jeanne de Salzmann*. Halifax, Nova Scotia: Shaila Press, 2002.

Rimbaud, Arthur. *Œuvres complètes*. Paris: Gallimard, Paris, 1972.

Sabina, Maria. *Selections*. Edited by Jerome Rothenberg. Berkeley, Calif.: University of California Press, 2003.

Salzmann, Jeanne de. "Le regard." In Bruno de Panafieu, *G. I. Gurdjieff*. Paris: L'Âge d'Homme, 1993.

Salzmann, Michel de. "Gurdjieff." In Mircea Eliade, *The Encyclopedia of Religion*. New York: Macmillan, 1987.

———. "Les miettes du festin." In *Gurdjieff, textes et témoignages inédits, Question de*, no. 50 (1982).

Shirley, John. *Gurdjieff: An Introduction to His Life and Ideas*. New York: Penguin, 2004.

Schuré, Edouard. *Les Grands Initiés*. Paris: Perrin, 1960.

Tchechovitch, Tchesslav. *Tu l'aimeras, souvenirs sur G. I. Gurdjieff*. Paris: L'Originel, 2003.

Tereshchenko, Nicolas. *Au-Delà de la Quattrième Voie*. Paris: Guy Trédaniel Éditeur, 1996.

———. *Fragments de Gnosis*. Paris: Guy Trédaniel Éditeur, 1993.

———. *Gurdjieff et la Quattrième Voie*. Paris: Guy Trédaniel, 1991.

———. *Le Message de Gurdjieff*. Paris: Guy Trédaniel Éditeur, 1995.

———. *Les Trésors du tarot*. Paris: Guy Trédaniel Éditeur, 1986.

Thompson, Claude G. *Enseignement de G. I. Gurdjieff*. St. Zenon, Québec: Louise Courteau, 2005.

Tonnac, Jean-Philippe de. *René Daumal, l'archange*. Paris: Grasset, 1998.

Tracol, Henri. *La vraie question demeure—G. I. Gurdjieff: un appel vivant*. Arcueil: Édition Éolienne, 1996.

Val, Nicolas de. *Daddy Gurdjieff, quelques souvenirs inédits*. Geneva: Georg, 1967.

Waldberg, Michel. *Gurdjieff: An Approach to his Ideas*. Translated by Steve Cox. London: Routledge and Kegan Paul, 1981.

———. *Gurdjieff hors les murs*. Paris: La Différence, 2001.

———. *La Parole putanisée*. Paris: La Différence, 2002.

Welch, Louise. *Gurdjieff et A. R. Orage en Amérique*. Paris: Albin Michel, 1990.

Wellbeloved, Sophia. *Gurdjieff, Astrology and Beelzebub's Tales*. New Paltz, N.Y.: Solar Bound Press, 2002.

———. *Gurdjieff, The Key Concepts*. New York: Routledge, 2003.

Witkiewicz, S. I. "Le peyotl." In *Les Narcotiques suivi de Les Âmes mal lavées*. Lusanne: L'Âge d'Homme, 1980.

Zuber, René. *Qui êtes-vous Monsieur Gurdjieff?* Arcueil: Éolienne, 1997.

COLLECTED WORKS

Les Dames de Gurdjieff. Paris: Éditions de la Table Ronde, 2005.

Dossiers H. G. I. Gurdjieff. Paris: L'Âge d'Homme, 1993.

Dossiers H. René Daumal. Paris: L'Âge d'Homme, 1993.

Gurdjieff à Avon. Avon: Les Amis du prieuré des Basses-loges, 2004.

Gurdjieff, textes et témoignages inédits, Question de, no. 50 (1982).

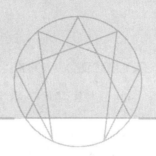

Index

BOOKS OF RELATED INTEREST

A Mystical Key to the English Language
by Robert M. Hoffstein

Iamblichus' Life of Pythagoras
by Thomas Taylor

Nature Word
by R. A. Schwaller de Lubicz

On a Spaceship with Beelzebub
By a Grandson of Gurdjieff
by David Kherdian

Music and the Power of Sound
The Influence of Tuning and Interval on Consciousness
by Alain Daniélou

Harmonies of Heaven and Earth
Mysticism in Music from Antiquity to the Avant-Garde
by Joscelyn Godwin

The Primal Force in Symbol
Understanding the Language of Higher Consciousness
by René Alleau

Shakespeare's Window into the Soul
The Mystical Wisdom in Shakespeare's Characters
by Martin Lings

Inner Traditions • Bear & Company
P.O. Box 388
Rochester, VT 05767
1-800-246-8648
www.InnerTraditions.com

Or contact your local bookseller